Essays in Applied Price Theory
by Reuben A. Kessel

REUBEN A. KESSEL, 1923–1975

Photograph by Manning Nash

ESSAYS IN APPLIED PRICE THEORY
BY REUBEN A. KESSEL

EDITED BY
R. H. Coase & Merton H. Miller

THE UNIVERSITY OF CHICAGO PRESS   *Chicago and London*

The late REUBEN A. KESSEL was a member of the faculty of the University of Chicago from 1957 to 1975, first in the Department of Economics and then in the Graduate School of Business, where he was professor of economics.

THE UNIVERSITY OF CHICAGO PRESS, CHICAGO 60637
THE UNIVERSITY OF CHICAGO PRESS, LTD., LONDON

© 1980 by The University of Chicago
All rights reserved. Published 1980

Printed in the United States of America
84 83 82 81 80   9 8 7 6 5 4 3 2 1

All of the chapters in this book appeared originally in journals or research monographs and are reproduced here by permission of the original publishers. The full publication history of each appears in the Bibliography at the end of the book.

R. H. COASE is Clifton R. Musser Professor in the University of Chicago Law School and is editor of the *Journal of Law and Economics*.

MERTON H. MILLER is Edward Eagle Brown Professor in the Graduate School of Business of the University of Chicago.

Library of Congress Cataloging in Publication Data

Kessel, Reuben A
  Essays in applied price theory.

  "Bibliography of major publications of Reuben A. Kessel, compiled by Shirley Kessel": p.
  Includes index.
  CONTENTS: Price discrimination in medicine.—The A.M.A. and the supply of physicians.—Higher education and the nation's health.—Transfused blood, serum hepatitis, and the Coase theorem.—The cyclical behavior of the term structure of interest rates, [etc.]
  1. Microeconomics—Addresses, essays, lectures. 2. Medical economics—Addresses, essays, lectures. 3. Finance—Addresses, essays, lectures. 4. Industrial organization (Economic theory)—Addresses, essays, lectures. 5. Trade regulation—Addresses, essays, lectures. I. Coase, Ronald Harry. II. Miller, Merton H. III. Title.
HB171.K435   338.5'2'01   80-12974
ISBN 0-226-43200-9

Robert Manning Strozier Library

26 1981

Tallahassee, Florida

Contents

Foreword, by R. H. Coase and Merton H. Miller   vii

PART I: HEALTH ECONOMICS
1 Price Discrimination in Medicine (1958)   3
2 The A.M.A. and the Supply of Physicians (1970)   37
3 Higher Education and the Nation's Health: A Review of the Carnegie Commission Report on Medical Education (1972)   55
4 Transfused Blood, Serum Hepatitis, and the Coase Theorem (1974)   69

PART II: THE CAPITAL MARKETS
5 The Cyclical Behavior of the Term Structure of Interest Rates (1965)   97
6 The Allocation of Mortgage Funds (1969)   217
7 A Study of the Effects of Competition in the Tax-Exempt Bond Market (1971)   233

PART III: MONOPOLY AND COMPETITION
8 Economic Effects of Federal Regulation of Milk Markets (1967)   269
9 Competition, Monopoly, and the Pursuit of Money. With Armen A. Alchian (1962)   297

PART IV: INFLATION
10 Redistribution of Wealth through Inflation. With Armen A. Alchian (1959)   327
11 The Meaning and Validity of the Inflation-Induced Lag of Wages behind Prices. With Armen A. Alchian (1960)   337

Bibliography of Major Publications of Reuben A. Kessel. Compiled by Shirley Kessel   361
Index   365

Foreword

Reuben Kessel, professor of economics in the Graduate School of Business of the University of Chicago, died in 1975 at the untimely age of fifty-two. The papers in this volume represent his major contributions to economics and exhibit the essential characteristics of his thought and style.

Born in Chicago and educated in the Chicago public schools, Reuben Kessel made his acquaintance with the University of Chicago during World War II, when he attended a meteorological school the United States Army was conducting on the campus. After his discharge from the Army in 1946, he entered the university as an undergraduate and went on to earn the M.B.A. degree from the Graduate School of Business in 1948. Characteristically, he chose to forgo the Bachelor's degree because of the additional cost. After graduation, he served for a year as an instructor in the Department of Economics of the University of Missouri before returning to the University of Chicago in 1949 to take his Ph.D. in the Graduate School of Business.

Kessel's high standards of craftsmanship and his relish for relating price theory to the everyday business of life led him to Milton Friedman, whose teaching contributed greatly to Kessel's development. Friedman's work on the relation between money and prices inspired Kessel's doctoral dissertation, "Inflation-Caused Wealth Redistribution: A Test of a Hypothesis," and several follow-up articles on inflation.

Kessel's intellectual kinship with Frank Knight and Henry Simons is equally evident, and through long and close association with Aaron Director and George Stigler, both of whom were students of Knight and colleagues of Simons, Kessel sharpened his logical and analytical skills. When it came to refining his hypotheses, Kessel usually consulted H. Gregg Lewis, whose technical proficiency in presenting empirical materials he greatly admired.

After finishing his course work at Chicago, Reuben Kessel spent the next four years as a staff member in the Economics Division of the RAND Corporation in Santa Monica. Armen Alchian was a colleague at RAND, and they began there a fruitful collaboration, some notable examples of which appear in the present volume. Following a brief stay in the School of Business Administration at UCLA, Kessel returned to Chicago, first to the Department of Economics, in 1957, and subsequently to the Graduate School of Business, in 1962. Promotion to the rank of professor came in 1965.

To his teaching in the Graduate School of Business, Reuben Kessel brought the same craftsmanlike qualities and skeptical attitudes that characterized his writings. He had little tolerance for abstract theorizing about unobservables. His characteristic question to students (and colleagues) was always: "What is your evidence for that proposition?" The empirical research papers he demanded from the students enrolled in his courses received serious and thorough professional criticism, and the papers that survived it often became the nucleus of a doctoral dissertation or journal article.

In addition to his work with doctoral students, Kessel served from 1963 to 1965 as director of the doctoral program of the Graduate School of Business and later as director of research; in the latter position he was essentially the administrator of the School's program of faculty research grants.

His ability to master specialized institutional detail without losing his perspective as an economist created a substantial demand for his services outside academia. Noteworthy among these engagements was his service in the landmark General Electric price-fixing case as economic advisor to Judge Robeson in the task of assessing damages. Kessel also enjoyed a long association, first as a consultant and later as a director, with the Bell Federal Savings and Loan Association, one of the largest in the United States; this close working relationship with the management of a large financial institution stimulated his own research on the money and capital markets, and the insights gained from his insider's knowledge about this class of financial intermediaries are easily discerned in several of the papers in this volume.

The papers selected for inclusion here have been grouped under four broad headings: Health Economics; The Capital Markets; Monopoly and Competition; and Inflation. Despite the seeming diversity of the topics, the categories overlap, and several themes, both substantive and methodological, recur in all four areas.

Part I, Health Economics, opens with what is perhaps Kessel's best-known paper, "Price Discrimination in Medicine." Included in many collections of essays on price theory over the past twenty years, it takes on added interest today, when price theory has spread beyond its customary boundaries. Kessel was not the first to treat the hallowed field of medicine as just another industry, nor was he even the

Foreword

first to call attention to the price discrimination built into the structure of fees for medical services. His contribution lay rather in suggesting a mechanism that would keep the discriminatory differentials from being eroded by competition; in the process he showed how one very simple price-theoretic explanation could account for a wide variety of empirical phenomena that had hitherto been given only separate, ad hoc rationalizations if, indeed, they were regarded as requiring any explanation at all. Kessel's list of these phenomena ranged from the institution of "professional courtesy" to the overrepresentation of specialists in the hierarchy of organized medicine and, further, to the discrimination against Jews, Blacks, and women in admissions to medical schools.

The mechanism that Kessel saw keeping the discriminatory fee structure from unraveling was the control of hospital affiliations by the American Medical Association—a control buttressed by the A.M.A.'s control over the educational process through its power to withhold accreditation from medical schools. In the second paper, "The A.M.A. and the Supply of Physicians," Kessel traces this control back to the much-praised Flexner Report of 1910. This report, he argues, was the instrument by which organized medicine enlisted the prestigious Carnegie Foundation for the Advancement of Teaching in its campaign to discredit and destroy the proprietary (i.e., tuition-supported) schools of medicine. Kessel savages the logic underlying the Flexner Report, especially its obsessive concern with the inputs rather than the outputs of the educational process.

The paper "Higher Education and the Nation's Health" was occasioned by still another report from the (now) Carnegie Commission, which hoped to play as great a role in solving the problems of medical education in the 1970s as it had earlier, with its Flexner Report of 1910. To Kessel, this was the sheerest gall, since he believed that the serious "doctor shortage" to which the second report was addressed had been caused in considerable part by the universal adoption of the recommendations contained in the first report. Kessel demolishes the pretensions of this second report on medical education, and he does so in a way that illuminates the basic economics of graduate professional education both in medicine and more generally.

The final paper in Part I, "Transfused Blood, Serum Hepatitis, and the Coase Theorem," challenges the widely held view that a blood-delivery system relying on paid donors is incapable of ensuring a supply of blood that is both adequate and safe. Kessel argues that the supposed failures of the price system in blood delivery are really failures to place the burden of product liability for bad blood on those who can bear it most efficiently, to wit, the hospitals and attending physicians.

Part II, The Capital Markets, opens with the monograph "The Cyclical Behavior of the Term Structure of Interest Rates," undertaken while Kessel was a visiting research associate at the National Bureau of Economic Research in 1961–62. Kessel made this study the core of his teaching in the finance and capital-market area for many years, particularly in his doctoral courses, and it inspired a considerable flow of subsequent research, both from Kessel's own students (notably Richard Roll and J. Huston McCulloch) and from his colleagues (among others, Charles Nelson).

The monograph itself was undertaken, in part, in response to David Meiselman's pathbreaking study of the term structure. Kessel argued that Meiselman's empirical tests in support of the strict-expectations hypothesis were seriously flawed and that a combination of the expectations hypothesis with the Keynes-Hicks liquidity-preference hypothesis could account better for the observed behavior of interest rates and the observed practices of financial intermediaries. Kessel's demonstration of the bias in forward rates as predictors of future short-term spot rates—a finding inconsistent with the strict-expectations hypothesis—has been supported by later investigators.

Many of the themes of Kessel's term-structure monograph are elaborated in the next paper, "The Allocation of Mortgage Funds." Kessel's version of liquidity preference depended heavily and explicitly on the actions of banks, savings and loan associations, and similar financial intermediaries, who made their living by borrowing short and lending long. The liquidity premium to him was essentially the compensation the owners received for bearing the attendant capital risk in a world where long-term bond prices varied substantially more than short-term bond prices. Yet, as Kessel's interest-rate monograph had shown, an investor who had continually invested in short-term bills during the postwar period would actually have earned substantially higher average rates of return than an investor in long-term bonds. Kessel argues, however, that returns on longs during the period were abnormally depressed because the market had for the most part failed to anticipate the secular rise in interest that actually occurred. Superimposed on this unanticipated drift was a series of sharp cyclical variations (also amply documented by the term-structure monograph) with yield relations at the peaks and troughs that, if not actually unanticipated, were at least relatively rare by the standards of past experience. The two types of movements in interest rates, and their interactions, are then invoked to explain some of the otherwise puzzling aspects of the postwar mortgage market and the behavior of the savings and loan firms that are satellite to it.

The third paper in Part II, "A Study of the Effects of Competition in the Tax-Exempt Bond Market," might equally well have been grouped with the papers on competition and monopoly in Part III. Kessel's previous work on the term structure, especially his analysis of the role of financial intermediaries in the money markets, provides the background against which the issues are discussed, but the central parts of the argument relate to the nature and extent of competition among underwriters. Kessel invokes search theory and the economics of information in a novel way to develop testable hypotheses about the effect of the number of bids on reoffering yields. His case against the Glass-Steagall Act's prohibition of the underwriting of municipal revenue bonds by commercial banks is based on his economic analysis of the restriction, not on a mere reflex ideological commitment to free entry. He describes carefully the conditions under which the removal of entry restrictions might be ineffectual, and he uses his firsthand knowledge of the institutional side of banking to explore the extent to which banks do or do not have comparative advantages in the underwriting of municipals.

The paper "Economic Effects of Federal Regulation of Milk Markets," which introduces Part III, Monopoly and Competition, is reminiscent of the papers in Part I on medical economics. Once again the central problem is that of elucidating the mechanism that permits price discrimination to be maintained; but here, in the milk case, unlike the situation in the medical field, Kessel shows that the devices preventing price-cutting have led to an output that is too large rather than too small.

The paper "Competition, Monopoly, and the Pursuit of Money" (written with Armen Alchian) can be seen today as one of the foundations of that area of economics falling under the rubrics of "property rights" and "agency costs." The paper is thoroughly empirical in spirit. Its objective is to show that invoking "utility maximization" as an alternative to "wealth maximization" in explaining the choices of "monopolists" is more than an empty tautology. The cutting power of the postulate comes by specifying the arguments of the utility function, and Kessel and Alchian show by many examples how careful specification of the objects of choice can lead to definite and often surprising predictions about behavior.

Part IV, Inflation, comprises two papers, both written jointly with Armen Alchian, that focus on the redistribution of wealth brought about by unanticipated inflation. The concern with inflation, both within and outside the economics profession, is now so strong that it is hard to believe that these articles, when they first appeared in the late 1950s, were considered far out of the mainstream of economics. Kessel and Alchian set out neither to praise nor to blame; their purpose was to test hypotheses about who gains from inflation, who loses, and why. The first paper tests the view, found in the writings of J. M. Keynes and Irving Fisher, that the owners of business firms gain from unanticipated inflation. Kessel and Alchian show, first, that this conjecture does not agree with the facts; second, that it fails because Keynes and Fisher mistakenly assumed that business firms are always debtors; and, third, that the Keynes-Fisher hypothesis can be rehabilitated by restating it in terms of the *net* debtor status of the firm. The paper is noteworthy, among other things, for being among the first to exploit data on changes in stock prices for testing economic propositions.

The final paper in the volume focuses on the view, held widely at the time both within and outside the economics profession, that wages systematically lag behind prices during inflations so that entrepreneurs gain at the expense of workers. Kessel and Alchian trace the wage-lag hypothesis back to two influential empirical studies of price and wages, one by Wesley C. Mitchell, covering the Civil War period in the United States, the other by Earl J. Hamilton for the period following the discovery of gold and silver sources in the Americas in the sixteenth century. The evidence for the wage-lag hypothesis in these studies is subjected to detailed reexamination by Kessel and Alchian, and the Hamilton-Mitchell thesis is shown to have far too little empirical or theoretical support to merit the canonical status it had achieved.

As with any collection of papers written over so long a span, some dating has inevitably occurred, but here the dating also reflects how often Kessel's pieces have become significant links in the chain of subsequent professional developments in each of the fields represented.

R. H. Coase
Merton H. Miller

I Health Economics

1 Price Discrimination in Medicine*
(1958)

MANY distinguished economists have argued that the medical profession constitutes a monopoly, and some have produced evidence of the size of the monopoly gains that accrue to the members of this profession.[1] Price discrimination by doctors, i.e., scaling fees to the income of patients, has been explained as the behavior of a discriminating monopolist.[2] Indeed this has become the standard textbook example of discriminating monopoly.[3] However this explanation of price discrimination has been incomplete. Economists who have subscribed to this hypothesis have never indicated why competition among doctors failed to establish uniform prices for identical services. For any individual doctor, given the existing pattern of price discrimination, income from professional services would be maximized if rates were lowered for affluent patients and increased for poor patients. However, if many doctors engaged in such price policies, a pattern of prices for medical services would be established that would be independent of the incomes of patients. Yet despite this inconsistency between private interests and the existing pattern or structure of prices based on income differences, this price structure has survived. Is this a contradiction of the law of markets? Why is it possible to observe in a single market the same service sold at different prices?

The primary objective of this paper, which is an essay in positive econom-

---

* The author is indebted to A. A. Alchian, W. Meckling, A. Enthoven, and W. Taylor of the RAND Corporation, W. Gorter, A. Nicols, and J. F. Weston of UCLA, H. G. Lewis and A. Rees of the University of Chicago, and Gary Becker of Columbia University for assistance.

[1] M. Friedman and S. Kuznets, Income from Independent Professional Practice (1945); M. Friedman in Impact of the Trade Union, p. 211, edited by D. M. Wright (1951); Also K. E. Boulding, Conference on the Utilization of Scientific and Professional Manpower, p. 23 (1944).
The results of the Friedman-Kuznets study, at p. 133, using pre-war data, indicate that the costs of producing doctors are seventeen per cent greater than the costs of producing dentists, while the average income of doctors is thirty-two per cent greater.

[2] J. Robinson, Economics of Imperfect Competition, p. 180 (1933). For example, the world famed Mayo Clinic discriminates in pricing. Albert Deutsch, The Mayo Clinic, 22 Consumer Reports 37, 40 (Jan. 1957). A finance department makes inquiries into the patient's economic status and scales the bills accordingly. Fees are not discussed in advance.

[3] E. A. G. Robinson, Monopoly, p. 77 (1941); C. E. Daugherty and M. Daugherty, Principles of Political Economy, p. 591 (1950); T. Scitovsky, Welfare and Competition, p. 408 (1941); K. E. Boulding, Economic Analysis, p. 662 (1955); S. Enke, Intermediate Economic Theory, p. 42 (1950); G. Stigler, The Theory of Price, p. 219 (1952).

ics, is to show by empirical evidence that the standard textbook rationalization of what appears to be a contradiction of the law of markets is correct. It will be argued that the discriminating monopoly model is valid for understanding the pricing of medical services, and that each individual buyer of medical services that are produced jointly with hospital care constitutes a unique, separable market. In the process of presenting evidence supporting this thesis, other closely related phenomena will be considered. These are (1), why the AMA favors medical insurance prepayment plans that provide money to be used to buy medical services, but bitterly opposes comparable plans that provide instead of money, the service itself and (2), why the AMA has opposed free medical care by the Veterans Administration for veterans despite the enormous increase in the quantity of medical services demanded that would result from the reduction to zero of the private costs of medical care for such a large group.

The second half of this paper represents an attempt, by means of an application of the discriminating monopoly model, to further our understanding of many unique characteristics of the medical profession. If the medical profession constitutes a discriminating monopoly, what inferences can be drawn concerning the relationship between this monopoly and other economic, sociological and political aspects of the medical profession? In particular, does the discriminating monoply model shed any light upon, (1) why a higher percentage of doctors belong to professional organizations than is true of other professions, (2) why doctors treat one another and their families free of charge, (3) why doctors, compared with any other professional group, are extremely reluctant to criticize one another before the public, (4) why specialists are over-represented among the hierarchy of organized medicine, (5) why a transfer of membership in good standing from one county society to a second sometimes requires serving a term as a probationary member, (6) why advertising that redounds to the interest of the medical profession as a whole is approved whereas advertising that is designed to benefit particular individuals or groups is strongly opposed, (7) why malpractice insurance is less expensive for members of organized medicine than it is for non-members, and finally (8) why minority groups, particularly Jews, have been discriminated against in admission to medical schools.[4]

The body of this paper is divided into five sections. These are, in order of presentation, a hypothesis alternative to the price discrimination hypothesis, a history of the development of the powers that enable organized medicine to

[4] It is worth noting that there is no inconsistency between the validity of the explanation to be presented and the inability of any or all members of the medical profession, past, present or future, to understand the economic arguments that follow. All that is required of doctors is the ability to engage in adaptive behavior of a very rudimentary character. Consult A. A. Alchian, Uncertainty, Evolution, and Economic Theory, 58 J. Pol. Econ. 211 (1950).

organize effectively a discriminating monopoly, evidence supporting the validity of the discriminating monopoly model for understanding the pricing of medical services, and lastly an application of the discriminating monopoly model to rationalize many characteristics of the medical profession that have been hitherto thought of as either anomalies or behavior that could best be explained as non-economic phenomena.

I. A Hypothesis Alternative to the Discriminating Monopoly Model

The standard position of the medical profession on price discrimination is in conflict with what might be regarded as the standard position of the economics profession. Economists argue that price discrimination by doctors represents the profit maximizing behavior of a discriminating monopolist; the medical profession takes the contrary position that price discrimination exists because doctors represent a collection agency for medical charities.[5] The income of these charities is derived from a loading charge imposed upon well-to-do patients. This income is used to finance the costs of hiring doctors to provide medical care for the poor who are sick. The doctor who is hired by the medical charity and the medical charity itself are typically the same person. Since the loading charge that is imposed upon non-charity patients to support the activities of medical charities is proportional to income or wealth, discriminatory prices result. The following quotation from an unnamed but highly respected surgeon presents the position of the medical profession.

I don't feel that I am robbing the rich because I charge them more when I know they can well afford it; the sliding scale is just as democratic as the income tax. I operated today upon two people for the same surgical condition—one a widow whom I charged $50, the other a banker whom I charged $250. I let the widow set her own fee. I charged the banker an amount which he probably carries around in his wallet to entertain his business friends.[6]

It is relevant to inquire, why have we had the development of charities operated by a substantial fraction of the non-salaried practitioners of a profession in medicine alone? Why hasn't a parallel development occurred for

[5] However, there is not a unanimity of views either among economists or medical men. Means, a retired professor of clinical medicine at Harvard and a former president of the American College of Surgeons, takes the point of view of the economists. He describes this price policy as charging what the traffic will bear. J. H. Means, Doctors, People and Government, p. 66 (1953).

[6] Seham, Who Pays the Doctor?, 135 New Republic 10, 11 (July 9, 1956). Those who favor price discrimination for this reason ought to be in favor of a single price plan with a system of subsidies and taxes. Such a scheme, in principle, could improve the welfare of both the poor and the well-to-do relative to what it was under price discrimination.
The equity of a tax that is imposed upon the sick who are well-to-do as contrasted with a tax upon the well-to-do generally has not troubled the proponents of this method of taxation.

5

such closely related services as nursing and dental care? Why is it possible to observe discrimination by the Mayo Clinic but not the A and P? Clearly food is as much of a "necessity" as medical care. The intellectual foundation for the existence of price discrimination and the operation of medical charities by doctors appears to rest upon the postulate that medicine is in some sense unlike any other commodity or service. More specifically, the state is willing to provide food, clothing, and shelter for the indigent but not medical care.[7] Since medical care is so important, doctors do not refuse to accept patients if they are unable to pay. As a consequence, discrimination in pricing medical services is almost inevitable if doctors themselves are not to finance the costs of operating medical charities.

The foregoing argument in defense of price discrimination in medicine implies that a competitive market for the sale of medical services is inconsistent with the provision of free services to the indigent. This implication is not supported by what can be observed elsewhere in our economy. Clearly there exist a number of competitive markets in which individual practitioners provide free goods or services and price discrimination is absent. Merchants, in their capacity of merchants, give resources to charities yet do not discriminate in pricing their services. Similarly many businesses give huge sums for educational purposes. Charity is consistent with non-discriminatory pricing because the costs of charity can be and are paid for out of the receipts of the donors without recourse to price discrimination.

However the fact that non-discriminatory pricing is consistent with charity work by doctors doesn't imply that discriminatory pricing of medical services is inconsistent with the charity hypothesis. Clearly what can be done without discrimination can, *a fortiori*, be done with discrimination. Therefore, it is pertinent to ask, is there any evidence that bears directly on the validity of the charity interpretation of price discrimination? The maximizing hypothesis of economics implies that differences in fees can be explained by differences in demand. The charity hypothesis propounded by the medical profession implies that differences in fees result from income differences. The pricing of medical services to those who have medical insurance provides that what might be regarded as a crucial experiment for discriminating between these hypotheses. Whether or not one has medical insurance affects the demand for medical service but does not affect personal income. Consequently if the charity hy-

---

[7] H. Cabot contends that the community is unwilling to provide for the medical care of the indigent. Therefore the system of a sliding scale of fees has evolved; pp. 123, 266 ff. He estimates that the more opulent members of the community pay ". . . from five to thirty times the average fee . . ." p. 270, The Doctors Bill (1935).

Robinson has defended discriminatory pricing of medical services in sparsely populated areas by using an argument based on indivisibilities. A Fundamental Objection to Laissez-Faire, 45 Economic Journal 580 (1935). For a refutation of this position, see Hutt, Discriminating Monopoly and the Consumer, 46 Economic Journal 61, 74 (1936).

pothesis is correct, then there should be no difference in fees, for specified services, for those who do and those who do not have medical insurance. On the other hand, if the maximizing hypothesis of economics is correct, then fees for those who have medical insurance ought to be higher than for those who do not have such insurance. Existing evidence indicates that if income and wealth differences are held constant, people who have medical insurance pay more for the same service than people who do not have such insurance. Union leaders have found that the fees charged have risen as a result of the acquisition of medical insurance by their members; fees, particularly for surgery, are higher than they would otherwise be if the union member were not insured.[8] Members of the insurance industry have found that ". . . the greater the benefit provided the higher the surgical bill. . . ."[9] This suggests that the principle used for the determinations of fees is, as Means pointed out, what the traffic will bear. Obviously fees determined by this principle will be highly correlated with income, although income will have no independent predictive content for fees if the correlation between income and what the traffic will bear is abstracted.[10]

Other departures from the implications of the hypothesis that price discrimination results from the desires of the medical profession to finance the costs of medical care for the indigent exist. These are: (1) Doctors typically do not charge each other for medical care when clearly inter-physician fees ought to be relatively high since doctors have relatively high incomes. (2) The volume of free medical care, particularly in surgery, has declined as a result of the rise in real per capita income in this country in the last twenty years. Yet there has been no change in the extent of price discrimination. As real per capita income rises, price discrimination ought to fade away. There is no evidence that this has been the case.[11] (3) There exists no machinery for matching the receipts and disbursements of medical charities operated by

---

[8] E. A. Schuler, R. J. Mowitz, and A. J. Mayer, Medical Public Relations (1952), report the attitude of lay leaders of the community towards the medical profession. For the attitudes of union leaders and why they have these attitudes, see p. 97 ff.

[9] Lorber in Hearings Before the House Committee on Interstate and Foreign Commerce on Health Inquiry, 83d Cong. 2d Sess. pt. 7, p. 1954 (1954); Also Joanis, Hospital and Medical Costs, Proceedings of the Fourth Annual Group Meeting of the Health and Accident Underwriters Conference, p. 18 (Feb. 19–20, 1952).

[10] The principle of what the traffic will bear and the indemnity principle of insurance are fundamentally incompatible and in principle make medical care uninsurable. This has been a real problem for the insurance industry and in part accounts for the relative absence from the market of major medical insurance plans. See the unpublished doctoral dissertation of A. Yousri, Prepayment of Medical and Surgical Care in Wisconsin, p. 438, University of Wisconsin Library (1956).

[11] Berger, Are Surgical Fees Too High?, 32 Medical Economics 97, 100 ff. (June 1955).

individual doctors. There are no audits of the receipts and the expenditures of medical charities and well-to-do patients are not informed of the magnitude of the loading charges imposed. Moreover one study of medical care and the family budget reported ". . . no relation in the case of the individual doctor between the free services actually rendered and this recoupment, the whole system is haphazard any way you look at it."[12]

II. History of the Development of the Medical Monòpóly

A necessary condition for maintaining a structure of prices that is inconsistent with the maximization by doctors of individual income is the availability and willingness to use powerful sanctions against potential price cutters. When one examines the problems that have been encountered in maintaining prices that are against the interests of individual members of a cartel composed of less than fifteen members, one cannot help being impressed with the magnitude of the problem confronting a monopoly composed of hundreds of thousands of independent producers. Yet despite the fact that medicine constitutes an industry with an extraordinarily large number of producers, the structure of prices for a large number of medical services nevertheless reflects the existence of discrimination based on income. This implies that very strong sanctions must be available to those empowered to enforce price discipline. Indeed, *a priori* reasoning suggests that these sanctions must be of an order of magnitude more powerful than anything we have hitherto encountered in industrial cartels. What are the nature of these sanctions? How are they employed? In order to appreciate fully the magnitude of the coercive measures available to organized medicine, it is relevant to examine the history of medicine to understand how these sanctions were acquired.

Medicine, like the profession of economics today, was until the founding of the AMA a relatively competitive industry. With very few exceptions, anyone who wanted to practice was free to hang out a shingle and declare himself available. Medical schools were easy to start, easy to get into, and provided, as might be expected in a free market, a varied menu of medical training that covered the complete quality spectrum. Many medical schools of this time were organized as profit making institutions and had stock outstanding. Some schools were owned by the faculty.

In 1847, the American Medical Association was founded and this organization immediately committed itself to two propositions that were to lead to sharp restrictions upon the freedom of would-be doctors to enter the medical profession and the freedom of patients to choose doctors whom the AMA felt were not adequately qualified to practice medicine. These propositions were (1) that medical students should have acquired a "suitable preliminary education" and (2) that a "uniform elevated standard of requirements for the

[12] Deardorff and Clark, op. cit. supra note 9, pt. 6, p. 1646.

degree of M.D. should be adopted by all medical schools in the United States.[13]

These objectives were achieved in two stages. During the first stage, the primary concern of the AMA was licensure. In the second, it was accrediting schools of medicine. During the first stage, which began with the founding of the AMA and lasted until the turn of the century, organized medicine was able by lobbying before state legislatures to persuade legislators to license the practice of medicine. Consequently the various states set up boards of medical examiners to administer examinations to determine whether or not applicants were qualified to practice medicine and to grant licenses to those the State Board deemed qualified to practice. Generally speaking, organized medicine was very successful in its campaign to induce states to license physicians. However, the position of organized medicine was by no means unopposed. William James, in testimony offered before the State House in Boston in 1898 when legislation concerned with licensing of non-medically trained therapists was being considered, adopted a nineteenth century liberal position. To quote from this testimony:

> One would suppose that any set of sane persons interested in the growth of medical truth would rejoice if other persons were found willing to push out their experience in the mental healing direction, and to provide a mass of material out of which the conditions and limits of such therapeutic methods may at last become clear. One would suppose that our orthodox medical brethren might so rejoice; but instead of rejoicing they adopt the fiercely partisan attitude of a powerful trade union, they demand legislation against the competition of the "scabs." ... The mind curers and their public return the scorn of the regular profession with an equal scorn, and will never come up for the examination. Their movement is a religious or quasi-religious movement; personality is one condition of success there, and impressions and intuitions seem to accomplish more than chemical, anatomical or physiological information. ... Pray, do not fail, Mr. Chairman, to catch my point. You are not to ask yourselves whether these mind-curers do really achieve the successes that are claimed. It is enough for you as legislators to ascertain that a large number of our citizens, persons whose number seems daily to increase, are convinced that they do achieve them, are persuaded that a valuable new department of medical experience is by them opening up. Here is a purely medical question, regarding which our General Court, not being a well-spring and source of medical virtue, not having any private test of therapeutic truth, must remain strictly neutral under penalty of making the confusion worse. ... Above all things, Mr. Chairman, let us not be infected with the Gallic spirit of regulation and regimentation for their own abstract sakes. Let us not grow hysterical about law-making. Let us not fall in love with enactments and penalties because they are so logical and sound so pretty, and look so nice on paper.[14]

[13] A. Flexner, Medical Education in the U.S. and Canada, Bull. No. 4, Carnegie Foundation for the Advancement of Teaching, p. 10 (1910).

[14] 2 Letters of W. James, 66–72 (edited H. James, 1920). Dollard reports that James took this position at the risk of being drummed out of the ranks of medicine. Dollard, Monopoly

However, it was not until the second stage that economically effective power over entry was acquired by organized medicine. This stage began with the founding in 1904 of the Council on Medical Education of the AMA. This group dedicated itself to the task of improving the quality of medical education offered by the medical schools of the day. In 1906, this committee undertook an inspection of the 160 medical schools then in existence and fully approved of the training in only 82 schools. Thirty-two were deemed to be completely unacceptable. As might be expected, considerable resentment developed in the medical colleges and elsewhere as a result of this inspection. Consequently the council withheld publication of its findings, although the various colleges were informed of their grades.[15] In order to gain wider acceptance of the results of this study, the Council solicited the aid of the Carnegie Foundation. "If we could obtain the publication and approval of our work by the Carnegie Foundation for the Advancement of Teaching, it would assist materially in securing the results we were attempting to bring about."[16] Subsequently Abraham Flexner, representing the Carnegie Foundation, with the aid of N. P. Colwell, secretary of the Council on Medical Education, repeated the AMA's inspection and grading of medical schools. In 1910, the results of the labors of Flexner and Colwell were published.[17] This report, known as the Flexner report, recommended that a substantial fraction of the existing medical schools be closed, standards be raised in the remainder, and admissions sharply curtailed. Flexner forcefully argued that the country was suffering from an overproduction of doctors and that it was in the public interest to have fewer doctors who were better trained. In effect, Flexner argued that the public should be protected against the consequences of buying medical services from inadequately trained doctors by legislating poor medical schools out of business.[18]

---

and Medicine, speech delivered at Medical Center, UCLA, to be published by the University of California Press as one of a series of papers presented in celebration of Robert Gordon Sproul's 25th anniversary as President of the University of California. The significance of consumers' sovereignty has been recognized by at least one other maverick doctor. Means, op. cit. supra note 5, at p. 72.

[15] Johnson in Fishbein, A History of the American Medical Association, p. 887 ff. (1947).

[16] Bevan, Cooperation in Medical Education and Medical Service, 90 Journal of the American Medical Association 1175 (1928).

[17] Flexner, op. cit. supra note 13.

[18] Flexner, op. cit. supra note 13, at p. 14. Two errors in economic reasoning are crucial in helping Flexner establish his conclusions. One is an erroneous interpretation of Gresham's Law. This law is used to justify legislation to keep low quality doctors out of the medical care market by interpreting it to mean that second-class doctors will drive first-class doctors out of business. The other is that raising the standards of medical education is necessarily in the public interest. Flexner fails to recognize that raising standards implies higher costs of medical care. This argument is on a par with arguing that we should keep all cars of a quality below Cadillacs, Chryslers, and Lincolns off the automobile market.

If impact on public policy is the criterion of importance, the Flexner report must be regarded as one of the most important reports ever written. It convinced legislators that only the graduates of first class medical schools ought to be permitted to practice medicine and led to the delegation to the AMA of the task of determining what was and what was not a first class medical school. As a result, standards of acceptability for winning a license to practice medicine were set by statute or by formal rule or informal policy of state medical examining boards, and these statutes or rules provided that boards consider only graduates of schools approved by the AMA and/or the American Association of Medical Colleges whose lists are identical.[19]

The Flexner report ushered in an era, which lasted until 1944, during which a large number of medical schools were shut down. With its new found power, the AMA vigorously attacked the problem of certification of medical schools. By exercising its power to certify, the AMA reduced the number of medical schools in the United States from 162 in 1906 to 85 in 1920, 76 in 1930 and 69 in 1944.[20] As a result of the regulation of medical schools, the number of medical students in school in the United States today is 28,500, merely 5,200 more than in 1910 when Flexner published his report.[21]

The AMA, by means of its power to certify what is and what is not a class A medical school, has substantial control over both the number of medical schools in the United States and the rate of production of doctors.[22] While the control by the AMA over such first class schools as, say, Johns Hopkins

[19] Hyde and Wolff, The American Medical Association: Power, Purpose, and Politics in Organized Medicine, 63 Yale L. J. 969 (1954).

[20] These figures are from R. M. Allen, Medical Education and the Changing Order, p. 16 (1946). Allen imputes this decline in the number of medical schools to a previous error in estimating the demand for doctors. The decline in the number of schools in existence represented an adjustment to more correctly perceived demand conditions for medical care.

[21] Dollard, op. cit. supra note 14. This result was far from unanticipated. Bevan, the head of the AMA's Council on Medical Education, clearly anticipated a decline in both medical students and schools. "In this rapid elevation of the standard of medical education with the increase in preliminary requirements and greater length of course, and with the reduction of the number of medical schools from 160 to 80, there occurred a marked reduction in the number of medical students and medical graduates. We had anticipated this and felt that this was a desirable thing. We had an over-supply of poor mediocre practitioners." Bevan, op. cit. note 16, at p. 1176. Friedman and Kuznets state, "Initially, this decline in the number of physicians relative to total population was an unplanned by-product of the intensive drive for higher standards of medical education." Op. cit. supra note 4 at pp. 10–11. It may have been a by-product, and there are some grounds for doubts on this count, but it surely was not unanticipated.

[22] Dr. Spahr contends that there is a ". . . widespread but erroneous belief that the AMA governs the profession directly and determines who may practice medicine." Medicine's Neglected Control Lever, 40 Yale Rev. 25 (1950). She correctly contends that this power belongs to the state but fails to recognize that it has been delegated to the AMA by the state. Mayer on the other hand recognizes both the power in the hands of the AMA and its source. He argues that the AMA has life and death powers over both medical schools and hospitals. 180 Harpers 27 (Dec. 1939).

is relatively weak because it would be ludicrous not to classify this institution a a class A school, nevertheless control over the aggregate production rate of doctors is great because of its more substantial power over the output of less distinguished medical schools.

The delegation by the state legislatures to the AMA of the power to regulate the medical industry in the public interest is on a par with giving the American Iron and Steel Institute the power to determine the output of steel. This delegation of power by the states to the AMA, which was actively sought and solicited, placed this organization in a position of having to serve two masters who in part have conflicting interests. On the one hand, the AMA was given the task of providing an adequate supply of properly qualified doctors. On the other hand, the decision with respect to what is adequate training and an adequate number of doctors affects the pocketbooks of those who do the regulating as well as their closest business and personal associates. It is this power that has been given to the AMA that is the cornerstone of the monopoly power that has been imputed by economists to organized medicine.[23]

III. Evidence Supporting the Discriminating Monopoly Model

The preceding analysis tells us nothing about the mechanism for controlling the price policies of individual doctors; it only implies that the rate of return on capital invested in medical training will be greater than the rate of return on capital invested in other classes of professional training. This difference in returns is imputable as a rent on the power of the AMA to control admissions to the profession by means of control over medical education. Here it will be argued that control over the pricing policies of doctors is directly and immediately related to AMA control of medical education. The relationship is that control over medical education is the primary instrumentality for control over individual price policies. More specifically, control over post-graduate medical training—internship and residency, and control over admission to specialty board examinations—is the source of the power over the members of the medical profession by organized medicine.

A. THE CONTROL MECHANISM

Part of nearly every doctor's medical education consists of internship and for many also a period of hospital service known as residency. Internship is a necessary condition for licensure in most states. This training is administered by hospitals. However, hospitals must be approved by the AMA for

[23] Dollard, op. cit. supra note 21, concedes that medicine is a monopoly but argues that the AMA has used its power, by and large, in the public interest. Therefore, he implies that the monopoly power of the AMA has been unexploited, and the profession has acted against its own self interest.

intern and residency training, and most non-proprietary, i.e., nonprofit, hospitals in this country are in fact approved for at least intern training. Each approved hospital is allocated a quota of positions that can be filled by interns as part of their training. Hospitals value highly participation in internship and residency training programs. These programs are valued highly because at the prevailing wage for intern services, it is possible to produce hospital care more cheaply with interns than without them. Interns to hospitals are like coke to the steel industry: in both cases, it is perfectly possible to produce the final product without these raw materials; in both cases, the final product can be produced more cheaply by using these particular raw materials.

There exist some grounds for suspecting that the wages of interns are maintained at an artificially low level, i.e., that interns receive compensation that is less than the value of their marginal product: (1) Hospitals are reporting that there is a "shortage" of interns and have been known to send representatives to Europe and Asia to invite doctors to serve as interns.[24] (2) University hospitals are more aggressive bidders for intern services than non-university hospitals. The fraction of the available intern positions that are filled by university hospitals is greater than by non-university hospitals.[25] If controls are exercised over what hospitals can offer in wages to interns, university hospitals are apt to be less vulnerable to the threat of loss of their class A hospital ratings than non-university hospitals. This would be true for the same reason that Johns Hopkins would have a freer hand in determining the size of its freshman class. The status of university hospitals is stronger because these hospitals are likely to be among the better hospitals in the country. Therefore, if controls over intern wages exist then it seems reasonable to suspect they would be relatively weaker over the wages of interns in university hospitals. For this reason, one would expect university hospitals to be more aggressive in bidding for interns.

However, whether or not interns are underpaid, the AMA has control over the supply of a vital, in an economic sense, agent of production for producing hospital care. Revocation of a hospital's Class A rating implies the loss of interns. In turn, the loss of interns implies higher costs of production. Higher costs of production result in a deterioration of the competitive position of any given hospital vis-à-vis other hospitals in the medical care market. This control over hospitals by the AMA has been used to induce hospitals to abide by the Mundt Resolution.[26] This resolution advises hospitals that are certified for intern training that their staff ought to be composed solely of members of

---

[24] Congress to Probe Doctor Shortage, 33 Medical Economics 141 (June 1956).

[25] 162 Journal of the American Medical Association 281 (1956).

[26] "By a long record of authoritative inspection and grading of facilities, organized medicine has placed itself in a position to deny alternatively the services of doctor and hospital to each other." O. Garceau, Political Life of the American Medical Association, p. 109 (1941).

local medical societies.[27] As a result of this AMA control over hospitals, membership in local medical societies is a matter of enormous importance to practicing physicians. Lack of membership implies inability to become a member of a hospital staff.[28]

County medical societies are for all practical purposes private clubs with their own rules concerning eligibility for membership and grounds for expulsion. A system of appeals from the rulings of county medical societies with respect to their members is provided. On the other hand, for non-members attempting to obtain membership in county medical societies, there is no provision for appeal. The highest court in the medical judicial system is the Judicial Council of the AMA. Between this council and the county medical societies are state medical societies. Judicial review is bound by findings of fact made at the local level.[29] For doctors dependent upon hospitals in order to carry out their practice, and presumably this constitutes the bulk of the profession, being cut off from access to hospitals constitutes a partial revocation of their license to practice medicine. Consequently, more doctors belong to their county medical associations than is true of lawyers with respect to local bar associations. More significantly, doctors are subject to very severe losses indeed if they should be expelled from their local county medical associations or be refused admission to membership. It is this weapon, expulsion from county medical associations, that is probably the most formidable sanction employed to keep doctors from maximizing their personal incomes by cutting prices to high income patients. "Unethical" doctors, i.e., price cutters, can be in large part removed as a threat to a structure of prices that discriminates in terms of income by the use of this weapon.[30] For potential unethical physicians, it pays not to cut prices if cutting prices means being cut off from hospitals.

Thus far we have argued that control over the individual price policies of the members of the medical profession has been achieved by the AMA through its control over post-graduate medical education. By means of its power to

---

[27] Hyde and Wolff, op. cit. supra note 19, at 952. The certification of hospitals for nursing training and the value of nursing training programs to hospitals may be on a par with intern training.

[28] The strike is another instrument for control over hospitals by the AMA. Doctors have refused to work in hospitals that have admitted osteopaths to their staff. Hyde and Wolff, op. cit. supra note 19, at 966; M. M. Belli, Ready for the Plaintiff, p. 115 (1956). The threat of a strike has also been used to induce hospitals to refuse staff membership to "unethical" doctors. Group Health Etc. v. King Co. Med. Soc., 39 Wash. 2d 586, 624, 237 P. 2d 737, 757–758 (1951).

[29] Hyde and Wolff, op. cit. supra note 19, at 949–950.

[30] "Ethics has always been a flexible, developing, notion in medicine, with a strong flavor of economics from the start." Garceau, op. cit. supra note 26, at p. 106. Also consult the Hippocratic Oath.

certify a hospital for intern training, the AMA controls the source of supply of a crucial agent for the production of hospital care. Control over the supply of interns has been used to induce hospitals to admit to their staffs only members of county medical associations. Since membership in the county medical associations is in the control of organized medicine, and membership in a hospital staff is extremely important for the successful practice of most branches of medicine, the individual doctor can be easily manipulated by those who control membership in county medical associations.

Members of the medical profession are also subject to another type of control, derived from AMA control over post-graduate medical education, that is particularly effective over younger members. Membership in a county medical society is a necessary condition for admission to specialty board examinations for a number of specialties, and passing these examinations is a necessary condition for specialty ratings.[31] Non-society members cannot win board membership in these specialties. This is a particularly important form of control over newcomers to the medical profession because newcomers tend to be young doctors who aspire to specialty board ratings.[32] Consequently the AMA has particularly powerful sanctions over those who are most likely to be price cutters. These are young doctors trying to establish a practice.[33]

B. THE EVIDENCE

Just as one would expect an all-out war to reveal a country's most powerful weapons, substantial threats to the continued existence of price discrimination ought to reveal the strongest sanctions available to organized medicine. For this reason, the opposition or lack of opposition to prepaid medical plans that provide medical service directly to the patient ought to be illuminating.

Generally speaking, there exist two classes of medical insurance. One is the cash indemnity variety. Blue Cross and Blue Shield plans fall within this class.[34] Under cash indemnity medical insurance, the doctor and patient are

---

[31] Hyde and Wolff, op. cit. supra note 19, at p. 952.

[32] A statement of sanctions similar to that noted above appears in Restrictions on Free Enterprise in Medicine, p. 9 (April 1949), pamphlet, Committee on Research in Medical Economics.

[33] "Other things being equal, old well-established concerns tend to be more hostile to price cutting than younger concerns." G. Stocking and M. Watkins, Monopoly and Free Enterprise, p. 117 (1951).

[34] Most of these plans have services provisions; that is, they agree to provide the service required to treat particular ailments only if the subscriber's income is below some pre-assigned level. Of the 78 plans approved by organized medicine, 58 have service provisions. Of these, only 3 provide service to all income classes. The remainder provide a cash indemnity to subscribers whose income exceeds the relevant pre-assigned income levels. Therefore, these plans do not interfere with the discriminatory pricing policies of doctors. Consult Voluntary Prepayment Medical Benefit Plans, American Medical Association (1954).

able to determine fees jointly at the time medical service is sold just as if there were no insurance. Therefore, this class of medical insurance leaves unaffected the power of doctors to discriminate between differences in demand in setting fees. If anything, doctors welcome insurance since it improves the ability of the patient to pay. On the other hand, for non-indemnity type plans, plans that provide medical services directly as contrasted with plans that provide funds to be used to purchase desired services, payments are typically independent of income. Costs of membership in such prepayment plans are a function of family size, age, coverage, quality of service, etc., but are independent of the income of the subscriber. Consequently, such plans represent a means for massive price cutting to high income patients. For this reason, the reception of these plans by organized medicine constitutes an experiment for testing the validity of the discriminating monopoly model. If no opposition to these plans exists, then the implication of the discriminating monopoly model —that some mechanism must exist for maintaining the structure of prices— is invalid. On the other hand, opposition to these plans by organized medicine constitutes observable phenomena that support this implication. If such opposition exists, then it supports the discriminating monoply hypothesis in addition to providing evidence of the specific character of the sanctions available to organized medicine.

A number of independent observers have found that a systematic pattern of opposition to prepaid medical service plans, as contrasted with cash indemnity plans, exists. "In many parts of the county, organized medical bodies have been distinctly hostile to group practice. This is particularly true where the group is engaged in any form of prepaid medical care."[35] "Early groups were disparaged as unethical. But within recent years active steps have been taken only against those groups offering a plan for some type of flat-fee payment."[36] "There is reason to believe that the Oregon, the San Diego, and the District of Columbia cases exemplify a nationwide pattern of behavior by the American Medical Association and its state and county subsidiaries. What has come into the open here is working beneath the surface in other states and counties."[37] This systematic pattern of opposition to single price medical plans has taken two distinct courses. These are (1) using sanctions in an effort to terminate the life of prepaid medical plans already in existence and (2) lobbying for legislation that would abort their birth.

There have been a number of dramatic battles for survival by prepaid non-price discriminatory medical plans resulting from the efforts of organized medicine to destroy them. These struggles have brought into action the most

[35] Building America's Health, report to the President by the Commission on the Health Needs of the Nation, V. I, p. 34 (1952).

[36] Hyde and Wolff, op. cit. supra note 19, at p. 977.

[37] Op. cit. supra note 32, at p. 14.

powerful sanctions available to organized medicine for use against price cutters. Consequently, the history of these battles provides valuable evidence of the character of the weapons available to the participants. For this purpose, the experiences of the following organizations are particularly illuminating: Farmers Union Hospital Association of Elk City, Oklahoma, the Kaiser Foundation of San Francisco and Oakland, Group Health of Washington, Group Health Cooperative of Puget Sound, Civic Medical Center of Chicago, Complete Service Bureau of San Diego, and the medical cooperatives in the State of Oregon. These plans are diverse, from the point of view of location, organization, equipment, sponsorship and objective. However, they all have one crucial unifying characteristic—fees or service charges are independent of income.[38] Similarly, the experiences of Ross-Loos in Los Angeles and the Palo Alto Clinic in California are illuminating because these organizations both operate prepayment single price medical plans and nevertheless continue to stay within the good graces of organized medicine.

The founder and director of the cooperative Farmers Union Hospital in Elk City, Oklahoma, Dr. Michael A. Shadid, was harassed for a number of years by his local county medical association as a consequence of founding and operating this price cutting organization. He was ingeniously thrown out of the Beckham County Medical Society; this organization was dissolved and reconstituted apparently for the sole purpose of not inviting Shadid to become a member of the "new" organization. Before founding the cooperative, Shadid had been a member in good standing in his county medical association for over a decade.

The loss of hospital privileges stemming from non-county society membership was not sufficient for the task of putting Shadid out of business, because his organization had its own hospital. Therefore, organized medicine turned to its control over licensure to put the cooperative out of business. Shadid was equal to this challenge. He was shrewd enough to draw members of the politically potent Farmers Union into his organization. Therefore, in the struggle to take away Shadid's license to practice medicine, the farmers were pitted

---

[38] The Health Insurance Plan of New York is not included in the foregoing enumeration because charges are not completely independent of income. For determining premiums, families are divided into two groups, those with incomes above $6,500 are assessed premiums twenty per cent greater than those applicable to the lower income group. Consult M. M. Davis, Medical Care for Tomorrow, p. 237 (1955). However, as a threat against the structure of prices for medical services based on income, this plan is almost as potent as those listed. Consequently, the opposition to it ought to be just about as severe and the weapons employed just as interesting for gaining insights into the nature of the sanctions over the behavior of individual doctors by organized medicine.

Available evidence suggests that HIP is under attack. See the testimony of G. Baehr, President and Medical Director of HIP in Hearings, op. cit. note 9, at pp. 1604, 1642, and 1663. Legislation that would outlaw such plans as HIP has been sponsored by organized medicine. Consult N.Y. Times, p. 15, col. 5 (Feb. 21, 1954).

against the doctors. The doctors came out of this political battle the losers because the state governor at the time, Murray, sided with the farmers.[39] However, the Beckham County Medical Society has been powerful enough to keep doctors who were known to be coming to Oklahoma to join Shadid's organization from getting a license to practice, powerful enough to frighten and cause the departure of a doctor who had been associated with Shadid's organization for a substantial period of time, powerful enough to keep Shadid out of a two-week postgraduate course on bone fractures at the Cook County Graduate School of Medicine (the course was open only to members in good standing of their local county medical societies), and was able to get enough of Shadid's doctors drafted during the war to endanger the life of his organization.[40] In recent years, the tide of battle has turned. The Hospital Association brought suit against the Beckham County Medical Society and its members for conspiracy in restraint of trade. This case was settled out of court. As part of this settlement, the county medical association agreed to accept the staff of the cooperative as members.

The experience of the Kaiser Foundation Plan is parallel to that of the Farmers Union. Both were vigorously opposed by organized medicine. The medical staff in each case could not obtain membership in local county medical societies. In both cases, the plans were able to prosper despite this obstacle, since they operated their own hospitals. In both cases, the doctor draft was used as a tool in an attempt to put these plans out of business.[41]

Control by organized medicine over licensure was used as a weapon in an attempt to kill the Kaiser Plan. Dr. Sidney Garfield, the plan's medical director, was tried by the State Board of Medical Examiners for unprofessional conduct. Garfield's license to practice was suspended for one year and he was placed on probation for five years. However, the suspension was withheld pending good behavior while on probation. This ruling by the State Board of Examiners was not supported in Court. Superior Court Judge Edward P. Murphy ordered the board to rescind all action against Garfield. The judge ruled that the board was arbitrary in denying Garfield a fair trial. Subsequently the appellate court reversed the decision of the trial court on one count but not the second. Nevertheless the judgment of the trial court in

[39] Davis argues that Shadid would have lost his license to practice if he had not had the powerful political support of the farmers. Op. cit. supra note 38 at p. 229.

[40] The story of Shadid and his organization may be found in M. A. Shadid, A Doctor for the People (1939), and Doctors of Today and Tomorrow (1947). In Two Harbors, Minnesota, doctors associated with a medical society disapproved plan could not win admission to their local county medical society and a doctor associated with this plan could not get into the same school from which Shadid had been barred—the Cook County Graduate School of Medicine. 71 Christian Century 173 (Feb. 10, 1954).

[41] For evidence on this point for the Kaiser Plan, see Hearings before a Subcommittee of the Senate Committee on Education and Labor, pt. 1, p. 338 ff., 77th Cong. 2nd Sess. on S. Res. 291 (1942).

rescinding the decision of the board of examiners was upheld. The entire matter was sent back to the board for reconsideration of penalty.[42]

Subsequently, Garfield was tried by the county medical association for unethical practices, namely advertising, and found guilty. However, he came away from this trial with only a reprimand and not the loss of his license.[43] By virtue of having its own hospitals and legal intervention by the courts against the rulings of organized medicine, the Kaiser Foundation has been able to resist the onslaughts of its foes. However, the battle is not over yet. Although Kaiser Foundation doctors are now admitted to the Alameda County Society, the San Francisco County Society still excludes them.[44]

Group Health in Washington was not as fortunate as Kaiser or Farmers Union with respect to hospitals. Unlike these other two organizations, Group Health did not have its own hospital and therefore was dependent upon the existing hospitals in the community. Consequently, when Group Health doctors were ejected from the District Medical Society, Group Health was seriously crippled. Nearly all the hospitals in the district were coerced into denying staff privileges to Group Health doctors and bed space to their patients. Moreover, many doctors were deterred from becoming members of the Group Health staff because of fear of punitive action by the District Medical Society. Still other doctors who were members of the Group Health medical staff suddenly discovered attractive employment possibilities elsewhere and resigned their Group Health positions.[45]

It was fortunate for Group Health that it was located in Washington, D.C. and therefore under the jurisdiction of federal laws, in particular the Sherman Act. The tactics of the District Medical Society and the AMA came to the attention of the Justice Department. This led to the successful criminal prosecution of organized medicine under the Sherman Act. The opinion of the Supreme Court delivered by Mr. Justice Roberts pinpoints the primary concern of the petitioners, the District Medical Society and the AMA. "In truth, the petitioners represented physicians who desired that they and all others should practice independently on a fee for service basis, where whatever arrangement for payment each had was a matter that lay between him and his patient in each individual case of service or treatment."[46]

---

[42] P. DeKruif, Life Among the Doctors, p. 416 (1949). The last two chapters of this book deal with the activities of organized medicine against the Kaiser Plan. For the decision of the appellate court, see Garfield v. Medical Examiners, 99 C. A. 2d 219, 221 P. 2d 705 (1950).

[43] Mayer reports that Dr. Louis Schmidt, the urologist, was expelled from organized medicine for advertising his venereal disease clinic. 180 Harpers 27 (Dec. 1939).

[44] Means, op. cit. supra note 5, at p. 131. Opposition to Kaiser also exists in Los Angeles area where this plan also operates. 83 Bulletin of the Los Angeles County Medical Society 501 (1953) contains a condemnation of the Kaiser Plan and a call-to-arms.

[45] Hyde and Wolff, op. cit. supra note 19, at p. 990.

[46] American Medical Association v. United States, 317 U.S. 519, 536 (1943).

As a result of this victory, consumer sovereignty with respect to Group Health was restored. As might be suspected from the intense opposition of the AMA and the District Medical Society, Group Health has shown unusual survival properties and flourishes in competition with fee-for-service medical care. Since its victory at court, good relations with the District Medical Society have been achieved by the Group Health staff.[47]

In view of the previous cases cited, the experience of the Group Health Cooperative of Puget Sound, Washington, takes on a familiar cast. The King County Medical Association objected to this prepayment plan. They claimed it was "unethical" because under the terms of the plan subscribers could not employ any doctor in the community. Subscribers could use only doctors who were members of the health plan. Staff members of Group Health were expelled from the county medical association and new additions to the Group Health staff were found ineligible for society membership. The local medical society refused to accept transfers of membership from other county medical associations of doctors who expected to join the staff of the cooperative. The Group Health staff was unable to use the existing hospitals of the community, thereby limiting the value of the plan to many members and potential members. Moreover, the staff was cut off from many scientific meetings and was unable to consult with the orthodox members of the profession. However, the cooperative survived despite the hostility of the county medical society.

As a direct consequence of these harassing measures adopted by the King County Medical Society, the cooperative brought action against the county medical society, charging that the defendants had conspired against them in an effort to force the cooperative out of business. This case went to the state supreme court and was won by the cooperative although no damages were allowed.[48] Mr. Justice Hamley said that "The purpose of the Society . . . has been primarily to benefit the members of the Society and its affiliates through the elimination of such competition. The means employed has . . . been oppressive in the extreme. . . ."[49] Subsequently, the justice went on to argue that the activities of the county medical association against Group Health were designed to eliminate competition in the contract medicine field.[50] The court ruled that the defendants should not exclude applicants from membership in the county medical society or hospitals because of their affiliation with Group Health, and should cease discouraging doctors from joining Group Health or consulting with its staff.[51]

[47] Becker, President, Group Health Association, Hearings before Senate Committee on Education and Labor, pt. 5, p. 2528, 79th Cong. 2nd Sess. on S. Res. 1606 (1946).

[48] Group Health Etc. v. King Co. Med. Soc., 39 Wash. 2d 586, 237 P. 2d 737 (1951).

[49] Ibid., at p. 622 and 757.

[50] Ibid., at p. 640 and 766.

[51] Ibid., at p. 664 and 780; Consult Means, op. cit. supra note 5, at pp. 177–181.

In testimony before a Senate Committee, Dr. Lawrence Jacques of the Civic Medical Center in Chicago reported that none of the staff of this medical center (it numbered fifteen at that time) had succeeded in being admitted to the county medical association.[52] Repeated applications for admission had either been ignored or rejected by the Chicago Medical Society. Appeals to the Illinois State Medical Society and the American Medical Association proved to be fruitless. A direct appeal by a committee of patients of the Civic Medical Center to the county medical association on behalf of their doctors was of little avail.

The doctors associated with the Complete Service Bureau of San Diego could not obtain membership in the county medical society and the patients and doctors associated with the plan were barred from the major hospitals of San Diego County. The county society published paid advertisements in the current editions of the San Diego telephone directory designating the members of the San Diego Medical Society among the physicians listed in the directory. These advertisements contained statements that gave the impression that non-society members were not qualified to practice medicine for professional and moral reasons. As a result of society opposition, the bureau had difficulty in hiring doctors at the going market price for their services.[53]

In Oregon, doctors serving on the staff of medical cooperatives were expelled from county medical societies and hospital facilities were made available only to doctors and the patients of doctors who were members in good standing of their local medical societies. Moreover, society members systematically refused to consult with non-society members and spread false propaganda in an effort to discredit society opposed plans.[54] The government brought action against the Oregon Medical Society under the Sherman Act and lost.[55]

The Civic Medical Center in Chicago did not have its own hospital. The members of the center were able to practice in only two hospitals in the entire Chicago area, and in neither of these two hospitals did they have full staff privileges. These limited staff privileges seriously hampered the operations of the group in the two hospitals in which they could practice. For example, in one of the hospitals surgical cases could not be scheduled for more than two days in advance by a physician unless he was a full staff member. In the words of Jacques, "The handicaps of nonmembership in the local medical society are serious and far-reaching and in effect amount to a partial revoca-

[52] Hearings, op. cit. supra note 47, at p. 2630 ff.

[53] Op. cit. supra note 32, at p. 11.

[54] Ibid.

[55] For the reasons for this loss, see United States v. Oregon Med. Soc., 343 U.S. 326 (1952) and the discussion of the case in Hyde and Wolff, op. cit. supra note 19, at p. 1020. One gets the impression from reading this case that the practices of the state society that would have led to victory for the government were discontinued in 1941.

tion of licensure to practice medicine."[56] During the war, some of the men in this group were disqualified for service as medical officers in the Navy, but nevertheless draftable as enlisted men, because applications to serve as medical officers were automatically rejected unless accompanied by a letter certifying that the candidate was a member in good standing of his local county medical society.[57] When Jacques was asked why his group was being excluded from the county medical association, his response was: "The evidence at hand suggests . . . that we are being excluded because of our prepayment plan."[58]

Apparently the value of price discrimination is deemed to be so great that the AMA has opposed "free" medical care to veterans by the Veterans Administration.[59] Free VA care for veterans would increase enormously the quantity of medical services demanded by making the marginal costs of these services zero for veterans.[60] Moreover opposing free care to veterans comes at a great cost to organized medicine.[61]

---

[56] Hearings, op. cit. supra note 47, at p. 2642.

[57] Apparently this rule is no longer in effect. Consult Hyde and Wolff, op. cit. supra note 19, at p. 951 n. 84.

[58] Hearings, op. cit. supra note 47, at p. 2644.

[59] It seems likely that the value of price discrimination has increased in recent years. In the last two decades, there has been a widespread development of consumer credit. This development has made it possible for credit bureaus to collect extensive and reliable data on consumer incomes. Such data are available to subscribers to credit bureau services. Therefore, doctors that belong to credit bureaus are able to price discriminate more precisely than would have been possible if they had to rely on the unsupported testimony of patients for income data. ". . . routine credit check of patient who had always been billed at modest rates—and learned that he was in fact the owner of thirty oil wells!" Mills, Credit Ratings: How You Can Use Them, 33 Medical Economics 171, 172 (May 1956).

[60] AMA opposition to free medical care for veterans constitutes evidence against the hypothesis that the AMA opposes direct service non-indemnity type group plans because they increase the efficiency with which medical resources are employed and therefore effectively increase the supply of doctors.

Still stronger evidence against the rationalization of opposition to direct service prepayment plans as a manifestation of opposition to changes that increase the efficiency with which the existing stock of doctors can be utilized, i.e., increase the supply schedule of physicians services, is the relative lack of opposition to group practices. Therefore, unless one is willing to postulate that it is the method of payment associated with prepayment medical plans that is a source of efficiency, one cannot argue that opposition to prepayment plans is on a par with the destruction by workers of machines that improve workers' efficiency.

"Group practice of medicine on a fee-for-service basis is tolerated and even admired by most doctors. The entire profession also strongly advocates voluntary medical insurance. Yet many physicians and some local medical societies violently disapprove of the combination of group practice with pre-payment and do everything in their power to prevent or destroy it." Baehr, Hearings, op. cit. supra note 9, at p. 1642.

[61] This opposition has won organized medicine a powerful foe. A. J. Connell, an ex-National Commander of the American Legion has attacked organized medicine as a "most powerful and monopolistic medical guild." N.Y. Times, p. 17, col. 3 (Jan. 29, 1954). In opposing "socialized medicine" these two groups were allies.

If price discrimination is in fact highly valued by organized medicine and prepayment direct service medical plans have been opposed in order to maintain a structure of discriminating prices, doesn't the existence of the prepayment plans unopposed by the AMA constitute an anomaly?[62]

How can the Ross-Loos and Palo Alto Clinic cases be explained?[63] The Ross-Loos plan in Los Angeles is a prepaid medical plan that is a profit-seeking organization. It was started in 1929 and by the end of 1952 had 127,000 members.[64] The Ross-Loos plan does not have hospitals of its own and is therefore forced to rely on the existing hospitals of the community. Consequently, the condemnation of this plan by organized medicine which occurred after it won acceptance from consumers in the medical care market, represented an enormous threat to its continued existence. The Ross-Loos plan doctors were expelled from the Los Angeles County Medical Association. Among the doctors to lose their county society membership was a former President of the Los Angeles County Medical Society. As a result of a number of appeals to higher courts, all within the judicial machinery of organized medicine, the decision that would have crippled if not destroyed this plan was reversed.

An excellent reason for this reversal is suggested by the testimony of Dr. H. Clifford Loos, a co-founder of Ross-Loos. In response to the question, "Are you handicapped to any extent by the fact that you are not able to advertise," Dr. Loos replied:

> As far as that goes, we do not care to be big, or bigger. If I had accepted all of the groups who applied to us, we would need our city hall to house us. We have put the brakes on. We can't accept too many. We feel we can't be too big.[65]

This constitutes strange behavior indeed for a profit-seeking institution that certainly ought to have no fears of Justice Department action for either being too large or monopolizing an industry. One cannot help suspecting that the

---

[62] Evidence of opposition to price cutting on a more modest scale exists. Individuals who have cut prices have either encountered the sanctions of organized medicine or a threat to employ these sanctions. Consult, Medical Group's Protests Stop Polio Shot Project in Brooklyn, N.Y. Times, p. 33M (Sept. 12, 1956). The Los Angeles Times reports that Dr. Sylvan O. Tatkin filed a complaint in the Superior Court of Los Angeles charging that the local association was engaging in unlawful rate fixing. Tatkin charged that he was refused membership in the local society and therefore dropped from the staff of Behrens Memorial Hospital in Glendale as a result of price cutting. L.A. Times, sec. 2, p. 30, col. 4 (June 29, 1956).

Economic theory implies that there would be no point for a monopolist that has control over supply being concerned with prices directly. For a non-discriminating monopolist, control over supply implies control over prices.

[63] There is evidence that opposition to prepayment plans is not merely local society policy. In Logan County, Arkansas, the entire county society was expelled from the state society by means of charter revocation. The local society was dominated by physicians participating in a disapproved plan. 27 Journal of the Arkansas Medical Society 29 (1930).

[64] Hearings, op. cit. supra note 9, at p. 1451.   [65] Ibid., at p. 1469.

amicable relations with the Los Angeles County Medical Society may have been acquired at the cost of a sharply curtailed rate of expansion.[66]

The Palo Alto Clinic in California provides prepaid medical care that is non-income discriminating to the students, employees, and faculty of Stanford University. This constitutes a small fraction of the clinic's business. Eighty-five per cent of the receipts of the clinic are attributable to conventional fee-for-service practice that lends itself to discriminatory pricing. This clinic continues to stay within the good graces of organized medicine. When questioned about extending the prepaid non-discriminatory service, Dr. Russel V. Lee, Director of the Clinic and Professor of Medicine in the School of Medicine of Stanford University, threw some light upon this apparent anomaly. "Several of the industries in the area have come to us for such service. We have been trying to get our county medical society approval before we go into these things, and we are doing a little job of county medical education because in general the county medical society will not approve of anything that smacks of a closed panel."[67] This suggests that the Palo Alto Clinic is in the position of having to go to its principal competitors for permission to sell its services to new customers. This is comparable to a requirement that a Ford dealer must first obtain the permission of his competing Chevrolet dealer before he can sell Fords to non-Ford owners who have asked for the opportunity to buy them. Probably the county medical society that includes the Palo Alto Clinic does not feel that the present level of sales of prepaid medical services by this clinic is high enough to justify the costs and risks of punitive action.

Organized medicine, i.e., the AMA and its political subdivisions, has opposed prepaid non-price-discriminatory medical plans not only directly by fighting against them but also indirectly by lobbying for legislation that would make such plans illegal. State medical societies have achieved a fair degree of success in sponsoring legislation designed to prevent price cutting in the medical care market caused by prepaid medical plans. As of 1954, "there are at least 20 states that have had such laws passed at the instigation of medical societies, which are designed to prevent prepaid group practice and to keep medical practice on a fee-for-service solo basis."[68] Another source says:

[66] Loos has also served as an expert witness for the San Diego County Society during its struggle with another prepayment plan. Complete Service Bureau v. San Diego County Med. Soc., 43 C. 2d 201, 212, 272, P.2d 497, 504 (1954). Hyde and Wolff, op. cit. supra note 19, at p. 985 impute the tolerance of Ross-Loos by organized medicine to the fact that it is physician sponsored as contrasted with being lay or non-physician sponsored. The theory outlined in this paper implies that this is not a relevant distinction.

[67] Hearings op. cit. supra note 9, at p. 1559.

[68] Baehr, Hearings, op. cit. supra note 9, at p. 1594. Very unorthodox lobbying tactics have been successfully employed by distinguished doctors to achieve the legislative goals of organized medicine. See Osler's forthright description in H. Young, A Surgeons' Autobiography, p. 407 (1940).

"Most of the states now have restrictive statutes permitting only the medical profession to operate or to control prepayment medical care plans."[69] Hansen lists as one of the primary objectives of this legislation "to preserve the fee-for-service system as far as possible by controlling the financial administration of the plans."[70]

IV. IMPLICATIONS OF THE DISCRIMINATING MONOPOLY MODEL

In the preceding section, this paper has been concerned with establishing the validity of the discriminating monopoly model for understanding the pricing of an important class of medical services—those produced by doctors in hospitals. Evidence of the existence of a pattern of relatively direct and obvious controls was presented. Yet it was argued that maintaining a structure of discriminatory prices for this large number of independent producers represents a fantastically difficult control problem. Does the existence of this difficult control problem shed any light upon other aspects of the medical profession? Our concern is largely with the more subtle or less obvious methods of control over the price policies of individual doctors.

The controls previously discussed are analogous to surgery; the controls to be discussed are analogous to preventive medicine. In particular, we explore the possibilities of a relationship between maintaining a structure of prices based on income differences and: the representation of specialists in power positions within organized medicine; discrimination against minority groups in admission to medical schools; the free treatment by doctors of other doctors and their families; the position of organized medicine on advertising; the defense of county medical association members against malpractice suits; the *no-criticism rules* that forbid unfavorable comment by one physician of another physician's work before a member of the lay public.

Specialists have more to gain from price discrimination than non-specialists because their work is more likely to be associated with hospitals. The power to withhold hospital facilities from doctors constitutes the strongest weapon for maintaining price discipline within the medical profession. Therefore, discrimination in pricing ordinary office visits as compared with services rendered in a hospital is much less pronounced. In fact, prices charged for office visits ought to be relatively independent of patient's incomes. Office care can be provided by doctors with no hospital connections whatsoever. Consequently, specialists, particularly those who do most of their work in hospitals, have a

[69] Hansen, Laws Affecting Group Health Plans, 35 Iowa L. Rev. 209, 225 (1950).

[70] Ibid., at p. 209. Yet in his conclusion, Hansen argues that "Farsighted medical societies should find no valid reason for opposing group health enabling legislation. Instead they should welcome experimentation in the field of medical economics with the same spirit they welcome it in the field of medical science." pp. 235-36. It is one of the implications of this paper that the more farsighted medical societies provide the strongest opposition to experimentation in the field of medical economics.

greater interest in maintaining price discrimination than general practitioners. Therefore, the fact that specialists are over-represented, as measured by the ratio of specialists to all doctors, in the AMA hiararchy is no accident.[71] This is precisely the group that has the greatest economic interest in maintaining price discipline and for this reason, are "naturals" for the job.[72]

Newcomers, even if they were formerly presidents of county societies elsewhere, are probationary members when they join some county societies.[73] They achieve full membership only after a successful term as probationary members. Relegating newcomers to a probationary status is a means for segregating from the general membership those who have a relatively high probability of being price cutters.[74] Newcomers represent a group whose members are trying to acquire practices and therefore are more likely to be price cutters than society members who have well established practices. Consequently newcomers require both an extraordinary degree of surveillance and a strong indication of the costs of non-compliance. Probationary membership achieves both of these objectives.[75]

The advertisement of medical services is approved by the medical profession if and only if such advertisements redound to the interest of the profession as a whole. Advertisements in this class are, for example, announcements of the availability for sale of Blue Cross type medical plans. These plans allow their subscribers the choice of any licensed practitioner. Organized medicine consequently takes the position that these advertisements are of benefit to the entire profession. On the other hand, advertisements that primarily redound to the interests of a particular group, for example, advertisements by a closed panel medical group, are frowned upon. Advertisements in this class are, by definition, resorted to only by "unethical" doctors. Why this difference in the

---

[71] Garceau, op. cit. supra note 26, at pp. 55–58. Hyde and Wolff, op. cit. supra note 19, at p. 947.

[72] Some observers have explained the over-representation of specialists in the AMA hierarchy as attributable to their greater incomes. Larger incomes imply that specialists are better able to afford the "luxury" of political activity. This explanation implies that psychiatrists and dermatologists ought to be just as over-represented as surgeons, abstracting from income differences. On the other hand, the argument advanced here implies that surgeons ought to be more strongly represented because membership in the AMA hierarchy can be more useful for advancing the economic interests of surgeons than it can be for those other specialties. This difference stems from the fact that psychiatrists and dermatologists do not use hospitals to the same extent in their practices.

There exists some reason for believing that among specialists, surgeons are over-represented in medical politics. One observer reports, "Our medical societies are not merely specialist-dominated; they are surgeon dominated." Berger, op. cit. supra note 11, p. 272.

[73] Hyde and Wolff, op. cit. supra note 19, at p. 941 n. 20 and p. 951 n. 83.

[74] Stocking and Watkins, op. cit. supra note 33, at p. 117.

[75] Some societies have indoctrination programs for newcomers. Drennen, They Help Young Doctors Get Started Right, 32 Medical Economics 104 (June, 1955). Drennen observes that for the newcomer such a program ". . . helps keep him on the path of righteousness." p. 108.

position of organized medicine with respect to these two classes of advertising? The approved class, insofar as it achieves its objective, tends to increase the aggregate demand for medical care. On the other hand, the disapproved variety will have the effect of reallocating patients from the profession as a whole to those who advertise. Consequently, advertising in this class constitutes competitive behavior and leads to price cutting. It tends to pit one doctor or one group of doctors against the profession as a whole with respect to shares of the medical care market. Active competition for increased shares of the medical care market by doctors would tend to eliminate price discrimination based on income differences.

The significance of advertising as a means for maintaining free entry is revealed by two bits of interrelated evidence. These are the strong opposition of organized medicine to advertising calling the public's attention to the services of a particular group of doctors and the willingness of some prepaid medical plans to incur the wrath of organized medicine by undertaking such advertising. Kaiser, the Civic Medical Center, and the Complete Service Bureau at one time or another advertised.[76] The use of advertising in the face of strong opposition by organized medicine implies that advertising plays a crucial role in enabling these groups to capture part of the medical care market. Consequently the ban on such advertising by organized medicine constitutes a barrier to entry into this market and is a means for keeping doctors from competing with one another and thereby incidentally destroying the structure of prices.

County medical societies play a crucial role in protecting their members against malpractice suits. Physicians charged with malpractice are tried by their associates in the private judicial system of organized medicine. If found innocent, then local society members are available for duty as expert witnesses in the defense of those charged with malpractice. Needless to say, comparable services by society members for plaintiffs in such actions are not equally available. By virtue of this monopoly over the services of expert witnesses and the tacit coalition of the members of a society in the defense of any of their members, the successful prosecution of malpractice suits against society members is extremely difficult.

On the other hand, for doctors who are persona-non-grata with respect to organized medicine, the shoe is on the other foot. Expert witnesses from the ranks of organized medicine are abundantly available for plaintiffs but not for defendants. Therefore the position of a plaintiff in a suit against a non-society member is of an order of magnitude stronger than it is for a suit

---

[76] "For the first ten months of its existence, with a considerable reluctance it continued the policy of institutional advertising, because it was felt that the clinic could not survive unless it was brought actively to the attention of the public." Jacques, Hearings, op. cit. supra note 41, at p. 2634. Complete Service Bureau v. San Diego County Med. Soc., 43 C.2d 201, 214–216, 272 P.2d 497, 504–506 (1954).

against a society member. Consequently it should come as no surprise that the costs of malpractice insurance for non-society members is substantially higher than it is for society members. Apparently some non-society members have experienced difficulty in obtaining malpractice insurance at any price.[77]

This coalition among the members of the medical profession not to testify against one another, like structured prices, puts some doctors in a position of pursuing a policy that does not maximize personal returns. Therefore more than just professional ethics makes this coalition viable. As might be expected, the ability of organized medicine to expel doctors from hospital staffs plays a crucial role in keeping doctors from testifying against one another. Belli reports that a doctor who acted as an expert witness in a malpractice suit he tried was subsequently barred from the staff of every hospital in California.[78] It is because of sanctions of this character that we can find reports of patients with strong prima facie evidence of negligence and yet unable to hire expert witnesses from the ranks of the medical profession.[79]

As a result of this coalition among society members for malpractice defense, two effects are achieved. The more direct and obvious consequence is an increase in the monopoly returns to the members of this profession over what they otherwise would be. The other is the welding together of the medical profession as an in-group. In this latter role, the coalition for malpractice defense is a force that has the same effect as a reciprocity, that is, the free treatment by doctors of other doctors and their families, and the rule that doctors are not to criticize one another in public.[80] The function of reciprocity and *no-criticism* is to induce the members of the medical profession to behave towards one another as if they were members of an in-group. Doctors are subtly coerced into personal relations with one another. Insofar as these measures bear fruit, doctors view themselves as a large association in which members deal with one another on a personal level. In relation to the general public, i.e., outsiders, the in-group, doctors, are united.

But what does the medical profession achieve by subtly coercing its mem-

---

[77] Garceau, op. cit. supra note 26, at p. 103 ff; Jacques, Hearings, op. cit. supra note 47, at p. 2642; Hyde and Wolff, op. cit. supra note 19, at p. 951 n. 86; Belli, op. cit. supra note 28, at p. 109.

[78] Belli, op. cit. supra note 28, at p. 98; The California Malpractice Controversy, 9 Stanford L. Rev. 731 (1957).

[79] See the story by Ullman in the Toledo Blade of June 12, 1946, about a surgery patient who was unable to hire an expert witness for demonstrating negligence in a case involving a sponge that a surgeon forgot to remove before sewing up the patient. Belli reports no such problem in hiring expert witnesses for legal malpractice cases. Op. cit. supra note 28, at p. 95.

[80] N. S. Davis, History of Medicine, ch. 14 (1907); Wylie, Conspiracy of Silence, 29 Medical Economics 167 (April 1952); Doctor Fights Expulsion on Slander Charge, 32 Medical Economics 269 (Dec. 1954). This is the story of a doctor expelled from his county medical society for expressing opinions about the professional competence of his colleagues, to patients.

bers into in-group relations with one another? The relationships among members of a family, an in-group par excellence, reveal the importance of these subtle controls. Members of a family are relatively reluctant to criticize one another before outsiders, tend not to charge each other market prices for services extended to one another, and try to avoid being in direct competition. The essence of in-group behavior is personal relationships among its members. On the other hand, the essential property of market place relationships is impersonality. Consequently insofar as a non-market place attitude can be fostered and maintained within the medical profession, such an attitude constitutes a barrier against doctors thinking of one another as competitors in the medical care market. This in itself constitutes a barrier against such market place activities as cutting prices.[81]

To the extent that the culture of members of an in-group is distinct from that of non-members, this difference reduces the probability that non-members can successfully "join" the in-group. Differences in culture and values constitute a natural barrier to integration. This is particularly important for medicine because it is both a social and an economic club and the returns of the economic club are related to the degree of social cohesion that exists within the social club. Consequently, members of culturally distinct minority groups would be more difficult to assimilate into such an in-group and it is likely that many would never feel that they were completely members under the best of circumstances. This implies that members of such minority groups would be more difficult to control by means of the informal controls characteristic of in-groups. Being thrown out of a country club is not much of a loss if one is only the janitor; for informal controls to be effective, they must be exercised over those who belong. Insofar as some minority groups are more difficult to assimilate, there exists an *a priori* basis for discrimination. It is to keep out those who have a higher probability of not being willing to go along with the majority. Minority groups whose culture and values are different from those of the majority could rationally be discriminated against in admission to medical schools because they are more difficult to control by informal controls after they are out in medical practice than is characteristic of the population at large.

The discrimination against Jews in admission to medical schools has been

---

[81] If the hypothesis presented here is correct, then it should be possible to observe a difference between the variance of surgical and psychiatric fees after abstracting from variations caused by differences in skills, type of operation and difficulty of particular cases. This difference would be imputable to the strong control over the pricing of surgical services by means of control over hospitals. Since reciprocity and *no-criticism* rules are viable because they help maintain structured prices, they should not be observed as rigorously by psychiatrists as surgeons. On this latter point, there exists evidence consistent with the hypothesis presented here. Psychiatrists have been the first, and thus far the only group within the medical profession to abandon reciprocity. Miller, Doctors Should Pay for Medical Care!, 30 Medical Economics 82, 84 (Jan. 1953).

explained, by both Jews and non-Jews alike, as a consequence of irrational prejudice.[82] Yet Jews might be regarded as the prototype of a minority group with cultural properties that, given the special problems of maintaining internal discipline within the medical profession, would make them undesirable candidates for admission to this profession. These cultural attributes evolved as a consequence of centuries of unparalleled persecution. This persecution, which by and large was economic, took the form of laws that barred Jews from particular product and labor markets in many of the most important countries in the history of western civilization. Cartels such as guilds followed similar policies. This exclusion policy channelled Jews into highly competitive markets, markets characterized by free entry, and forced them to develop their commercial skills to a higher level than was characteristic of the population at large in order to survive economically. For Jews, a medieval guild type share-the-market attitude was a non-survival property whereas a policy of vigorously competing was a survival property. The process of adaptation by Jews to laws constraining their economic activities led them to develop considerable ingenuity in minimizing the impact of such laws upon their economic well being. Jews developed into robust competitors with little respect for rules, either government or private, that regulated economic activities and with a substantial body of practical experience in implementing this point of view.[83] These attitudes became a part of Jewish cultural tradition

[82] For direct evidence on discrimination against Jews in admission to medical schools, consult, Hart, Anti-Semitism in Medical Schools, 65 American Mercury 53 (July 1947); Kingdon, Discrimination in Medical Colleges, 60 American Mercury 391 (Oct. 1945); Bloomgarden, Medical School Quotas and National Health, 15 Commentary 29 (Jan. 1953); Goldberg, Jews in the Medical Profession—A National Survey, 1 Jewish Social Studies 327 (1939); Shapiro, Racial Discrimination in Medicine, 10 Jewish Social Studies 103 (1948).

The indirect evidence on this point seems to be more convincing than the direct evidence. Practically all of the Americans who study medicine abroad are Jews. No comparable evidence for the study by American Jews of law, dentistry, accounting, engineering, etc. in foreign countries exists. Therefore, the hypothesis that Jews prefer to study abroad is not tenable. On the other hand, this evidence is consistent with the hypothesis that Jews are strongly discriminated against in this country. Consult Levinger, Jewish Medical Students in America, 2 Medical Leaves 91, 94 (1939) and Goldberg, supra at p. 332.

Some observers have used a Noah's Ark approach to determine whether or not discrimination against Jews in admission to medical schools exists or existed. Because the ratio of Jewish medical students to all medical students exceeds the ratio of all Jews to our total population, some observers have concluded discrimination is absent. D. S. Berkowitz, Inequality of Opportunity in Higher Education. (1948).

[83] The same problem of survival in a hostile world has led a number of observers to argue that the frequency of Jews among alcoholics, dope addicts, and child deserters is low relative to the non-Jewish population. This same argument has been used to conclude that the frequency of Jews among neurotics is higher. Morrison, A Biologic Interpretation of Jewish Survival, 3 Medical Leaves 97 (1940); Meyerson, Neuroses and Alcoholism Among the Jews, 3 Medical Leaves 104 (1940); Liber, The Behavior of the Jewish and the Non-Jewish Patient, 5 Medical Leaves 159 (1943).

There exists evidence that Jews are under-represented among prison inmates. Levinger, A Note on Jewish Prisoners in Ohio, 2 Jewish Social Studies 210 (1940). This is what the sur-

and at least in this respect, distinguished Jews from non-Jews. This was particularly true of Jews that came from Czarist Russia and Poland where discrimination against them was particularly strong.[84]

Because of these special cultural properties, which are vestigial in the United States and therefore are in the process of fading away, the discrimination against Jews in admission to medical schools is far from irrational if one is concerned with maintaining price discrimination in medicine. The *a priori* probability of a Jew being a price cutter because of the special attributes developed in an effort to survive in a hostile environment is greater than that for a non-Jew. The Jewish doctor is more likely to have a commercial market place attitude towards other members of his profession than is the non-Jew. From the point of view of the medical profession, as one doctor expressed it, Jews ". . . spoil everything they go into by turning it into a business."[85]

If, as this analysis implies, admission to medical schools is influenced by the desire to select candidates who will not become price cutters, then it ought to be possible to observe similar policies for postgraduate education. In particular, it should be possible to observe evidence of bias against Jews in surgical relative to non-surgical specialties. Consequently Jews ought to be under-represented in surgery relative to other fields of specialization. Converse results ought to hold for psychiatry. A study of physicians who were diplo-

---

vival hypothesis suggests. It is significant to note, however, that this under-representation is not uniform for all categories of crime. The representation of Jews among prison inmates convicted of crimes of scheming, i.e., fraud, larceny, possession of stolen property, etc., is relatively large. Laws regulating economic affairs, unlike most laws, were directed against Jews. Hence one should expect to find respect by Jews for this category of laws weakest. By this argument a post-war study of prison populations ought to show a relatively large representation of Jews among OPA violators.

[84] J. W. Parkes, The Jewish Problem in the Modern World, (1946) recognizes the unique experiences of Jews in modern history and the impact of these experiences upon Jewish culture in his first chapter, Why Is There a Jewish Question?

[85] Hall, Informal Organization of the Medical Profession, 12 Canadian Journal of Economics and Political Science 38 (1946). This article suggests that young doctors 'buy' positions on hospital staffs by providing free medical care in hospital clinics. The older members of the profession have an interest in maintaining this method of admission to hospital staffs because it helps maintain the acceptability of price discrimination with the public.

Similarly there exist controls over the maximum fees charged, price ceilings in effect, in order to minimize the possibility of fees that the public will regard as outrageous and thereby endanger the existence of structured prices. This function is performed by county medical society review committees that deal with the complaints of excessive fees. For an example of the functioning of such a committee, consult Phillips, Doctor Cancels $1,500 Bill for Hoopers at Medical Group's Urging, N. Y. Times, p. 1, col. 2, (June 23, 1957). For a reflection of public attitudes in this case, consult 70 Time 34 (July 1, 1957). A. Ruppin suggests that Jews developed modern competitive attitudes in commerce before the industrial revolution as a result of their exclusion from medieval guilds, in an effort to survive commercially in this hostile environment. With the onset of the industrial revolution and the weakening of trade barriers, the relative economic position of Jews improved. Jews in the Modern World, p. 110 (1934).

mates in various specialties was made for the year 1946 for Jews and non-Jews for the cities of Brooklyn, Newark, Buffalo, and Hartford-Bridgeport. It was found that thirty-two per cent of the surgeons in Brooklyn were Jews, twenty-five percent in Newark, eight in Buffalo, and six in Hartford. Of the ten specialties considered for Brooklyn, the representation of Jews among the surgeons was lowest. For the other three cities, eleven specialties were considered. For all three of these cities, the representation of Jews among specialists was also lowest in surgery (453 Jewish specialists were considered in Brooklyn, the other three cities added 122). On the other hand, for the category neurology-psychiatry, the representation of Jews among the specialists practicing in this field ranked third for Brooklyn. For the other three cities, the rankings were one tie for fourth place, one first place and one fourth place.[86]

The distinction between psychiatry and surgery is a special case of the general distinction between surgical and non-surgical specialties. Hospital connections are far more important for the practice of surgical than non-surgical specialties. Therefore controls over the members of the medical profession in surgical specialties are stronger. If, as it has been argued, price discrimination is stronger in the surgical specialties, then there should be a significant difference in the frequency of Jews in surgical and non-surgical specialties. Two independent studies provide evidence that is consistent with this implication. For the state of Pennsylvania, one observer found that the frequency of Jews in non-surgical specialties was forty-one percent larger than in surgical specialties. The probability of a sample of this size, 1,175, of which 190 were Jews, being a random sample of a population characterized by an absence of a difference in the frequency of Jews in the surgical and non-surgical specialties is less than one half of one percent.[87] For Brooklyn the frequency of Jews in the non-surgical specialties was thirty percent greater than for the surgical specialties. This difference could occur by chance with a probability of less than one percent if this were a random sample of a population that failed to exhibit this property. Similar results hold for a combination of the other three cities.[88] The hypothesis that there exists a difference between surgical and non-surgical specialties with respect to the admission of

[86] Consult Shapiro, op. cit. supra note 82, at p. 125, table IV.

[87] Weinberg, Jewish Diplomates in Pennsylvania, 4 Medical Leaves 159 (1942). The non-surgical specialties were dermatology and syphilology, pediatrics, psychiatry and neurology, internal medicine, radiology, pathology; the surgical specialties were orthopedic surgery, ophthalmology, otolaryngology, obstetrics and gynecology, surgery, and anesthesiology.

[88] Shapiro, op. cit. supra note 82, at p. 125. One entry for all ophthalmologists in Brooklyn is missing and another entry for all radiologists in Hartford was obviously in error. Therefore Hartford radiologists and Brooklyn ophthalmologists, both Jewish and non-Jewish, were not represented in the foregoing calculations. Personal communication with the author of this article failed to elicit a clarifying response.

Jews is consistent with the qualitative observation found in another report. This source observes that "fair play" exists in the admission of Jews to non-Jewish hospitals for training in the non-surgical specialties but not for training in the surgical specialties.[89] Apparently the Jews who do get into medical schools are "dumped" in the non-surgical specialties.[90]

Another piece of evidence consistent with the price cutting explanation of the discrimination against Jews in medicine is the drop in admissions of Jews to medical schools between 1933 and 1938. During that time, there was a decrease in over-all admissions to medical schools of about five percent and a decrease in admission of Jewish students of about thirty percent.[91] Between 1928 and 1933, the prices of medical services dropped sharply and the real income of doctors as a group decreased. The depression produced a reduction in the size of the pie available to the profession. This smaller pie was contended for quite vigorously by the existing members. The Jews as price cutters were probably relatively successful, and in the process the structure of discriminatory prices was jeopardized. As a result, the threat of Jews to the aggregate income of the profession was brought home in a very forceful way at this time. Therefore the sharp curtailment in admission of Jews to medical schools resulted in an effort to reduce the vulnerability of structured prices to destruction by competitive behavior.[92]

The evidence used to support the proposition that discrimination against certain minority groups results from the desire to maintain price discrimina-

[89] Facilities of Jewish Hospitals for Specialized Training, 3 Jewish Social Studies 375, 378 (1941).

[90] These data are also consistent with at least two other hypotheses worth considering. One is that Jews simply lack the physical dexterity required for success in surgery. This seems to be inconsistent with the frequency of Jews in such fields as dentistry. Levinger, Jews in the Professions in Ohio, 2 Jewish Social Studies 401, 430, table XXXIII (1940). The other is that there exists no more discrimination against Jews in surgical specialties than non-surgical specialties but that there does exist at least an additional barrier that must be surmounted in order to get into the surgical specialties that is absent for the non-surgical specialties. No evidence of the existence of such a barrier has been detected.

[91] Goldberg, op. cit. supra note 82, at p. 332. Another distinguished member of the medical profession who has encountered the disapproval of his colleagues for unorthodox views, recognized the economic motivation for this policy and properly describes it as a trade union tactic. He also recognized the conflict of interest position of organized medicine resulting from its control over admissions to the profession. Cabot, op. cit. supra note 7, at p. 263.

[92] A decrease in the frequency of Jews among medical students could occur for reasons other than an increase in the intensity of discrimination. However only an increase in the intensity of discrimination would (1) increase the frequency of Jews in schools of osteopathy, and (2) increase the frequency of Jews among all Americans studying abroad. Between 1935 and 1946, the frequency of Jews in schools of osteopathy more than doubled (9.1 to 20.3%). A Report of the President's Commission on Higher Education, pt. II, pp. 38 ff. (1947). This report imputes to the blocking of opportunities in medicine the rise in the frequency of Jews in osteopathic schools. The President's Commission concluded that a substantial part of the responsibility for the discriminatory practices of medical schools belongs to professional associations.

tion is also consistent with the implications of simple monopoly theory. If medicine is a monopoly, then it follows that the number of candidates that would like to win entry into the medical profession exceeds the number that in fact are permitted to enter. Therefore unless the number of openings in the profession are sold or auctioned off, a practice that has not been unknown in the American labor movement, non-price rationing is inevitable. This leaves those who have the job of rationing available openings the opportunity to indulge in their tastes for the kind of people that they would like to see in the profession without any effective constraints in the form of costs or positions that must be filled. Under these circumstances, as contrasted with the free entry characteristic of competitive markets, nepotism, discrimination against unpopular cultural groups such as Jews and Negroes, and discrimination against those who hold unpopular ideas such as communists, thrives.[93] Therefore discrimination against Jews and others in admission to medical schools can be rationalized as a manifestation of non-price rationing. Since the surgical specialties are presumed to have more monopoly power than the non-surgical specialties, there is more non-price rationing in the former and as a result, more discrimination.[94] The increase in the tempo of discrimination in the thirties can also be rationalized as a consequence of an increase in the extent of non-price rationing. The demand for medical services is probably highly income elastic and as a result of the depression and admission policies geared to a demand schedule for medical services that existed in the twenties, the monopoly returns in medicine declined during the early depression years. Therefore admissions were subsequently curtailed in order to redress the effects of too liberal admission policies in the past. Consequently the extent of non-price rationing increased.

CONCLUSION

If different prices for the same service exist, then economic theory implies that there must also exist some means for enjoining producers of this service from acting in their own self interest and thereby establishing uniform prices. Observable phenomena abundantly support this implication. Available evidence suggests that the primary control instrument of organized medicine is the ability to cut off potential price cutters from the use of resources complementary to doctors' services for producing many classes of medical care. How-

[93] On theoretical grounds, there is a sound basis for the belief that generally speaking, the A.F.L. craft unions have more monopoly power than the C.I.O. industrial unions. Wright, op. cit. supra note 1, pp. 207 ff. Observers of discrimination in the American labor movement find that Negroes are discriminated against more frequently by A.F.L. unions than by C.I.O. unions. H. E. Northrop Organized Labor and the Negro, ch. 1. (1944).

[94] If it were found that the surgical specialties had no more monopoly power than the non-surgical specialties, this would be evidence against the simple monopoly hypothesis, but would be consistent with the discriminatory monopoly hypothesis.

ever, techniques other than the withdrawal of staff privileges in hospitals are also employed to maintain discipline in the medical profession. These include *no-criticism rules,* professional courtesy or the free treatment by doctors of other doctors and their families, prohibition of advertising that might reallocate market shares among producers, preventing doctors from testifying against one another in malpractice suits, and the selection of candidates for medical schools and post graduate training in the surgical specialties that have a relatively low probability of being price cutters. All of these sanctions can be rationalized as means for maintaining price discrimination. Therefore the use of these sanctions is consistent with the hypothesis that the medical profession constitutes a discriminating monopoly.

If being cut off from the use of a complementary agent of production, hospital services, is the chief means of disciplining the existing members of the medical profession, then there ought to be a difference in the price discipline maintained in the surgical and non-surgical specialties. Consequently there ought to be a significant difference between the surgical and the non-surgical specialties in the frequency of discriminatory pricing. There are no grounds for believing that there is any difference between the surgical and non-surgical specialties with respect to the effectiveness of the more subtle means of control. Therefore as a result of the relatively weaker impact on the non-surgical specialties of the loss of hospital staff privileges, it should be possible to observe that the non-surgical specialties have not only more price cutters in their midst but also are relatively freer in criticizing other members of the profession, serving as expert witnesses, and violating professional courtesy. Similarly this analysis implies that before the turn of the century, price discrimination in medicine was less pervasive, doctors criticized each other more freely, were more willing to act as expert witnesses against one another, did not as readily provide free medical care to other members of the profession, and did not discriminate against potential price cutters in admission to medical training.[95]

The economic interest of the medical profession in maintaining price discrimination has led to opposition directed against new techniques for marketing medical services that offer promise of utilizing the existing stock of physicians more efficiently than heretofore. Consequently the opposition by organ-

[95] Fee splitting, according to the hypothesis presented in this paper, should have been more prevalent at this time. Splitting fees makes for freer entry into the surgical care market. Newcomers can offer large rebates to referring physicians and thereby win patients away from established surgeons. There seems to be evidence that fee splitting was prevalent in medicine around the turn of the century and it was indeed employed by newcomers as a means for winning entry into the surgical care market. Rongy, Half a Century of Jewish Medical Activities in New York City, 1 Medical Leaves 151, 158 (1937). This implies that the older, more established surgeons oppose fee splitting. This is consistent with the evidence. Williams, A. C. S. Closes In On Fee Splitters, 31 Medical Economics 161 (1954).

Berger, op. cit. supra note 17, at p 141 contends that surgeons object to fee splitting for economic reasons.

ized medicine to prepaid service type medical plans probably has resulted in higher economic costs of medical care for the community than would otherwise have been the case. Similarly the incompatibility of the indemnity principle of insurance and the "what the traffic will bear" principle of pricing medical services has inhibited the development of major, medical catastrophe insurance in this country and consequently has limited the ability of individuals to insure themselves against these risks. Insofar as freer criticism by the members of the medical profession of one another before the public is of value to consumers in helping them distinguish between better and poorer practitioners and in raising standards within the profession, the public has obtained a lower quality of medical service than would otherwise have been obtainable at existing costs. And insofar as being a potential price cutter weeds out candidates from medical schools and post graduate training in the surgical specialties who were better potential doctors than those accepted, then the quality of the medical services that could have been achieved at existing costs was reduced.

Economic theory implies that prepaid medical service plans imperil the existence of price discrimination. Consequently theory also implies that in geographical areas where such plans exist, price discrimination ought to be relatively less prevalent. In California, the Kaiser Plan has captured a substantial fraction of the medical care market and is the largest single producer in the state. In an effort to meet this competition, service-type plans have been offered by orthodox members of the medical profession that are non-discriminatory with respect to income. Competition has had the effect of reducing the extent of discriminatory pricing in the area. This has been true in a number of counties in California where the Kaiser Plan is particularly strong.[96] Therefore both economic theory and empirical evidence suggest that if there were more competition among doctors in the sale of medical services, i.e., if doctors were individually freer to pursue their self-interest, there would be less discrimination in the pricing of medical services.

[96] Oakley, They Met the Challenge of Panel Medicine, 32 Medical Economics 122 (Feb. 1955); Olds, Usual Fee Plan Put to Test, 31 Medical Economics 131, but especially p. 206 (July, 1954); Andrews, How They're Fighting the Kaiser Plan, 31 Medical Economics, 126 (Sept. 1954).

2 The A.M.A. and the Supply of Physicians*
(1970)

INTRODUCTION

This paper deals with two related topics: first, the role of the American Medical Association (AMA) in determining the rate of output of physicians and, as a consequence, the current stock of physicians, and, second, the role of organized medicine —that is, the AMA—in circumscribing the choice of contractual relationships between physicians and their patients. Because it is my thesis that the famous Flexner report of 1910 constituted the key to achieving control over the output of physicians by the AMA, a substantial portion of this paper is devoted to this report and its implications for understanding how our society produces physicians.

The history of public intervention in the market for medical services can be conveniently divided into two periods. The earlier begins with the publication of the Flexner report and ends with the conclusion of World War II. During this period, public intervention in the market for medical services had its principal effect on the supply of physicians' services. Organized medicine—again, the AMA—, using powers delegated by state governments, reduced the output of doctors by making the graduates of some medical schools ineligible to be examined for licensure and by reducing the output of schools that continued to produce eligible graduates. This led to the demise of the schools producing ineligible graduates, since training doctors was their *raison d'être*. For the surviving schools, their costs of producing doctors increased enormously.

The later period, which begins with the end of World War II and continues to the present moment, may be characterized as a period when governmental intervention, through programs such as Kerr-Mills, Medicaid, and Medicare, operated to increase the demand for the services of doctors.

I
THE FLEXNER REPORT

The Flexner report has been hailed, even by critics of the AMA, as an action of the AMA in the public interest. For example, Dr. John H. Knowles has said,

> At the turn of the century, the AMA stood at the forefront of progressive thinking and socially responsible action. Its members had been leaders in forming

---

* Editor's Note: This article was prepared prior to the appearance of CARNEGIE COMMISSION ON HIGHER EDUCATION, REPORT ON MEDICAL EDUCATION (1970), which deals with some of the same subject matter and reaches similar conclusions.

much-needed public health departments in the States during the last half of the nineteenth century. It formed a Council on Medical Education in 1904 and immediately began an investigation of proprietary medical schools. Because of its success in exposing intolerable conditions in these schools, the Carnegie Foundation, at the AMA's request, commissioned Abraham Flexner to study the national scene. His report in 1910 drove proprietary interests out of medical education, established it as a full university function with standards for admission, curriculum development, and clinical teaching. Our present system of medical education, essentially unchanged since the Flexner (and AMA) revolution—and acknowledging its current defects—was accomplished through the work of the AMA. Surely this contribution was and is one of its finest in the public interest.[1]

This interpretation of history is challenged here; an alternative interpretation is that the "success" of the Flexner-AMA revolution accounts for the current scarcity of physicians.

The decline in the number of medical schools and in the output of physicians as a consequence of the Flexner report has been amply documented. Shryock interprets the history of medical education during the period from 1870 to 1910 as a struggle between existing practitioners, represented by the AMA, and medical educators for control over the output of doctors and hence over the medical schools themselves.[2] The victor in this struggle was the AMA, and its most powerful weapon in the battle was the Flexner report on medical schools, which was undertaken and published under the aegis of the prestigious Carnegie Foundation.[3] This report discredited many medical schools and was instrumental in establishing the AMA as the arbiter of which schools could have their graduates sit for state licensure examinations. Graduation from a class A medical school, with the ratings determined by a subdivision of the AMA, became a prerequisite for licensure.[4] This victory completed the long campaign of the AMA against medical educators. The first triumph in this campaign was the elimination of the power of medical schools to license their own graduates.

It is the thesis of this essay that Flexner and the Carnegie Foundation were, to use the language of the Left of the 1930s, "dupes of the interests." In other words, they unwittingly served the highly parochial interests of organized medicine. Flexner's work consisted of a grand inspection tour of the medical schools of the time—some were evaluated in an afternoon—to determine how they produced their outputs. His model of how doctors should be produced was the medical school of Johns Hopkins University.[5] There was no attempt to evaluate the outputs of medical

---

[1] Knowles, *Where Doctors Fail*, SATURDAY REVIEW, Aug. 22, 1970, at 21, 22.

[2] R. SHRYOCK, MEDICAL LICENSING IN AMERICA: 1650-1965, at 92-93, 108-09, 113 (1967).

[3] A. FLEXNER, MEDICAL EDUCATION IN THE UNITED STATES AND CANADA (1910) [hereinafter cited as FLEXNER REPORT].

[4] The power of the AMA over medical schools is described by H. MARGULIES & L. BLOCK, FOREIGN MEDICAL GRADUATES IN THE UNITED STATES 25-27, 44-45 (1969).

[5] This is brought out in Flexner's autobiography. *See* A. FLEXNER, AUTOBIOGRAPHY 74 (rev. ed. 1960).

schools; there was no investigation of what their graduates could or could not do.[6] Nor was there any discussion of what a graduate of a medical school *should* be able to do, or of the possibility of raising standards of medical education through stiff licensure examinations. The entire burden of improving standards was to be borne by changes in how doctors should be produced—that is, how students, facilities, and faculty ought to be combined to generate physicians. He implicitly ruled out all production functions other than the one he observed at Johns Hopkins.

It is a paradox that a group ostensibly so concerned as the AMA with the qualifications of doctors for the practice of medicine failed to be disturbed by Flexner's lack of qualifications for the task he undertook. Flexner was neither a physician nor a scientist, and had no qualifications as a medical educator. He had an undergraduate degree in arts from Johns Hopkins and had operated a small, private, and apparently profitable preparatory school in Louisville for fifteen years. It is unlikely, if not inconceivable, that he would have been accepted in a court of law as an expert witness in the field of medical education before he undertook his study.[7]

Virtually all the work Flexner undertook had already been done by the AMA, and N. P. Colwell, the secretary of the AMA's Council on Medical Education at the time, accompanied Flexner in some of his inspections and provided him with the results of the AMA's previous labors.[8] Indeed Flexner spent many hours at the Chicago headquarters of the AMA. It was clearly recognized that Flexner, or more properly the Carnegie Foundation, had a comparative advantage over the AMA in publishing an attack on the medical schools of the time. The Carnegie Foundation was comparatively invulnerable to a self-interest charge. "[I]f we could obtain the publication and approval of our work by the Carnegie Foundation for the Advancement of Teaching, it would assist materially in securing the results we were attempting to bring about."[9]

As a result of the implementation of the Flexner report, medical education became considerably more expensive and exhibited relatively little variation from school to school. To this day, there probably is less variation in medical training than in almost any other field. The implementation of Flexner's recommendations made medical schools as alike as peas in a pod. In their first year, medical students almost invariably took anatomy, biochemistry, and physiology; in the second, microbiology, pathology, and pharmacology. The next two years consisted of supervised contacts with patients in the major clinical specialties of a teaching hospital. Often this training pattern was written into state laws.[10]

---

[6] Significantly, Flexner's brother, who became a very distinguished physician, graduated from one of the schools put out of business.

[7] See A. FLEXNER, *supra* note 5, at 78, 79.

[8] The AMA's Council on Medical Education rated 82 schools class A in 1906. Flexner rated only 72 schools that high a few years later. See Dodds, *Adventures in Medical Education*, 32 J. MED. EDUC. 781, 787-88 (1957).

[9] Bevan, *Cooperation in Medical Education and Medical Service*, 90 J.A.M.A. 1173, 1175 (1928).

[10] The Crisis in Medical Services and Medical Education 7, report on an exploratory conference

The implementation of the Flexner report has, until relatively recently, sharply reduced experimentation in the training of physicians. As a result, there was a hiatus of over forty years in the search for better curricula and teaching methods, and in the utilization of the talents of scientists outside of medical schools for the training of physicians. It is only in recent years, in the decade of the 1960s, that the fetters imposed by the Flexner report have been loosened. As a consequence, medical education is currently in a state of flux, and the number of electives open to medical students has increased enormously. In addition, the economic cost of acquiring the MD degree has started to decrease, because some medical schools have relaxed their requirements for a bachelor's degree as a condition for admission. Moreover, as a result of student pressure, medical schools have increased their willingness to substitute undergraduate courses for preclinical courses.

A little recognized consequence of the Flexner report was its effect on the frequency of Negro doctors in the population and on the number of Negro medical schools. As a result of the AMA's and Flexner's endeavors, the number of medical schools declined from 162 in 1906 to sixty-nine in 1944, while the number of Negro medical schools went from seven to two. Moreover, the number of students admitted to the surviving schools decreased. Flexner's views on medical education for Negroes were patronizing: "A well-taught negro sanitarian will be immensely useful; an essentially untrained negro wearing an M.D. degree is dangerous"; "the practice of the negro doctor will be limited to his own race . . . ."[11] According to census figures, the frequency of Negro physicians among all physicians increased sharply from 1900 to 1910 (from 1.3 per cent to 2.0 per cent) and leveled off afterwards. In the absence of Flexner's, or more properly the AMA's, repression of medical schools, one would have expected the frequency of Negro physicians to rise as their educational disadvantages were overcome. The problem of obtaining medical education for Negroes was intensified by the development of intern and residency programs, because many hospitals refused to hire Negroes for their house staffs for purely racial reasons. The usual argument was that white patients, particularly obstetrical patients, do not wish to be treated by Negro doctors.[12]

Not by chance, 1910 was also a high water mark for women physicians. "By 1940 the number of women physicians (including osteopaths) was 8,810, which was somewhat smaller than it had been at a high point in 1910."[13]

For those interested in the motive of the AMA in seeking control over medical schools, an unambiguous answer was provided by the former head of the AMA's Council on Medical Education:

---

sponsored by the Commonwealth Fund and the Carnegie Corporation of N.Y., Fort Lauderdale, Fla., Feb. 1966.

[11] FLEXNER REPORT, *supra* note 3, at 180.

[12] Often Negro medical students took their first two years of training in Northern medical schools and then went South for their clinical training.

[13] Shryock, *Women in American Medicine*, 5 J. AM. MED. WOMEN'S ASS'N 371, 377 (1950).

> In this rapid elevation of the standard of medical education ... with the reduction of the number of medical schools from 160 to eighty, there occurred a marked reduction in the number of medical students and medical graduates. We had anticipated this and felt that this was a desirable thing. We had ... a great oversupply of poor mediocre practitioners.[14]

According to Shryock,

> Competing within a free economy they observed that the scientific motive for educational reform coincided with their own professional ambitions. They became increasingly aware that too many schools were turning out too many graduates to make practice profitable.[15]

The advent of licensure and the closure of the medical schools that failed to meet AMA standards was of course justified as a measure to protect the public from the ministrations of unqualified or incompetent physicians.[16] But when higher standards were imposed, there was no immediate change in quality since the graduates of those medical schools that were put out of business continued to practice. As is commonplace whenever licensure is imposed upon a previously unlicensed activity or new standards are imposed, there were no substantial changes in the quality of the outstanding inventory of practitioners. Grandfather clauses protected the rights of existing physicians to continue to practice medicine regardless of the adequacy of their training. Hence the effects of the change in training standards for physicians could not have been realized for many years after Flexner's labors.

The restriction on opportunities to study medicine in this country were particularly oppressive for Jews and Negroes.[17] There was a large decrease in demand for medical services caused by the great depression of the 1930s. As a result, there was a cutback in admissions to medical schools, with Negroes and Jews bearing a disproportionate share of the reduction.[18] Probably females also bore a disproportionate share of the reduction in admissions.[19]

---

[14] Bevan, *supra* note 9, at 1176.

[15] R. SHRYOCK, *supra* note 2, at 57 (footnote omitted).

[16] Lawrence Friedman, *Freedom of Contract and Occupational Licensing 1890-1910: A Legal and Social Study*, 53 CALIF. L. REV. 487, 493 *et seq.* (1965), explains the growth in licensure during this period as being largely economic, a function of the desire to restrict entry. He uses the same explanation for physicians and barbers. By contrast, Milton Friedman, Kuznets, and Rayack view the AMA's shutting down of medical schools as having the unintended effect of restricting entry as well as the desired effect of increasing standards. *See* M. FRIEDMAN & S. KUZNETS, INCOME FROM INDEPENDENT PROFESSIONAL PRACTICE 11-12 (1954); E. RAYACK, PROFESSIONAL POWER AND AMERICAN MEDICINE: THE ECONOMICS OF THE AMERICAN MEDICAL ASSOCIATION 70 (1967).

[17] For an explanation of why this should occur, see Alchian & Kessel, *Competition, Monopoly, and the Pursuit of Money*, in ASPECTS OF LABOR ECONOMICS 157 (National Bureau of Economic Research, 1962). It would be interesting to see if there was an increase in the frequency of children of physicians being admitted to medical school.

[18] *See* Goldberg, *Jews in the Medical Profession—A National Survey*, 1 JEWISH SOC. STUDIES 332 (1939); J. BURROW, AMA: VOICE OF AMERICAN MEDICINE 187 (1963). For slightly different periods both groups were cut back by about 30% while the over-all reduction in students admitted was about 17%. It also became considerably more difficult for graduates of foreign medical schools to win licensure in the United States during the 1930s.

[19] If one allows for a secular trend upwards in the frequency of females among medical students, the

As a result of the Flexner report and the restrictions of opportunities for medical education in this country, foreign medical schools, particularly in the late 1930s, were deluged by American applicants. If one divides graduate training in United States institutions into the categories of business administration, agriculture, education, engineering, physical and natural sciences, economics, and medicine, then foreign enrollments in American institutions exceed American enrollments in foreign institutions by a wide margin for all fields but one—medicine. Americans studying abroad range from one-fourth to one-thirtieth of foreigners studying in the United States for six of the seven categories. But the ratio of Americans studying medicine abroad to foreigners studying medicine in the United States exceeded three to one for the year 1966.[20] Apparently the restriction of opportunities in this country continues to affect the number of Americans studying medicine abroad.

II

Educational Costs and Physicians' Fees

It is of course a well-known axiom that an increase in quality requires an increase in price. And an increase in price implies an increase in efforts to economize on a resource that has become more scarce.[21] Hence, an increase in quality implies a greater effort to economize on physicians' services. What this means specifically is that people tend to substitute self-diagnosis and treatment for the services of a physician. This tendency manifests itself at the onset of an illness or suspected illness, and going to a physician is deferred until the symptoms become alarming. Consequently, increasing the quality of physicians does not necessarily imply that the quality of medical care that the public as a whole receives also increases, since the public receives a mixture of professional attention and self-treatment.

The foregoing argument about the effect of quality improvements on price has been countered with the argument that higher standards protect all of the public. Those too poor "to afford" good medical care, so the argument runs, would and do

---

1930s appear to be overrepresented among observations below the trend line. The relevant numbers appear in C. LOPATE, WOMEN IN MEDICINE app. I, at 193 (1968).

[20] *See* INSTITUTE ON INTERNATIONAL EDUCATION, OPEN DOORS (1967); AMERICAN COUNCIL ON HIGHER EDUCATION, A FACT BOOK ON HIGHER EDUCATION (1967). One source reports that in the late 1930s 90% of the Americans studying medicine abroad were Jewish. *See* Goldberg, *supra* note 18, at 332.

[21] Flexner was aware of this argument and countered it with the proposition that the country was encumbered with too many doctors. He decided, aided by reasoning not apparent to this reader, what was the "right" ratio of physicians to population. Given this constant, he inferred that the output of physicians ought to be reduced and that medical schools were "frequently set up regardless of opportunity or need." He also believed that it was necessary to drive low quality doctors out of business if the market was to support high quality doctors. This position was buttressed by an erroneous interpretation of Gresham's law. *See* FLEXNER REPORT, *supra* note 3, at 6, 14. Chapter 1 of the report deals with the economics of the medical profession.

receive it free. Money is not a barrier to receiving medical services. Since these views have received wide acceptance by both the public and economists, they deserve attention.

Both economists and noneconomists have inferred, incorrectly, that if care is provided by physicians at no out-of-pocket or pecuniary cost to the patient, an act of charity has occurred. They have forgotten that transactions at a zero price can be economically profitable for everyone involved.[22] Most of the "free" care that was traditionally provided by the medical profession fell into three categories: (1) work done by neophytes, particularly in the surgical specialties, who want to develop their skills and therefore require practice; (2) services of experienced physicians in free clinics who wish to develop new skills or maintain existing skills so they can better serve their private, paying patients; and (3) services to maintain staff and medical appointments which are of great value financially. The advent of Medicare has reduced the availability of "charity" patients used as teaching material, and has led to readjustments in training procedures, particularly for residents.[23]

To see that the free care argument can not be taken seriously, all one needs to do is examine the relationship of infant mortality to income. The infant mortality rate is highly sensitive to the absence or presence of medical care, particularly prenatal care. Clearly Negroes have lower incomes and higher infant mortality rates than whites, for they have not been provided with enough free care to offset the effects of income differences.[24] Moreover, infant mortality rates in the United States do not compare favorably with a number of European countries, including some that use midwives extensively. Charity, with or without quotation marks, can not be regarded as an important means for offsetting the effects of restriction on entry into the practice of medicine.

The argument that restriction on entry and licensure has raised standards of medical practice has great appeal and acceptance. Unfortunately there does not appear to be any empirical study available to support this view, and it is striking that organized medicine has not investigated the effects of licensure on the quality of care of the community. The usual statement one sees is that Americans have the best medical care in the world—if the contention were "the most expensive," it would probably be easier to buttress.

---

[22] My article, Kessel, *Price Discrimination in Medicine*, 1 J. LAW & ECON. 20, 23 *et seq.* (1958), contains this error, and Arrow, *Uncertainty and the Welfare Economics of Medical Care*, 53 AM. ECON. REV. 941, 957 (1963), follows me in it.

[23] CITIZENS COMMISSION ON GRADUATE MEDICAL EDUCATION, THE GRADUATE EDUCATION OF PHYSICIANS 75, 77 (1966). This document is also known as the Millis Report.

[24] Evidence showing a relationship between medical care and health status, setting aside public health measures dealing with infectious diseases, is difficult to obtain even for infant mortality. Diet plays an important role in preventing infant mortality, and dietary information is typically provided by physicians as part of prenatal care. For those unwilling to accept the foregoing argument, it is relevant to point out that access to the medical establishment does vary with income. Therefore either the well-to-do "need" more medical care than the poor, or free care does not offset the effect of income differences.

III

RESTRICTION OF ENTRY AND QUALITY OF CARE

Many distinguished writers, some in the field of political economy, have argued for free entry into the practice of medicine—for giving the public freedom to choose anyone as a physician without constraints imposed by the state. This view appears in the famous letter of Adam Smith to Cullen[25] and in a letter of William James to his fellow physicians in Boston.[26] It is also Milton Friedman's position.[27] This view was expressed as well by Samuel Clemens as by anyone. When he found out that MDs were trying to put osteopaths out of business in his state, he said,

> I don't know that I cared much about these osteopaths until I heard you were going to drive them out of the State; but since I heard that I haven't been able to sleep.
> Now, what I contend is that my body is my own, at least I have always so regarded it. If I do harm through my experimenting with it, it is I who suffer, not the State.[28]

By using licensure as a barrier to entry, our society has to a large extent abandoned freedom of choice of physicians. It is pertinent to turn to an examination of this professed policy of protecting the public from making poor choices of physicians. How consistent has organized medicine been in adhering to the implications of its arguments about protecting the public from incompetent doctors?

(1) There is a substantial body of evidence that there has been discrimination in terms of race, creed, and color in admission to medical schools.[29] This discrimination became especially severe when there was a cutback in the production of doctors in the mid-1930s as a result of the onset of the great depression. Negroes and Jews (and possibly women) seem to have borne a disproportionate share of the reduction in admissions to medical schools.[30] Clearly the cutback in output can not be justified as an effort to maintain quality of medical care, since discrimination in terms of race, creed, and color reduces the quality of student inputs into medical schools.

(2) When higher standards were instituted, they were not made applicable to existing practitioners. Hence, it was future and not current medical problems that would benefit from any improvement of standards. Yet, so far as the public is

---

[25] *See* Guttmacher, *The Views of Adam Smith on Medical Education*, 47 BULL. JOHNS HOPKINS HOSP. 164, 171 (1930).

[26] 2 H. JAMES, THE LETTERS OF WILLIAM JAMES 66 *et seq.* (1920).

[27] M. FRIEDMAN, CAPITALISM AND FREEDOM 149 (1962).

[28] Quoted in Andrews, *Medical Practice and the Law*, 31 FORUM 542, 547 (1901).

[29] 2 REPORT OF THE PRESIDENT'S COMMISSION ON HIGHER EDUCATION 38 *et seq.* (1947). The Commission concluded that a substantial part of the responsibility for the discriminatory practices of medical schools belongs to the professional associations.

[30] One of the ironies surrounding Flexner's study is the fact that, because of his work in 1910, in the 1930s Jews from family circumstances similar to his own—immigrant parents, poverty, high education aspirations—were unable to get into medical schools.

concerned, there are no grounds for distinguishing between mistreatment by recent as distinguished from less recent graduates of medical schools.

(3) There is no re-examination procedure for doctors. Once a doctor wins a license to practice, it is almost never revoked unless he is convicted of law-breaking. It is pertinent to ask why holders of automobile drivers' licenses are subject to re-examination and holders of licenses to practice medicine are not. Is medicine less important? Why are commercial airline pilots subject to re-examination but not physicians? Clearly, to be consistent in one's concern about maintaining high quality, there should be periodic re-examination of physicians with recertification to insure that physicians keep current on what constitutes good practice.[31]

(4) Politics has been intertwined with decisions that should be based on quality considerations alone. An important instance has been the requirement that a doctor be a member of his county medical society in order to qualify for membership in a specialty board. Obviously membership in the AMA has nothing to do with a doctor's qualifications for membership on a specialty board.[32]

(5) Doctors run most hospitals, in the sense that they have de facto control over staff appointments. For most medical specialists, being on the staff of a hospital is an imperative for successful practice. Yet appointment decisions are not based solely on considerations of skill and talent, but are similar to admissions procedures to a country club—race, religion, family, type of practice, and so forth are often important.[33]

(6) Within the medical profession there exists great internal solidarity and cohesion. This is much stronger in medicine than in a field characterized by free entry such as the profession of economics. As a consequence, there tends to be a closed loop of referrals of patients from one doctor to another, and patients are unable to form effective coalitions with doctors in buying the services of other doctors. It is very difficult to obtain the judgment of the profession about the relative ranking of doctors in particular fields and parts of the country. The difficulty of obtaining doctors to testify as expert witnesses for plaintiffs in malpractice suits is so widespread that lawyers assert that a "conspiracy of silence" exists. For these reasons, the incentive to produce quality work and to develop an outstanding reputation is not as strong as it would be in a world in which such information could be more easily obtained.

For all these reasons, it is difficult to take very seriously the protestations of the medical profession that its concern in establishing control over medical schools was quality. Improvements in the quality of the output of medical schools probably

---

[31] Driving proprietary interests out of medical education is alleged to be one of Flexner's great achievements. See Knowles, supra note 1, at 22. This is factually incorrect. They have been driven out of pre-MD training, but in fact they play an important role in the training of the practicing physician. The detail men of pharmaceutical companies provide the continuing education of many practicing physicians. See The Crisis in Medical Services and Medical Education, supra note 10, at 12.

[32] Comment, *The American Medical Association: Power, Purpose, and Politics in Organized Medicine*, 63 YALE L.J. 938, 952 (1954).

[33] *Id.*

did occur. Yet, if the experience of law schools is relevant, improvements undoubtedly would have occurred without the efforts of organized medicine. It was this promised improvement in the quality of the output that "sold" the public and/or legislators on giving powers to regulate output to organized medicine. Economic gains to the medical profession resulting from restriction on output constitutes an explanation of the shutting down of medical schools with fewer loose ends than the "desire to raise standards" explanation.

However, even if one prefers to reject the foregoing explanation and to accept the view that those responsible for restricting the output of physicians were not economically motivated, one can hardly deny that the output of doctors has in fact been unresponsive to market forces. The increases in demand for medical services, particularly those brought about by Medicare and Medicaid, have had relatively little impact upon the output of doctors by American medical schools. As a consequence, the prices of physicians' services have risen dramatically, and there has been a shift of medical resources away from the population at large and towards the beneficiaries of Medicare and Medicaid.[34] This analysis suggests that the proposed measures to increase the demand for medical care, such as the extension of Medicare to the under-sixty-five population, would not increase the availability of physicians to the population generally and, if anything, would be more likely to reduce than increase availability.

IV

INNOVATIONS IN MEDICAL EDUCATION

The current problem of the relative unavailability of physicians had its origin in the victory of organized medicine over educators in their battle for control of medical education. Educators have a much stronger interest in producing doctors than has organized medicine and, if given the opportunity, would act to make the output of physicians responsive to consumer desires. Unfortunately, the options open to medical educators have been narrower than is true in most academic disciplines.

To see what can be done to increase output, it is useful to contrast post- with pre-MD training. There seems to be a plethora of facilities in the United States for post-MD training. Approved spaces in hospitals for post-MD training, that is, training more advanced than medical schools' training, exceed the output of American medical schools by quite a wide margin. As a result, one finds large numbers of non-American graduates of foreign medical schools taking intern and residency training in this country.[35] Despite these imports, many unfilled vacancies exist. Intern

---

[34] Some writers believe that the output of physician services has declined and leisure has replaced work as real income increased—that is, that the supply of physician services is backward bending. This view has been seriously considered by Professor Martin Feldstein of Harvard, who has circulated it in a working paper.

[35] About 20% of all approved internships and residencies in the United States are unfilled despite the use of foreign-trained physicians in one-third of these positions. *See* PUBLIC HEALTH SERVICE, HEALTH MANPOWER SOURCEBOOK table 28, § 20 (1968).

and residency programs have never been regarded as difficult to expand. Approved residencies in hospitals increased six hundred per cent between 1940 and 1960, while the output of medical graduates rose only thirty-five per cent.[36] These advanced programs are under the aegis of hospitals rather than medical schools, although university-affiliated hospitals are overrepresented in post-MD training. It is an anomaly educationally that, the more advanced the training, the greater is the availability of facilities and that the more specialized and advanced training often takes place outside medical schools.

Why should the facilities for post-MD training be disproportionately large relative to pre-MD training? An explanation of this phenomenon rests on the hypothesis that there exist economic benefits to the medical profession for post-MD training that are virtually nonexistent for pre-MD training. The interns and residents of a hospital, the so-called house staff, are hospital employees, and a large part of their duties consists of aiding the attending staff in the care of their patients. Despite the time costs involved in instruction, the attending staff can on balance gain time by delegating duties to the house staff that they would otherwise have to perform for themselves. Hence, doctors that are members of the attending staff of a hospital with a large intern and residency training program have an important competitive advantage stemming from their lower costs of producing patient care. Needless to say, the prized positions for attending staffs are in hospitals with extensive intern and residency training programs. Consequently the staffs of hospitals without educational programs push hard to obtain such programs. No economic benefit of a comparable magnitude exists for pre-MD programs. It is true that third- and fourth-year medical students have some value around a hospital, but they are not worth as much as post-MD students. First and second year medical students are a dead weight with respect to instructional costs and, in the past, have provided no useful output in a hospital. Indeed, costs of instruction are relatively high for the first two years of medical school because of small classes and expensive facilities.

The foregoing suggests that the bottleneck in medical education is the first two years of medical school when, under the Flexner curricula, medical students take their so-called basic science courses. Serious questions can be raised as to whether or not these courses ought to be taught in a medical school at all. They are relatively elementary and are often taught by faculties that are undistinguished when compared with the faculties of biological and physical sciences in many universities. Indeed many medical students have already completed some of these courses in their premedical studies and find "ordinary medical school teaching inferior to the teaching of science in the better undergraduate institutions"[37] in addition to being duplicative and hence a waste of time. It is difficult to understand why medical schools could not divest themselves of this elementary instruction and con-

---

[36] R. SHRYOCK, *supra* note 2, at 91.
[37] The Crisis in Medical Services and Medical Education, *supra* note 10, at 9.

centrate in their field of comparative advantage—clinical teaching, both pre- and post-MD.

If medical schools were to divest themselves of responsibility for preclinical teaching of basic sciences, then (*a*) the resources of institutions which do not have medical schools but do have outstanding science departments could play a role in physician training; (*b*) the science departments of schools with medical schools could play a more active role in training doctors; (*c*) the preclinical years of training could become part of undergraduate training, thereby shortening the period of production of doctors by two years and effecting an enormous reduction in the costs of producing MDs; and (*d*) the resources liberated from training in basic sciences could be employed to expand the numbers trained by medical schools and to increase the quality of post-MD training which is now largely outside the province of existing medical schools and almost wholly didactic.

The important social problem currently is how to make medical schools responsive to the demands of the market for physicians. One solution is to enlist the aid of the nonmedical sector of the educational establishment in providing basic science training and to utilize the resources liberated in medical schools for expansion of enrollments of third- and fourth-year medical students. However, this is but one suggestion in a field of education that has been relatively stagnant for many years. Consequently, one does not have the natural experimentation in educational techniques that otherwise would have been available. An unfortunate heritage of Flexner's work is the overspecification of how doctors are to be produced. If Flexner had specified what knowledge and capabilities a physician should have and had given medical educators the freedom to search for efficient techniques for producing the desired output, we would currently know a great deal more about how to produce physicians efficiently. Undoubtedly we would also have many more physicians, because the costs of their production would be considerably lower and because production would not have been cut back in the 1930s. Medical education has been made artificially expensive because of the overspecification of how it was to be produced, particularly (but not exclusively) during the first two years of medical school.[38] As a result, many writers on the subject explicitly or implicitly accept the view that medical education is extremely costly, just as if this were a natural constant like the speed of light.

Search for efficiency in medical education could be stimulated by opening state licensure examinations and/or national boards to all applicants without concern over how they received their medical education or the rating, if any, of the schools attended. To insure that this examination is not used by the medical profession as a barrier to entry, it should bear a reasonable resemblance to the examination that existing practitioners are asked, from time to time, to pass. Such a move could

---

[38] The report on graduate medical education suggests that the internship no longer performs any educative function. THE GRADUATE EDUCATION OF PHYSICIANS, *supra* note 23, at 58. It also suggests that the length of residencies is related to the desires for house staff and is not determined solely by educational considerations. *Id.* at 70.

increase both the output of physicians and their quality. It could enable the community to move closer to economic efficiency in the production of physicians, since both quality and quantity could be increased without any change in aggregate expenditures for the production of physicians.

V

THE AMA AND HEALTH CARE DELIVERY

Rigidity in medical education has been matched, if not surpassed, by rigidity in the marketing of medical services. The AMA long ago discovered that fee-for-service is the ideal way of marketing medical care. Moreover, its confidence in the correctness of this view was so great that any other method of marketing medical care was opposed actively in order to prevent less intelligent brethren from falling into error. This opposition took two forms: (*a*) working for legislation to prohibit alternative methods of marketing medical care, and (*b*) refusing hospital staff appointments to physicians associated with such unapproved methods.

More specifically the AMA, or organized medicine, opposed bitterly comprehensive prepaid group medical plans such as Kaiser, Ross-Loos, Group Health, and HIP. Plans of this type are illegal in seventeen, or about one-third, of the states.[39] Where they were legal, they were opposed nevertheless, and the chief weapon used to fight these plans was to deny access to hospitals for patients of physicians in such plans. As a consequence the AMA was prosecuted under the Sherman Act in Washington, D.C., and under state antitrust laws elsewhere.[40] Physicians without a taste for martyrdom were deterred from joining such programs, and there is little doubt that the commitment of organized medicine to fee-for-service has inhibited search for and experimentation with alternatives to this method of marketing medical care. Hence, as with medical education, there is less experimental knowledge about the marketing of medical services than would have been available if organized medicine were less powerful and there were more freedom to innovate.[41]

Nevertheless, not all prepaid group plans have been aborted, and much can be learned from those that have been born, and especially from the ones that have survived. One of the most interesting aspects of these plans is the lower frequency of surgeons (and surgery) than exists in the usual fee-for-service practice.[42]

The lower frequency of surgery for prepaid group plan members has been explained as a consequence of differences in economic incentives. In comprehensive pre-

---

[39] Faltermayer, *Better Care at Less Cost Without Miracles*, FORTUNE, Jan. 1970, at 80, 127.

[40] *See* Kessel, *supra* note 22, at 36. *See also* Phelan, Erickson & Fleming, *Group Practice Prepayment: An Approach to Delivering Organized Health Services*, in this symposium, pt. 2 (forthcoming).

[41] *See* Forgotson & Cook, *Innovations and Experiments in Use of Health Manpower—The Effect of Licensure Laws*, 32 LAW & CONTEMP. PROB. 731 (1967), for a discussion of legal restrictions on the use of paramedical personnel in the delivery of health care.

[42] *See* Donabedian, *An Evaluation of Prepaid Group Practice*, INQUIRY, Sept. 1969, at 14; Roemer, *On Paying the Doctor and the Implications of Different Methods*, J. HEALTH & Soc. BEHAV., Spring 1962, at 4.

paid plans, the cost of a marginal unit of surgery (hospitalization and surgical service) are borne by the plan, with the marginal revenue from this surgery being zero. By contrast, under fee-for-service the marginal revenue of an additional unit of surgery to the surgeon is positive, since he receives a surgical fee; hospital costs are borne by the patient or his insurer. Consequently, it has been argued that some surgery is performed under fee-for-service that would not have occurred under prepaid medical care. An alternative interpretation of these same findings is that members of prepaid plans go outside their plans to buy surgery, foregoing rights to surgery at zero marginal costs in order to shop at positive marginal costs in the fee-for-service medical market.[43]

Another aspect of this problem, which has not been explored in the literature is that surgeons in comprehensive prepaid plans undertake relatively more surgery per month or per year than surgeons in fee-for-service. The number of surgical procedures per surgeon, aggregated by using Blue Cross or Medicare fee schedules as index numbers, seems to be greater under prepaid medical plans than it is under fee-for-service. To understand why this should be the case, it is helpful to examine the anomalous characteristics of the surgical market.

There are virtually no contracts the consumer enters into involving expenditures as large as those involved in surgical fees in which the price is not carefully specified and well known to the consumer before the purchase. Yet surgeons' fees are almost never discussed by patients with their surgeons before operations; one in twenty would probably be a high estimate of the frequency of patients who know their surgeon's fee before they commit themselves to surgery.[44] This alone suggests that surgery is not characterized by a high degree of price competition; price wars are undoubtedly more common in gasoline.

The argument that price competition is absent in surgery does not depend upon consumer ignorance. The presence of systematic price discrimination in the provision of surgical services is evidence of the absence of price competition,[45] made possible by organized medicine's control over access to hospital beds. Comparable control over fees for office visits does not exist, and consumer knowledge of the prices for office visits is considerably greater. Consequently the rate of exchange of surgical for nonsurgical services in the market fails to reflect the rate of exchange in production. Therefore, too many physicians are attracted into surgery, and they are apt to be underemployed relative to physicians in the nonsurgical specialties.[46] This misallocation has been aggravated by the onset of Medicare and Medicaid, which

---

[43] *See* Klarman, *Effect of Prepaid Group Practice on Hospital Use*, 78 PUB. HEALTH REP. 955 (1963). "Zero costs" may make this an overstatement of the point, since time costs are neglected.

[44] If there is a case for state intervention to require a window-sticker for consumers in buying cars, then a fortiori there is a case for providing comparable knowledge for the purchasers of surgical services.

[45] Kessel, *supra* note 22, at 29-42.

[46] This misallocation is not new. *See* Bunker, *Surgical Manpower in the United States and in England and Wales*, 282 N. ENG. J. MED. 135, 143 (1970).

typically have more generous surgical fee schedules than Blue Cross. It is not unknown for patients to be charged surgical fees as much as fifty per cent greater than the Medicare rate, which is supposed to reflect the prevailing rate in the community. Medicare has increased the ability of some members of the community to pay for surgery and consequently increased the price of surgery.[47]

A great virtue of prepaid group medical plans is that the marginal costs of the time of surgeons to such plans is lower than it is to the public. The price per surgical procedure under fee-for-service is regulated; the price of a surgeon's time to a plan that will convert this time into surgical procedures is not. Hence, prepaid plans represent a means of cutting prices for surgical services. Alternatively, prepaid plans constitute means for buying surgical and nonsurgical services at prices that reflect their relative costs of production.

Many writers have found fault with our medical care delivery system on the grounds that it is a "cottage industry," characterized by a large number of small firms that, in their judgment, are operating at less than optimal size. One of the striking pieces of evidence obtained from our experience with comprehensive prepaid group medical plans, which are relatively large-scale enterprises, is that advertising is crucial for getting started and generating sufficient volume to justify attempts to achieve scale economies. Many of the successful and unsuccessful prepaid plans ran into trouble with organized medicine because they advertised. Why advertising should not be permitted has never been made clear, though it is usually roundly condemned by the AMA as being unethical. It appears that freedom to advertise is important if we want to encourage innovation in the marketing of medical care.[48]

CONCLUSION

In summary, both the production (education) of physicians and the delivery of health care have suffered from common problems—inability of institutions and individuals to innovate because of the restraints imposed by organized medicine.[49] In the production of physicians, it was a mistake to specify how physicians were to be produced instead of specifying what the product should be and allowing schools to compete in efficiently producing that product. State licensure examinations or

---

[47] It is not a complete surprise to find that unfilled vacancies in the surgical residencies are generally smaller than they are in the nonsurgical specialties. *See* AMA, DIRECTORY OF APPROVED INTERNSHIPS AND RESIDENCIES, 1968-69, at 8, 9. The over-all percentage filled is 81%. For thoracic surgery, it is 91%; surgery, 89%; plastic surgery, 87%; colon and rectal surgery, 92%; neurologic surgery, 91%. By contrast, general practice is 48% filled, pathology 56%, and psychiatry 76%.

[48] Kessel, *supra* note 22, at 36.

[49] There exist many parallels between medicine and AFL building trade unions—discrimination in admissions, training techniques that are over-specified and excessively protracted, and archaic work rules. There has been great public dissatisfaction with the performance of both. In the case of the building trades, this dissatisfaction has led to measures that increase the demand for housing (FHA and VA loans); for medicine, it has been instrumental in bringing about Medicare and Medicaid. Public intervention has thus far served the interests of these monopolists. In neither field has a frontal attack been made on the basic problem—restriction on the supply of crucial agents of production.

the national board examinations constitute an appropriate vehicle for specifying what physicians can be expected to do. Medical schools should be free to decide how to produce whatever it is that constitutes a physician without intervention by the state or the AMA.

Similarly, in the case of medical care delivery, individuals and groups should be free to innovate alternative delivery systems. There is no case for sanctifying fee-for-service and making prepaid plans illegal. Nor is there any good reason for prohibiting advertising by physicians.

In the decade of the 1960s, and particularly in the last five years, the AMA began openly to admit that a "doctor shortage" exists. Many new medical schools have been started, restrictions on the use of paramedical personnel have been relaxed, and some innovations in the medical curricula have occurred that have reduced the time it takes to produce an MD. This behavior is subject to two interpretations—either the AMA has changed its spots or the times are embarrassingly good financially for the medical profession and hence a more relaxed attitude is appropriate. This history of the AMA suggests that the latter interpretation is more correct. During the prosperity of the late 1920s, the AMA was less restrictive than it was during the great depression.[50] It is important to remember that, whatever the times, the AMA has an inevitable conflict of interests. It has presumed simultaneously to represent (1) the public, in maintaining standards for the production of physicians and in determining the quantity to be produced, and (2) the medical profession, the purveyors of medical services. In other words, the AMA represents both the buyers and the sellers of physician services in determining the output of physicians. Given this anomalous position, it is difficult to believe that the AMA will ever permit the number of physicians to be produced that the public is willing to support with its patronage.[51] Consequently its power to determine output via the rating of medical schools should be withdrawn and graduation from an AMA-approved medical school should not be a condition for admission to licensure examinations.[52]

It is important to remember that physicians, not Congressmen, produce medical care. An extension of Medicare to include everyone would increase the demand for medical care and probably reduce the availability of physicians. The problem that exists in medicine is largely a consequence of the severe restriction in the output of

---

[50] In the 1930s there was a "little" Flexner report on medical education known as the Weiskotten Survey, which found that some schools had become lax in their standards and admitted too many students. See Dodds, *supra* note 8, at 790.

[51] "It must be recognized, however, that it is not likely that America will ever be able to produce all the physicians the nation would like to have." L. COGGESHALL, PLANNING FOR MEDICAL PROGRESS THROUGH EDUCATION 26, 98 (1965). Coggeshall goes on to argue that it is uneconomic to have the public's desire satisfied.

[52] In part this has already occurred with respect to graduates of schools other than the Canadian and American institutions—the graduates of the so-called foreign medical schools. The AMA did rate these schools at one time. See MARGULIES & BLOCK, *supra* note 4, at 46.

physicians that was caused by the AMA and abetted, probably unwittingly, by Flexner and the Carnegie Foundation. Hence, the solution to our medical problems lies in increasing the output of physicians, in making the number of physicians in the community responsive to the desires of the community. To accomplish this goal, the AMA should be stripped of its power to control the output of physicians.

3 Higher Education and the Nation's Health: A Review of the Carnegie Commission Report on Medical Education (1972)

THE Carnegie Commission's report is ". . . concerned with the serious shortage of professional health manpower, the need for expanding and restructuring the education of professional health personnel, and the vital importance of adapting the education of health manpower to the changes needed for an effective system of delivery of health care in the United States."[1] The Commission, to put matters succinctly, finds that a deplorable state of affairs exists with respect to the production and delivery of medical care and that the output of physicians ought to be increased by fifty per cent in the next decade.[2]

With few exceptions, this report implicitly views the current state of affairs with respect to the supply of medical care as if it were a consequence of a natural event such as an earthquake or hurricane. Therefore, the Commission's report contains virtually no analysis of how the current state of affairs came into existence. This omission constitutes a serious deficiency; it is usually necessary to understand the cause of a social problem in order to deal with it effectively.

Generally it is a mistake to ignore the causes of a social problem. For the Carnegie Commission to largely ignore the causes of our present difficulties in the medical field is self-serving. It is our thesis that most of our present difficulties, in particular the so-called "shortage" of physicians is attributable to the Carnegie Foundation's previous endeavors in the field of medical education—that is, the famous Flexner report on medical education and the widespread implementation of its recommendations.[3]

The focus of the Commission's recommendations is ". . . the contributions of university health science centers" and they report they know of ". . . no

---

[1] Carnegie Comm'n on Higher Education, Higher Education and the Nation's Health; Policies for Medical and Dental Education, Foreword at v (1970).
[2] *Id.* at 5.
[3] Abraham Flexner, Medical Education in the U.S. and Canada (Carnegie Foundation for the Advancement of Teaching, Bull. No. 4, 1910).

55

single area in all of higher education where more constructive action can be taken now than in medical and dental education."[4] The current report regards medical education and research as now undergoing a second great transformation, comparable to that brought on by the Flexner report, ". . . and the United States, once again, will greatly benefit."[5] Hence, by implication, the Commission argues that the present difficulties would even be greater, if that is conceivable, if the Flexner report had not been produced. One can search in vain for evidence in the current report, or elsewhere, to support this view.

The Flexner "model," which constituted the prevailing pattern for medical education in the United States until relatively recently and which emphasized research output, is criticized only as being self-contained and ignoring health care delivery. By self-contained, the Commission means that science in a medical school is set apart from science generally in a university. It also reports that it is now desirable (it avoids saying whether it was desirable in the past), to have diversity in our medical schools.[6] The research or Flexner model is only one of three models the Commission finds desirable. The others are the health care delivery "model" in which medical schools orient themselves to external services, and the integrated science "model" in which the "science" component of medical education, typically given in the first two years of a medical school curriculum, is taught by the science departments of a university.[7] By contrast, the clinical, or third and fourth years, are to be taught within medical schools, which may be essentially teaching hospitals.

Briefly, the Commission recommends that: (1) the time required to become a practicing physician be reduced from eight to six years by reducing from four to three years the medical school curriculum and reducing residency requirements by one year; (2) the output of physicians be increased by fifty per cent by 1978; (3) an intermediate degree be made available for those who have completed the two years of basic science, the equivalent of the first two years of medical school, who then will choose between science and research, or medical schools and careers as physicians; (4) the federal government subsidize the production of physicians through aid to medical students and/or medical schools.[8]

The Commission offers virtually no explanation of the "shortage" of physicians, how or why it came into existence receives almost no attention. The report notes that the supply of physicians is inelastic in the short run and

---

[4] Carnegie Comm'n, *supra* note 1, at 2.
[5] *Id.* at 3.
[6] *Id.* at 4. The absence of diversity is clearly a consequence of Flexner's work.
[7] *Id.* at 4.
[8] *Id.* at 9.

with the advent of Medicare and Medicaid, medical costs rose because ". . . the supply of both physicians and hospital capacity tends to be inelastic and respond slowly to increases in demand."[9] Whether or not a "shortage" of physicians existed before the advent of Medicare and Medicaid is not considered.

The mechanism by which the increase in demand for physicians' services, generated by Medicare and Medicaid, gets translated into an increase in the number of physicians produced is nowhere spelled out. Nor is there discussion of the more general problem of how the desires of the public for physician's services get translated into practicing physicians. The implicit view of the Commission, if it says anything at all on this point, is that some agency, like the Carnegie Foundation, should survey the consumers of medical care, decide how many doctors are required, and then assign production goals to the medical schools.

The Commission also reports that frequently used criteria or indexes of the health status of a nation indicate that the United States does not compare favorably with many European countries. Moreover, it points out that the unfavorable comparison with respect to infant mortality cannot be wholly accounted for by the blacks in the American population. No explanation is offered for this unfavorable comparison.[10] Willingness to spend for medical care is implicitly ruled out as an explanation by citing the fact that seven per cent of the gross national product goes to the medical sector.

The report tacitly assumes that the frequency of minority groups among physicians should be the same as their frequency in the population. Hence, the Commission finds that there are enough Japanese and Chinese medical students but not enough blacks and women. The implications of these recommendations for minority groups over-represented among physicians relative to their frequency in the population are not explicitly considered. The arithmetic of the position the Commission takes indicates that too many of some unspecified groups become physicians.

The defense for the position taken on minority groups by the Commission is that physicians can "relate" better to patients if both the patient and physician belong to the same minority group.[11] Presumably a symmetrical argument leads to the conclusion that not enough women are physicians. The consequences of this view for physicians who treat children, octogenarians, patients with cancer, etc., are not considered.

The Commission's recommendations with respect to admissions policies for

[9] *Id.* at 21.
[10] *Id.* at 15.
[11] *Id.* at 29.

medical schools border on inconsistency and are less than straightforward. They suggest that medical schools: "Refrain from discrimination on the basis of race, creed, or sex and also pursue positive policies to encourage the admission of members of minority groups."[12] What policies should be pursued with respect to members of non-minority groups? Do they mean all minority groups regardless of race, creed or color? If so, what about the groups they implicitly argue are over-represented among physicians?

The evidence that the Commission presents for the existence of what it describes as a physician "shortage" is that approximately eleven per cent of all American MD candidates attend foreign schools (Canadian medical schools are not defined as foreign for this purpose.).[13] If the Commission regards this "shortage" as antedating Medicare and Medicaid (this point is unclear in the report), then no explanation is contained in the report of why it came into existence.

The absence of educational opportunities for the study of medicine in the United States is anomalous; it is true for virtually no other field. The Commission failed to ask why medicine is unique; it is the only major field in which more Americans study abroad than foreigners study in the United States. Why is it that a country which spends such vast sums, both publicly and privately, for higher education in such diverse fields as agriculture, insurance, veterinary medicine, etc., has failed to provide comparable opportunities for medicine? Conversely, why do foreign countries provide relatively more abundant opportunities for study of medicine? This question, and its answer, fall within the domain of causes of the current crisis in medicine, a subject that is almost studiously avoided.

The report recommends federal subsidies to medical students and medical schools with a uniform level of tuition for all schools of one thousand dollars.[14] For many if not most of the private schools this would represent a substantial reduction in tuition, that is, in excess of fifty per cent since tuition currently is about $2,500 per year. It would also result in the premier medical schools getting virtually all of the best students because the lesser schools would be unable to use financial inducements to offset differences in faculty quality.

It is amazing that the Commission would recommend a course of action that represents a subsidy from the poor to the rich. Indeed, the Commission fails to acknowledge that this is in fact what is being recommended. Admission to medical school implies subsequent admission to the upper ten per cent, or better, of the income distribution. Hence, attending medical schools

[12] *Id.* at 69.
[13] *Id.* at 37.
[14] *Id.* at 68.

is equivalent to undertaking a very profitable investment. The Commission is in fact recommending the subsidization, or more properly the further subsidization, of what already constitutes one of the most profitable investments in our society.

The profitability of an investment in medical education may be estimated by comparing the investment required to win a license to practice medicine in the United States for an American by studying abroad with the costs of obtaining this same license through study in the United States or Canada. On average, Americans who study medicine abroad receive their licenses three years after they graduate from medical schools; by contrast, their more fortunate brethren who get into American medical schools receive their licenses, on average, one year after graduation. Moreover, the average age at licensure of Americans who study abroad is 32, in contrast to 27 for those who study in the United States. (Many foreign medical schools require six years of attendance for graduation.[15]) Assuming that the Americans who study medicine abroad earn a rate of return on their investment in education that is competitive with investments in legal education, science, economics, etc., then by an *a fortiori* argument, Americans who study medicine in the United States must receive rates of return in excess of the competitive rate. This conclusion has been reached from a wholly different approach, using data from the 1930's by other investigators.[16] There clearly exist returns to physicians trained in the United States that are greater than competitive returns. Alternatively, there exist monopoly returns to an investment in medical education.

The magnitude of these monopoly returns is a function of what one regards as the relevant rate of interest and the pattern of earnings over time following licensure. Assuming a thirty year career following licensure for foreign trained physicians, and a thirty five year career for the local product, a six per cent rate of interest implies returns to American trained physicians forty per cent greater than those realized by foreign trained Americans. (For convenience,

[15] This is based on AMA data used to produce their directory of physicians. Physicians trained abroad that were both born in the United States and live here are defined to be Americans that went abroad for medical training. There are almost six thousand physicians in this population. Americans who study abroad have usually been unable to win admission to American medical schools. Assuming they constitute inferior raw material, should one attribute all of the delay in winning licensure to lack of educational opportunities as has been done above? A test of whether this attribution is correct is the absence of a relationship between age at licensure of graduates of American medical schools and the quality of student inputs. Since the best schools typically get the best medical students, school quality can function as a proxy for student quality. The absence or presence of such a relationship is currently under investigation.

[16] Milton Friedman & Simon Kuznets, Independent Income from Professional Practice (Nat'l Bur. of Econ. Res., Pub. No. 45, 1945).

uniform and identical income streams following licensure were assumed.) As the rate of interest used increases, estimates of the advantage of training in the United States also increase. If foreign trained Americans are getting a competitive rate of return on their investment in education, then these results strongly imply monopoly returns for American trained physicians.

The argument against the would-be rich monopolists paying for the investment that will make them rich monopolists that is offered by the Commission is: there exist ". . . psychological barriers to incurring indebtedness on the part of students from low-income families, an attitude that is undoubtedly explained in part by the tendency for low-income families to experience income instability."[17] The evidence to support the view that students from low-income families are incapable of recognizing their financial self-interest is not cited. Elsewhere, the Commission cites its approval of equity-type financing of medical education but nevertheless concludes that the training of medical students should be subsidized because subsidization would be ". . . more even-handed in its impact."[18]

The study of medical schools and the financing of medical education, on which the Commission says it relies, comes to the same conclusion—have the poor subsidize the rich insofar as they are students of medicine.[19] The justification for this conclusion is less patronizing and more sophisticated—that the social or economic benefits of physicians exceed the private returns.[20] The evidence of the existence of monopoly returns presented here and elsewhere suggests that the converse view—that the economic or social returns are less than the private returns—is more correct.

Because the Commission dodges the question of how the "shortage" of physicians came into being, it also deals circumspectly with the licensure issue. It wants the development of a national system of licensure (which to a great extent already exists for physicians by virtue of the acceptance by states of the national board results) by the government with the aid of the American Medical Association.[21] If the historical record is any guide, this is on a par with having spiders run an orphanage for flies; the AMA is in no position to represent the public interest in this matter. There is no glimmer of recognition in the Commission's report that the current "shortage" of physicians is related to the past activities of the American Medical Association aided by the Flexner report.[22]

[17] Carnegie Comm'n, *supra* note 1, at 64.
[18] *Id.* at 68.
[19] Rashi Fein & Gerald I. Weber, Financing Medical Education, 191 (Carnegie Comm'n on Higher Education, 1971).
[20] *Id.* at 217.
[21] Carnegie Comm'n, *supra* note 1, at 78.
[22] For evidence on the role of the AMA, see Reuben A. Kessel, The AMA and the Supply of Physicians, 35 Law & Contemp. Prob. 267 (1970).

The Commission never faces up to the role of licensure laws in creating the "shortage" which it acknowledges. If it did, many of the problems that it addresses would vanish. To be more specific, the Commission is exercised over the high cost of medical education. Estimates of educational costs per medical student of between $6,000 and $16,000 per year are cited. Student-to-faculty ratios of one to one compared with six to one in graduate education generally are also cited. An alternative to the exhortation of the Carnegie Commission to reduce costs is to stimulate competition in medical education.

Currently, medical students trained in the United States take Part I of their national boards, or for that matter, Part I of state licensure examinations, after two years of medical education. A prerequisite, to repeat, a necessary condition for admission to these examinations, is attendance at an AMA approved medical school. Clearly only knowledge of basic science and not how, why, or where it was acquired is relevant. Certainly attendance at an AMA approved school is not. If the irrelevant admission requirements to this examination were dropped, then medical schools would be forced to compete with liberal arts colleges, science departments of universities, and scientific institutes in providing basic science training. As a consequence, there would be, as the old socialists were fond of saying, a rationalization of the production of physicians at least with respect to the first two years of training. Moreover, the basic science requirement could be substantially completed during the undergraduate years.

Similarly with respect to the second two years of medical training, the so-called clinical years, hospitals with post-MD training programs, that is, internships and residencies, could by an *a fortiori* argument provide pre-MD clinical training. Moreover, given the willingness of hospitals to incur enormous costs for these post-MD programs, it is difficult to see why tuition charges for third and fourth year medical students could not be reduced substantially if not eliminated. The faculty could be practicing physicians who would be part-time teachers. For all practical purposes, this would represent little or no change from current practice; third and fourth year students are typically instructed by clinical professors who are practicing physicians and who buy titles in exchange for part-time teaching services.[23] (In the student-faculty ratio cited earlier, only full-time faculty were counted.) The real obstacle to such a development is the state licensure laws; only those who attend AMA approved medical schools can take Part II of the national boards or the state licensure examination. Again, if knowledge and not attendance at an AMA approved medical school were relevant for admission to licensure

---

[23] There is only one medical school without part-time clinical faculty, that is, with medical students instructed only by full-time faculty. This maverick school is in the process of acquiring some part-time clinical faculty along with a new hospital affiliation.

examinations, this country would now have more physicians, lower costs of producing physicians and, consequently, lower costs of medical care.

Graduation from approved medical schools became a necessary condition for sitting for licensure examinations as a result of the Flexner-AMA "reforms" generated by the famous Flexner report. The schools that Flexner and the AMA disapproved could and did turn out graduates that passed state licensure examinations. Hence, these schools had to be legislated out of existence. Flexner defended such legislation with this patronizing argument: "The law that protects the public against the unfit doctor should in fairness protect the student against the unfit school."[24]

One cannot help wondering why the Commission is not concerned that different examination standards exist for Americans who study medicine abroad as compared with those who study in either the United States or Canada. Americans who study medicine abroad are clearly discriminated against—they must complete their medical education and be eligible for licensure in the country in which they received their training and must pass an admission examination, the so-called ECMFG, before being admitted to licensure examinations in the United States. Hence, they are at a substantial disadvantage in taking their basic science examination since the time gap between training and examination is several years. Since the Commission is concerned with the "shortage" of physicians, it is puzzling that it failed to be concerned with the double standard for licensure examinations, and the irrelevant criteria used to admit foreign-trained American medical graduates to licensure examinations. Clearly these barriers reduce the availability of qualified physicians in the United States.

The Commission feels that health personnel are "inefficiently" used and hospital personnel often wastefully used and cites, with implicit approval, the view that our health care delivery system is a "non-system."[25] Evidence of the existence of inefficiency or waste is not mustered. Moreover, it is not clear whether the term "non-system" is the slave or the master of the Commission. Do we have a system for the delivery of groceries, meats, shoes, clothes, houses, barber services? If the present arrangement for the delivery of medical care is a "non-system," what is a system? Explicit answers to this question are not provided and one can only surmise from the Commission's recommendations and analysis what a system for the delivery of medical care would be.

If one tries to infer what a system would be from the Commission's recommendations, it would largely consist of more of what has already failed. The

[24] Abraham Flexner, *supra* note 3, at 167.
[25] Carnegie Comm'n, *supra* note 1, at 20.

medical schools, whose income from student tuition is about four per cent, and which are now heavily dependent upon governmental funds, would become more financially dependent upon the government. They would in effect become wards of the state. With the reduction in medical school tuition, non-price rationing of admissions would become more severe than it has been in the past. The record of the medical schools with respect to discrimination in terms of race, creed, or color has been a shameful one. Lessening the dependence of medical schools upon student fees will increase the latitude for discrimination in terms of race, creed or color.[26]

Yet the Commission is in a sense correct when it says that we have a "non-system." There exists no mechanism for bringing into equality the number of physicians which the public desires and is willing to support with the number in fact available. At one time, before the advent of Flexner, such a mechanism existed. Flexner and the medical profession, but not the public, argued that the medical schools of the time were producing a surplus of physicians. He also contended that there was no desire on the part of the public for the physicians being produced. Flexner cited with approval the view that the greed of the medical schools' owners or faculties for tuition fees and the desires of the public accounted for the production of unwanted physicians.[27] The medical schools in the early 1900's, so Flexner argued, through advertising and other blandishments, seduced students into making unprofitable investments in medical education.[28] Moreover, in the introduction to Flexner's work by the then head of the Carnegie Foundation, Pritchett, he contended that there had been over-production of physicians for twenty-five years.[29]

What is the right number of physicians for a society? Pritchett suggested that some optimal constant exists. To use his words: "It is evident that in a society constituted as are our modern states, the interest of the social order will be served best when the number of men entering a given profession reaches and does not exceed a given ratio." What is this ratio and how is it obtained?

For example, in law and medicine one sees best in a small village the situation created by the over-production of inadequately trained men. In a town of two thousand people one will find in most of our states from five to eight physicians where two well trained men could do the work efficiently and make a competent livelihood. When, however, six or eight ill-trained physicians undertake to gain a

---

[26] For an explanation why this should be true see Armen A. Alchian & Reuben A. Kessel, Competition, Monopoly, and the Pursuit of Money [Pecuniary Gain], in Aspects of Labor Economics. ([Universities] Nat'l Bur. of Econ. Res., Special conf. ser. no. 14, 1962).

[27] Abraham Flexner, *supra* note 3, at 35.

[28] *Id.* at 19.

[29] *Id.* at x. Clearly "over-production" does not mean being out of long run equilibrium.

living in a town which can support only two, the whole plane of professional conduct is lowered in the struggle which ensues, each man becomes intent upon his own practice, public health and sanitation are neglected, and the ideals and standards of the profession tend to demoralization.[30]

Clearly Pritchett's concept of optimality, abstracting from quality or professional competence, is economic. It is determined by that ratio of physicians to population which will provide physicians with a "competent livelihood." Since the mechanism by which the desires of the public for physicians was producing a surplus of physicians, as viewed by the Carnegie Foundation and the AMA using the "competent livelihood" criterion, this mechanism had to be destroyed. The key to its destruction was the destruction of the linkage between the willingness of students to pay for a medical education and the interests of medical schools in catering to these desires. The Flexner revolution emancipated the medical schools from dependence upon student fees. As a consequence, it created a non-system; the desires of the public could not be translated into physicians willing to provide medical services.

The proposed reduction in tuition for medical students, which if adopted would make tuition in medical schools lower than tuition in virtually all private non-church supported preparatory schools, would further weaken if not totally destroy the linkage between the desire for physicians by the public and the incentives of medical schools to produce physicians. Before the advent of Flexner, the returns to being a physician led would-be physicians to seek out medical schools that were largely or totally supported by tuition fees and hence had powerful incentives, too powerful in Flexner's view, to produce physicians to meet the desires of the public.

From the time of Flexner's report to the present day there has been a downward trend in the fraction of the income of medical schools derived from student fees. Currently this fraction is, according to Fein and Weber, about four per cent and would obviously go lower if the recommendations of the Commission with respect to tuition were adopted.[31] About half of the income of medical schools is derived from sponsored research grants from government, governmental agencies, and private foundations.[32] Clearly the principal product produced by medical schools is research, not medical education.

Moreover, it is not clear whether past financial support of medical school research by governmental and private agencies has led to an improvement or a deterioration of the health status of this nation. Clearly the increment to medical knowledge from research must have been positive. However, if there

---

[30] *Id.* at xiv.
[31] Rashi Fein & Gerald I. Weber, *supra* note 19, at 58, table 9.
[32] *Id.*

had been less research money available, medical schools would have been more dependent upon tuition fees, and hence, would have had stronger incentives to produce physicians. The additional physicians that would have been produced would presumably also have had a beneficial effect upon the health status of the nation.

The creation of this non-system for the production of physicians has been justified on the grounds that high quality physicians and hence high quality medical care is insured. The evidence to support this view is embarrassingly absent; certainly it would be hard to argue that the international comparisons cited earlier buttress this view. The other scanty evidence available on the quality of medical care does not provide much support either. More specifically, the famous study by Peterson of general practice in North Carolina does not indicate that we reached, many decades after the Flexner reforms were initiated, the level of competency in medical practice that was promised.[33] Indeed, the views of the American College of Surgeons—that about one-half the surgery is undertaken by unqualified physicians—raises grave doubts about what the Flexner reforms have achieved other than raising the incomes of physicians.[34] Two independent sources provide additional and related pieces of evidence on the quality of medical care. International comparisons of the frequency of surgical procedures in the United States and in England reveal a higher frequency of surgical procedures in the United States that cannot be explained by differences in the natural incidence of ailments.[35] Comparisons of the frequency of surgery in fee-for-services and prepaid group practices, recently renamed health maintenance organizations, indicate a higher frequency of surgery under fee-for-service.[36] These differences can be explained, of course, as a consequence of differences in tastes for surgery, or of members of prepaid groups buying surgery in the fee-for-service market. However, the interpretation most consistent with the international evidence leads to serious questions about the quality of the medical advice being purveyed in this country.

The issue of consumer protection from the ministrations of the unqualified physician or bad advice from good physicians is not raised by the Commission. We suffer from obsolete licensing laws that grant lifetime rights to phy-

[33] Osler L. Peterson, *et al.*, An Analytic Study of North Carolina General Practice 1953-1954, 31 J. Medical Ed. No. 12, pt. 2 (Dec. 1956).

[34] Milton I. Romer, On Paying the Doctor and the Implication of Different Methods, 3 J. Health & Human Behavior 4, 7 (1962).

[35] John P. Bunker, Surgical Manpower: A Comparison of Operations and Surgeons in the United States and in England and Wales, 282 N. Eng. J. of Medicine 135, 137 (1970).

[36] The marginal returns of an additional surgical procedure are negative for pre-paid plans, and positive when payment is in fee-for-service.

sicians to offer a wide range of medical treatments and surgical procedures which many physicians are unqualified to undertake. To the Commission's credit, it does suggest that physicians be re-licensed periodically. With the development of modern medicine, specific purpose licenses rather than general licenses should be considered. These licenses should correspond with the major fields in medicine and surgery and be subject to re-examination. To prevent abuse, licensure examinations for new entrants and for existing practitioners should bear a reasonable resemblance to one another.[37]

CONCLUSIONS

Before the advent of Flexner, the principal product line of most medical schools was physicians and the principal source of income for these schools was tuition. Schools were beholden to their students and deans had to attract and keep students to survive. Indeed, Flexner complained that the deans of some of these schools ". . . know more about modern advertising than about modern medical teaching."[38] Over time, the schools that survived the Flexner reforms, a minority of those in existence at the time his report was published, became less and less dependent upon tuition income. Currently less than five per cent of all income is derived from tuition. Governments, governmental agencies, and foundations account for more than one-half of the income of medical schools. If the Commission's recommendations are implemented, tuition will be virtually eliminated as a source of medical school income.

The change in the sources of income for medical schools has transformed medical school deans from business men, possibly advertising experts who catered to the desires of students, to mendicants who cater to governments and governmental agencies which have replaced students as a source of medical school income. This transformation has weakened incentives to produce physicians efficiently if at all.

The courses medical students take in the first two years are very similar to courses offered in university science departments, and the clinical training in the third and fourth years is similar to the clinical training of interns and residents for which there exist negative tuition fees. Why are the costs of producing physicians so great? Because there is an absence of incentives to produce physicians efficiently. The Commission implicitly recognizes the relevance of the foregoing argument by suggesting that some of the basic science training take place outside medical schools and within university science departments, and that hospital-schools be developed to provide the third and fourth years of training.

[37] Reuben A. Kessel, *supra* note 22, at 278.
[38] Abraham Flexner, *supra* note 3, at 19.

If this society is to increase the supply of physicians, then the linkage between the desires of the public for physicians and the incentives to produce physicians by medical schools must be re-established. This suggests that medical schools should be more dependent upon student tuition for income and less dependent on governmental largesse or welfare which the Commission recommends.

The recommendations of the Commission, that the education of physicians be subsidized, implies that the poor will be subsidizing the rich. The Commission has been unwilling to recognize the redistributive implications of its proposals. Either it fails to understand the rudiments of modern capital theory, that medical students have transitorily low income but embody a large capital value or present worth, or else it feels that equity considerations are irrelevant. Certainly equity is not explicitly considered. Moreover, evidence on what students are in fact willing to pay for medical education, as demonstrated by the behavior of Americans who study medicine abroad, clearly indicates that substantially higher tuition charges are feasible and would not reduce the output of physicians in this country. Indeed, both tuition and output could be simultaneously increased; higher tuition charges would simply reduce the monopoly returns to the new entrants into medicine.

To the Commission's credit, it does recognize the inadequacy of present licensure arrangements and understands that a re-licensing procedure should be established. However, turning to the AMA for assistance is turning in the wrong direction. The AMA represents the existing establishment and will act to protect this establishment and not the public.

Reform of licensure examinations is a critical and largely ignored subject. The licensure examination should test medical and scientific knowledge, and admission should not be restricted to those who have attended AMA approved schools. How knowledge is acquired is irrelevant; hence, the admission requirements to licensure examinations are also irrelevant. If admission requirements to licensure examinations were dropped, there would develop strong incentives for schools to efficiently train physicians because of the competition among schools that would develop. A giant step towards eliminating the "shortage" of physicians and reducing their costs of production would be to eliminate admission requirements to licensure examinations.

4 Transfused Blood, Serum Hepatitis, and the Coase Theorem* (1974)

THE late Professor Richard M. Titmuss, in a volume entitled *The Gift Relationship*, delivered a scathing indictment of the system of collecting and delivering blood in the United States by comparing unfavorably the American blood delivery system with the one that prevails in England.[1] The key to Titmuss's objection to our blood delivery system, which utilizes both voluntary and paid donors, is the fact that patients contract hepatitis, more specifically serum hepatitis, substantially more frequently in the United States than in England as a result of blood transfusions.[2] According to Titmuss, about three and one-half per cent of all transfused patients in the United States subsequently contract hepatitis; in England, the corresponding number is under one per cent.[3] This is equivalent to saying that the frequency of hepatitis as a result of transfusion in the United States exceeds England by a factor of about four.

Commercialism in blood procurement—the utilization of paid as an alternative to unpaid (which is not equivalent to Titmuss's altruistic) donors—is held responsible for the higher frequency of transfusion hepatitis in the United States. (It is widely believed that the frequency of hepatitis among recipients of blood from paid donors is roughly ten times greater than it is for unpaid donors.)[4] Commercial donors, according to Titmuss, discourage

---

* The author wishes to acknowledge the assistance of Professor Ronald Coase. An earlier version of this paper was presented at the Industrial Organization Workshop at the University of Chicago.

[1] Richard M. Titmuss, The Gift Relationship: From Human Blood to Social Policy (1971).

[2] There are two types of hepatitis, serum or transfusion (type B) and infectious (type A). These names were derived from beliefs about how these maladies were transmitted which subsequent findings do not wholly support. Hence they have been renamed in a manner that is not suggestive of how they are transmitted or acquired. Both attack the liver. Type B has a substantially longer incubation period, and is more lethal.

[3] Richard M. Titmuss, *supra* note 1, at 146 & 154.

[4] See National Heart and Lung Institute (NHLI) Blood Resources Studies Summary Report 63 (U.S. Dep't Health, Ed. & Welfare, NIH 73-416, June 30, 1972) [hereinafter cited as NHLI Summary Report]. The full NHLI report is published in 3 volumes. Vol. 1: Supply and Use of the Nation's Blood Resource; vol. 2: Regulation of the Nation's

or eliminate voluntary donors; bad blood suppliers drive good blood suppliers out of business. Moreover, he regards malpractice suits as undesirable commercialism which he contends, along with organized medicine in the United States, leads to wasteful "defensive" medicine.[5]

Titmuss also uses economic criteria to compare the "economic efficiency" of the English and American blood delivery systems and finds the American system less efficient.[6] Consequently, Titmuss is less than enamoured with the price mechanism as a means of organizing the production and marketing of blood. Indeed, Titmuss has great reservations about the virtues of the price mechanism for organizing the production and allocation of scarce resources generally; it is his view that the world needs more love and less pecuniary calculation.

The thesis that the price mechanism should not be used for the organization and production of anything arouses the ire of Arrow and Solow.[7] However, they either do not object to or endorse the view that the commercial donor should be outlawed and replaced by the volunteer donor in order to reduce the incidence of hepatitis.[8]

Blood Resource; vol. 3: A Pilot Study of Hemophilia Treatment in the United States (U.S. Dep't Health, Ed. & Welfare, 1973).

[5] Richard M. Titmuss, *supra* note 1, ch. 9, and 197. Although not explicit, it appears that he would attribute "unnecessary" surgery to commercialism in the medical care market. It is unclear whether Titmuss would hold corresponding views about the effects of malpractice suits for lawyers and consulting economists.

[6] A relevant test of Titmuss's hypothesis—that commercialism increases economic inefficiency—is to look for a relationship between the degree of commercialism in an area or region and the measure Titmuss uses to gauge economic efficiency. Titmuss asserts that Seattle has a relatively non-commercial source of blood; hence, if Titmuss is right, an investigation ought to show it to be an area in which blood is efficiently allocated.

[7] See Kenneth J. Arrow, Gifts and Exchanges, in 1 Philosophy & Public Affairs 343 (1972); Robert M. Solow, Blood and Thunder, 80 Yale L.J. 1696 (1971).

[8] Michael H. Cooper & Anthony J. Cuyler, The Price of Blood (Inst. of Econ. Affairs, 1968) advocate thoroughgoing commercialism in the organization and distribution of blood. However, they do not deal with the issue of transfusion hepatitis except for one discussion question following the conclusion of their paper, and a reference to a paper by J. Garrott Allen (& Wynn A. Sayman, Serum Hepatitis from Transfusions of Blood, 180 J. Am. Med. Ass'n 1079 (1962)) who has done as much as anyone to alert the medical profession to the incidence and risks of serum hepatitis.

Another possible exception is Marc A. Franklin who has written two important papers dealing with this subject. They are entitled: Tort Liability for Hepatitis; An Analysis and a Proposal, 24 Stan. L. Rev. 439 (1972); and Hepatitis, Blood Transfusions and Public Action, 21 Catholic Univ. L. Rev. 683 (1972). In the second article, Franklin is mostly concerned with alternative legal and social arrangements for providing blood.

E. R. Jennings, Not All Paid Donors Pose Hepatitis Risks, 2 Lab. Medicine July, 1971, at 8, argues that it is the socio-economic status of donors, not whether or not they are paid, that matters. Hence, the selection of donors, paid or unpaid, ought to be by socio-economic class. He unambiguously disagrees with Titmuss on this critical point.

The NHLI study, vol. 1, *supra* note 4, app. C, at 4 concludes: "The incidence of post-transfusion hepatitis is apparently associated with the specific socio-economic conditions

Arrow points to the absence of a mechanism to equilibrate the quantity of blood demanded with the quantity supplied in Titmuss's explanation of the working of the English system.[9] This is of some relevance because it deals with the principal piece of empirical evidence in Cooper and Cuyler—a survey of blood availability when surgeons wish to operate—which Titmuss dismisses out of hand. Over one-third of the surgeons surveyed reported that they sometimes postpone operations for want of blood.[10]

Support for Cooper and Cuyler's explanation of the equilibrating mechanism appears in a review article by Surgenor:

> In England, an order by a physician for a blood transfusion is usually conditional upon the availability of blood. In the United States, this is not so; an order for blood is generally not negotiable by a hospital and must be carried out.[11]

Surgenor does not take seriously Titmuss's conclusion that the English system of blood distribution is more efficient because of the absence of data bearing on the question and the failure by Titmuss to take account of the foregoing ". . . fundamental difference between British and American medical practice."[12]

It is the thesis of this paper that Titmuss can be interpreted in a way which makes his conclusion correct. More specifically, Titmuss can be interpreted as arguing that the mechanism for supplying blood to patients is not responsive to their desires—that too low a quality has been supplied. This has been attributed by Titmuss to excessive commercialism; it is explained here as a consequence of insufficient commercialism. Titmuss is correct for the wrong reason.

The first section of this paper deals with the value of hepatitis-free blood; the second with how a system of blood supply, which is responsive to consumer desires, would operate; the third with why the current system, which is moving towards a wholly voluntary system of blood procurement, has come into existence.

A. The Value of Hepatitis-Free Blood

Given the current state of medical technology, there exists no practical way to test effectively for the presence of hepatitis in the blood of all donors.

---

of the donor population rather than with the incentives used in collecting the material." This position is somewhat at variance with what is said on this subject elsewhere in this volume, for example, p. 13, as well as in the summary volume.

[9] Kenneth J. Arrow, *supra* note 7, at 356.

[10] Michael H. Cooper & Anthony J. Cuyler, *supra* note 8, at 17.

[11] D. MacN. Surgenor, Human Blood and the Renewal of Altruism: Titmuss in Retrospect, in 2 Int'l J. Health Sciences, 443, 444 (1972).

[12] *Id.*

The capability of transmitting transfusion hepatitis via blood is detected by testing for the presence of a hepatitis-associated antigen, HBA_g. The best testing method in current use reveals about twenty-five per cent of all hepatitis carriers. Other tests in the wings offer the promise of detecting a maximum of fifty per cent.[13] (There seems to be discreet silence on the question of how much good blood it falsely rejects.) The risk associated with hepatitis rises monotonically with age. It is believed that many infants, particularly infants raised in crowded and relatively unsanitary conditions, incur hepatitis subclinically, that is, no one knows it. By contrast, one study shows that about twenty per cent of those who contract transfusion hepatitis after the age of forty die as a result.[14]

Of the set of transfused patients who manifest symptoms of hepatitis, one HEW report estimates that half convalesce at home for a month without hospital treatment. The other half are hospitalized for about a month and convalesce at home for another month provided they are not among the ten per cent of those hospitalized who die as a result of hepatitis.[15] The costs of (1) subclinical cases, which is estimated to exceed the clinical cases by a factor of five, (2) the transmission of other ailments such as malaria, (3) physician fees, (4) those who never fully recover, estimated to be about equal in number to those who die, and undergo a lifetime of both treatment and sub-par health, and (5) home care are all ignored.[16] For those who never fully recover, their life length is shortened and characterized by tiredness, irritability, lassitude, etc. Clearly hepatitis, unlike warts and athlete's foot or feet, is an extremely costly ailment. Moreover, those who incur this disease typically become more irritable and difficult to live with, a consideration which is not trivial for the marital partners and others associating with hepatitis patients.

The value to patients of high quality blood can be illustrated by very primitive cost calculations. Costs associated with transfusion hepatitis are: (1) for those hospitalized, thirty days at $125 per day taking account of physician fees, laboratory work, etc., which comes to $3,750; (2) the opportunity costs of being out of the labor market, which HEW estimates at $450 a month after adjusting for average participation in the labor market;[17]

[13] See Martin Goldfield, et al., Hepatitis Associated with the Transfusion of HBA_g-Negative Blood, in Hepatitis and Blood Transfusion, Proceedings of a Symposium held at Univ. of Calif. 320 (Girish N. Vyas, Herbert A. Perkins, & Rudi Schmid eds. 1972) [hereinafter cited as Hepatitis and Blood Transfusion].

[14] J. Garrott Allen & Wynn A. Sayman, *supra* note 8, at 1079, 1084.

[15] Posttransfusion Hepatitis: Cases, Deaths, and Costs, in U.S. Dep't Health, Ed. & Welfare, Conference on the National Blood Policy 4 (unpublished reports, 1973).

[16] *Id.* at 1-10.

[17] *Id.* at 5.

(3) home nursing care at $450 per month; (4) treatment for the non-hospitalized at $500; (5) $200,000 as the value of human life which is also used as the cost of being permanently disabled and is obtained from estimates of the value workers place on their lives as inferred from their own behavior.[18] The foregoing implies that the expected costs of hepatitis are $23,225.[19]

The probability of getting hepatitis in the United States as a result of a transfusion of blood seems to depend upon the socio-economic class of the donors, the number of pints involved in a transfusion, and whether or not one has had hepatitis or has natural immunity. The average size of transfusions appears to be rising as a result of the development of open-heart surgery which is a very blood-intensive procedure using up to twenty pints. For open-heart surgery patients transfused with paid donor blood, one study reports about half incurred hepatitis.[20]

An extensive and recently reported study of the incidence of hepatitis among open-heart surgery patients at fourteen so-called university hospital centers contains a body of data useful for estimating the value of a marginal shift in blood sources.[21] These data, reproduced in Table 1, imply that the frequency of symptomatic hepatitis is 8.8 cases per one thousand units of the lowest quality of blood transfused against 2.0 per thousand for the best quality. Hence, a shift from the worst to the best blood implies a reduction in the risk of hepatitis of 6.8 parts per thousand. What would such

---

[18] Richard Thaler & Sherwin Rosen, Estimating the Value of Saving a Life: Evidence from the Labor Market 36 (Nat'l Bur. Econ. Res., Conf. on Res. in Income & Wealth, Dec. 1, 1973) estimate the value of a human life at $200,000 in 1967 dollars.

[19] The expected costs of hospitalization and inpatient treatment are $1875; death and permanent disability, $20,000; home nursing, $425; absence from the labor market, $675; outpatient medical treatment, $250. These numbers are derived from Richard Thaler & Sherwin Rosen, *supra* note 18; and Posttransfusion Hepatitis, *supra* note 15, except for permanent disability and outpatient medical treatment which are added by the author.

[20] John H. Walsh, *et al.*, Post Transfusion Hepatitis After Open-Heart Operations, 211 J. Am. Med. Ass'n 261 (1970).

[21] George F. Grady, Ann J. E. Bennett, *et al.*, Risk of Posttransfusion Hepatitis in the United States, 220 J. Am. Med. Ass'n 692, tab. 4, at 695 (1972). The reported lethality—eight deaths out of 135 severe cases of hepatitis or 6%—may be at variance with the findings of J. Garrott Allen & Wynn A. Sayman, *supra* note 8. No information is provided on the age of patients other than the fact that those who died were all over sixty. Similarly no information was provided on the average length of hospital stay.

This study surprisingly reported the use of pooled plasma and fibrinogen. Since one contaminated unit in a pool is sufficient to contaminate the entire pool, it is difficult to reconcile this practice with concern for the welfare of patients. (The incidence of hepatitis requiring hospitalization of a week or more was 6% for those receiving plasma and 16% for the recipients of fibrinogen.) Multiple-donor plasma was removed from inter-state commerce by government order in 1968; however, multiple donor fibrinogen continues to be used to the puzzlement of the authors of this paper. Titmuss viewed with horror the existence of such pooling and argued that it is absent in England. See Richard M Titmuss, *supra* note 1, at 149.

a reduction be worth? If the expected costs of hepatitis are $23,000, a reduction in the probability of getting hepatitis by one part in one thousand is worth $23, and a shift from the lowest to the highest quality source would be worth approximately 156 additional dollars per unit, that is, 156 additional dollars above and beyond what is now the cost of the lowest quality blood. The foregoing calculation is highly sensitive to the assumptions made about the opportunity costs of time, cost of home nursing care, the magnitude of the blood quality differences that exist, and above all the value of a marginal extension of life.

The evidence presented by Titmuss to support his contention that the frequency of transfusion hepatitis is greater in the United States leaves something to be desired. Differences in standards of reporting, size of transfusions, use of blood derivative products, representativeness of the sample observed, and the definition of commercialism are all problems largely ignored.

TABLE 1
POSTTRANSFUSION VIRAL HEPATITIS ACCORDING TO SOURCE OF DONOR BLOOD

	Average No. of Units of Blood[a] Per Patient	Patients at Risk	Hepatitis Cases		
			All	Symptomatic	Severe
In Patients Receiving All Transfusions From a Single Category					
Group 1: Red Cross donors only	7.4	715	10(1.4%)	10(1.4%)	9(1.3%)
Group 2: Other volunteer donors only	6.4	354	6(1.7%)	6(1.7%)	6(1.7%)
Group 3: Paid donors, known to transfusionist	6.3	396	13(3.3%)	12(3.0%)	11(2.8%)
Group 4: Prebottled blood from paid donors	4.9	625	33(5.3%)	27(4.3%)	19(3.0%)
In Patients Receiving Transfusions From Mixed Sources					
Groups 1, 2, 3 above but no prebottled blood from paid donors	9.3	1,550	35(2.3%)	35(2.3%)	28(1.8%)
Prebottled blood from paid donors and some blood from groups 1, 2, or 3	8.1	1,314	57(4.3%)	47(3.6%)	38(2.9%)
Single Sources and Mixed Sources					
Totals	7.7	4,954[b]	154(3.1%)	137(2.8%)	111(2.2%)

Source: George F. Grady, Ann J. E. Bennett, *et al.*, Risk of Posttransfusion Hepatitis in the United States, 220 J. Am. Med. Ass'n 692 (1972).

[a] Includes single-donor transfusion products.
[b] Among the 4,984 patients receiving single-donor transfusion products the sources of blood were unspecified regarding 30 including 3 who developed hepatitis.

The widespread acceptance of Titmuss's conclusion that national differences in the incidence of transfusion hepatitis exist and are explained by the use of commercial donors is evidence of strong prior beliefs about the deficiencies of commercialism. According to Titmuss, the reason that the incidence of hepatitis from blood transfusions is lower in England than in the United States is that in England blood is collected from relatively hepatitis free donors, while in the United States some of the blood purchased comes from those members of our society who have extremely high, perhaps the highest, *a priori* probability of having had hepatitis and thus of having contaminated blood.[22]

Some, but far from all, of our purchased blood has been acquired from the derelicts of our society, drug addicts, alcoholics, and prisoners. The difference in the incidence of hepatitis in the blood of paid and unpaid donors is correlated with social status. Transfused blood in England is supplied completely, according to Titmuss, by unpaid altruistic donors. Given this evidence, Titmuss concludes that it is the system of paid donors that is the source of our difficulties and more broadly, the price mechanism which is responsible for many of our social ills.[23] Solow concurs in the view that the use of paid donors is the source of our difficulties. "We can all agree on one point, that the use of paid donors must be responsible for the substantial and growing risk of hepatitis from transfusion."[24] This analysis is not without its apparent impact. In Illinois, paid donor blood has been virtually outlawed as a result of a blood labeling law enacted in 1972, which subjects physicians and hospitals transfusing commercial blood to greater risk of lawsuits and burdens them with additional record keeping. The American Association of Blood Banks is moving towards complete elimination of the use of paid donor blood.[25] "Several states are attempting to pass laws to prohibit *payment for blood*."[26]

It is widely believed that the *a priori* probability of transmitting serum hepatitis varies by a factor of ten. Despite this expected variation in the quality of blood transfused, price variations that correspond with quality

---

[22] Titmuss implicitly rejects the proposition that a difference in the natural incidence of hepatitis exists. Some evidence exists that supports this view. See Howard F. Taswell, Incidence of HBA_g in Blood Donors: An Overview, in Hepatitis and Blood Transfusion 272.

[23] Glazer accepts this interpretation and suggests that selling blood be outlawed. See Nathan Glazer, Blood, Public Interest No. 24, at 86, 93 (Summer 1971).

[24] Robert M. Solow, *supra* note 7, at 1703.

[25] NHLI Summary Report, at 64.

[26] *Id.* at 2. Outlawing paid donors is supported by the American Red Cross. See Allen Kleiman, Gold Versus the Gift of Blood, 287 New Eng. J. of Med. 51 (1972). In effect the American Red Cross would like to create a new class of victimless crimes.

variations have not been observed in the retail blood market. Moreover, the lowest quality blood seems to travel the greatest distance. Hospital patients are more likely to be offered choices in room accommodations than in the quality of blood transfused.[27] For hospitals dependent upon the single largest supplier of blood, the American National Red Cross, the quality provided has been highly variable. The Red Cross, despite its support of noncommercialism in blood acquisition, has, according to an HEW sponsored study, supplied blood acquired from paid donors.[28] Typically, patients do not have access to information relevant for evaluating the quality of blood to be transfused. Although there exists evidence of significant differences between hospitals with respect to the incidence of hepatitis (hospitals are a proxy for quality), there also exists evidence of great quality differences within particular hospitals and, in the case of multi-unit transfusions, in the quality of the blood transfused to a given patient.[29]

B. The Economics of Blood Supply

Paid blood need not per se be impaired blood. Whether in fact it is impaired depends, as E. R. Jennings has pointed out, not upon whether it was paid for, but from whose veins it comes.[30] There is no reason why paid donors could not come from the same social class that the voluntary donors come from. If so, the two classes of blood would be indistinguishable. Unpaid blood is not, of course, free blood in an economic sense. Advertising, providing a suitable atmosphere for donors, waiting arrangements, opportunity costs of donors' time, etc., are not free.[31]

It is important to recognize that not only in principle is it correct that commercial blood need not be low quality blood, it is true in fact. The world famed Mayo Clinic has a low incidence of transfusion hepatitis and purchases a substantial fraction of the blood its physicians transfuse from suppliers whose sources are the population of small towns in Minnesota.[32] Nor is this an isolated example:

---

[27] Often there is no explicit charge for blood. More frequently, there is an explicit charge only for blood not replaced by donors provided by the transfused patient.

[28] See NHLI Summary Report, at 134.

[29] See George F. Grady, Ann J. E. Bennett, et al., supra note 21, tabs. 8 & 9, at 697 & 698.

[30] E. R. Jennings, supra note 8, at 8.

[31] Advertising for unpaid donors of blood, which often appear in the editorial pages of the nation's most distinguished newspapers, has a pronounced seasonal pattern that reflects the seasonal pattern in noncommercial giving. There appears to be two seasonal lows in gifts of blood, one around mid-year and the other paradoxically during the Christmas season.

[32] The low incidence in transfusion hepatitis is confirmed by George F. Grady, Ann J. E. Bennett, et al., supra note 21, tab. 9, at 698.

Due to the University's location in a comparatively small town of about 50,000 inhabitants, we are greatly dependent on outside sources of blood and blood components. Because of the increasing awareness of the transmission of hepatitis by transfusion of "commercial" blood, blood banks throughout the country have been rapidly decreasing the use of blood from paid donors in an effort to avoid this problem. Similar trends have been evident at the University of Iowa even though the commercial sources of blood used seemed remarkably free of hepatitis risk. The largest amount of commercial blood was purchased in 1967 when almost 7,600 pints of blood were obtained from such sources. After that time this source of supply has been reduced gradually until April, 1972, when University Hospitals stopped using any commercial blood.[33]

This switch from paid donor to volunteer blood, it is significant to note, occurred despite what are regarded as good results with paid donor blood.[34]

In principle one cannot say whether unpaid blood is cheaper (when blood is explicitly purchased, prices seem to range from five dollars to thirty dollars a unit), as measured by the economic value of the resources used in blood acquisition, or more expensive than paid blood.[35] The evidence presented by Titmuss and confirmed by other investigators indicates that the derelicts of society produce low quality blood and probably should not be paid as much for their blood as their middle class cousins receive. Unless one is prepared to argue that the supply of good quality blood is completely insensitive to price, the evidence presented earlier suggests that a shift away from sources of low quality to sources of high quality blood would reduce the economic costs of medical procedures involving transfusions. Moreover, this shift would seem to be profitable at prices substantially higher than prices currently paid. Low quality blood is, at the margin, more expensive than high quality blood. It is difficult to rationalize the use of low quality blood for anyone who has not had hepatitis. Moreover, if blood costs are covered by third party payers, it is virtually impossible to explain its use.[36]

The experience with transfusion hepatitis suggests that the way to mini-

[33] John A. Koepke (Medical Director, Transfusion Service, University of Iowa Hospitals and Clinics, Iowa City, Iowa), The Variables Affecting Blood Costs in a Large Multi-Source Transfusion Service, in Tri-State Blood Bank Ass'n, First National Symposium on Blood Banking Costs 23, 24 (May, 1973).

[34] Others also report good results with commercial blood. See William V. Miller, Paid Blood Donors, 286 New. Eng. J. Med. 895 (1972). The prestigious Massachusetts General Hospital also uses commercial blood. See Morton Grove-Rasmussen, Gold Versus the Gift of Blood: Fact versus Fiction, 287 New Eng. J. Med. 360 (1972).

[35] The NHLI's study, vol. 1, *supra* note 4, at 131, reports that the after-tax profit margin of a proprietary blood bank studied was less than that of some of the not-for-profit blood banks.

[36] Feldstein argues that medical insurance has induced undesirable increases in the quality of services provided by the medical establishment, particularly hospitals. The evidence on blood fails to sustain this view. See Martin S. Feldstein, The Medical Economy, in Scientific Am., Sept., 1973, at 151, 154.

mize its incidence is to (1) solicit donors from the socio-economic classes that have a low *a priori* probability of having hepatitis, (2) test for the presence of the hepatitis associated antigen, (3) have a donor pool that is as small as possible consistent with not endangering the health of donors and obtaining the output of blood desired, (4) utilize the information obtained when a transfused patient incurs hepatitis to eliminate tainted blood suppliers from the donor pool.[37]

The foregoing suggest screening would-be donors by socio-economic class and developing sources of blood from regions of the country with a low natural incidence of hepatitis.[38] And within any particular region, there exists evidence that inhabitants of slums have a higher rate than in suburbs. Perhaps the clearest evidence of the differential incidence of hepatitis exists for drug addicts vis-à-vis the nonaddict population: ". . . there are abundant data indicating that narcotic addiction is the principal cause of the high HBA_g-positive rate among people who sell their blood."[39] The foregoing suggests that much of the difference between commercial and noncommercial blood in transmitting serum hepatitis is accounted for by the presence of addicts in the population of commercial donors.

There apparently exists little or no utilization of the knowledge about the incidence of hepatitis in a donor pool from transfused patients who subsequently contract serum hepatitis.[40] Utilization of this knowledge presents some problems—many, if not most, transfusions utilize the blood of more than one donor. Hence new entrants in donor pools should have their blood used in relatively small transfusions or with the blood of other donors for whom there exists, based on past history, a great deal of evidence that they supply hepatitis-free blood. The blood of new entrants in a pool probably ought to be used in transfusions involving children where the risks and hence the costs of hepatitis are low.[41] This, of course, suggests that the value of a donor's

---

[37] The normal or accepted shelf life of whole blood is twenty-one days. However, for open-heart surgery, there is a premium for fresh blood, because its oxygen-carrying capacity decays with time. Hence the economic value of blood declines monotonically with age. See NHLI's Summary Report, at 138.

[38] See R. Y. Dodd, *et al.*, American National Red Cross Experience with HBA_g Testing, in Hepatitis and Blood Transfusion, 175, 177 reports, based on the presence of HBA_g antigen, a variation of from .2 per 1000 in Waterloo, Iowa, to 3.44 per 1000 in Puerto Rico. For cities an incidence of .29 per 1000 in St. Paul, Minnesota and 3.10 per 1000 in Savannah, Georgia are reported.

[39] Thomas C. Chalmers, Carrier Blood Donors, in Hepatitis and Blood Transfusion 281.

[40] *Id.* at 285-86.

[41] George F. Grady, Ann J. E. Bennett, *et al.*, *supra* note 21; and J. Garrott Allen & Wynn A. Sayman, *supra* note 8, suggest that the lethality of transfusion hepatitis rises with age.

blood, whether or not it is explicitly recognized through a pricing mechanism, rises as the number of hepatitis-free transfusions he supplies increases.

C. PRESENT ARRANGEMENTS FOR SUPPLYING BLOOD

1. *Introduction*

There exist great regional variations in the extent to which commercial blood, that is, blood bought and paid for with dollars, is utilized. Seattle, as previously noted, is on a completely voluntary system.[42] Until relatively recently and for the country as a whole, about one-third of all whole blood transfused was obtained from commercial donors.[43] This is the blood that is generally regarded as the source of much if not most of the serum hepatitis contracted and is being phased out as a source of whole blood for transfusions.

The opposition to commercialism in blood supply is an opposition to the facade of commercialism, not to its substance.[44] Blood assurance programs— which are being expanded—constitute an arrangement by which blood today is bartered for the assurance of blood in the future.[45] A donor, by supplying blood periodically, guarantees blood supplies for himself and his family in the future should they be desired for medical purposes. Similarly patients receiving transfusions are charged "replacement" fees for the blood they receive which are forgiven if they can get enough friends and relatives to replace the blood received. (The rate of transformation of blood so "donated" to blood received often exceeds one-to-one.) Indeed, there are efforts afoot to get insurance companies, particularly Blue Cross, not to cover the cost of blood transfusions in order to induce the friends and relatives of a patient receiving transfusions to "donate" blood.[46] Less than ten per cent of all blood used in the United States is, in Titmuss's language, altruistically given.[47]

---

[42] Constance Holden, Blood Banking: Money is at the Root of the System's Evils, 175 Science 1344, 1347 (1972).

[43] Richard M. Titmuss, *supra* note 1, at 94.

[44] There seems to be a lack of symmetry in the opposition to commercialism in the procurement of whole blood as distinguished from blood derivative products such as plasma and fibrinogen which also transmit transfusion hepatitis. Typically blood derivative products or components are supplied by commercial drug companies who use the services of paid donors in order to obtain the necessary raw materials. The drive is to eliminate the commercial donor as a source of whole blood but not plasma and fibrinogen. See An Evaluation of the Utilization of Human Blood Resources in the United States 22 (Nat'l Academy of Sciences, Nat'l Res. Council, 1970).

[45] One source estimates that replacement donors at an inner city hospital serving a low-income population have an incidence of HBA_g, the hepatitis-associated antigen whose presence in blood is believed to be highly correlated with the capability of transmitting long incubation hepatitis, about two and a half times greater than the same type of donor at a hospital serving a higher income group. See Howard F. Taswell, *supra* note 22.

[46] See Ron Hasterok, The Insurance Viewpoint on Blood Services, and Arlene E. Kane,

Clearly the opposition is not to commercialism per se in the acquisition of blood for transfusions, but only a certain aspect of commercialism—the payment for blood intermediated by money.[48] The opposition to commercialism intermediated by monetary transactions can be rationalized if one accepts the premise that this type of transaction is a proxy for the acquisition of tainted blood and a finer discrimination against tainted blood would cost more than its benefits. (It is also important that there be no easy transference from one category of commercialism to another.)

It is difficult to accept this explanation because there seems to be no reason why drug addicts, derelicts, prisoners and others with a high *a priori* probability of having hepatitis cannot be screened out directly. Furthermore, the evidence provided by the Mayo Clinic and the Iowa City Blood Bank shows that they can be screened out easily.[49] What then is the explanation for the almost uniform opposition to the acquisition of blood by direct payment?

It is the thesis of this paper that avoiding liability for transfusion hepatitis by the medical establishment explains the opposition to "commercialism" in acquiring blood to be transfused. Eliminating commercialism in blood acquisition is an important plank in the program of the medical establishment for eliminating strict liability in tort for blood.

The recent history of litigation and legislation in Illinois constitutes a

---

The 'Non-Replacement Fee' as a Source of Income, in Tri-State Blood Bank Ass'n, *supra* note 33, at 64 and 103. Many Blue Cross-Blue Shield contracts do not cover the cost of blood. J. Garrott Allen, Commercial Blood in Our National Blood Program, 102 Archives of Surgery 122, 124 (1971) apparently opposes the insurance of blood costs on the grounds that the absence of insurance would encourage "voluntarism" in the supply of blood.

The Southern California Kaiser pre-paid plans, and this is probably true of Kaiser plans in other areas, are not pre-paid with respect to blood. If transfused blood is not replaced, then a replacement fee of twenty-five dollars is charged. Similarly, Medicare does not cover the first three units of a transfusion creating incentives to engage in barter.

Even in Seattle where replacement fees are not levied, the King County Blood Bank makes a great effort to get relatives of patients receiving transfusions to donate blood. The cost of collection and solicitation of blood is buried in a processing charge that includes the cost of cross matching and testing for the presence of the hepatitis associated antigen. Hence, although there is no formal charge for blood, there is a de facto blood charge.

[47] See Marc A. Franklin, Tort Liability for Hepatitis, *supra* note 8, at 441, n.13.

[48] It should be made clear that Titmuss opposed all forms of commercialism in the procurement of blood and the foregoing is meant to describe the views of the American medical establishment which has adopted the facade but not the substance of Titmuss's position.

[49] This does not imply that these organizations are consciously screening. It could simply be attributable to their location in a relatively hepatitis-free area and acquiring blood locally. But it does indicate that by confining blood donors to those in certain socio-economic classes or areas, it is possible to make large reductions in the probability of giving hepatitis producing blood to patients.

piece of evidence in support of the foregoing thesis. In *Cunningham v. MacNeal Memorial Hospital*, the State Supreme Court upheld a decision of a lower court that strict liability in tort held in the case of a patient, Francis Cunningham, who had contracted serum hepatitis as a result of a transfusion received at MacNeal Memorial which left the patient with permanent disabilities.[50]

As a result of this decision, organized medicine in Illinois, in particular the hospitals, medical societies and blood suppliers, lobbied for and won from the State Legislature exemption from strict liability in tort for blood.[51] Part of the legislative package won by organized medicine is a blood labeling law. This law burdens physicians transfusing commercial blood. (Explanations of why commercial blood was used must be provided in medical records.) As a result of the blood labeling law, commercial blood is now only rarely used in Illinois, and its use occurs only when noncommercial blood is unavailable. Most states have laws exempting the medical establishment from strict liability for transfusion hepatitis and those that do not are contemplating such laws.[52] The State of Washington provides for strict liability for transfused blood only if the donor is compensated, that is, paid with money, and Idaho provides for liability if the donor is compensated or if the blood bank is a for-profit organization.[53]

This legislation, whose enactment runs counter to the trend towards greater product liability declares that the commercial standards of supplier responsibility typically observed in the product market are inoperative for blood. Although caveat emptor is dying in product markets, particularly those served by profit seeking organizations, it is experiencing a renaissance in the blood market.[54] Some of the reasons advanced for this legislation, which is

---

[50] Cunningham v. MacNeal Memorial Hospital, 47 Ill. 2d 443, 226 N.E.2d 897 (1970).

[51] The legislation produced is: Ill. Rev. Stat. ch. 111½, §§ 620-1 *et seq.* Florida seems to have followed a similar pattern. In March, 1967, the Florida State Supreme Court ruled that strict liability in tort held for blood in a case similar to the Cunningham case. See Richard M. Titmuss, *supra* note 1, at 162, n.2. Subsequently, legislative relief from the ruling of the court was obtained. See NHLI, Summary Report at 85-86.

[52] NHLI Summary Report at 86. 120 Modern Hospitals, March, 1973, at 48, reports that 45 states have such laws. They define a transfusion of blood as a service and not a product. This is also the position of the American College of Legal Medicine; see Arthur Colemen & James R. Abernathy, Legal Evolution Strikes Blood Banking and Hospitals, 64 J. Nat'l Med. Ass'n 469, 470 (1972).

[53] NHLI Summary Report at 86, Exhibit XXI. The Washington legislation, enacted in 1971, came about as a result of a suit, Reilly v. King County Blood Bank, 6 Wash. App. 172, 492 P.2d 246 (1971), in which strict liability in tort was declared operative for transfusion hepatitis.

[54] Two articles (David L. Rados, Product Liability: Tougher Ground Rules, Harv. Bus. Rev., July-August, 1969, at 144; and Lawrence A. & Arnold I. Bennigson, Product Liability: Manufacturers Beware!, *id.*, May-June, 1974, at 122) argue that caveat emptor

supported by the Red Cross in addition to the medical establishment, is that strict liability for tort will raise the price of blood.[55] But this should not, of course, determine policy; what matters are the full costs of treatment including the costs associated with serum hepatitis. This position can have merit only if the increased price of blood exceeds the reduction in costs of those (a) unfortunate enough to contract transfusion hepatitis and (b) who avoid contracting hepatitis as a result of strict liability.

An argument advanced in support of exemption is the absence of any way of being sure that any particular unit of blood is hepatitis-free. The Illinois Supreme Court rejected this argument in the Cunningham case. The Court held that the same defense applies to typhoid bacilli in clams sold commercially; there is no way of being sure they are not present. Nevertheless, it shall be argued here, they correctly upheld the applicability of the strict liability doctrine.[56]

As a practical matter, strict liability in tort for blood does not exist in the United States. In the states in which legislatures have not granted exemptions to the medical establishment, they have not been needed; the courts have accepted either the view that hospitals are charities and not business establishments or that it is "inherently" impossible to be absolutely certain of blood quality given the present state of knowledge or that blood transfusion is a service and not a product.[57] Only for prepaid groups, the so-called health

---

has been replaced with caveat venditor in the latest ten to fifteen years. For a similar interpretation of trends in the real estate market, see, Robert Kratovil, Courts Shift Their Stance on Real Estate, The Guarantor (Chicago Title & Trust Co., Winter, 1974).

This trend in product liability has implications for the behavior of casualty insurance premiums over time as well as the measurement and/or interpretation of time series of prices.

[55] See the letter by James B. Hartney, M.D., who was Chairman of the Chicago Medical Society's Blood Bank Committee, in the Chicago Tribune, October 17, 1970, at sec. 1, p. 10, col. 5. Also Marc A. Franklin, Hepatitis, Blood Transfusion and Public Action, *supra* note 8, at 702, n.86.

The American Red Cross maintains two positions that appear to be inconsistent. They support outlawing commercial donors in order to protect transfused patients. Yet they simultaneously oppose product liability for blood.

[56] Cunningham v. MacNeal Memorial Hospital, 47 Ill. 2d 443, 266 N.E.2d 897, 903 (1970). An even stronger position supporting strict liability was taken by the Court in Hoffman v. Misericordia Hospital of Philadelphia, 439 Pa. 501, 267 A.2d 867 (1970).

Marilyn J. Ireland, The Legal Framework of the Market for Blood, in the Economics of Charity, 176 & ff. (Institute of Economic Affairs, 1973) has overlooked the legislation nullifying the judicial decisions that held for strict liability. She therefore concluded that product liability exists in these states and as a consequence, the quality of blood either has been or will be improved. In this same volume, David B. Johnson, recognizes the existence of these legislative enactments. *Id.* at 163.

[57] Marc A. Franklin, Tort Liability for Hepatitis, *supra* note 8, at 474, asserts only 9 states still regulate liability for transfusion hepatitis under common law. The remainder, 41, have enacted statutes to limit such liability to negligence. Franklin's count is greater

maintenance organizations, is there any liability at all. Because of their contractual obligations, they bear some, but far from all, of the costs of transfusion hepatitis of their subscribers.

It is clear that the views of legal scholars who have studied product liability have not been sought by state legislators. Calabresi and Bass declare: "... what seems clear is that the last person whom we would want to see bear the costs is the individual patient who is unlucky enough to get the bad blood."[58] They regard the incentive to discover better tests of the purity of blood as the principal allocative effect of their view on where liability should be placed.[59] They do not consider the possibility that liability rules can reduce the social or economic costs of serum hepatitis or the therapeutic choice between whole blood and blood components. In this important sense, they differ from the views espoused here or in Franklin's papers.

2. Implications of Coase's Work for Liability Rules

In the abstract zero transactions cost world that Coase investigates in the first part of his famous paper, it is irrelevant where liability is placed because one can costlessly contract out of any initial legal position.[60] The choice of the initial position does not affect the allocation of resources. If liability for serum hepatitis is placed on the physician, then his fees to patients being transfused will be sufficiently higher to pay for the expected costs of the liabilities being incurred. If liability is placed on the patient, then the physician's fees will be lower and the difference in physician fees in these two instances will pay for the expected costs of the risks of hepatitis that are assumed. Similar analysis is relevant and probably more appropriate for hospitals and blood suppliers. (The defendants in the Illinois, Pennsylvania, Florida and Washington cases were either hospitals, blood suppliers, or both.) It is on a

---

than the count of the NHLI Summary Report, despite the fact that the Summary Report has a later publication date and the trend has been towards greater state intervention. A later count in Modern Hospitals, March 1973, at 49, has the number up to 45.

Hospital Week, published by the American Hospital Association, reports that the California appellate court has affirmed a lower court decision and ruled that the transfusion of blood is a service and not the sale of a product. 9 Hospital Week, Aug. 10, 1973.

[58] Guido Calabresi & Kenneth C. Bass, Right Approach, Wrong Implications: A Critique of McKeon on Products Liability, 38 U. Chi. L. Rev. 74, 86 (1970). Franklin does not cite Calabresi and Bass on this point and seems to have, not surprisingly, reached similar conclusions. He devotes a lot of space in this Stanford Law Review article, supra note 8, to the question: Where in the medical establishment—the hospital, physician, blood bank—should liability be placed? In his Catholic University Law Review article, supra note 8, he views with regret the fact that most courts have been immobilized by statutory controls from imposing liability for hepatitis upon the medical establishment.

[59] Guido Calabresi & Kenneth C. Bass, supra note 58, at 84.

[60] R. H. Coase, The Problem of Social Cost, 3 J. Law & Econ. 1 (1960).

par with buying a car with the choice of a one or a two year warranty with appropriate differences in price. If one buys a car with a one year warranty, then liability for the second year is borne by the owner. By contrast, buying a car with a two year warranty implies the seller bears the liability in the second year.

Where liability in the foregoing world is placed is an accounting detail. It is very hard to believe this full knowledge, transaction-cost free world is a prototype for the blood market. The costs incurred by the medical establishment in escaping from liability for tainted blood—there is no free legislation —suggests that they have a strong stake, presumably financial, in avoiding liability for hepatitis.

In recent years there has been a tremendous shift in liability to the hospital and physician from the patient.[61] This shift, in part a result of the development of *Res Ipsa Loquitur* and the greater availability of expert witnesses for plaintiffs, has been opposed on the grounds that it encourages the practice of defensive medicine. Whatever the merits of this argument in other contexts, it is difficult to apply it to blood procurement. Strict liability in tort for serum hepatitis, a form of product liability, does not involve showing whether or not the medical establishment behaved prudently, according to acceptable standards, etc. If a patient is transfused and subsequently becomes ill with transfusion hepatitis, then liability is established. What sorts of records the hospital and/or the attending physician maintained, who he consulted, what tests he ran, are irrelevant. It is not necessary to demonstrate negligence. Hence it is difficult to visualize any role for defensive medicine in warding off liability for tainted blood. Moreover, it is difficult to see how the cost of conducting business between the patient and the physician or the hospital can increase if liability is shifted from the patient.[62]

Is there an argument from the individual consumer's or patient's point of view for not having liability for medical malpractice imposed upon the medical establishment? Would such an imposition increase the relevant costs of blood for consumers by forcing them to buy a higher quality of blood than they desire? For the small class who already have known immunity to transfusion hepatitis, there exists a case for arguing that such legislation is against their interests. Because of the large amounts of blood used in treating hemophilia, a substantial fraction of all hemophiliacs have contracted serum hepa-

[61] Between 1960 and 1970, premiums for physicians increased six-fold; surgeons ten-fold; and hospitals three-fold. See the appendix to U.S. Dep't Health, Ed. & Welfare, Report of the Secretary's Commission on Medical Malpractice 48 (January 16, 1973).

[62] The argument Coase used in explaining the opposition to imposing liability upon railroads for fire damage to crops along the right of way, formidable costs of transacting between the railroad and farmers, seems to be inapplicable here. See R. H. Coase, *supra* note 60, at 31.

titis in the past and are immune to this ailment.[63] Hemophiliacs with immunity to serum hepatitis constitute the only natural market for low quality addict blood. Hence, they would lose unless they could recontract with health care providers to assume the risk of hepatitis and this market was large enough to be catered to by blood suppliers.[64]

3. Where Should Liability Be Placed?

Consider a situation in which liability is placed on a patient and he buys and pays for blood with three chances in one thousand of incurring hepatitis per unit purchased. Further assume that he subsequently contracts transfusion hepatitis. It is very difficult *ex post* to determine whether or not he bought three chances in one thousand blood or three chances in one hundred. He has an expensive and virtually insurmountable gap in knowledge to overcome, particularly in a world in which data on the incidence of hepatitis is not easy to come by, in finding out whether or not the product purchased is in fact the product delivered. Hence, civil remedies are virtually precluded unless strict liability exists.

Moreover, it must not be forgotten that not all blood is transfused as a result of elective surgery or other elective procedures. A non-trivial fraction of all blood is transfused to patients that are found in trauma as a result of accidents and are in no position to weigh alternatives in the blood market. Under such circumstances, it is somewhat ludicrous to expect patients to take responsibility for the quality of the blood they receive; whatever virtues caveat emptor may have in other contexts, it is difficult to argue that it should prevail here.

Both the physician and the hospital can more cheaply obtain the knowledge required to determine whether the quality of blood ordered for a patient is in fact received. They are in a better position, as compared with the patient, to obtain the information relevant for evaluating the medical experiences of all patients transfused with blood from a particular supplier. Hence, if liability is placed with either the hospital or the physician, which almost surely will involve some subsequent transference to the blood supplier, those who have the cheapest access to the relevant information will be making the choice and evaluating the performance of blood suppliers. This information will be used in setting fees and hospital charges to the patient who in turn

---

[63] See Blood Banking—Major Findings by HEW Task Force 5, in U.S. Dep't of Health, Ed. & Welfare, Conference on the National Blood Policy (unpublished reports, 1973).

[64] Presumably physicians or hospitals might also want to contract with blood banks to transfer some of the liability for serum hepatitis. In Illinois, hemophiliacs have won, through the exercise of political muscle, the right to barter blood donated on their behalf, by friends, relatives and others, for hospital costs they incur. For everyone else, blood can only be bartered for blood.

will be in a better position to evaluate alternatives in the medical care market than he would be if he were self-insured.

The case for placing liability directly on the physician rather than on the hospital or the blood supplier rests on the fact that he chooses among alternative modes of treatment. Hence he is in the best position to evaluate whether blood or blood substitutes ought to be used, and in what quantities, and to evaluate the risks to specific patients. Therefore, he can, at a lower cost than anyone else, obtain the information relevant for decisions involving the risks of hepatitis and compare them with other medical risks.

4. *Why is Strict Liability Opposed?*

If defensive medicine, which raises the costs of medical care without a commensurate increase in the utility of medical care to consumers, is rejected as a rationale for the opposition of the suppliers of medical care to the transference of liability from the patient to the suppliers, how is this opposition to be explained? The imposition of product liability upon the consumer is the result of a coalition between the medical societies, hospitals, and blood banks. The blood legislation won by this coalition is a testimonial to its political power. However the question remains: Why was this legislation sought?

Eliminating caveat emptor from the blood market would require the current suppliers of blood to adapt to a wholly new set of rules for survival. Whenever liability is placed on the supply side of the medical care market, it is bound to be shifted around so that the supplier of blood will have to effectively guarantee the quality of the product supplied. Hence, standards of supplier responsibility which are characteristic of commercial markets, in particular the drug market, will be imposed upon charitable institutions such as the American Red Cross or hospital blood banks.

Currently the comparative advantage of these organizations in the blood market is solicitation, that is, begging for blood and money. The value of this comparative advantage in a market in which suppliers could not evade product liability would decline sharply; indiscriminate solicitation, because the donor pool is so large, yields too much tainted blood. Hence, imposing strict liability upon these volunteer agencies would be on a par with permitting the practice of nudism only in the polar regions; it is doubtful the cult could survive the rigours of this constraint. Since the supply of blood is the principal product line of the American Red Cross and many other groups such as the King County Blood Bank in Seattle, their place in the sun would either be eliminated or sharply reduced. Therefore, it is not difficult to understand why both the hospitals and blood suppliers (and many hospitals are blood suppliers) oppose strict liability.

The opposition of the medical profession to strict liability is more difficult to understand.[65] The American Red Cross and hospital and community blood banks prefer, in common with most economic enterprises, to exclude competitors. However, for the medical profession, blood is a complementary resource like hospitals. Hence, it appears to be in the self-interest of physicians for a highly competitive blood market to exist. Consequently, promoting voluntarism for blood donors, fighting product liability, and working to eliminate commercial donors does not appear to make economic sense.

What then is the explanation of the position of the AMA? Marshall's theory of joint demand implies that the lower the prices of resources complementary to the services of a monopolist, the higher the monopoly returns. Hence for medicine which is characterized by highly restricted entry and monopoly returns, there exists strong economic incentives to promote economic conditions that minimize the costs of blood for every quality level. In a subsidy free world, this would surely be a highly competitive blood market.

It is important to recognize that within the membership of the AMA are physicians associated with both the production and the consumption of blood. As employees of blood banks, physicians are overrepresented among banks using volunteer blood. Per unit of blood produced by blood banks, those using volunteer blood employ relatively physician-intensive procedures. Indeed, standards for the accreditation of blood banks have been set up that require that these organizations be run by physicians if not pathologists.[66] Hence, the job opportunities of these physicians are threatened by commercialism in the supply of blood.

The interests of physicians engaged in the production of blood, in contrast to the interests of the general membership of the AMA, is to drive commercialism out of the blood business. Moreover, the interests of these physicians are concentrated whereas the interests of the general membership in a competitive blood market are diffuse. It is not unusual in political organizations to find that the interests of producers are overrepresented relative to consumers because the transactions costs in making diffuse consumer interests politically effective are greater than they are for concentrated producer interests. In other words, the decision-making structure of the AMA with respect to blood is dominated by producer interests that are employed by blood banks using volunteer blood.

As a result of the political power of the coalition of physicians, hospitals,

---

[65] Organized medicine has expressed its opposition to strict liability for blood in an editorial entitled Blood Money, in 215 J. Am. Med. Ass'n 109-110 (Jan. 1971). Its support for voluntarism appears in Am. Medical Ass'n, Comm. on Transfusion & Transplantation, Guide for Hospital Committee on Transfusion 3 (undated).

[66] See NHLI Study, vol. 1, *supra* note 4, at 373.

and volunteer blood banks, product liability for blood-derivative products, some supplied by large national drug companies, are either in doubt or nonexistent. Many blood derivative products, such as plasma and fibrinogen, are supplied by both voluntary agencies such as the Red Cross and commercial drug companies and, like whole blood, have the capability of transmitting transfusion hepatitis. The laws declaring blood transfusions to be a service and not a product also declare or imply that the transfusion of blood derivatives is a service and not a product. (In Illinois, all blood derivative products are exempt by statute even if supplied by an avaricious and highly profitable drug company.) Hence, the usual commercial standards of supplier responsibility for drug products exacted from the drug companies are suspended for blood derivatives. However, even if the normal commercial standards were applied to drug companies for blood derivative products, the exemption for whole blood creates difficult problems in assessing liability because whole blood and blood derivatives are often jointly used to treat patients.

5. *Why is Too Low Quality of Blood Now Being Provided?*

If the figures on the marginal value of low risk over high risk blood are correct, then there still remains the question: Why have not hospitals developed better sources of blood? After all, both physicians and hospitals are concerned with the welfare of their patients. A large part of the answer to this question must be that the dangers of transfusion hepatitis are relatively new on the medical scene and neither patients nor physicians are as alert to this problem currently as they will be when more experience with this complication of transfusions is accumulated. Hence, one can argue that in the long run, the Coase theorem will hold. Under this interpretation, suppliers of blood should be currently moving in the direction of improving blood quality.

A role of strict liability, given the foregoing interpretation, is to influence the pace at which the medical establishment adjusts to the relatively recently developed knowledge about the relationship of blood sources to the transmission of transfusion hepatitis. Currently whether or not a hospital develops good sources seems to be relatively insensitive to pressures from either patients or physicians. Grady asserts:

... in my experience, most hospitals have been successful in improving the quantity and quality of their blood sources only insofar as it was of concern to the local prime figure in the clinical teaching and bedside care hierarchy. For example, if the Chief of Surgery of an outstanding surgical service thinks it is important to have low risk blood, it is usually provided by one means or another. If hepatitis risk is considered a relatively minor problem and has to compete and take its place among thousands of other problems, then improvements are unlikely in spite of technological advances. It is simply a question of leadership.[67]

Because of the absence of advertising competition among hospitals, the fact that some hospitals are alert to the dangers of hepatitis to their patients and obtain low risk blood does not force other hospitals to find sources of blood of equal quality in order to remain economically viable. Hence the claims and litigation arising out of the existence of strict liability are especially important in this particular market as a means of exerting pressure on the prime figures in the medical hierarchy of hospitals to obtain low risk blood. Strict liability would reduce the survival properties of hospitals with a medical hierarchy that was insensitive to or ignorant of the risks of hepatitis for their patients. Consequently, they would move faster towards providing the quality of blood their patients want.

In the absence of strict liability, the pace at which the medical establishment will move towards providing low risk blood for patients will be much slower. Eventually enough information is generated by the experience of relatives and friends, by articles and books, by radio and TV, and by newspapers so that both the public and physicians, both sides of the market, will become informed of the risks and only low risk blood will be used. This is a more expensive way of disseminating the relevant information, hence the movement towards long-run equilibrium will be slower than it would be if strict liability existed.

The desire to avoid product liability explains the inconsistency between the opposition to commercialism in blood procurement on the one hand and the promotion of barter as a means of providing blood on the other. In order to avoid product liability, the patient is induced to provide his own blood via blood assurance programs and the hospital provides transfusion services. For the same reason medical insurors controlled by the medical establishment, such as Blue Cross and Blue Shield, do not provide coverage of blood costs, nor do many pre-paid groups, that is the so-called health maintenance organizations. They all wish to establish that the provision of blood is a service and not a product. The desire to avoid product liability also explains why the medical establishment has not imposed quality standards upon their blood suppliers. Such standards would inevitably be defined in terms of the risks of

---

[67] G. F. Grady, HBA_g in Blood Donors, in Hepatitis and Blood Transfusion 310. It should be pointed out that Grady must be regarded as a relatively knowledgeable observer since he is the senior author of one of the most, if not the most, extensive empirical studies of the relationship between blood sources and transfusion hepatitis using data derived from many hospitals. Hence he ought to be well aware of hospital procurement practices.

hepatitis and therefore would increase the risks that courts and/or legislators would impose similar standards upon the medical establishment.

A test of the explanation offered for the unwillingness of the medical establishment to accept strict liability in tort for blood is provided by the legislation in Idaho and Washington which imposes strict liability if commercial blood is transfused. One would expect if the hypothesis presented is correct, that the frequency with which commercial blood is used in these two states will be significantly lower than it is for the country as a whole. Blood procurement practices in both of these states support this implication.

Whether or not blood is obtained from volunteers, paid donors, or altruistic donors in the Titmuss sense of the term, is irrelevant. Similarly, whether or not paid donors drive altruistic donors out of business is also irrelevant.[68] What is relevant is the quality of blood transfused and the incentive to obtain good blood for this purpose. Imposing strict liability upon the attending physician or the hospital or the blood supplier will accelerate the achievement of this end. By virtue of this liability there will be additional financial incentives, incentives that have been absent, to obtain less dangerous blood for transfusions. The drug addict, but not necessarily the paid donor, will be driven out of the blood business as a result of efforts to keep malpractice insurance costs and premiums down. This conclusion should hold if liability is placed upon physicians, whether or not they contract out some or all of their liability to either hospitals or blood banks.[69]

The additional financial incentives of strict liability will mobilize the resources of the market to find and utilize economical supplies of high quality blood.[70] Probably a thoroughgoing system of professional blood donors will develop, professionals being usually better than amateurs. The analysis presented implies that voluntarism in blood procurement is a *deus ex machina* which makes possible the anomalous rule of liability for blood that currently prevails. Hence imposing strict liability for blood would eliminate voluntarism and explains the hostility towards commercial blood procurement by voluntary agencies.

[68] The theorem that in one market only one price can exist implies that paid and unpaid donors cannot simultaneously coexist unless unpaid donors have utility functions that are rare in nature. In the absence of such utility functions, payment for blood will simply increase the producer's surplus of would-be unpaid donors. This suggests that voluntary donors would be recruited by blood donor services willing to pay. Hence, a natural antipathy towards the organizations that pay for blood by institutions such as the Red Cross is implied by this analysis.

[69] Franklin apparently rejects applying strict liability to physicians for reasons difficult to understand. See Marc A. Franklin, Tort Liability for Hepatitis, *supra* note 8, at 472.

[70] There exists some evidence that suggests non-profit hospitals respond relatively slowly to changes in demand conditions. See Bruce Steinwald & Duncan Neuhauser, The Role of the Proprietary Hospital, 1970 Law & Contemp. Prob. 815, 837.

The fact that the Mayo Clinic pays for blood is suggestive of the direction of the medical establishment would move in a world of strict liability.[71] Moreover, more screening by social class, absence or presence of slum background, and medical history would occur. Implicit prices would become explicit; the price of the blood supplied by a given donor would rise as the number of trouble-free units previously supplied increased. Professional donors would have incentives to stay healthy and blood banks would have incentives to weed unsatisfactory donors out of their pools. Moreover, more thought would go into designing programs for administering transfusions that would make it easy and hence less expensive to detect donors of tainted blood.[72]

Conclusions

It has been argued that Titmuss is correct in the sense that too low a quality of blood has been provided by the medical establishment to patients.[73]

---

[71] This is not regarded as commercialism by those who study the relationship between blood sources and hepatitis. The Mayo Clinic or the hospitals servicing the Mayo Clinic buy blood from churches in small towns in Minnesota. These churches, in turn, procure this blood as gifts from their members. Hence gifts of blood are an alternative to gifts of money. By giving blood instead of money, church members escape taxes on their earnings as blood donors. If blood were sold directly by donors instead of indirectly through churches, only the aftertax receipts from the sale of blood would be available for church support. Hence taxes are escaped whose magnitude is a function of the marginal tax brackets of donors. This source of blood is defined to be other volunteer donors in George F. Grady, Ann J. E. Bennett, *et al.*, *supra* note 21, tab. 8, at 697. One can search in vain in this article for the definition of other volunteer donors only.

At times one has the feeling that commercialism is defined as that method of procuring blood that has the highest incidence of transfusion hepatitis. For example, group three in George F. Grady, Ann J. E. Bennett, *et al.*, *supra* note 21, tab. 8, at 697, is referred to as paid non-commercial donor in Posttransfusion Hepatitis, *supra* note 15, at 8. This category is ignored by Howard F. Taswell, *supra* note 22, at 272, when he compares the risks of hepatitis from volunteer and commercial blood. He averages the incidence of hepatitis for the two classes of volunteer donors and compares the number obtained with the risks associated with the blood described in group four. His comparison is more inept than misleading since he fails to adjust for differences in the average size of transfusion.

Commercial blood is defined by the Illinois law as blood obtained from a donor in exchange for money. If blood is not procured from a donor through monetary incentives, it can be subsequently resold an indefinite number of times and still remain non-commercial blood.

[72] The problem of supplying blood is in many ways symmetrical with the problem of supplying semen for artificially inseminating human females. The suppliers of semen are solicited and paid by the medical establishment and effort is expended in discovering males who will provide a high quality set of genes. The usual source is medical students. In the past, they were an important source of blood for transfusions.

[73] The evidence on blood quality is not the only empirical support for Titmuss's view that our blood procurement program works badly. Section III, Blood Banking, in U.S. Dep't Health, Ed., & Welfare *supra* note 63, at 5, reports that some plasma pools come

Titmuss has interpreted this finding as a consequence of too much commercialism; in our view it is a consequence of too little commercialism. The acquisition of an exemption from product liability for blood by the medical establishment delays the development of low risk sources of blood by emasculating short-run financial incentives to undertake such development.

It is doubtful that many of the institutions involved in blood procurement today, such as the American Red Cross, would be viable in a world in which the usual commercial standards of supplier responsibility existed. Similarly the management of blood procurement by hospitals would become more difficult and hence it is likely that some managers would not be viable in this more difficult world. Hence, there exists powerful special interest groups, apart from physicians, whose economic interests are served by opposing strict liability.

Because of the absence of strict liability, it is possible to observe patients in major hospital centers, all obviously viable producers of open heart surgery, incurring vastly different frequencies of transfusion hepatitis. For example, the two largest producers of open heart surgery in Grady's study, and it is not unlikely that they are the two largest producers in the world, differ by a factor of eight in the incidence of symptomatic hepatitis.[74]

The recommendation for changes in liability rules essentially argues that the standards of product liability taken for granted in the commercial world should be applied to transfused blood. The present liability rule is highly anomalous, exists because of the pressures upon state legislatures by organized medicine and is, in our view, anti-consumer legislation. It is hard to defend caveat emptor for blood but not for cars, soup, and the hundreds of products found in the market place. If state legislatures had not intervened, that is, if they had done nothing, strict liability in tort for blood and blood derivatives would exist in many if not most of the states in the United States. "The

---

from as many as a thousand donors. This implies that the pool is almost certain to be contaminated even if the probability of any one donor's blood being contaminated is on the order of one or two chances in a thousand. Clearly the procedure to follow if one wished to raise the probability of contaminating a pool is to increase its size. It is difficult to believe that government intervention to eliminate the use of pooled plasma would either be necessary or occur in a world in which strict liability for hepatitis existed.

This source also estimates that 25% of all whole blood collected for transfusion is never transfused and most of these non-transfused units are wasted through outdating. This view may also be found in An Evaluation of the Utilization of Human Blood Resources, *supra* note 44, at 21. However, this source, *id.* at 37, suggests that this waste is inherent in voluntarism whereas Titmuss argues that it is produced by commercialism.

[74] George F. Grady, Ann J. E. Bennett, *et al.*, *supra* note 21, tab. 6, at 696 reports a difference of a factor of six. However, the average size of transfusions in the poorer center, Cleveland Clinic, is seven units against over nine in the better one, Mayo Clinic. See *id.* tab. 9, at 698. Of the patients transfused at the poorer center, 3.4% exhibited symptomatic hepatitis. In one of the poorest centers, the rate was 8.1%. *Id.* tab. 6, at 696.

kind of situation which economists (and others) are prone to consider as requiring corrective Government action is, in fact, often the result of Governmental action."[75] The desire to maintain a highly anomalous product liability rule for blood explains why commercial blood is relatively absent in Washington and Idaho. It also explains the opposition to paid donors and the promotion of barter among the potential patient population as a means of acquiring blood for transfusions. Moreover, it explains the lower standards for blood derivative products supplied by drug companies.

It is important to recognize that the long-run supply function of information to patients about the risks of hepatitis from transfusions, or the potential benefits and risks of any other medical procedure is flatter than the short-run supply function. Eventually enough information is generated by the experience of relatives and friends, by articles and books, by radio and TV, and by newspapers so that the public can make relatively accurate evaluations cheaply. However, the transfusion of whole blood is a relatively new medical development growing out of our experience during World War II and the discovery of transfusion hepatitis came relatively recently. Hence if transfusion hepatitis were an old established ailment, the case for strict liability would be weaker but not nonexistent.

Currently the favored method of assuring the provision of low risk blood for transfusions is to regulate donors—more specifically, to outlaw "commercial donors."[76] Hence product liability, a form of direct control over the output of blood suppliers that is enforced by the users of blood, is an alternative to indirect control over inputs of blood suppliers enforced by government regulation. The history of legislation regulating medical care delivery suggests that such regulation of inputs is more likely to represent the interests of the medical establishment than the transfused patient.

[75] R. H. Coase, *supra* note 60, at 28. (Brackets added.)

[76] Volunteer donors are alleged to be better than paid donors because paid donors have an incentive to conceal facts about their health that would make them unacceptable donors. The proponents of this view have not recognized that the same argument is relevant for replacement donors or candidates for membership in blood assurance programs. Indeed, hospitals in areas serving a large number of ghetto dwelling patients who require blood as a result of trauma will probably have low quality blood provided by their replacement donors.

II The Capital Markets

5 The Cyclical Behavior of the Term Structure of Interest Rates (1965)

ACKNOWLEDGMENTS

Earlier versions of this paper were presented at the money workshop of the University of Chicago, faculty seminars at the Universities of Pennsylvania and California at Los Angeles, and the Econometric Society meetings in Pittsburgh in 1962. I have greatly benefited from the comments of colleagues at both the National Bureau and the University of Chicago.

David Meiselman of the Office of the Comptroller of the Currency, Paul Cootner of the Massachusetts Institute of Technology, and John M. Culbertson of the University of Wisconsin provided invaluable criticism in their roles as discussants at the Econometric Society meetings in 1962.

REUBEN A. KESSEL

CONTENTS

    INTRODUCTION AND SUMMARY OF PRINCIPAL FINDINGS   103

1. EXPLANATIONS OF THE TERM STRUCTURE OF INTEREST RATES   107
   What Is the Expectations Hypothesis, 107
   Existing Evidence, 109
   New Evidence, 124

2. WHY LIQUIDITY PREFERENCE EXISTS   146

3. HOW SHORT- AND LONG-TERM INTEREST RATES HAVE BEHAVED CYCLICALLY   161

4. THE APPLICATION OF THE LIQUIDITY PREFERENCE AND EXPECTATIONS HYPOTHESES TO THE CYCLICAL BEHAVIOR OF INTEREST RATES   183
   Applications of the Lutz-Meiselman Model, 183
   Applications of the Hicks Model, 186

5. CONCLUSIONS AND IMPLICATIONS FOR FURTHER RESEARCH   198

    DIRECTOR'S COMMENT   203

    APPENDIX A   205

    APPENDIX B   208

TABLES

1. Meiselman's Error Term and Forecast Revisions — 122
2. Distribution of Errors in Predicting Treasury Bill Rates — 126
3. Correlation of Forecast Revisions with Errors as Defined by Meiselman, 1958–61 — 140
4. Coefficients of Correlation Between Weekly Seasonal Factors in Treasury Bill Rates, 1959–61 — 142
5. Cyclical Changes in Yields of Government Securities, October 1945–February 1961 — 162
6. Variation in Yields of Government Securities During Four Business Cycles, October 1945–February 1961 — 164
7. Average Yield of Government Securities During Four Business Cycles, October 1945–February 1961 — 164
8. Timing of Short- and Long-Term Yields of Government Securities at Business Cycle Peaks and Troughs, October 1945–February 1961 — 165
9. Timing of Peaks and Troughs in Bill Rates Using Seasonally Adjusted and Unadjusted Data — 167
10. Cyclical Changes in Yields of Government Securities, 1921–45 — 172
11. Average Yield and Standard Deviation in Yields of Government Securities During Five Business Cycles, 1921–45 — 172
12. Timing of Short- and Long-Term Yields of Government Securities at Business Cycle Peaks and Troughs, 1921–45 — 173
13. Basic Yields on Corporate Bonds During Business Cycles, 1900–61 — 179
A-1. Comparison of Actual and Forecast Term Structures of Interest Rates, Measured by Areas Under Curves — 206

A-2. Types of Term Structures, Thirty-Seven Selected Years
(1900–42), and Actual Changes in One-Year Rates   207
B-1. Spot and Forward One-Year Rates   209
B-2. Yields of Fixed-Maturity Treasury Securities   210
B-3. Spot and Forward One-Year Rates Adjusted for
Liquidity Premiums   215

CHARTS

1. Marginal Rates of Interest with Stable Expectations — 117
2. Average Yield as a Function of Term to Maturity, Durand Data, 1900–1954 — 120
3. Market Expectations of Future 91-Day Bill Rates — 132
4. Forward and Spot One-Year Rates on Government Securities — 137
5. Yields of U.S. Government Securities, 1942–53 — 166
6. Yields of U.S. Government Securities, 1954–61 — 168
7. Yields of U.S. Government Securities, 1920–33 — 170
8. Yields of U.S. Government Securities, 1934–41 — 171
9. Average Pattern of Long-Term and Short-Term Interest Rates in the United States During Fourteen Business Cycles, 1858–1914 — 174
10. Average Pattern of Long-Term and Short-Term Interest Rates in the United States During Five Business Cycles, 1914–33 — 175
11. Average Pattern of Long-Term and Short-Term Interest Rates in the United States During Four Business Cycles, 1945–61 — 177
12. Average Pattern of Long-Term and Short-Term Interest Rates in the United States During Two Business Cycles, 1933–45 — 178
13. Basic Yields of Corporate Bonds, First Quarter, Durand Data, 1900–61 — 181
14. "Normal" or Average Yield Curve — 187
15. Yield Curve at Cyclical Troughs — 188
16. A Flat Yield Curve — 189
17. Yield Curve at Cyclical Peaks — 190
18. Effects of Alternative Expectations of Falling Rates upon the Shapes of Yield Curves — 191

INTRODUCTION AND SUMMARY OF PRINCIPAL FINDINGS

THE TERM STRUCTURE of interest rates, i.e., the relationship between yields or internal rates of return and maturities of default-free securities, has been analyzed by what can be regarded as three independent theories. One that has had widespread appeal for theoretical economists has been called the expectations theory. According to this theory, long-term rates are an average of expected short-term rates; the holder of a long-term security will earn, on average, just as much as the holder of a series of short-term securities over any specified time interval. To illustrate: if one bought a one-year security today and another when the first matures, the expected return would be equal to the return that would have been obtained if a two-year security had been bought initially.

Another widely accepted theory, not necessarily inconsistent with the expectations hypothesis, is liquidity preference. This theory of the term structure of interest rates, which often is treated as a modification of the expectations hypothesis, rests on the postulates that (1) the risks associated with holding long maturities are greater than those of holding short maturities, (2) the community prefers to avoid risk, and (3) there are positive costs to society of obtaining the services of speculators. It implies that the expected yield to be derived from holding a two-year security is greater than that of holding a one-year security, or series of one-year securities, for identical periods of time. The greater risks associated with long-term securities imply that, on average, they yield more. This view, which has been associated with the name of Keynes, may be found in Hicks where it is linked with the expectations theory. Hicks treats the term structure of interest rates as being jointly determined by liquidity preference and expectations. Meiselman, in his recent investigation, rejected the liquidity preference element of the Hicksian theory.

The third theory is based on the premise that the market for default-free securities is largely "segmented," i.e., that there is little or no switching among securities with different maturities by the large institutional buyers that dominate this market. To put the same point in somewhat different language, the cross elasticity of demand is low, possibly zero; securities of different maturities are poor substitutes for one another; what happens in the bill market has little or no relationship to what happens in the long-term bond market. This suggests that variations in inventories or stocks of securities by term to maturity produce variations in relative yields. Yields of short- and long-term securities need bear no necessary relationship to one another; yields of short maturities can either be greater or less than the yields of long maturities depending upon the inventories of each that are outstanding.

The first chapter of this study deals with the evidence relevant for examining the validity of these three hypotheses. The evidence bearing on the first two is quantitatively greater and can be interpreted more unambiguously than that for the market segmentation hypothesis. This chapter begins by explaining what the expectations hypothesis is. This is followed by an evaluation of the evidence developed by other investigators for and against this theory. Then the evidence produced as part of this investigation is presented. Finally, all of this data is evaluated insofar as it bears on all three theories.

In the second chapter market institutions are considered. An attempt is made to rationalize the existence of liquidity preference by examining the evidence on the costs of speculative services, assuming that the market prefers on balance to avoid risk.

The third chapter is a description of the behavior of interest rates for default-free securities over the cycle, particularly for the period since the end of World War II when data have been relatively plentiful. The business cycle is the unit for organizing, whenever possible, the data on yield variance, average yields, timing of peaks and troughs, and yield differentials as they are related to term to maturity.

The Hicksian theory of the term structure of interest rates is applied to the cyclical behavior of the term structure of rates in the fourth chapter. The first part represents a working out of the implications of the Hicksian theory. The latter part is expository; it illustrates the implications of the Hicksian theory for the term structure of interest rates at business peaks and troughs.

The principal finding of this investigation is that a combination of two hypotheses—liquidity preference and expectations—must be employed to interpret the term structure of interest rates. Taken by itself, the expectations hypothesis implies that forward rates are the spot rates expected by the market. Yet available evidence indicates that forward rates are high estimates of future spot rates. Hence it is difficult to interpret forward rates as expected rates. Similarly, liquidity preference alone implies that short rates ought always to be below long rates; this implication is contradicted by short rates above long rates, i.e., by the so-called "humped" yield curve. By interpreting forward rates as the sum of expected rates plus liquidity premiums, that is, by using both hypotheses, the rates expected by the market can be detected. Moreover, this more complex hypothesis explains both the bias in the estimates of a pure expectations hypothesis and short rates that are higher than long rates.

Correlations between forward and spot rates suggest that the market does have some power to foresee, up to a year in the future, spot rates from a month to a year to maturity. This same conclusion is reached if forward rates, adjusted for liquidity premiums, are used to predict subsequently observed spot rates, and if the mean square error is computed. Using either criterion, expectations seems to predict better than an inertia model.

The behavior of interest rates in the United States over the last century indicates that, relative to long-term rates, short-term rates are typically high about cyclical peaks and low at troughs; that is, they rise relatively during expansions and fall during contractions. Hence, the common belief that the shorter the term to maturity, the greater the cyclical variability in yields is, in general, correct.

Data reflecting the prices of government securities during the last forty years, and high-grade corporate securities during roughly the same period, show that short maturities typically yield less than long maturities. On the average, yield curves have been positively sloped. Nevertheless, yield curves with negative slopes were not uncommon during the period from 1900 to 1930.

These observations of the cyclical behavior of the term structure of rates can be rationalized, assuming the market has some modest ability to predict the course of short-term rates over the cycle. High short-term relative to long-term rates—a characteristic of cyclical peaks—indicates that the market regards current short-term rates as abnormally high, and expects them to be lower in the future. Humped or declining yield curves imply that the market expects short-term rates to fall sharply. Low short-term relative to long-term rates—a characteristic of cyclical troughs—indicates that the market regards current short-term rates as abnormally low and expects them to be higher in the future. For at least the latest nine cycles, or since 1921, short-term rates for governments have been, on average over the full cycle, lower than long-term rates; this is a manifestation of the less than perfect substitutability of long- for short-term securities in the market. It can be explained by liquidity preference and the costs of providing the speculative services required to "convert" longs into shorts.

1

EXPLANATIONS OF THE TERM STRUCTURE OF INTEREST RATES

IT IS THE THESIS of this investigation that the term structure of interest rates can be explained better by a combination of the expectations and liquidity preference hypotheses than by either hypothesis alone. Alternatively, these two hypotheses can be viewed as complementary explanations of the same phenomenon—the term structure of interest rates. The evidence to be examined in support of this view falls into two classes. One is the findings of previous investigators; the works of Macaulay, Culbertson, Meiselman, Walker, and Hickman contain evidence relevant for evaluating the substantive merits of this thesis. The other class consists of evidence gathered as part of the present investigation.

A. *What Is the Expectations Hypothesis*

The expectations hypothesis has been enunciated by Fisher, Keynes, Hicks, Lutz, and others.[1] It has had widespread appeal for theoretical economists primarily as a result of its consistency with the way similar phenomena in other markets, particularly futures markets, are explained. In contrast, this hypothesis has been widely rejected by empirically minded economists and practical men of affairs. It was rejected by economists because investigators have been unable to produce evidence of a relationship between the term structure of interest rates and expectations of future short-term rates. (Others

---

[1] See Friedrich A. Lutz, "The Structure of Interest Rates," in the American Economic Association, *Readings in the Theory of Income Distribution*, Philadelphia, 1946, p. 499; and Joseph W. Conard, *An Introduction to the Theory of Interest*, University of California Press, 1959, Part III.

have found it difficult to accept the view that long- and short-term securities are perfect substitutes for one another in the market.) Meiselman contends that previous investigators have not devised operational implications of the expectations hypothesis. Moreover, he contends, they have examined propositions which were mistakenly attributed to the expectations hypothesis, and when these propositions were found to be false, they rejected the expectations hypothesis.[2]

Briefly, the expectations hypothesis asserts that a long-term rate constitutes an average (a weighted average in the case of coupon-bearing securities) of expected future short-term rates. It says that forward rates (or marginal rates of interest) constitute unbiased estimates of future spot rates.[3] It is based on the assumption that short- and long-term securities, default risks aside, can be usefully viewed as identical in all respects except maturity. It implies that the expected value of the returns derived from holding long- and short-term securities for identical time periods are the same.

The word *future* should be emphasized in discussing the expectations hypothesis, since it concerns the effects of expectations about future short-term rates upon the current term structure of interest rates. To illustrate with a simplified example: assume that two-year securities yield 3 per cent and one-year securities 2 per cent. The forward rate on one-year money one year hence, or the marginal cost of extending a one-year term to maturity for an additional year, is 4 per cent; this is arithmetic, not the expectations hypothesis. The expectations hypothesis, as interpreted by Lutz and Meiselman, but not by Hicks, states that the forward rates are unbiased estimates of future short-term rates. For the preceding example, it implies that the market expects the rate on one-year securities one year hence to be 4 per cent. Four per cent is not only the forward rate—it is the expected one-year rate one year hence; i.e., it is what the market thinks the one-year rate will be one year hence.

[2] David Meiselman, *The Term Structure of Interest Rates,* Englewood Cliffs, New Jersey, 1962, pp. 10 and 12.

[3] A spot rate is a rate on funds for immediate delivery; it is today's rate for money to be delivered today for a specified period of time. In contrast, a forward rate is today's rate for money to be delivered in the future for a specified period of time. This time period could be anything, a day, a year, or a decade.

Conversely, assume a 2 per cent rate on two-year maturities and a 3 per cent rate on one-year maturities. Then the yield on one-year securities one year hence which will equalize the net yield from holding two one-year securities successively with that of holding one two-year security is 1 per cent. This must follow if one accepts the view that securities are alike in all respects except term to maturity.[4]

B. Existing Evidence

1. MACAULAY

Macaulay was among the first to produce empirical evidence that related long-term rates to expectations of future short-term rates. Before the founding of the Federal Reserve System, there existed a pronounced and well-known seasonal in the call money rate. The widespread knowledge of the existence of this seasonal implied that time money rates, which are loans from one to six months that are otherwise similar to call money loans, should turn up before the seasonal rise in call money rates. Macaulay found that time money rates did in fact anticipate the seasonal rise in call money rates and concluded that this constituted "... evidence of definite and relatively successful forecasting."[5] Macaulay was unable to uncover additional evidence of successful forecasting. He warned against concluding that forecasting was not attempted. Macaulay's contention was that evidence of successful forecasting is rare because successful forecasting is also rare.[6]

2. HICKMAN

W. Braddock Hickman, in a preliminary, unpublished, but nevertheless widely cited and read, NBER manuscript prepared in 1942, reports the results of his tests of the expectations hypothesis.[7] Like Macaulay, he sought evidence of successful forecasting; unlike Macaulay, he failed to find it. He compared observed or actual yield curves with those predicted one year or more ahead by the

---

[4] These calculations ignore compounding of interest and intermediate payments in the form of coupons.

[5] Frederick R. Macaulay, *Movements of Interest Rates*, p. 36. The reappearance of a seasonal in the money market in recent years has made it possible to reproduce Macaulay's experiment with a new body of data.

[6] *Ibid.*, p. 33.

[7] W. Braddock Hickman, "The Term Structure of Interest Rates: An Exploratory Analysis," National Bureau of Economic Research, 1942, mimeographed.

term structure of interest rates, as interpreted by the Lutz-Mieselman variant of the expectations hypothesis. For such a comparison, expected yield curves must be determined at one point and actual yield curves at a later point of time. If the expectations hypothesis is valid, Hickman reasoned, then expected yield curves will be correlated with observed yield curves.

Hickman found that simply assuming that this year's yield curve will be the same as next year's gave what he regarded as better predictions of subsequently observed yield curves than the expectations hypothesis. This was one of the early uses of an inertia hypothesis as a benchmark for evaluating the predictive content of a substantive hypothesis. Hickman did not employ correlation analysis. If he did, as shall be shown, his conclusion that inertia is the better predictor would be more difficult if not impossible to sustain. In addition, he subjected the expectations hypothesis to two additional tests. (These tests, and the data employed are described in Appendix A.) All of his tests are based on the view that the validity of the expectations hypothesis hinges upon accurate forecasts. Meiselman does not regard this finding as relevant. "Anticipations may not be realized yet still determine the structure of rates in the manner asserted by the theory." [8]

3. CULBERTSON

Culbertson's empirical research is similar to Hickman's; both ran tests based on the assumption that forward rates are accurate predictions of future spot rates. Culbertson examined the yields of short- and long-term governments for identical periods of time. He argued that if the expectations hypothesis is valid, then yields to investors ought to be the same whether short- or long-term securities are held. (His calculations take into account both income streams and capital gains and losses.) He found marked differences in returns for the same holding periods. Since he found it difficult

[8] Meiselman, *Term Structure of Interest Rates,* p. 12. Hickman also had some doubts about the relevance of his test or any other test. The difficulties in conceiving of a means for testing the expectations hypothesis led Conard to contend erroneously, as Meiselman's work demonstrates, that only by assuming the market predicts accurately is it possible ". . . to build a theory whose predictions can be meaningfully tested." See Conard, *Theory of Interest,* p. 290.

to believe that speculators would operate in the government securities markets and predict as badly as his results suggested, he rejected the expectations hypothesis.[9]

4. WALKER

Walker's test of the expectations hypothesis also was based on the assumption that the market could predict accurately. However, it was more like Macaulay's work in this respect than that of Hickman and Culbertson. Both he and Macaulay revealed the consistency between the implications of accurate expectations and the expectations hypothesis; both observed instances in which the expectations of the market could be presumed to be accurate; and both found the behavior of the market was consistent with the expectations hypothesis.[10]

Walker's work deals with governmental interest rate policy during World War II. Around the beginning of that war, the Federal Reserve System and the Treasury embarked upon a policy of stabilizing, through open market operations and the maturity composition of new issues, the existing levels of rates on government securities. At that time, the yield curve was sharply rising; the bill rate was three-eighths of 1 per cent, one-year securities yielded 1 per cent, and long-term securities 2.5 per cent. If the expectations hypothesis is correct, the prestabilization term structure implied that future short-term rates were expected to be higher than existing short-term rates. In contrast, the stabilization policy implied that future short-term rates would be the same as current short-term rates. When the financial community became convinced that the monetary authorities could and would make this policy effective, it also became convinced that existing long-term rates were inconsistent with revised expectations of future short-term rates:

[9] "... the explanation of broad movements in the term structure of rates must be sought principally in factors other than behavior governed by interest rate expectations." See John M. Culbertson, "The Term Structure of Interest Rates," *Quarterly Journal of Economics*, November 1957, p. 502.
Meiselman, *Term Structure of Interest Rates*, p. 12, regards this and Hickman's work as tests of nonexistent implications of the expectations hypothesis.

[10] Charls E. Walker, "Federal Reserve Policy and the Structure of Interest Rates on Government Securities," *Quarterly Journal of Economics*, February 1954, p. 19.

long-term rates were too high. Hence, there was a tremendous shift out of short- and into long-term securities by the holders of governmental obligations. Such a shift is implied by the expectations hypothesis, given the prewar term structure and its wartime stabilization.[11] This shift in large part converted the stabilized yield on bills to a nominal rate similar to some other wartime prices.

Walker's results, unlike Macaulay's findings, cannot be interpreted as providing unambiguous support for the expectations hypothesis because they are also consistent with an implication of the liquidity preference hypothesis. Liquidity preference as a theory of the term structure of interest rates implies that the longer the term to maturity of a security, the higher its yield. Yield differentials between long- and short-term securities constitute equalizing differences that reflect differences in risks of capital losses. The establishment of a ceiling on long-term bond yields implies a floor or support price for their capital values. A price support program for long-term bonds implies that much of the risk of capital loss is eliminated. Therefore, long maturities become relatively more attractive investment media.

Although Walker's results do not discriminate between expectations and liquidity preference, they do discriminate between expectations and liquidity preference on the one hand and market segmentation on the other. If the holdings of governments by the major institutions of the financial community changed as much as Walker reports they did, this constitutes evidence against the market segmentation hypothesis; if the market segmentation hypothesis is correct, Walker should not have observed a shift in the maturity distribution of governments by the major institutions of the financial community.[12]

---

[11] If a rising yield curve exists, long-term securities yield more than short-term because the market anticipates offsetting losses on capital account attributable to holding long-term securities. The elimination of these anticipated capital losses implies that the yield of long-term securities is truly greater than that of short-term securities.

Conversely a declining yield curve implies that future short-term rates will be lower. Hence the holders of long-term securities trade a lower income on current account for anticipated capital gains. The stabilization of such a yield curve means that these anticipated capital gains cannot be realized, hence, that the yield of short-term securities is truly greater than that of long-term securities.

[12] This interpretation of Walker's findings as well as the contention that his results are consistent with liquidity preference does not appear in the original

The expectations hypothesis has been rejected for its unrealistic assumptions, particularly the assumption that short- and long-term securities of equivalent default risk can be treated as perfect substitutes. Many practitioners in financial markets, committing the fallacy of composition, reason that no one regards bills and long-term bonds as alternatives because they observe that many institutions specialize in a particular maturity spectrum. As long as some ranges of maturities are considered as alternatives by individual participants in this market, and in the aggregate these ranges cover the entire maturity spectrum, the market will act as though bills and bonds are alternatives. Yet every participant in this market may deal in a highly circumscribed maturity spectrum.

Mrs. Robinson has contended that the purchasers of a consol must know the course of future interest rates for ". . . every day from today till Kingdom Come." [13] Hickman and Luckett have enunciated, less colorfully, essentially the same argument.[14]

Presumably the size of the bonus a promising high school or college baseball player receives in exchange for his affiliation with a major league club is a function of his expected performance as a ball player. This interpretation, which is widely accepted, implies that the market predicts the performance of a ball player over his entire career. In order to properly calculate the size of these bonuses, the market must predict batting averages, fielding performance, and, in the case of pitchers, pitching effectiveness. Emotional stability, which appears to be irrelevant for determining future short-term rates, must also be predicted for ball players, since many become emotionally unstable in the face of severe competition and hence lose some of their economic value.[15]

---

paper. Walker regarded his evidence as supporting the Lutz variant of expectations. For another statement of what the market segmentation hypothesis is, see Conard, *Theory of Interest*, p. 304.

[13] See Joan Robinson, "The Rate of Interest," *Econometrica*, April 1951, p. 102.

[14] Dudley G. Luckett, "Professor Lutz and the Structure of Interest Rates," *Quarterly Journal of Economics*, February 1959, p. 131. Hawtrey also seems to be a member of the school that rejects the expectations hypothesis because of difficulties in predicting short-term rates. He argues that short- and long-term rates are determined in completely segregated and independent markets. See Ralph G. Hawtrey, "A Rejoinder," *The Manchester School*, October 1939, p. 156.

[15] The objection to the expectations hypothesis for the lack of "realism" in its assumptions has led to an attempt to find an alternative, more realistic set

5. MEISELMAN

Meiselman is the first investigator to employ an operational test of the expectations hypothesis that does not depend upon accurate foresight for its validity. If a relationship exists between expectations and the term structure of interest rates, then its existence can be detected despite inaccurate predictions. The understanding by economists of how expectations are formed and revised in the light of new information has improved enormously in recent years. Meiselman, by utilizing this knowledge, was able to make the expectations hypothesis operational even when the market could not anticipate future rates of interest correctly. He showed that expectations, whether or not they are correct, nevertheless affect the term structure of rates. His results constitute striking evidence that the expectations hypothesis has empirical validity.[16]

The expectations hypothesis implies that the term structure of interest rates constitutes at one moment of time a set of predictions of short-term rates at various moments of time in the future. For every instant of time, there exists a term structure or yield curve and a set of implicit forward rates. These forward rates are, if the hypothesis is correct, expected short-term rates. If two term structures separated temporally are compared, the earlier contains predictions of future short-term rates and the later the data, i.e., the realized or actual short-term rates necessary for an evaluation of the accuracy of these predictions. Recent work on expectations suggests that if a realized or actual short-term rate is above its predicted level, then the predictions for other rates, yet to be realized, will be revised upward. Conversely, if the actual rate is below the predicted, then other predicted rates will be revised downward during the time interval between observations.

---

of assumptions. See Burton G. Malkiel, "Expectations, Bond Prices, and the Term Structure of Interest Rates," *Quarterly Journal of Economics*, May 1962, No. 2, p. 197. The author claims his model is ". . . in closer conformity with the practices of bond investors who had always considered the Lutz theory chimerical." (See p. 218.) Conformity here should not be interpreted as predicting better; there is no test of the predictive powers of the models in the Malkiel paper. Conformity refers to the conformation of the assumptions of Malkiel's model with descriptions of how bond investors behave.

[16] Meiselman, *Term Structure of Interest Rates*, Chapter 2.

The Cyclical Behavior of the Term Structure of Interest Rates

To illustrate: Assume at T_0, say January 1, 1960, the following relationships between yield and term to maturity are revealed by the market:

Yields as a Function of Term to Maturity at T_0

1-year governments yield	1.0 per cent
2	2.0
3	3.0
4	4.0

The expectations hypothesis, given this data at T_0, implies that the market expects future one-year rates to be higher than the current one-year rate. Since the one-year rate is 1 per cent and the two-year rate 2 per cent, the forward rate on one-year money one year hence must be 3 per cent for the returns on these alternatives to be equal. Analogously, if the current two-year rate is 2 per cent and the three-year rate 3 per cent, then the forward rate on one-year money two years later must be high enough to compensate for the difference between 2 and 3 per cent for two years. Therefore, a one-year rate of 5 per cent is implied for two years hence.

Market Predictions at T_0 of Expected One-Year Rates

Expected one-year rate for T_1, the year beginning 1/1/61, is 3.0 per cent
T_2, 1/1/62, 5.0
T_3, 1/1/63, 7.0

Assume at T_1, a year later, that the following relationships between yield and term to maturity are revealed by the market:

Yields as a Function of Term to Maturity at T_1

1-year governments yield	2.0 per cent
2	3.3
3	4.0

Clearly the one-year rate observed in the market at T_1 (2 per cent) is less than it was expected to be a year ago (3 per cent). The difference between the anticipated one-year rate one year hence at T_0 and the realized one-year rate at T_1 (both rates are for an identical moment of time but are measured one year apart) is defined as the error. If recently acquired knowledge on the formation of expectations is correct, then forecasts of expected one-year rates for T_2 and

115

T_3, i.e., for January 1, 1962, and 1963, will have been revised downward during the year 1960, or between T_0 and T_1.

One can infer from the term structure of interest rates at T_0 and T_1 how much these estimates of future short-term rates have been revised.

Market Predictions at T_0 and T_1

Expected One-Year Rate for One Year, Beginning on	T_0	T_1	Change in Forecast, or Magnitude of Forecast Revision (per cent)
January 1, 1962 (T_2)	5.0	4.6	−0.4
January 1, 1963 (T_3)	7.0	5.4	−1.6

At T_1 the expected one-year rates beginning at T_2 and T_3 are 4.6 and 5.4 per cent respectively. The difference between 5.0 and 4.6 per cent measures the change in the forecast one-year rate for T_2; the difference between 7.0 and 5.4 measures the change in the forecast one-year rate for T_3. Hence, if the expectations hypothesis is correct, then errors and forecast changes should be positively correlated.[17] Meiselman found that his error terms (i.e., the difference between predicted and actual one-year rates) and his forecast revisions were in fact positively correlated.

The distinction between anticipated and unanticipated interest rate changes is crucial for an understanding of how Meiselman tested the expectations hypothesis. If forward rates a year apart are as depicted by Chart 1, then the expectations hypothesis would imply that there has been no change in the rates forecast. Yet the rates for one-, two-, and three-year maturities must have changed during this year; yield curves were not constant. Nevertheless the expected one-year rates for particular moments of time were unchanged. The observations that are correlated, i.e., the error term and the forecast revision, refer to interest rates for particular dates.[18]

---

[17] Meiselman defines the error as the spot minus the forward; the revision of the forecast is defined as the later forecast less the earlier.

[18] An implication of this distinction is the proposition that stock prices can vary over time with no change in expectations of future earnings, if the market expects earnings to fluctuate. Hence, insofar as investors anticipate cyclical changes in the profitability of enterprises, anticipated cyclical variations in stock prices should exist.

Meiselman correlated errors with contemporaneous revisions in forecasts. For the example used, there are two forecast revisions, − 0.4 and 1.6, that are correlated with the error, − 1.0. The future spot rates whose estimates were revised will be observed in the market as spot, and not forward, rates one and two years after the spot rate in the error term can be observed. For the data Meiselman employed, the future spot rates whose estimates were revised will be observed in the market as spot rates one through eight years after the spot rate in his error term can be observed. In both the example and Meiselman's work, forward rates pertaining to subsequently observable one-year spot rates for particular moments of calendar time were observed a year apart. The difference between observations which pertain to the same spot rate are forecast re-

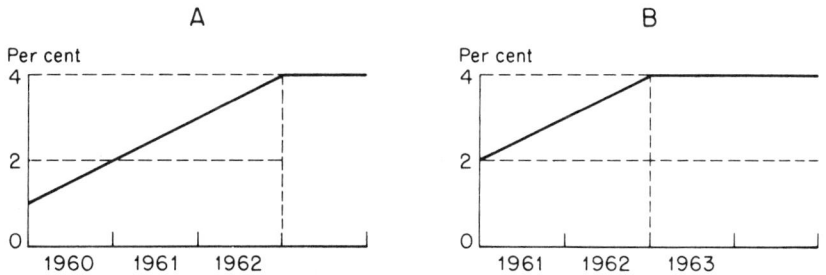

CHART 1

Marginal Rates of Interest with Stable Expectations

visions. Since Meiselman observed his forward and spot one-year rates yearly, he observed eight forward rate revisions and one error term every year (with, of course, the exception of the earliest year that his data encompasses). Meiselman produced eight regressions relating forward rate revisions to errors observed simultaneously. He found significant relationships for all eight, with correlation coefficients ranging from a low of .59 to a high of .95. All eight regression lines went through the origin, in the sense that the constant terms of the regressions were insignificantly different from zero.

This led to the inference that forward rates are unbiased estimates of future spot rates, which implies, when trends in interest rates are ignored, that yield curves are on the average flat. Short- and long-term rates will tend to be equal. If forward rates are biased upward, then yield curves, again ignoring trends, are on the average positively sloped. Hence, short-term rates will average less than long-term rates, and both, on the average, will rise with term to maturity. Such differentials between different terms to maturity, usually referred to as liquidity premiums, reflect the greater liquidity of short maturities.[19] Meiselman argues that the absence of a constant term in his regressions implies the absence of liquidity premiums. If the constant term is zero, a forward rate that is equal to the subsequently observed actual spot rate, i.e., a zero error term, implies no forecast revision. If forecasts are not revised when the error term is zero, then Meiselman infers that liquidity premiums are absent. To show that this inference is incorrect, consider the following formal statement of the hypothesis Meiselman tests:

$$_{t+m}E_t - {_{t+m}E_{t-1}} = \beta({_tR_t} - {_tE_{t-1}}) \tag{1}$$

Let E represent expected rates, R spot rates, F forward rates, and L liquidity premiums. The pre-subscript represents a year of calendar time. The post-subscript measures the moment a rate is either inferred from the term structure or observed as an actual spot rate. The forward and spot rates Meiselman considered were for one year only. Hence, $_{t+m}E_t$ is the expected one-year spot rate for the year $t+m$ that is inferred from the term structure of interest rates at moment t. The expected one-year spot rate for the year $t+m$ that is inferred from the term structure of interest rates at moment $t-1$ is $_{t+m}E_{t-1}$. The difference between the post-subscripts t and $t-1$ is, for Meiselman's study, one year.

One cannot observe expected rates directly; the term structure of interest rates reveals only forward rates. Whether or not $E = F$, or $E + L = F$ must be established by empirical evidence. Suppose liquidity premiums exist and they increase monotonically at a decreasing rate as a function of term to maturity. Then the longer the time interval between the moment a one-year forward rate is in-

---

[19] The Hicksian view of the term structure of interest rates implies that forward rates are biased and high estimates of future short-term rates. He viewed the "normal" yield curve as being positively sloped. See John R. Hicks, *Value and Capital*, London 1946, pp. 135–140. Lutz explicitly rejected the view that liquidity premiums exist because he could observe short-term rates above corresponding long-term rates and he regarded this as a contradiction of the liquidity preference hypothesis. See Lutz, in *Theory of Income Distribution*, p. 528.

ferred from a term structure and the moment it becomes a spot rate, the greater the liquidity premium. Similarly, year-to-year changes in forward rates for specific calendar years will increase as they get closer in time to becoming spot rates. The largest increase will occur during the year a forward rate becomes a spot rate.[20]

If the forward rate, F, is equal to the expected rate, E, plus a liquidity premium, L, then substituting in (1) yields

$$({}_{t+m}F_t - {}_{t+m}L_t) - ({}_{t+m}F_{t-1} - {}_{t+m}L_{t-1}) = \beta[{}_tR_t - ({}_tF_{t-1} - {}_tL_{t-1})].$$

Let $- {}_{t+m}L_t + {}_{t+m}L_{t-1} = \Delta L$. Then the restatement of Meiselman's hypothesis becomes

$${}_{t+m}F_t - {}_{t+m}F_{t-1} = \beta({}_tR_t - {}_tF_{t-1}) + \beta_t L_{t-1} - \Delta L.$$

Letting $a = \beta_t L_{t-1} - \Delta L$, results in

$${}_{t+m}F_t - {}_{t+m}F_{t-1} = \beta({}_tR_t - {}_tF_{t-1}) + a. \tag{2}$$

This is the regression equation Meiselman computed. He found that the observed constant was insignificantly different from zero. Hence, he inferred that a or $\beta_t L_{t-1} - \Delta L$ is also insignificantly different from zero.

A zero constant term is equally consistent with either $\beta_t L_{t-1} = \Delta L = 0$ or $\beta_t L_{t-1} = \Delta L > 0$. Hence, this piece of evidence is inappropriate for establishing the validity of the proposition that forward rates are unbiased estimates of expected spot rates; it is consistent with the existence of liquidity premiums. The proposition that forward rates are unbiased estimates of future spot rates remains untested.

Meiselman's own work, the work of Hickman, the time series of short- and long-term governments for the past forty years (to be presented in Chapter 3), and some new evidence presented here, all support the view that the term structure of interest rates, as interpreted by the expectations hypothesis, embodies biased and high estimates of future short-term rates. Meiselman used Durand's yield curves for high-grade corporates from 1900 through 1954 for his tests. For each of these years, Durand estimated a yield curve. If an

---

[20] For the purpose of determining whether or not forward rates are biased or unbiased estimates of spot rates, the liquidity content of spot rates is irrelevant. It is only the difference, if any, between the liquidity content of forward and spot rates that matters.

THE CAPITAL MARKETS

average is computed of the yields for each term to maturity, i.e., an average of all fifty-five one-year maturities, two-year maturities, etc., the composite yield curve which results, reflects average conditions for all fifty-five years. This curve is in fact positively sloped (see Chart 2). Since interest rates, if anything, were trending down

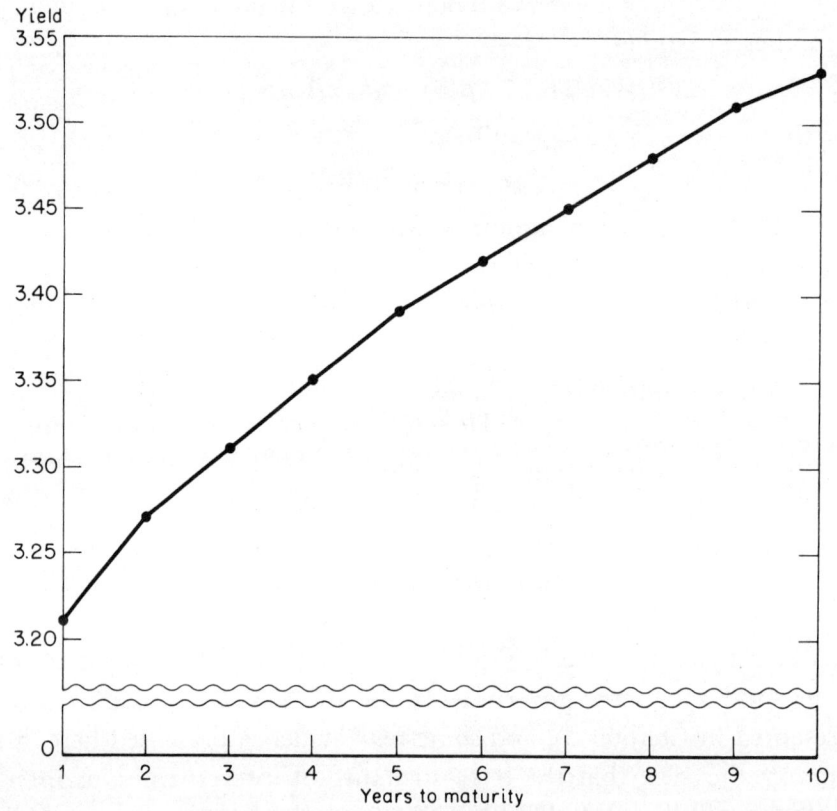

CHART 2
Average Yield as a Function of Term to Maturity, Durand Data, 1900–1954

SOURCE: 1900–42, Durand, *Corporate Bonds;* 1943–47, Durand and Winn, *Basic Yields of Bonds;* 1948–51, *The Economic Almanac, 1956* (National Industrial Conference Board).

during these fifty-five years, forward rates must have been arithmetically high estimates of spot rates.

If liquidity premiums exist, the frequency of high estimates ought to be greater than that of low estimates and the average of the differences between estimated and actual rates ought to be positive.

Hence, Meiselman's error terms ought to have a significantly higher frequency of minus than plus signs and their average ought to be negative. Tests of these implications with the Wilcoxon two-sample and signed-rank tests lead to their acceptance.[21]

The foregoing demonstrates that forward one-year rates were on the average greater than actual one-year rates. It suggests that they were also greater than expected one-year rates and that they systematically overstate what the market expects one-year rates to be. This conclusion is based on an analysis of the inputs for Meiselman's independent variable. What about the dependent variable, i.e., the forward-rate changes that are regarded by Meiselman as prediction changes? Since forward rate changes are the difference between observations, separated by a year, of forward rates that pertain to a specific spot rate observable in the future, the first forward rate must be inferred from data further out on a yield curve than the second. Hence, if liquidity preference is operative (if it produces positively sloped yield curves), then the first forward rate ought to be, on the average, greater than the second. Meiselman observed prediction changes separated by one through eight years from the moment of time relevant for the measurement of the error term. The first forward rate is, on the average, larger than the second for all eight regressions. It is hard to rationalize this observation as a chance event; the probability of drawing eight successive negative numbers from a population in which negative and positive numbers are equally represented is less than 1 per cent. On the whole, this evidence is consistent with a positively sloped yield curve that flattens out as term to maturity increases; it is what one would expect to be derived from data summarized by Chart 2.

Meiselman's changes in forward rates and error terms constitute a measure of the marginal costs, more precisely the rate of change of yield with respect to term to maturity, of reducing term to maturity by a year. The pecuniary values at the margin, as revealed by the market, of liquidity changes attributable to changes in term

---

[21] See W. Allen Wallis and Harry V. Roberts, *Statistics: A New Approach*, Glencoe, 1956, pp. 596–598. Significance levels of 6 and 2 per cent were produced using one tail of the normal distribution. Of the fifty-four forward one-year rates, thirty-five were high and nineteen were low.

to maturity of one year are computed. They behave, roughly speaking, as one would expect; the longer it takes for a forward rate to become a spot rate, the greater the premium of forward over spot. With but two exceptions out of a possible nine cases, liquidity premiums decrease monotonically as term to maturity increases (see Table 1).

TABLE 1

MEISELMAN'S ERROR TERM AND FORECAST REVISIONS[a]

	Years Until Second Observation Becomes a One-Year Spot Rate	Per Cent
Mean error term[b]	0	−.143
Mean forward rate revision[c]	1	−.101
	2	−.078
	3	−.065
	4	−.077
	5	−.054
	6	−.040
	7	−.049
	8	−.022

[a] These data were obtained through personal communication with Meiselman.

[b] Mean of differences between one-year forward and spot rates.

[c] Mean change in one-year forward rates as term to maturity decreases by one year.

Hickman's data are consistent with Meiselman's findings. Predicted yield curves for the years 1936 through 1942, with a year between the time predicted and actual yield curves are observed, were all high. Even more interesting, and this is consistent with Meiselman's data, Hickman's results show that the longer the interval between predicted and observed or actual yield curves, the greater the bias in the estimates.[22] This empirical finding is an implication of a positively sloped yield curve when trends in rates are absent.

The data (to be presented in Chapter III) on yields of governments for the nine most recent business cycles, a period of roughly forty years, clearly indicate that the average yields of

[22] There are twenty-eight predictions, all too high. See Table A-1 which reproduces Hickman's data.

short-term governments are less than long-term governments. All nine cycles, without exception, conform to this generalization. These data constitute additional evidence that the term structure of rates, as interpreted by the expectations hypothesis, yields biased estimates of future short-term rates. If forward rates are not expected rates, but expected rates plus a liquidity premium, one should expect these time series to show that yields of short-term governments are usually less than long-term governments. Since Meiselman and Hickman worked with Durand's data, which reflect the yields of high-grade corporates, these data on the relative yields of short- and long-term governments for these nine cycles constitute independent evidence of the existence of bias in the predictions of the expectations hypothesis.

Unfortunately, this evidence is not unexceptionable. The fifty-five yearly observations of Durand, which Meiselman used, have a downward trend. In 1900, Durand's basic thirty-year rate was 3.30 per cent; in 1954, it was 3.00 per cent. If declining short-term rates are unanticipated, the predicted rates of the expectations hypothesis will exceed actual rates. From 1935 through 1942, the downward trend is still greater; the thirty-year basic rate fell from 3.50 to 2.65. Hence, if the long-term downward trend in rates has been unanticipated by the market, the relationship between the yields of short- and long-term governments may be a consequence of forecasting errors.[23]

Meiselman, like Walker, produced evidence relevant for evaluating the validity of the market segmentation hypothesis; unlike Walker, Meiselman points out the relevance of his work for this hypothesis. ". . . the systematic behavior of the yield curve would appear to contradict the widely held view that the market for debt claims is 'segmented' or 'compartmentalized' by maturity and that rates applicable to specific maturity segments can best be analyzed by rather traditional partial equilibrium supply and demand analysis where transactors act on the basis of preference for specific

---

[23] Hickman found that a simple projection of the previous year's yield curve produced numerically closer predictions than the expectations hypothesis, which is consistent with the foregoing interpretation. His finding is also, of course, consistent with an upward bias in the predictions of the expectations hypothesis.

maturities. . . ." [24] The correlation between forward rate revisions and error terms demonstrates that changes in the yields of one- and two-year securities are related to changes in yields of maturities up to nine and ten years. Consequently, at least for this maturity range, the market is not segmented enough to invalidate this test of the expectations hypothesis.

C. New Evidence

Confining tests of the expectations hypothesis to circumstances for which expectations can be presumed to be accurate has produced only fragmentary evidence. Expectations can be presumed to be accurate only under very special circumstances. Hence, forward rates can equal expected spot rates and yet differ from realized spot rates. But even this limited approach has not been fully exploited. Clearly, in a world in which spot rates are positive, and this would surely encompass the two most recent decades, one could assume that the market never expects negative spot rates. Therefore, if negative forward rates were observed, this would constitute evidence against the expectations hypothesis. Conversely, if negative forward rates were not observed, this would be evidence for the hypothesis.

The behavior of the term structure of bill yields during September 1960 contradicts the expectations hypothesis. In that month the forward rate on one-week money, inferred from the term structure of bill yields with maturities on December 8th and 15th, was often negative.[25]

For nine of the twenty-one trading days in September 1960, negative forward rates for one-week money could be observed. To restate the foregoing, on these nine dates in September 1960 (and this same phenomenon could be observed in September 1959) there existed some bills whose asked prices were higher than the asked prices for bills with one week less to maturity. Since it is unreasonable to argue that the market expected the spot rate for one-week

---

[24] Meiselman, *Term Structure of Interest Rates*, p. 34.

[25] The asked prices reported on the quote sheets of C. J. Devine were the source of price data. Salomon Bros. and Hutzler quote sheets contained data that led to the same conclusion.

bills on September 8th, or any other week since the end of World War II, to be negative, it follows that forward rates are not expected spot rates.

Critics have rejected the expectations hypothesis because the predictions of future short-term rates implied by the theory differed from subsequently observed actual rates. Meiselman argues that these critics have rejected the hypothesis for the wrong reasons. His position, that expectations need not be correct to determine the term structure of interest rates, is, of course, valid. Yet, given free entry and competition in securities markets, should not one expect to find a relationship between expectations as inferred from the term structure of interest rates and subsequently observed actual rates? It is of course unreasonable to expect expectations or predictions of future short-term rates to be absolutely accurate. New information coming to the market after a prediction is made will lead to prediction revisions and less than perfect forecasts. Yet new information should not lead to biases in the estimates; a mean bias should not be present. Hence, the average difference between predicted and actual rates ought to be insignificantly different from zero. The absence or presence of a mean bias in the relationship constitutes a test of whether or not forward rates are expected rates. Similarly, for very short intervals between the inference of predictions and the observation of actual short-term rates, there should be some observable advantage for the expectations hypothesis over some form of inertia hypothesis as a predictor of future short-rates. If not, why should the market waste its time and energy, which are scarce resources, in trying to predict future short-term rates? [26]

To control for trends in rates, and to measure forward and actual rates uninfluenced by capital gain considerations, the forward and actual yields of Treasury bills were examined from the beginning of 1959 through March 1962. All of the forward rates implicit in the

---

[26] Meiselman went too far in dismissing the work of Hickman and Culbertson. The expectations hypothesis, as he and Lutz interpreted it, does imply that there ought to be equality in the yields of short- and long-term rates in the absence of trends. If there is not, either the people operating in this market are doing an unbelievably bad job or this constitutes evidence against the Meiselman version of the expectations hypothesis.

TABLE 2

DISTRIBUTION OF ERRORS IN PREDICTING TREASURY BILL RATES[a]

	14-Day Rates	28-Day Rates	42-Day Rates	56-Day Rates	63-Day Rates	91-Day Rates
No. of observations	124	143	146	137	113	125
Frequency of high predictions	93	132	135	120	91	119
Average size of errors (per cent)	.199	.567	.599	.444	.455	.669
Average actual rates (per cent)	2.34	2.39	2.54	2.67	2.79	2.91

[a] Bills with precisely 182 and 91 days to maturity were used to compute the forward 91-day rate. Ninety-one days after this computation, the spot 91-day rate was observed and compared with the forward rate. Similarly, bills with 126, 112, 84, 63, 56, 42, 28, and 14 days to maturity were used to compute forward rates and to measure spot rates.

Bid and asked prices, obtained from government bond dealers, were averaged to obtain the prices used. The daily quote sheets of Salomon Bros. & Hutzler, C. J. Devine & Co., were the sources of bid and asked prices. These daily price reports quote bid and asked prices of bills for specified days to maturity from the time payment is received.

Forward 91-day rates were computed by subtracting the current 91-day rate from twice the current 182-day rate. This method of computing forward rates increases the difficulties of detecting an upward bias in the estimates of the expectations hypothesis. It understates forward relative to spot rates. Indeed, if the estimates of the expectations hypothesis were unbiased, this computing procedure would show a downward bias. Bill yields are bankers discount yields, and equal discount yields for different maturities are not comparable. For example, a 4 per cent discount yield on a 90-day bill implies a yield on a 360-day basis of 4.04 per cent. In contrast, a 4 per cent discount yield on a 180-day bill implies a yield of 4.08 on a 360-day basis. In general, the longer the term to maturity of a bill, the more its discount yield understates its bond equivalent yield. Hence, the procedure followed produces lower estimates of forward rates than would be produced by a correct computation.

term structure of interest rates during that time for two-, four-, six-, eight-, nine-, and thirteen-week bill rates were computed and compared with actual yields. The time period under investigation began and ended with the 91-day bill rate at the same level, approximately 2.75 per cent, although it rose sharply to 4.50 per cent and fell to 2.25 before it came back to its original level. The results of this investigation are tabulated in Table 2.

These results, along with the evidence already cited, strongly support the belief that forward rates are biased and high estimates of future short-term rates. Hence they are not the predictions of the market. In addition, these findings support the common belief that there exists a preference for short-term over long-term securities in the market. This preference produces a yield differential that constitutes an equalizing difference. The greater pecuniary yield of long-term securities represents compensation for the nonpecuniary advantages associated with holding short-term securities.

These findings also suggest that the futures market for money may be unlike other futures markets. Generally, one finds that forward prices are below corresponding spot prices when spot prices are rising and above them when spot prices are falling. For the futures market for money, however, forward rates in the Treasury bill market are typically above spot rates even when the latter are rising. During an upswing, the extent to which this occurs narrows, and some reversals, i.e., spot rates in excess of forward rates, occur. However, these reversals are suprisingly infrequent.

On theoretical grounds, one should expect liquidity premiums to vary with the level of interest rates. Treasury bills, like other securities, can be viewed as providing two streams of income: one is a pecuniary yield measured by interest rates; the other is a nonpecuniary yield as a money substitute. The average difference in 28- and 56-day bill yields can be viewed as an equalizing difference that reflects the greater value of the former as a money substitute. Economists customarily think of a rise in interest rates as implying an increase in the cost of holding money. By parity of reasoning, an increase in interest rates should also imply an increase in the cost of holding money substitutes. Since 28-day bills are better money substitutes than 56-day bills, a rise in interest rates implies that the opportunity costs of holding the former should rise relative to that of holding the latter. For this condition to be satisfied, yields of 56-day bills must rise relative to those of 28-day bills. Such a rise implies an increase in liquidity premiums, i.e., an increase in the spread between forward and actual 28-day rates. This reasoning is consistent with the results obtained for the range of bill maturities studied; the opportunity costs of holding any specified maturity, instead of a longer and hence less liquid maturity, increases as interest rates rise. Conversely, these opportunity costs decrease when rates fall. Within the range of bill maturities observed, and contrary to what is true for the yield curve as a whole, yield curves are steepest when rates are high and flattest when rates are low.

If the spread between 28- and 56-day bills increases with a rise in rates, and if liquidity premiums increase, then the premium of forward over spot money should also increase. This implies that what Meiselman and Hickman erroneously regarded as error terms, the difference between forward and subsequently observed spot rates, should be a positive function of the current level of spot rates. To determine whether or not this inference is correct, the difference between forward and subsequently observed 28-day spot rates was regressed on current 28-day spot rates. This is equivalent to regressing liquidity premiums plus or minus a forecasting error on current 28-day rates. These results are consistent with the hypothesis that liquidity premiums rise with the level of spot rates. The premium of forward over spot 28-day rates increases by one basis point for every increase of about five basis points in the spot rate.

The foregoing conclusion was derived from 137 monthly observations during the three business cycles from October 1949 through February 1961. They are supported by the results obtained from a regression using 138 weekly observations of 91- and 182-day bills from January 1959 through February 1961. For the latter test, the regression coefficient was about twice the former. A rise of about two and a half basis points in the 91-day bill rate is associated with a rise of about one basis point in the premium of forward over spot 91-day rates.[27]

[27] For the 91-day bills, the weekly observations cover a period when there were 182- and 91-day bills outstanding simultaneously. The regression coefficient was .43 with a standard error of .05.

For the 28-day bills, observations were obtained once a month. Typically, more than one observation could have been used in any month. The observation chosen was the one closest to the middle of the month. The regression coefficient was .22 with a standard error of .03.

The effects of bankers discount were eliminated from these data.

The association of a rise in liquidity premiums with a rise in the level of rates can also be shown by regressing the difference between forward and subsequently observed spot rates upon their sum.

The validity of these tests depends upon the absence of positive correlation between forecasting errors and spot rates. Unfortunately it is difficult to disentangle forecasting errors from liquidity premiums.

Since both interest rates and business conditions vary with the cycle, the finding that liquidity premiums rise with interest rates raises the question, are liquidity premiums a function of the level of interest rates or of the stage of the business cycle? In order to investigate this question, forward and actual 28-day bill rates were computed monthly from the term structure of 56- and 28-day bills for the three latest complete business cycles. During these three cycles, there was an upward trend in interest rates. Therefore, if liquidity premiums vary with the level of rates, it should be possible to observe that they rise secularly. The regression of the difference between predicted and actual 28-day rates on time for these three cycles does indicate an upward trend. Hence, liquidity premiums are positively related to the level of interest rates.[28]

The existence of liquidity premiums implies that the expectations hypothesis yields biased and high estimates of future short-term rates. It does not reveal in any direct way whether or not the market has any power to correctly anticipate subsequently observed spot rates. If liquidity premiums are held constant, if expected and not forward rates are observed, does a significant relationship exist between these expected rates and subsequently observed spot rates?

Forward rates for specific periods of calendar time and subsequently observed spot rates for the same periods were subjected to correlation analysis. This corrects, in a very crude way, for bias in the estimates of future spot rates attributable to liquidity premiums. Forward rates, which can be regarded as market predictions when adjusted for liquidity premiums, were inferred from the term structure of 182- and 91-day bill rates. (These rates were computed using an average of bid and asked prices adjusted for bankers discount.)

The results of this test indicate that the expectations hypothesis definitely does have predictive content. For 138 predictions of 91-day bill rates from the beginning of 1959 through the first quarter of 1962, the expectations hypothesis explained 58 per cent of the observed variation. The question remains whether an inertia hypothe-

---

[28] Of 137 predictions of the Lutz variant of the expectations hypothesis, 121 were high, five low, and eleven were correct. The effects of bankers discount were eliminated from these data.

sis could do equally well or better. Perhaps the observed correlation could be attributable to serial correlation in the data.

To determine whether or not the results obtained should be imputed to correct expectations, two variants of an "inertia hypothesis" were considered. One "predicted" 91-day bill rates 91 days hence by assuming no change. The other extrapolated into the future the difference between current 91-day rates and those 91 days ago.

The correlations for both variants of the inertia hypothesis tested were the same; each explained 48 per cent of the observed variation. The expectations hypothesis explained approximately 20 per cent more of the observed variation. During most of the period of observation, from about the middle of 1959 through the middle of 1960, there was a sharp rise and fall in rates. For the remainder of the period, interest rates were roughly stable. If the two hypotheses are compared for the period when rates were highly unstable (this reduces the number of observations to fifty), then expectations explain 48 per cent of the observed variations, whereas the variants of inertia each explain 30 per cent. The comparative advantage of the theory was stronger, as one would expect, when interest rates were unstable.

Is the observed difference between these correlation coefficients significant? Could it have occured as a result of chance? To answer this question, forward and current spot rates were correlated with subsequently observed spot rates and the partial correlation coefficients were computed. The addition of current spot rates increased the fraction of the observed variation explained from 58 to 59 per cent. The partial regression coefficient for expectations was significant and positive (the partial regression coefficient was .86, with a standard error of .14). In contrast, the partial regression coefficient for inertia was negative and also significant (the regression coefficient was −.31, with a standard error of .18).

These results indicate clearly that the expectations hypothesis does have predictive content that cannot be attributed to inertia. However, the negative coefficient for inertia requires explanation. The hypothesis presented here views the forward rate as a function of expected spot rates plus a liquidity premium. But liquidity premiums are a function of the level of spot rates: when current spot rates are high, the premium over spot that is reflected in the forward rate is also high, and vice versa. Hence, the larger the spot rate, the larger the number that ought to be deducted from forward rates to obtain the expected rates of the market. Therefore, the negative coefficient which is observed is consistent with the view that liquidity premiums exist and vary directly with the level of interest rates, more specifically with spot rates.

To restate this argument more formally, using symbols already defined:

1. $_{t+1}F_t = {_{t+1}}E_t + {_t}LP_t$.
2. $_tLP_t = f(_tR_t)$.
3. $_{t+1}F_t - f(_tR_t) = {_{t+1}}E_t$.
4. $_{t+1}E_t = {_{t+1}}R_{t+1} + U$.
5. $_{t+1}F_t - f(_tR_t) = {_{t+1}}R_{t+1} + U$.

The data used to evaluate the predictive content of the expectations hypothesis are reproduced in Chart 3. The thick line depicts actual 91-day rates. The thin lines indicate forward rates adjusted and unadjusted for liquidity premiums. The point of origin of the thin lines at the thick line represents the moment a forward rate is inferred; the terminal point of the thin line measures the magnitude of the forward rate at the moment when the actual 91-day rate corresponding to this forward rate can be observed. Liquidity premiums were measured using the regression equation obtained by regressing the difference between forward and realized 91-day rates on current spot rates. These results suggest that within the range of maturities encompassed by Treasury bills, expectations do influence the term structure of interest rates, and the market forecasts future spot rates with some degree of accuracy. However, to obtain the expectations of the market, liquidity premiums must be deducted from forward rates.[29]

[29] The fact that forward rates are usually higher than actual spot rates may have led Hickman to abandon the search for a relationship between them. An inertia hypothesis could produce numerically closer predictions to spot rates than the expectations hypothesis, yet the latter could produce stronger correlations. It is the strength of the correlations, if one accepts the view that liquidity premiums exist, that is relevant for evaluating these alternatives. Insofar as liquidity premiums are a constant or linear function of forward rates, they do

CHART 3
Market Expectations of Future 91-Day Bill Rates

——— Forward rates
- - - - - Forward rates adjusted for liquidity premiums
——— Spot rates

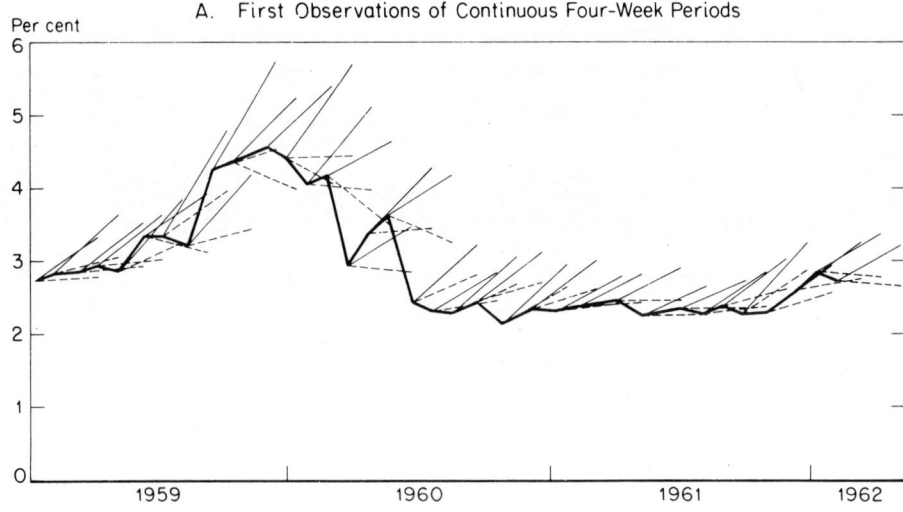

A. First Observations of Continuous Four-Week Periods

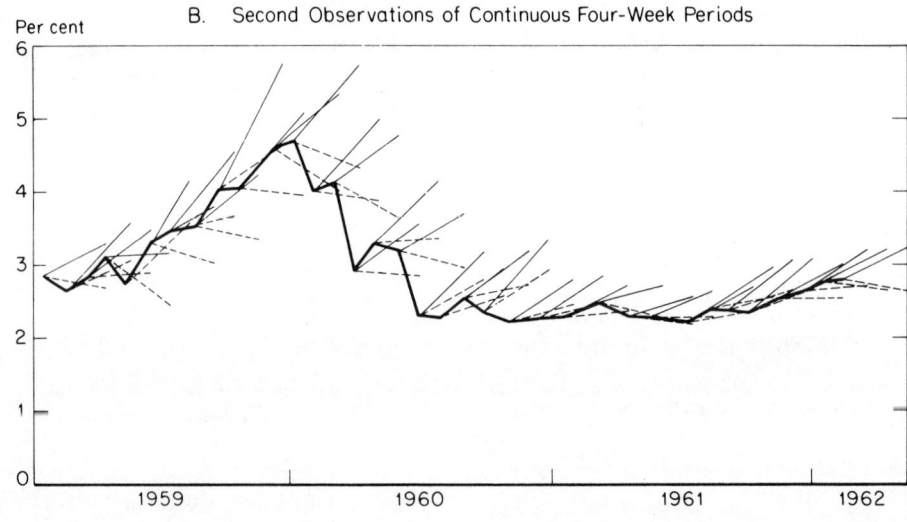

B. Second Observations of Continuous Four-Week Periods

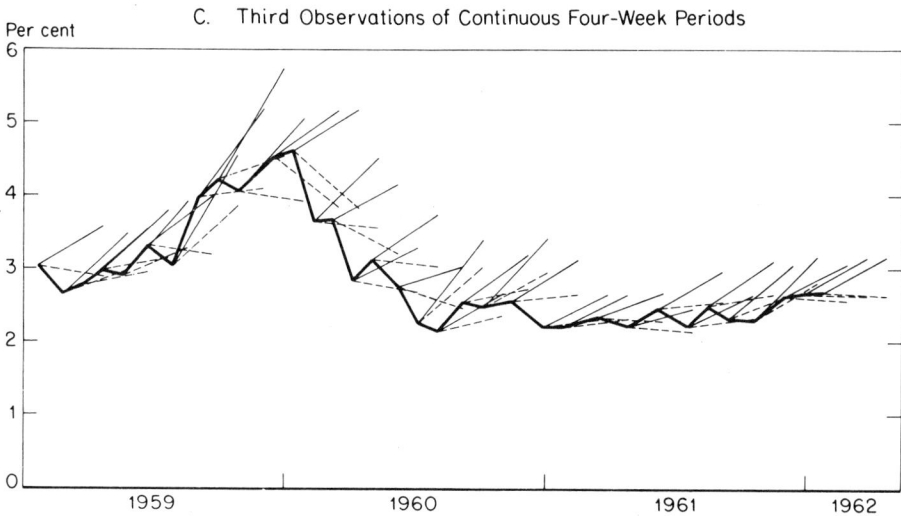

C. Third Observations of Continuous Four-Week Periods

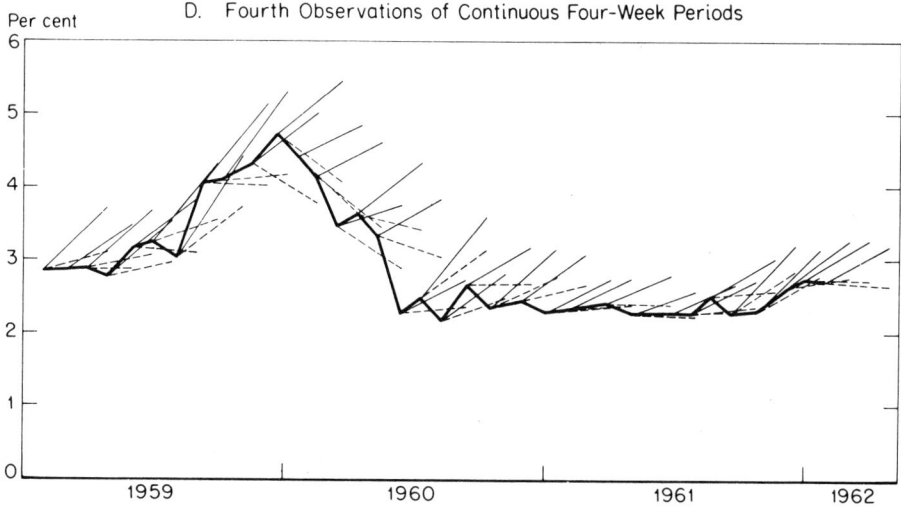

D. Fourth Observations of Continuous Four-Week Periods

Thus far, this analysis does not reveal how stable the liquidity preference function is. Is the relationship between spot rates and liquidity premiums stable enough to permit one to estimate liquidity premiums for one business cycle and use these estimates to uncover successfully the expectations of the market, as distinguished from forward rates, for a second cycle? To answer this question, the regression of the difference between forward and subsequently observed 28-day spot rates upon current 28-day spot rates, for the two cycles from October 1949 through April 1958, was used to estimate liquidity premiums for the following cycle. Then inertia and expectations were compared as a means of forecasting subsequently observed spot rates. Expectations was definitely the better predictor. The standard error of estimate was .50 for inertia against .38 for expectations. The partial regression coefficient for inertia was −.07; for expectations, it was .75. The standard error of the regression coefficient was .19 for inertia and .16 for expectations. Multiple correlation analysis, using forward rates adjusted for liquidity premiums, yields results almost identical with those obtained with unadjusted forward rates.[30]

These results suggested that the data Meiselman employed, which were compiled by Durand, should be reexamined to see if forward rates do predict subsequently observed spot rates. Hence forward and current spot rates were considered as independent variables and subsequently observed spot rates as the dependent variable in a multiple regression equation. This involves using the same data Meiselman used to compute what he regards as an error term. No evidence of successful forecasting was detected; inertia appeared to be the better independent variable.

To utilize more recent data that are qualitatively more com-

---

not influence the correlation of forward with spot rates. For the two sets of seven pairs of observations in Hickman's study, representing one-year forecasts, the correlation coefficient for expectations was .725; for inertia, .721. When both variables were included in a multiple correlation, neither had a significant partial correlation coefficient. Hence no basis is provided by correlation analysis for arguing that one or the other variable explained the observed variation. If one plots forward rates and the variant of inertia Hickman employed, there is almost a constant difference between them.

[30] For the three cycles, 1949 to 1961, the simple correlation coefficients indicated that expectations explained 88 per cent of the observed variation whereas inertia, i.e., extrapolating no change, explained 82 per cent.

The Cyclical Behavior of the Term Structure of Interest Rates

parable to the data Meiselman utilized, the experiment performed with forward and spot three-month Treasury bills was repeated using monthly forward and spot one-year governments for 1958 through 1961. One- and two-year rates were read off the fixed maturity yield curve published monthly in the Treasury Bulletin.[31] Again forward and current spot rates were treated as independent variables and subsequently observed spot rates as the dependent variable. The result is consistent with that using three- and six-month bills and reinforces the view that the market has some power to forecast successfully. However, taken by itself it does not constitute quite as convincing evidence of the existence of successful forecasting. This is what one would expect; it is harder to forecast a year into the future than it is to forecast for three months.

If the rationalization of the statistical findings using three- and six-month bills is correct, then forward rates should have a positive coefficient and current one-year rates a negative one. One should also expect to find that the partial correlation coefficient for expectations would be smaller in the case of one- and two-year Treasury securities than it was for three- and six-month bills.

These anticipations are in general borne out. The sign of the regression coefficient for one-year spot rates is negative. For three- and six-month bills, this regression coefficient is 75 per cent greater than its standard error; for one- and two-year governments, it is a third larger than its standard error. For three- and six-month bills, the regression coefficient for forward rates is positive and six times its standard error; in the case of one- and two-year governments, it is positive but only nine-tenths its standard error.

Possibly the most convincing evidence that the market can forecast, with modest accuracy, one-year spot rates one year into the future was obtained through the following experiment. Liquidity premiums embodied in one-year forward rates for the 1958–61 cycle were estimated from an equation derived from the difference between forward and subsequently observed spot rates regressed on current one-year rates for the 1954–58 cycle. The expected rates of the market for the 1958–61 cycle were then obtained by subtracting

[31] I am indebted to H. Irving Forman of the National Bureau staff for these measurements. They are reproduced, along with the related forward and spot rates, in Appendix Table B-1.

135

the estimated liquidity premiums from forward rates. The mean square errors in the implicit forecasts of the market, i.e., the difference between forward rates less liquidity premiums and subsequently observed spot rates were compared with those generated by assuming next year's one-year spot rates will be identical with current rates. Although neither independent variable appeared in some absolute sense to yield very good forecasts, it is clear that expectations was significantly better as an independent variable than inertia. For thirty-five monthly observations, the mean square error was 2.09 for inertia, .91 for expectations. The elimination of liquidity premiums contributed importantly to this reduction in error. Without such adjustment, the mean square error of the forward rates was 1.91, only slightly less than that for inertia. These results show that if one is predicting one-year rates one year hence, and the current one-year rate is known, adding the two-year rate to one's knowledge constitutes a valuable piece of information.

Time series of forward and spot one-year rates during the period 1958 to 1961 are reproduced as Chart 4. These data, as well as the data for forward and spot three-month bills, suggest that the market can detect spot rates that are abnormally high or low. All of the forward rates are biased estimates. However, if one examines the slopes of the lines connecting current spot rates with forward rates for one year into the future, these lines appear flattest when current spot rates are highest. Hence, if the market can abstract from liquidity premiums (which produce the bias) then it appears that the market can forecast. That is, when rates are high, the market expects them to fall, and conversely, as the adjusted forward rates in the lower part of the chart suggest. This is consistent with the view that the market has some notion of what constitutes a normal rate of interest.

What causes the observed difference between the results using Durand's data on corporates and the recent data on one- and two-year governments? The evidence provides the basis for highly speculative answers at best. Durand's data encompass fifty-five years and are yearly observations; the data on governments encompass five years and are monthly observations. Possibly the market cannot distinguish between cyclically and secularly high and low rates

CHART 4
Forward and Spot One-Year Rates on Government Securities

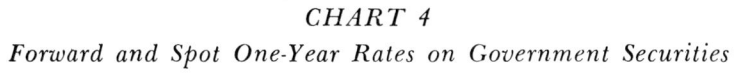

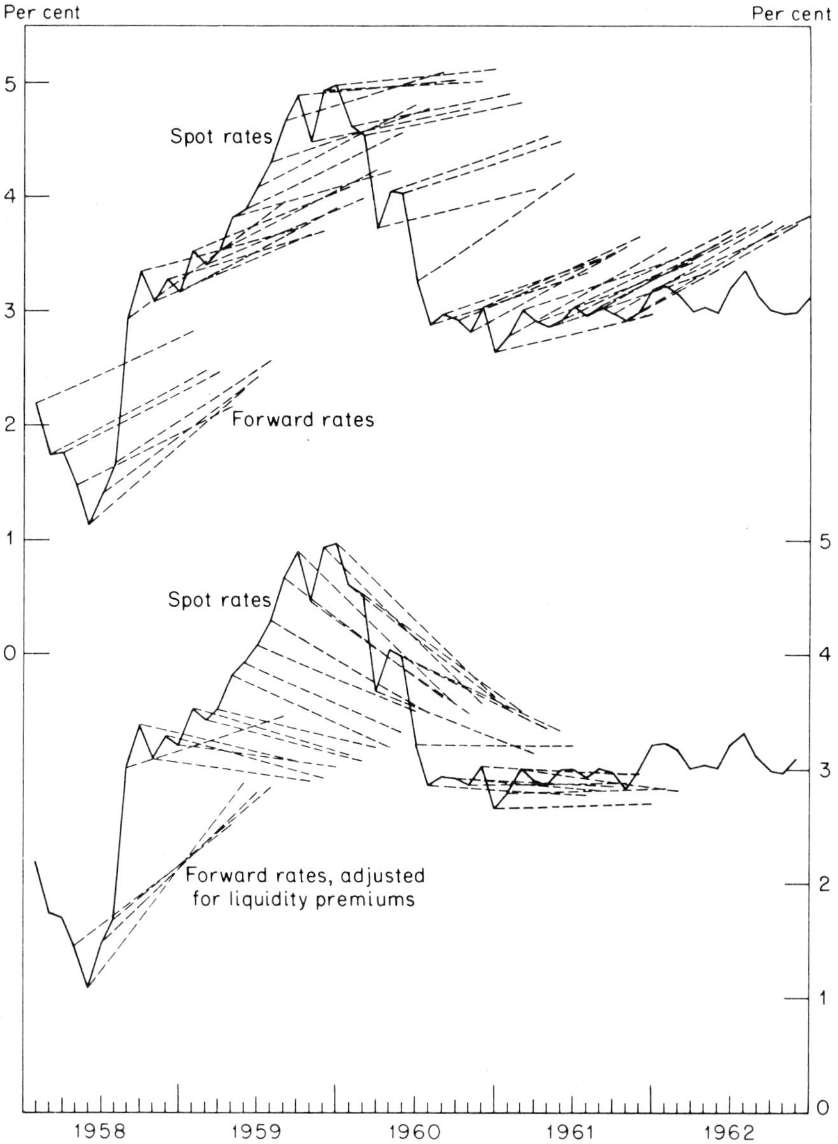

SOURCE: Derived from Treasury yield curves, using one- and two-year rates. The rates in the upper section of the chart are from Table B-1; those in the lower section, from Tables B-2 and B-3.

of interest. If the market could anticipate cyclical changes better than secular changes, there would be an observed difference in forecasting accuracy over one cycle as compared with many cycles. When spot rates are high cyclically, their subsequent change is quite different from that when they are high secularly. If the forecasts of the market are the same in either case, studies of the accuracy of forecasts will lead to different results depending upon the time period under investigation.

Another avenue for explaining secular and cyclical differences is the study of the stability of liquidity premiums over time. Before the 1930's, judging by Durand's data, liquidity premiums were much smaller or possibly nonexistent. There seems to have been a structural change in the economy in this respect since the early 1930's. Possibly this can be attributed to the abolition of interest on demand deposits, or perhaps to a change in attitude toward risk that led to changes in liquidity premiums. In any case, instability of liquidity premiums could account for the observed difference in the secular and cyclical correlations of forward and one-year spot rates.

Still another avenue for explaining these findings is data limitations. Durand did not use a criterion such as least squares for his curve fitting. He fitted only yield curves that do not have maximums or minimums. When his yield curves were not flat throughout, they either increased or decreased monotonically with term to maturity and then flattened out. By definition, Durand could not observe a yield curve with any other shape. He offers no explanation for this self-imposed constraint.

In the postwar period, when short-term rates have been above long-term rates, yield curves have been hump shaped. These curves at first rise with term to maturity, reach a maximum, and then fall and finally flatten out. It is difficult to believe that this was not also true during some of the fifty-five years encompassed by Durand's data. If one examines both the data and the curves fitted, it is clear that humped yield curves could just as correctly have been fitted some of the time. Since this was not done, one- and two-year rates derived from Durand's curves are probably high estimates of true one- and two-year rates, and are high relative to longer maturities.

The Cyclical Behavior of the Term Structure of Interest Rates

If one examines the yield curves Durand fitted to data in the 1920's, yield curves for governments and corporates have opposite slopes for three of these years. Indeed, the data on governments presented above show short-term governments yielding, on average, less than long-term governments in the 1920's. Durand's findings on corporates indicate just the opposite.

Another difficulty, ignored by both Hickman and Meiselman, is the fact that Durand's yield curves are drawn for coupon bonds. Hence, the Hicksian formula for internal rates of return or yield to maturity, which implicitly assumes the absence of coupons, is inappropriate for computing forward rates. To compute forward rates correctly, both coupons and yields to maturity, or internal rates of return, must be known.

If one accepts the view that yield curves were, on average, positively sloped during the fifty-five years Durand observed, then coupon rates for bonds with one or two years to maturity must have, on average, exceeded internal rates of return. If coupons exceed internal rates of return, then it can be shown that the Hicksian formula underestimates forward rates. However, the measurement errors which can be attributed to ignoring coupons seem to be small compared to those attributable to uncertainties regarding the shape of Durand's yield curves. Using coupons of 6 per cent, errors in computing forward rates seem to be on the order of two or three basis points.

The figures on bill rates collected provide new data to repeat Meiselman's experiments. The results of tests of the expectations hypothesis using Treasury bills are tabulated in Table 3. Treasury bills with terms to maturity of less than six months are the source of price data.

Since these correlations are all unambiguously significant, they provide additional support for Meiselman's view that a relationship between expectations and the term structure of interest rates exists. His major conclusion—that there is validity in the expectations hypothesis—is sound, despite his failure to isolate unanticipated changes in interest rates and to recognize that forward rates were not expected rates. What about the data Meiselman used? How are the liquidity premiums related to the level of rates for Durand's

TABLE 3

CORRELATION OF FORECAST REVISIONS WITH ERRORS
AS DEFINED BY MEISELMAN,
1958-61[a]

Type of Error	Correlation Coefficient	Regression Coefficient
1. Error in forecast of two-week rates with changes in expected two-week rates two weeks hence	.37	.40
2. Error in forecast of two-week rates with changes in expected two-week rates eleven weeks hence	.36	.26
3. Error in forecast of four-week rates with changes in expected four-week rates twelve weeks hence	.21	.27
4. Error in forecast of six-week rates with changes in expected six-week rates eighteen weeks hence	.59	.62
5. Error in forecast of eight-week rates with changes in expected eight-week rates sixteen weeks hence	.85	.59

Source

Line 1: Correlation of changes in predicted two-week bill rates with forecasting errors implied by the expectations hypothesis, i.e., with the difference between predicted and actual two-week rates. The error terms were obtained by comparing predictions implied by four- and two-week bill rates with actual two-week bill rates two weeks later. The prediction changes were obtained from the difference between the predicted two-week rate four weeks hence and then, two weeks later, two weeks into the future. The first prediction was obtained through the use of six- and four-week bills; the second was measured through the use of four- and two-week bills.

Line 2: Correlation of changes in predicted two-week bill rates as inferred from eleven- and nine-week bills and, two weeks later, from nine- and seven-week bills with the difference between predicted and actual two-week rates. The independent variables for this and the test described in Line 1 are identical.

Line 3: Correlation of changes in predicted four-week bill rates with the prediction errors implied by the expectations hypothesis. The independent variable is the difference between predictions implied by eight- and four-week bill rates and, four weeks later, actual four-week bill rates. The dependent variable--the prediction change--is the difference between the predicted four-week rate implied by the sixteen- and twelve-week bill rates and, four weeks later, the predicted four-week rate implied by the twelve- and eight-week bill rates.

Line 4: Correlation of changes in predicted six-week bill rates with prediction errors. The independent variable is the difference between predictions implied by twelve- and six-week bill rates and, six weeks later, actual six-week bill rates. The dependent variable, the prediction change, is the difference between the predicted six-week rate implied

NOTES TO TABLE 3 (concluded)

by the twenty-four- and eighteen-week rates and, six weeks later, the predicted six-week rate implied by the eighteen- and twelve-week bill rates.

Line 5: Correlation of changes in predicted eight-week bill rates with prediction errors. The independent variable is the difference between predictions implied by sixteen- and eight-week bill rates and, eight weeks later, actual eight-week bill rates. The dependent variable, the prediction change, is the difference between the predicted eight-week rate implied by the twenty-four- and sixteen-week rates and, eight weeks later, the predicted eight-week rate implied by the sixteen- and eight-week rates. This may be illustrated by the following sample calculation. On November 28, 1961, the sixteen-week rate was 2.61, and the eight-week rate 2.51. The expectations hypothesis implies that the eight-week rate eight weeks hence, on January 23, 1962, is expected to be 2.71. This is twice the sixteen-week rate less the eight-week rate. The actual eight-week rate on January 23, 1962, eight weeks after November 28, was 2.61. Hence the error is -.10. The first prediction in the data from which Line 5 was derived was inferred from the twenty-four- and sixteen-week rates on November 28, 1961. These were 2.72 and 2.61 respectively. Hence the predicted rate for March 20, 1962, which is three times the twenty-four-week rate less twice the sixteen-week rate, is 2.94. Eight weeks later, on January 23, 1962, the sixteen-week rate was 2.72, and the eight-week rate 2.61. Hence the predicted eight-week rate for March 20, 1962, was 2.83, and the prediction change -.11.

[a] The existence of liquidity premiums implies that the errors as defined by Meiselman are typically larger than the true errors the market committed. The true errors are the differences between forward rates minus liquidity premiums and spot rates; the true forecast revisions are the observed revisions net of liquidity differences.

data? The regression of the difference between forward and subsequently observed spot one-year rates against current one-year rates reveals little variation in the "error" with the level of spot rates. The regression coefficient is .09 with the standard error of .06, and only about 4 per cent of the variation is explained. In contrast, for the same regression using forward and spot one-year governments for the 1958–61 cycle, the regression coefficient is one, with a standard error of .10, and 70 per cent of the variation is explained. Clearly the different between forward and spot rates for the government data appears to be much more sensitive to variations in spot rates than it is for Durand's data.

The reappearance of a seasonal in the money market in recent years implies that it is possible to repeat Macaulay's experiment with a new body of data. If the expectations hypothesis is correct, seasonal adjustment factors ought to vary systematically with term to maturity. More specifically, just as the time money rates "anticipated" seasonal changes in call money rates, changes in, say, sixty-day seasonal adjustment factors ought to "anticipate" changes in thirty-day factors. Hence it should be possible to construct a set of seasonal adjustment factors for sixty-day rates if the factors for thirty-day rates are known; knowledge of seasonal adjustment factors for thirty-day bills implies knowledge of these factors for bills of longer maturity.

To test this hypothesis, weekly moving seasonal adjustment factors were computed for twenty-seven- and fifty-five-day bills for 1959, 1960, and 1961, using bid prices unadjusted for bankers discount. If the expectations hypothesis is correct, a set of seasonal adjustment factors for fifty-five-day bills constructed out of twenty-seven-day factors ought to be more strongly correlated with actual fifty-five-day factors than just twenty-seven-day factors alone. For every week, a simple average of twenty-seven-day factors for that week and for four weeks in the future was computed. This should be, according to the expectations hypothesis, a fifty-five-day seasonal. The correlation of this set of theoretical seasonal adjustments with actual fifty-five-day adjustment factors was stronger than the correlation between twenty-seven- and fifty-five-day factors. Converse results ought to hold for a fifty-five-day seasonal adjustment constructed out of twenty-seven-day factors, if the adjustment factors are obtained by averaging the current twenty-seven-day seasonal with that of four weeks in the past. This seasonal, when correlated with the fifty-five-day seasonal directly computed, ought to exhibit less correlation than exists for the relationship between twenty-seven- and fifty-five-day factors. Hence the rank ordering of cor-

TABLE 4

COEFFICIENTS OF CORRELATION BETWEEN WEEKLY SEASONAL FACTORS IN TREASURY BILL RATES, 1959-61

Type of Seasonal Program	Average of 27-Day Seasonals (Current and 4 Weeks Hence) with 55-Day Seasonal	27-Day Seasonal with 55-Day Seasonal	Average of 27-Day Seasonals (Current and 4-Weeks Past) with 55-Day Seasonal
Multiplicative	.844	.811	.520
Additive	.804	.750	.486

relations alone, quite apart from the question of whether or not there is a significant difference between the correlations, constitutes evidence that the market anticipates seasonal movements in rates. These findings are summarized in Table 4.

The Durand data and the data collected for this study provide a means for discriminating between expectations and liquidity preference on the one hand and market segmentation on the other. The market segmentation hypothesis implies that differences in maturity account for differences in substitutability between securities. If maturity differences are held constant, then the substitutability or the cross elasticity of demand ought also to be constant. In contrast, the expectations hypothesis implies that a seven-year security is more like an eight-year security than a one-year security is like a two-year security. The expectations hypothesis implies that the common element in two securities separated by a year in maturity increases monotonically as term to maturity increases.

Similarly, if one accepts the view that liquidity preference varies with the level of rates, then the premium increases as the level of rates increases. Hence, if securities separated by a year in term to maturity are examined, one should expect the common element to increase as term to maturity increases. Because both liquidity preference and expectations have common implications, this test does not discriminate between them. It does, however, produce evidence that must be regarded as discriminating between expectations and liquidity preference on the one hand and market segmentation on the other.

The foregoing tests were performed with two independent sets of data: the Durand data that Meiselman used and yields to maturity, for the latest cycle, read off the yield curve in the *Treasury Bulletin* by a draftsman. The test employed was a simple rank test. The expectations and liquidity preference hypotheses imply that the correlations between securities separated by a year in term to maturity ought to decrease monotonically as term to maturity increases. Hence the theory forecasts a set of ranks that can be compared with the observed ranks to see if they are positively correlated.

Consistent results were obtained using these independent sets of data. The ranks predicted by the expectations and liquidity preference hypotheses and the actual ranks were highly correlated. Each set of data consisted of nine pairs of ranks. Using the Olds rank correlation test, and interpreting the implications of the liquidity preference and expectations as implying a one-tail test, both significance levels were under 2 per cent.[32]

The foregoing analysis of the implications of liquidity preference and expectations for the correlation between the yields of securities separated by a constant time span as term to maturity increases also implies that yield curves ought to flatten out with maturity. Given that the weights assigned to marginal rates of interest, in the determination of average or internal rates of return, decrease with maturity, then yield curves must flatten out with maturity. This assumes that the variance in forward rates is independent of term to maturity.

The evidence presented supports the Hicksian theory of the term structure of interest rates; it supports the view that both expectations and liquidity preference determine the term structure of interest rates. These results show that forward rates should be interpreted as expected rates plus a liquidity premium. If forward rates are so interpreted, then the expectations of the market seem to forecast subsequently observed short-maturity spot rates; the relationship between expected and subsequently observed spot rates cannot be rationalized as the workings of chance.

With respect to the market segmentation hypothesis, the evidence is less clear. These findings show that this hypothesis is not of the same magnitude as liquidity preference and expectations in the determination of the term structure of rates. The fact that forward rates embody short-term forecasts of spot rates that have a perceptible degree of accuracy implies that liquidity premiums are stable. Hence the scope for the impact of market segmentation upon the term structure of rates must be limited. The Meiselman findings on the relationship between what he termed forecast revisions and errors support this view, as do the tests presented here.

[32] The test employed is described in W. Allen Wallis, "Rough-and-Ready Statistical Tests," *Industrial Quality Control*, March, 1952.

A proponent of market segmentation may argue that these tests, in particular, the test based on holding absolute maturity differences constant while varying relative maturity differences, are based on incorrect interpretations of market segmentation. Economic literature does not contain a statement of the market segmentation hypothesis that is as rigorous as those available either for liquidity preference or expectations. Therefore, the possibility of misinterpretation cannot be easily dismissed. The Walker findings which deal with the root of the market segmentation hypothesis are particularly relevant. He showed that institutions have sharply changed the maturity composition of their holdings in response to market forces. This seems to strike at the very foundation of the market segmentation thesis. The only contrary evidence uncovered—this is also subject to the same uncertainties about its relevance—is the existence of negative forward rates in the bill market. Such occurrences seem to be rare, and therefore relatively insignificant, but should not be dismissed entirely. There is always the possibility that more of such evidence exists or that the effects of market segmentation are relatively subtle and the tests employed too crude to detect its existence.[33]

---

[33] There were negative forward rates in the bill market in the 1930's. At that time rates were relatively low and taxes on bank deposits in Illinois were high enough to make it profitable to take a negative yield rather than be subject to taxation on deposits.

2

WHY LIQUIDITY PREFERENCE EXISTS

IT IS CLEAR from the analysis of the data used by Hickman and Meiselman and the evidence presented here (the historical data going back to 1920 in the next chapter and the comparisons of predicted and actual bill rates), that the expectations hypothesis alone does not explain the term structure of interest rates. The existence of upward bias in the estimates of future short-term rates suggests that at least one other variable is relevant—liquidity preference. Liquidity preference can be regarded as a force that causes forward rates to be biased and high estimates of short-term rates. Its effects can be measured by the difference between the mean value of forward and expected rates; i.e., by the difference between actual forward rates and the yields that short-term securities would have to have for the expectations hypothesis to yield unbiased estimates of future short-term rates. This raises the questions why does liquidity preference exist and how does it affect the term structure of interest rates?

Keynes, who introduced the term to economics, used liquidity preference to describe a preference of the market, abstracting from differences in yield, for assets that are immune to capital losses produced by interest rate changes. If uncertainty as to the future course of interest rates exists, then the market has a choice of taking risks with respect to capital values, income streams, or some combination of both. On balance, the evidence indicates that the market prefers to take risks of income stream changes. That is, the market prefers money to securities if differences in pecuniary yields are ignored.[1] Consequently, equalizing yield differentials exist be-

---

[1] See J. M. Keynes, *The General Theory of Employment, Interest and Money*, New York, 1936, pp. 168 ff. This view may also be found in Hicks, *Value and Capital*, p. 151.

tween money and securities that offset differences in relative vulnerability to capital losses through interest rate changes. Since the risk of capital losses attributable to holding securities is directly related to term to maturity, security yields ought also to vary directly with term to maturity. Just as the "interest rate" equilibrates the net return to holding money and "securities," the term structure of interest rates equilibrates the net return to holding securities of varying terms to maturity and money. The shorter the term to maturity of a security, the smaller is its vulnerability to capital loss, and hence the greater its liquidity and the smaller the yield differential between that security and money. Therefore, liquidity preference constitutes, by implication, a theory of the term structure of interest rates. It is a theory, not of the level of interest, but of interest differentials. Linked with risk avoidance, it implies a positively sloped yield curve.[2]

Short maturities, in addition to being less vulnerable to capital losses attributable to interest rate changes, have lower costs of conversion to cash than long maturities. Since the cost of converting securities to cash increases with term to maturity, the liquidity of securities, in this specialized sense, decreases with term to maturity. Consequently, the market ought to prefer short- to long-term securities. Like risk avoidance, transactions costs imply a rising yield curve as a function of term to maturity. Given the existence of this inverse relationship, is it strong enough to account for the normal difference in yields between long- and short-term governments? Over the three latest reference cycles, the average yield of the longest-term governments has been about one hundred basis points greater than the average yield of 91-day Treasury bills.[3] For three-

[2] This view of liquidity preference appears in David W. Lusher, "The Structure of Interest Rates and the Keynesian Theory of Interest," *Journal of Political Economy*, April 1942, p. 274. He says: "Each rate of interest in the structure of rates may be looked upon as balancing the advantages of holding cash." Similarly, Abba P. Lerner in *Economics of Control*, New York, 1944, p. 343, says: "Competition equalizes the *sum* of money and liquidity yields." Samuelson regards liquidity preference as an explanation of the existence and level, not of the interest rate, but of the differential between the yield on money and the yields on other assets. See Paul A. Samuelson, *Foundations of Economic Analysis*, Vol. 80, Harvard Economic Studies, Cambridge, Mass., 1947, pp. 122–124.

[3] If the first postwar cycle (October 1945 to October 1949) is included in this calculation, a greater average spread between bills and long-term governments

month Treasury bills, turnaround costs (that is, the costs of getting into and out of bills) typically are around one-sixty-fourth of 1 per cent of value at maturity, or about sixteen cents.[4] In contrast, corresponding costs for the longest of long-term governments are about eight-thirty-seconds, or $2.50. Insofar as bills are bought at the weekly auction and held to maturity, transactions costs for their holders are zero. If bills are bought at auction and not held to maturity, or if bought from a dealer and held to maturity, then the relevant transactions costs are about eight cents. Bonds can, of course, also be bought directly from the Treasury and held to maturity. However, bonds are sold by the Treasury relatively infrequently, and infrequently held to maturity.

The extent to which transactions costs can account for the observed difference in yields on three-month bills and longer maturities is a function of the holding period. In general, the longer the holding period, the less the relative disadvantage of longer maturities, and conversely. If bills and long-term bonds are compared for a holding period of three months, and if bills are bought at auction and held to maturity and long-term bonds are bought and sold through a dealer, then the equalizing yield differential is equivalent to 1 per cent per year. That is, 4 per cent is the net yield to the

---

results. The average size of the bill-bond spread is larger for the first than for any of the three succeeding cycles. It is excluded on the grounds that the bill rate for most of the first postwar cycle was largely a fictitious rate. The governmental policy that stabilized the prewar term structure of interest rates led to a bill yield that was low relative to the yield on bonds. The reduction in the size of the bill-bond spread between the first and the succeeding postwar cycles constitutes additional evidence that the reported bill rate was out of line with the yield on long-term governments and was, in effect, a nominal rate.

[4] The Commission on Money and Credit in their report, *Money and Credit*, Englewood Cliffs, New Jersey, 1961, p. 118, attributes the higher transactions costs to the greater risks to dealers of trading in long-term governments. This explanation implies that these costs must have been lower during the period when the structure of interest rates was pegged. In fact, the spreads between bid and asked prices were about half of what they are now.

Dealer operations are highly leveraged, more so than those of most banks, and the value of government securities as collateral is inversely related to term to maturity. The Joint Economic Committee, *A Study of the Dealer Market for Federal Government Securities*, Washington, D.C., 1960, p. 92, reports that dealer margin requirements for Treasury bills are one-quarter of 1 per cent. They are one-half of 1 per cent for certificates, 1 per cent for bonds under five years, 2 per cent for bonds between five and ten years to maturity, and 3 per cent for maturities over ten years.

holder of long-term governments, if the yield to maturity is 5 per cent; 3 per cent is the net yield, if the yield to maturity is 4 per cent, etc.[5] This implies that an investor who calculates on an expected value basis, and who wants to invest for three months and assumes that the yields of long-term securities will average 1 per cent more than bills, will find no difference between bills and long-term governments. Consequently, for holding periods less than three months, the equalizing yield spread between bills and bonds is in excess of an annual rate of 1 per cent. For more than three months, it is less than 1 per cent. For six months, the equalizing yield differential on an annual basis is one-half of 1 per cent, and for one year, one-quarter of 1 per cent.

If one assumes transactions costs for bills of one-thirty-second, which is a more realistic assumption, the equalizing yield differential between bills and nine- to twelve-month governments for a three-month holding period is twelve to thirteen basis points (this assumes a two-thirty-second turnaround cost for the longer maturity). When nine- to twelve-month governments are compared with three- to five-year governments for a one-year holding period, the equalizing yield differential is about six basis points (this assumes a two-thirty-second turnaround cost for the shorter, and a four-thirty-second cost for the longer maturity).

Actual yield differentials (implied by Table 7) have exceeded the equalizing yield differentials computed above. This suggests that pure transactions costs do not fully account for the observed yield differentials. However, one must be careful in making this comparison. During the period encompassed by Table 7, there was a secular trend upward in yields which caused holders of long-term securities to incur capital losses. Therefore, for the long bond-bill comparison, it is necessary to add the assumption that the market failed to anticipate the secular rise in rates.[6]

---

[5] A $2.50 transaction cost would come to $10.00 on an annual basis, hence it would reduce the gross yield by 10/1000, or 1 per cent.

[6] This assumption is consistent with a number of other observations. It is consistent with the observed difference between correlations of forward and one-year spot rates considered for just one cycle and for the entire 1901–54 period when a secular downward movement was followed by a secular upward movement in rates. It is consistent with the finding that the differential between bills and nine- to twelve-month governments cannot be explained by transactions cost

On the whole, this analysis suggests that yield differentials as a function of term to maturity cannot be rationalized completely as a consequence of transactions cost differences. Risk avoidance must be introduced. Unfortunately this statement and the calculations upon which it is based are not as straightforward as they appear. Typically, bid and asked prices overstate spreads; most transactions take place within this range and almost none outside of it. This tends to make the advantage of investing in long-term securities somewhat better than these calculations indicate. On the other hand, because the market for long-term governments is relatively thinner than that for short-term governments, the price at which a transaction takes place is more likely to be affected by its size. As a result, more transactions in long-term governments are brokerage transactions than is true of bills. Virtually all bills are bought and sold for the account and risk of dealers, whereas for long-term governments, dealers less frequently buy and sell from their own inventories for their customers.[7] Hence, an estimated 25 per cent of all trading in long-term governments represents brokerage transactions. From the point of view of the holders of long-term securities, this alone makes them less liquid than bills because it takes more time to consummate a brokerage transaction than a dealer

---

differences alone. For this comparison, trends in rates are virtually irrelevant. And finally, it is consistent with the composite yield curve for 1901–54 implied by the Durand data. The difference between the average yields of long- and short-term securities cannot be explained by transactions costs. Yet on balance, the trend in interest rates for this entire period is, if anything, down.

[7] This seems to be a direct result of a thin market. Dealers that expect long-term bond prices to fall would be willing to buy all offered for their own account if they could either turn around and sell them at the existing market price or sell short another issue very similar to the issue offered. To the extent that hedging is possible, dealers can win trading profits without incurring risks of capital losses. Since only three or four dealers deal extensively in long-term governments, it is not unusual to find that they all have the same price expectations. If they expect a fall in prices, they are willing to buy at current prices only what it is possible to hedge; they will buy the rest only at less than the current price.

Bid and asked prices widen when prices are expected to fall and narrow when they are expected to rise as a result of changes in the cost of carrying inventories. Of course, quoted bid and asked prices often are not meaningful numbers when dealers are unwilling to take positions.

Brokerage costs for a complete turnaround, a purchase and a sale, are usually two-thirty-seconds or less. However, would-be brokerage transactions are subject to the risk of never being consummated. They make sense when customer market expectations differ from those of dealers.

trade. Most of the time, and for most transactions, the difference between bid and asked prices for bills and long-term bonds measures the relative costs of transactions. For large transactions, however, say over two million (which would be regarded as a small transaction in bills), bonds are substantially less liquid than bills when dealers expect yields to rise. Hence, bid and asked prices with the usual spreads understate the relative costs of trading in the long-term bonds.[8]

Although ambiguities exist in the measurement of transactions costs for long-term securities, it seems fairly clear that average yield differentials as a function of term to maturity, if cyclical effects upon yield differentials are ignored, are too large to be solely explained by transactions costs. Hence, the Keynesian view, that short-term securities are preferred in order to avoid risks of capital losses, does have a role to play in explaining observed yield differentials. Motives other than transactions costs must be introduced to explain the observed yield differentials; the rationale for the holding of money substitutes is the same as the rationale for the holding of money proper.

The Keynesian view of the term structure of interest rates has implications that are, in a crude sense, consistent with observed yield differentials over the cycle. This view does more than imply that yield curves ought to rise with term to maturity. Vulnerability to capital loss is not a linear function of term to maturity; it increases at a decreasing rate with increases in maturity. Hence average yields ought to rise with term to maturity at a decreasing rate. To illustrate: an unanticipated permanent increase in short-term rates from 3 to 6 per cent implies, for securities bearing a 3 per cent coupon, that (a) a perpetuity would lose half its value, (b) a bond with a twelve-year term to maturity would fall in value by 25 per cent, and (c) a bond with four years to maturity would fall in value by about 10 per cent.[9]

---

[8] There is a danger of making too much of this point. It is clear that the market for long-term governments is characterized by a larger volume of trading than the most heavily traded corporate security, A. T. & T. bonds.

[9] This point appears in Harry C. Sauvain, "Changing Interest Rates and the Investment Portfolio," *Journal of Finance,* May 1959, pp. 235 ff., and Malkiel, *Quarterly Journal of Economics,* May 1962, p. 202, theorem 3.

These authors fail to point out that the greater variance in the prices of long-

The evidence for postwar business cycles shows that average yields rise at a decreasing rate as term to maturity increases. For the three latest cycles, the spread between bills and nine- to twelve-month governments is thirty basis points. This implies a rise in the average rate, for this segment of the yield curve, of about forty-eight basis points per year. The yield spread between nine- to twelve-month governments and three- to five-year governments is forty-three basis points, or a rise in the average rate of about seventeen basis points per year. The differential in yields between three- to five-year governments and twenty-year governments is twenty-eight basis points. Hence the average rate for the segment encompassed by these two maturities rises about one and three-quarter basis points a year. Similar conclusions are implied by the composite yield curve constructed from Durand's data [10] (see Chart 2).

The Keynesian view, that the market prefers short- to long-term securities to avoid the risks of capital losses, does not imply that participants in this market need be characterized as risk avoiders generally. An enterprise that is quite willing to speculate in what it regards as its principal line of economic activity may rationally be unwilling to run risks of capital losses on its holdings of money substitutes. As long as it can speculate more efficiently in its principal activities, there is no inconsistency between its risk aversion in bond markets and risk acceptance or preference in other markets.

This argument is symmetrical for money holders. Some money is held in preference to long- and short-term governments to avoid risk. Yet it does not follow that money holders are generally risk avoiders. To determine whether they are or not involves an over-all

---

term vis-à-vis those of short-term bonds is an economic, and not an arithmetic, proposition which rests on the assumption that errors in forecasting future spot rates are positively correlated. In principle, prices of long-term bonds could fluctuate less than short-term bonds. To illustrate: Consider the price behavior of a one- and a two-year bond, assuming that errors in forecasting the current one-year rate are negatively correlated with errors in forecasting the one-year rate one year hence. If long-term bonds did not fluctuate in price more than short-term bonds, then Meiselman would not have observed that forecasting errors and forecast revisions were positively correlated.

[10] Malkiel (*ibid.*, p. 206) also concludes that, as term to maturity increases, yield curves flatten out and the marginal vulnerability to interest rate changes decreases.

evaluation of their total risk positions. Knowledge of just money holdings, or money substitute holdings, is not enough.[11]

Acceptance of the Keynesian empirical judgment that the market for governments is largely composed of risk avoiders does not necessarily imply that short-term rates will be systematically lower than long-term rates. It suggests that speculative opportunities will exist for those who are willing to bear risks, i.e., those who are willing to calculate on an expected value basis. More specifically, it suggests that there ought to exist gains to be derived from being short on near maturities and long on distant maturities.[12]

Such a financing short is rarely undertaken. The going rate for borrowing securities is one-half of 1 per cent. This is, in effect, a call loan rate for governments. It can be terminated at the option of either the supplier of securities on loan or the borrower. Securities on loan usually can be recalled on twenty-four hours notice. Borrowers of securities must maintain collateral, in the form of other governments, with the lenders of securities. The borrower usually has the right to substitute from day to day among the securities held as collateral, subject to the constraint that the aggregate value of the collateral be equal to or greater than the securities borrowed.[13] The short seller must, when the lender wants his securities back, either arrange for another loan or close out his short position. In any case, he must reacquire the securities initially borrowed through a new loan or by buying them in the market. Since bills are held as money substitutes, the calling up of borrowed bills by lenders during their term to maturity is to be expected. Insofar as longer-term securities than bills are borrowed, the trans-

---

[11] Similarly, the fact that a firm holds cash balances does not imply that it is a creditor and is expecting deflation. Nor does the existence of bonds outstanding for a firm imply that it is a net debtor. A more complex analysis of the entire structure of monetary assets and monetary liabilities is necessary before such a judgment can be reached.

[12] It is important to recognize that this is not arbitrage. Changes in interest rates will produce dramatic effects on the net equity position of a speculator in such a position. A rise in rates implies capital losses, and a fall, capital gains.

[13] This is one of the principal factors that make the loan rate as high as one-half of 1 per cent. The lenders of securities, usually banks, incur clerical costs as a result of frequent changes in the collateral offered by borrowers, typically government bond dealers. Bond dealers usually offer the securities held in their position as collateral.

actions costs for borrowing and reborrowing are reduced at the expense of higher rates of interest. Consequently, the short seller has the choice of costs in the form of low interest rates (i.e., the yields of very short maturities) with borrowing and reborrowing problems, or somewhat higher rates and somewhat more stable borrowing arrangements.[14]

The costs of maintaining and financing a short position are usually so large that it is more economical for dealers to finance the holding of long-term governments through bank loans or repurchase agreements. As a consequence, the yields of short-term securities are brought into line with long-term yields, not directly through a short position in near-term maturities, but indirectly through borrowing in the money market (i.e., a short position in bank credit). For the suppliers of funds for the money market—banks and nonfinancial institutions such as industrial enterprises—providing credit to dealers is an alternative to holding bills. Consequently, the bill rate is linked to the cost of short-term dealer financing through both the demand and the supply side of the market. As a result of this interrelationship between the yield on long-term governments on the one hand and financing costs of dealers in the money market on the other, an equilibrium spread exists between the yields of short- and long-term governments. In equilibrium, the marginal costs of borrowing to finance the holding of long-term governments should equal the yield spread between bills and bonds. This spread measures the marginal costs of the resources required for additional commitments in long-term securities financed by short-term liabilities.

Insofar as costs of speculating on the spreads between bills and bonds exist, speculation will not operate to make the expected value of bond yields the same as bill yields. Bonds will yield more than bills and this differential will be a function of the costs of being short on near maturities and long on distant maturities. That such positive costs exist is strongly supported by the empirical evidence. Their existence implies that forward rates implicit in the

---

[14] Joint Economic Committee, *Study of the Dealer Market*, p. 59, reports that the probability of a transaction in a government security is inversely related to its term to maturity.

term structure of interest rates, if one accepts the expectations hypothesis, will be biased estimates of future short-term rates. The interesting question is, how large are the costs of simultaneously taking long positions on distant maturities and short positions on near maturities?

The government bond market does not exist in isolation. At the short end it is an integral part of the money market, and at the long end, of the capital market. A number of financial institutions (in particular, commercial banks, the Federal Reserve System, savings banks, investment banks, savings and loan associations, life insurance companies, government, municipal, and corporate bond dealers, and the Federal National Mortgage Association), although conventionally regarded as being extremely conservative, are speculators in the money and capital markets. The average maturity of their assets is greater than the average maturity of their nonequity liabilities. Hence, they are speculators in the sense that they are long on long-term money and short on short-term money and by and large, live on the carry. Their economic viability is a function of the spread in yields between their assets and their liabilities.

Each of these classes of financial institutions operates in distinct and overlapping portions of the money and capital markets. Moreover, the specifics of their modus operandi differ. Savings banks, savings and loan associations, and life insurance companies issue forms of time deposits to finance their acquisition of assets. Commercial banks and the Federal Reserve Banks hold many short-term assets, but they issue demand deposits. Dealers and investment bankers use bank loans and similar short-term credit instruments; life insurance companies hold extremely long-term assets. These institutions all operate the same way in one essential respect—they reduce the yields on long maturities and raise the yields on short maturities. The existence of an average yield differential between bills and bonds of about one hundred basis points over the three latest reference cycles reflects the marginal costs of speculation to reduce this yield differential. It emerges despite the work of all of these financial institutions and reflects the fact that speculative activity, like most economic activities, is not cost free.

This analysis suggests that there exists an equalizing difference in yields between short- and long-term governments. This yield differential measures, at the margin, the relative advantages of short- and long-term governments as money substitutes, i.e., as a means of avoiding risks of interest rate changes and keeping down transactions costs. It is analytically the same as the yield differential between cash and long-term bonds that is often referred to as "the rate of interest," but it is smaller because short-term governments are less than perfect substitutes for cash balances.

The analysis also suggests that the spread between long- and short-term governments need not be the same as the spread between long- and short-term corporate bonds. Corporates have higher transactions costs which limit the value of short-term corporates as money substitutes. Hence, the corporate short-long spread ought to be smaller than the corresponding yield spread for governments. The usual brokerage charge for buying and selling a corporate bond that is listed on the New York Stock Exchange and sells for about $1,000 is $5.00, or one-half of 1 per cent. However, there is some question as to whether the cost is comparable to the spread between the bid and asked prices for governments. The latter includes the cost of the services of the dealer who takes a position, whereas the former does not. A more relevant comparison is the over-the-counter, one-hundred bond corporate market. This is where most bonds are bought and sold. Dealers take positions and have buying and selling prices comparable to the bid and asked price for governments. For the bonds of A. T. & T., the corporate security with the widest market, the most frequently found spread is three-quarters, or $7.50 per bond for long-term bonds. This ranges down to about one-sixteenth for the very shortest-term bonds.

These findings strongly support the Keynesian theory of "normal backwardation" which rests on the premise that speculative services on net balance come at a positive pecuniary cost to society. This theory has common implications for commodity markets and the markets for government securities.[15] In commodity markets, the

---

[15] John M. Keynes, *A Treatise on Money*, Vol. II: *The Applied Theory of Money*, London, 1930, pp. 142 ff. This theory also appears in Hicks, *Value and Capital*, pp. 136 ff.

theory implies that forward prices are biased and low estimates of future spot prices; the prices of forward commitments rise as their term to maturity shortens. Similarly, in the money and capital markets, the theory implies that forward rates are biased and high estimates of spot rates; the prices of forward commitments rise as their term to maturity shortens.

Normal backwardation views speculators as selling insurance services to risk avoiders (or hedgers, in the case of commodity markets). This particular type of insurance, in common with insurance generally, comes at a cost to society; the nonpecuniary returns to speculators as a class are not large enough to compensate them for the opportunity costs of the resources used to provide their services. In contrast to this view, Professor Knight and, subsequently, Professor Telser enunciated the view that hedgers or risk avoiders provide the services of a casino to speculators.[16] Futures markets, in their view, are places where a speculator or gambler can get relatively favorable betting odds, i.e., where the house take is relatively small. Consequently, they contend that forward prices could represent unbiased or even high estimates of the spot value of future commitments. The nonpecuniary returns to speculators can be large enough to compensate or more than compensate for the opportunity costs of the resources employed in providing speculative services.

These views of futures markets imply that individuals choose either to bear risks or to hire speculators to bear risks, at either positive, zero, or negative cost. In fact the choice confronting the holders of governments is either to bear risks of capital losses or risks of income instability, or some combination of both. Given the stocks of long- and short-term securities that have been outstanding during the period under investigation, society has on balance chosen to bear the risks of income uncertainty and to hire speculators at positive costs to bear the risks of capital uncertainty.[17]

---

[16] Frank H. Knight, *The Economic Organization*, New York, 1951, p. 79; Lester G. Telser, "Reply," *Journal of Political Economy*, August 1960, p. 406.

[17] Although society has, on balance, paid for the service of bearing the risk of capital losses, this does not imply that those who have provided this service have been unable to hedge their risks. Insurance companies, because of the predictability of their expenditures, have been important suppliers of this service. Commonly, authors have referred to insurance company liabilities as long term. It is

The costs of bearing the risks of income uncertainty appear to have been negative. If "normal backwardation" is interpreted to mean avoiding the risk of capital losses and not risk avoidance per se, then these findings support the Keynesian view.[18]

The existence of bias in the estimates of future short-term rates, implied by the Lutz-Meiselman variant of the expectations hypothesis, implies that securities of different terms to maturity are not perfect substitutes for one another when the holding period yields are equal. The existence of positive costs of arbitrage and speculation is a necessary condition for the existence of liquidity premiums. Whether there exists any yield relationship for which securities of different maturities are perfect substitutes depends on the character of cost conditions in the production of speculative services.

The evidence presented suggests that the futures market for money is in a sense segmented into many markets that are partly isolated from one another through the existence of costs of converting long- into short-term securities. This market, like that for beer in the United States, is segmented by the existence of transportation costs.[19]

---

clear that these liabilities are not long term in the same sense that the issuer of a long-term bond has a long-term liability. The cash surrender value of an insurance policy is clearly a short-term liability, as are the rights to borrow against cash surrender values. Similarly, death benefits may be regarded as constrained short-term liabilities.

[18] The empirical evidence that has been brought to bear on the issue of bias in forward rates in commodity markets has not been interpreted as providing clear support for either the Knightian or Keynesian position. In large part, the source of the difficulty has been that a very small bias in forward prices could provide the going rate of return on capital to speculators. Yet the presence of a small bias, particularly in a world in which prices have not been absolutely stable, is very hard to detect. The relevant literature on this point includes Lester G. Telser, "Futures Trading and the Storage of Cotton and Wheat," *Journal of Political Economy*, June 1958, p. 233, a subsequent exchange between Cootner and Telser in the August 1960 issue of the same journal; and Holbrook Working, "New Concepts Concerning Futures Markets and Prices," *American Economic Review*, June 1962, pp. 449–454.

[19] Specialists in the market for government securities are fond of arguing that no one regards long- and short-term securities as perfect substitutes for one another (presumably when holding period yields are alike), hence they are not perfect substitutes in the market. Although this reasoning leaves something to be desired, the conclusion appears to be valid.

A striking piece of evidence, already cited, that corroborates the views of

The introduction of costs of converting long- into short-term securities implies that, if the provision of speculative services in this market is an increasing cost industry, the relative yields of short- and long-term securities can be affected by the maturity composition of outstanding stocks. Hence, these yields can be influenced by open market operations; whether or not the Fed (Federal Reserve System) follows a bills-only policy can make a difference. Insofar as the Fed buys bills, and bills only, the decrease in the stock of bills outstanding implies an increase in the volume of speculative services produced by financial intermediaries and hence a rise in yield differentials. Conversely, insofar as the Fed buys only long-term governments, the decrease in the stock of these securities outstanding implies a decrease in the volume of speculative services produced by financial intermediaries and hence a fall in yield differentials. How large this fall or rise will be depends upon the supply elasticity of speculative services.

Increasing costs of providing speculative services imply that variations in the stocks of long- and short-term governments outstanding will affect long-short yield differentials. This is a sufficient but not a necessary condition for open market operations to affect yield curves. The existence of constant costs for speculative services implies that a specified range of yield differentials will exist; this range will be analogous to gold points under a gold standard. Depending upon how wide the counterparts to gold points are, there still remains some scope for open market operations as a means of influencing the long-short yield differential. Probably the strongest grounds for believing that increasing costs are relevant is the argu-

---

market practitioners is the term structure of bill yields during September 1960. These observations show that positive costs of arbitrage must exist. Hence, by an a fortiori argument, positive costs of providing speculative services must also exist. Assuming that the market prefers to avoid risks of capital loss, these costs imply a positively sloped yield curve. The rarely observed negative forward rates were produced apparently by corporate treasurers who, to meet tax obligations on December 15, mechanically bought Treasury bills that matured on December 15 in order to match tax expenditures with receipts.

The existence of these costs of arbitrage or speculation implies that forward rates can vary from expected rates. Forward rates are usually higher than expected rates and the difference can be accounted for by risk avoidance and speculative costs. Insofar as this is what is meant by market segmentation, the position of specialists in the market is correct.

ment that there exist variations among investors with respect to their willingness to bear risk. Hence, as the volume of speculative services produced increases, the costs of financial resources to speculators will also increase.

A theoretical frame of reference similar to that enunciated in this section seems to be implicit in the writings of many economists in the field of debt management. For example, Simons believed that short-term debt is a better money substitute than long-term debt.[20] This implies that there must be a pecuniary yield differential between long- and short-term debt since aggregate or total yield on both types of debt must be equal. Hence, a positively sloped yield curve is implied.[21] An advocate of a pure expectations hypothesis would regard short- and long-term debt as having equal inflationary potential; variations in the maturity distribution of outstanding debt would have no effect on aggregate demand.

[20] See "On Debt Management," and "Rules Versus Authorities in Monetary Policy," in Henry C. Simons, *Economic Policy for a Free Society*, Chicago, 1948.
[21] Simons (*ibid.*, p. 225) recognizes this implication when he says, ". . . issue-yields will normally vary directly with maturities."

3

HOW SHORT- AND LONG-TERM INTEREST RATES HAVE BEHAVED CYCLICALLY

THE BEHAVIOR of the term structure of interest rates during business cycles can be summarized by:
1. Relative yields of short- and long-term securities at cycle peaks and troughs.
2. Variance in yields over the cycle as a function of term to maturity.
3. Average yields over the cycle as a function of term to maturity.
4. Correspondence of peaks and troughs in yields with business cycle peaks and troughs.

In the first part of this chapter, the behavior of the term structure of interest rates since the end of World War II is described. Then the yields on government securities during the period between the two world wars are examined. Finally, the cyclical variation and relative level of yields on long- and short-term non-governmental obligations since 1858 is reviewed.

Since the end of World War II, there have been pronounced specific cycles in interest-rate series. The peaks and troughs of these series have been closely associated with turning points in business conditions. For the first four complete business cycles following the war, intra-cyclical changes in interest rates were, on the average, 50 per cent greater than cycle-to-cycle changes. Although there was a strong trend upward in interest rates during this time, peak-to-trough and trough-to-peak changes in rates were large relative to secular changes (see Table 5).

Relative to secular trends, peak-to-trough changes in short maturities were especially large. From the trough in the earliest of

TABLE 5

CYCLICAL CHANGES IN YIELDS OF GOVERNMENT SECURITIES,
OCTOBER 1945–FEBRUARY 1961[a]

Business Cycle			Absolute Values (per cent)			Changes	
Trough	Peak	Trough	Trough	Peak	Trough	Trough to Peak	Peak to Trough
A. Three-month Treasury bills							
10/45	11/48	10/49	.38	1.12	1.05	.74	−.07
10/49	7/53	8/54	1.05	2.10	.88	1.05	−1.22
8/54	7/57	4/58	.88	3.59	1.16	2.71	−2.43
4/58	5/60	2/61	1.16	3.53	2.29	2.37	−1.24
B. Nine- to twelve-month governments							
10/45	11/48	10/49	.82	1.21	1.08	.39	−.13
10/49	7/53	8/54	1.08	2.40	.62	1.32	−1.78
8/54	7/57	4/58	.62	3.89	1.40	3.27	−2.49
4/58	5/60	2/61	1.40	4.32	2.79	2.92	−1.53
C. Three- to five-year governments							
10/45	11/48	10/49	1.15	1.67	1.36	.52	−.31
10/49	7/53	8/54	1.36	2.74	1.68	1.38	−1.06
8/54	7/57	4/58	1.68	3.95	2.41	2.27	−1.54
4/58	5/60	2/61	2.41	4.63	3.52	2.22	−1.11
D. Twenty-year governments							
10/45	11/48	10/49	2.07	2.42	2.20	.35	−.22
10/49	7/53	8/54	2.20	3.09	2.52	.89	−.57
8/54	7/57	4/58	2.52	3.62	3.11	1.10	−.51
4/58	5/60	2/61	3.11	4.24	3.77	1.13	−.47
Averages, Four Cycles, 1945–61							
Three-month Treasury bills							1.72	−1.24
Nine- to twelve-month governments							1.98	−1.48
Three- to five-year governments							1.60	−1.00
Twenty-year governments							.87	−.44

Source: Series are adjusted for seasonal variation by the National Bureau. All series, except the twenty-year government bond series, are compiled by the Federal Reserve Board and are reported monthly in the *Federal Reserve Bulletin*. The twenty-year government bond series is compiled by the Morgan Guaranty Trust Co.

[a] During this time, there was a half cycle of experience with six-month Treasury bills. For this half cycle, May 1960 through February 1961, 182-day bills decreased from 3.50 to 2.60, a change of 98 basis points. (A basis point is equal to .01 per cent.)

The three-month bill series is, strictly speaking, not directly comparable with the other series. Yields of bills are discount yields based on a 360-day, and not the usual 365-day year. Hence, bill yields understate correct yields, and the true yield differentials between bills and other securities is less than the differences reported here. In general, the higher the absolute level of bill rates, the greater the bias. For bill yields of 2.5 to 3 per cent, the bias is around eight basis points.

these four cycles to the trough in the latest, a period of more than fifteen years, interest-rate changes for bills and nine- to twelve-month governments were less than the trough-to-peak changes in the two latest cycles.

Since the trough-to-peak increases in short-term rates were greater than the corresponding increases in long-term rates, the former rose relative to the latter during expansions. Conversely, short-term rates fell relatively during contractions, since their peak-to-trough decreases were greater. Consequently, short-term rates were relatively high about cyclical peaks and low about troughs.

The relative changes in short- and long-term yields over the cycle imply systematic changes in yield differentials or spreads between maturity classes. Since short-term rates were typically below long-term rates, spreads between them narrowed during the course of an expansion and widened during a contraction. Absolute differences became smaller when rates increased and larger when rates decreased. For the three latest cycles (1949–61), an absolute increase in bill yields of one-hundred basis points was associated with an average decrease in the spread between bills and twenty-year government bonds of forty-three basis points.[1]

This evidence also indicates that short-term rates were more variable absolutely over the cycle (see Table 6). However, the general belief that the longer the term to maturity, the less volatile the yield, is not entirely supported. In each of the three latest cycles, nine- to twelve-month governments were more variable absolutely than three-month Treasury bills. This suggests that the absolute variability in yields over the cycle first increased and then decreased with the term to maturity.

In contrast to the spreads between bills and long-term governments, the yield differential between bills and nine- to twelve-month governments widened over the course of the post-World War II expansions and narrowed during the contractions. For the three latest cycles, an absolute increase of 1 per cent in the yields of bills was associated with an average increase of eighteen basis points in the differential.

[1] The slope of the regression equation relating the absolute size of the yield differential between bills and bonds to the absolute level of bill yields was .43.

TABLE 6

VARIATION IN YIELDS OF GOVERNMENT SECURITIES DURING FOUR BUSINESS CYCLES, OCTOBER 1945–FEBRUARY 1961

Business Cycle, Trough to Trough	Three-Month Bills	Nine- to Twelve-Month Governments	Three- to Five-Year Governments	Twenty-Year Governments
Standard deviation				
10/45 to 10/49	.334	.159	.197	.163
10/49 to 8/54	.375	.434	.405	.259
8/54 to 4/58	.817	.886	.605	.311
4/58 to 2/61	.874	1.031	.698	.321
Coefficient of variation[a]				
10/45 to 10/49	44.59	16.19	14.43	7.40
10/49 to 8/54	25.41	27.45	20.51	10.04
8/54 to 4/58	35.58	35.44	20.78	10.10
4/58 to 2/61	31.87	30.72	18.15	8.22

[a] Standard deviation stated as a percentage of the mean.

TABLE 7

AVERAGE YIELD OF GOVERNMENT SECURITIES DURING FOUR BUSINESS CYCLES, OCTOBER 1945–FEBRUARY 1961
(per cent)

Business Cycle, Trough to Trough	Three-Month Bills	Nine- to Twelve-Month Governments	Three- to Five-Year Governments	Twenty-Year Governments
10/45 to 10/49	.749	.982	1.365	2.203
10/49 to 8/54	1.476	1.581	1.975	2.580
8/54 to 4/58	2.296	2.500	2.912	3.079
4/58 to 2/61	2.742	3.356	3.846	3.904
Unweighted average of the cycle averages				
10/45 to 2/61	1.816	2.105	2.524	2.942

Unlike the variability in yields over the cycle, average yields varied monotonically with term to maturity (see Table 7). The longer the term to maturity, the higher the yield. This suggests that yield curves were, on the average, positively sloped during the four 1945–61 cycles.[2] Slopes were invariably positive from the end

TABLE 8

TIMING OF SHORT- AND LONG-TERM YIELDS OF GOVERNMENT SECURITIES AT BUSINESS CYCLE PEAKS AND TROUGHS, OCTOBER 1945–FEBRUARY 1961

	Lead (−) or Lag (+) in Months, at Business Cycle Peaks and Troughs								
	10/45 T	11/48 P	10/49 T	7/53 P	8/54 T	7/57 P	4/58 T	5/60 P	2/61 T
1. Three-month bills	a	a	a	−1	−2	−1	+2	−5	−2
2. Nine- to twelve-month governments	a	+4	−3	−1	0	0	+2	−4	−1
3. Three- to five-year governments	+5	−3	−3	−1	0	0	+2	−5	−5
4. Twenty-year governments	+4	−1	+2	−1	0	−1	0	−4	−5

[a] No specific cycle.

of the war through 1955, but in more recent years, curves with negatively sloped segments have been observed.

In general, the steepness or the degree to which yield curves were positively inclined decreased from trough-to-peak. Only about peaks could one observe yield curves with negative slopes (see Table 5 and Charts 5 and 6). Negatively sloped yield curves, or more

[2] Yield curves depict, at one point in time, average rates of interest as a function of term to maturity. They portray the average yield of securities that are homogeneous with respect to credit-worthiness and vary only in term to maturity. Marginal rate of interest curves bear the same relation to yield curves that marginal cost curves bear to average cost curves. These show marginal rates of interest as a function of term to maturity and are implied by yield curves. A one-to-one correspondence exists between points on marginal rate of interest curves and yield curves. Marginal rate of interest curves are usually referred to as forward rates; they are the incremental or marginal costs of borrowing for two years instead of one year, etc. The marginal cost of extending a one-year maturity for an additional year is the forward rate for one-year money one year hence. Estimates of current yield curves for government securities are reported monthly in the *Treasury Bulletin*.

CHART 5

Yields of U.S. Government Securities, 1942–53

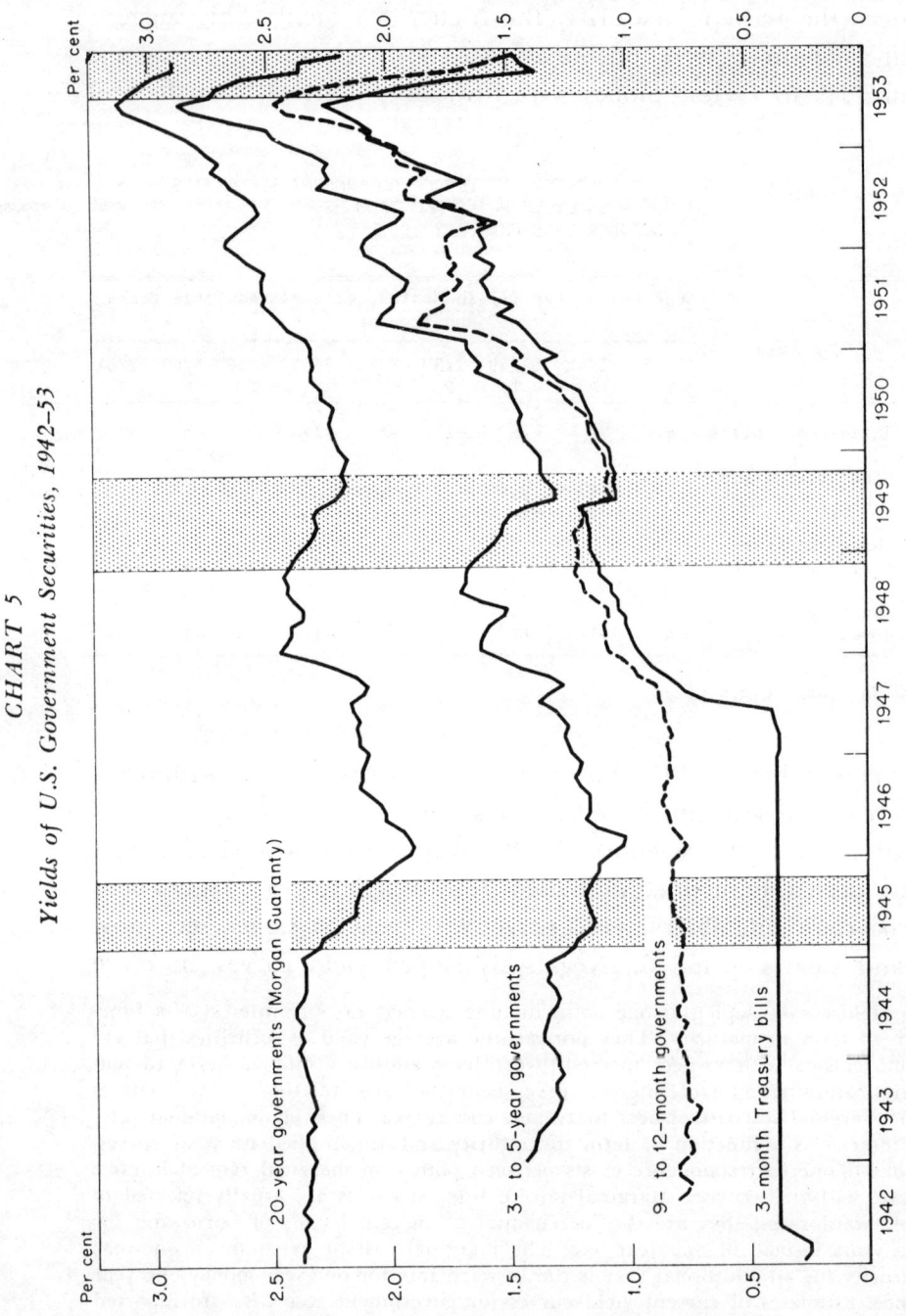

NOTE: Shaded areas represent business cycle contractions; unshaded areas, expansions.

correctly yield curves with negatively sloped segments, occurred about the 1957 and 1960 cyclical peaks.

During the 1945–61 business cycles, the peaks and troughs in the specific cycles of governments were roughly synchronous with those in business activity. For bills, the degree of synchronization is poorest for the earliest cycle and roughly on a par with longer-term governments for the three later cycles (see Table 8, and Charts 5 and 6). The striking coincidence of timing in specific and business cycles suggests that the forces that determine the peaks and troughs of business cycles must also play a role in determining those in the specific cycles of time series of government obligations.[3]

Seasonally adjusting the time series used had relatively little effect on the dating of specific cycle peaks and troughs. If anything the correspondence of specific with business cycle peaks was closer after adjustment (see Table 9).

TABLE 9

TIMING OF PEAKS AND TROUGHS IN BILL RATES USING SEASONALLY ADJUSTED AND UNADJUSTED DATA

Bill Rates	Business Cycle Turns					
	P	T	P	T	P	T
Unadjusted						
Date of specific cycle turn	4/53	6/54	10/57	6/58	12/59	1/61
Lead (−) or lag (+) in months, relative to business cycle turn	−3	−2	+3	+2	−5	−1
Adjusted						
Date of specific cycle turn	6/53	6/54	6/57	6/58	12/59	12/60
Lead (−) or lag (+) in months, relative to business cycle turn	−1	−2	−1	+2	−5	−2

The time series upon which these uniformities in the cyclical behavior of interest rates are based appear in Charts 5 and 6. These time series unfortunately do not go back before World War II. In the 1920's and 1930's, the interest on virtually all of the long-term governments outstanding was partially tax exempt, and on short-term governments wholly tax exempt. The issuance of Treas-

[3] Of the thirty-two specific cycle turning points, nineteen preceded the corresponding business cycle turning point, seven succeeded, and six were coincidental. On average, specific cycle turning points led by 0.9 months. At peaks, the average lead was 1.6 months; at troughs, 0.3 months.

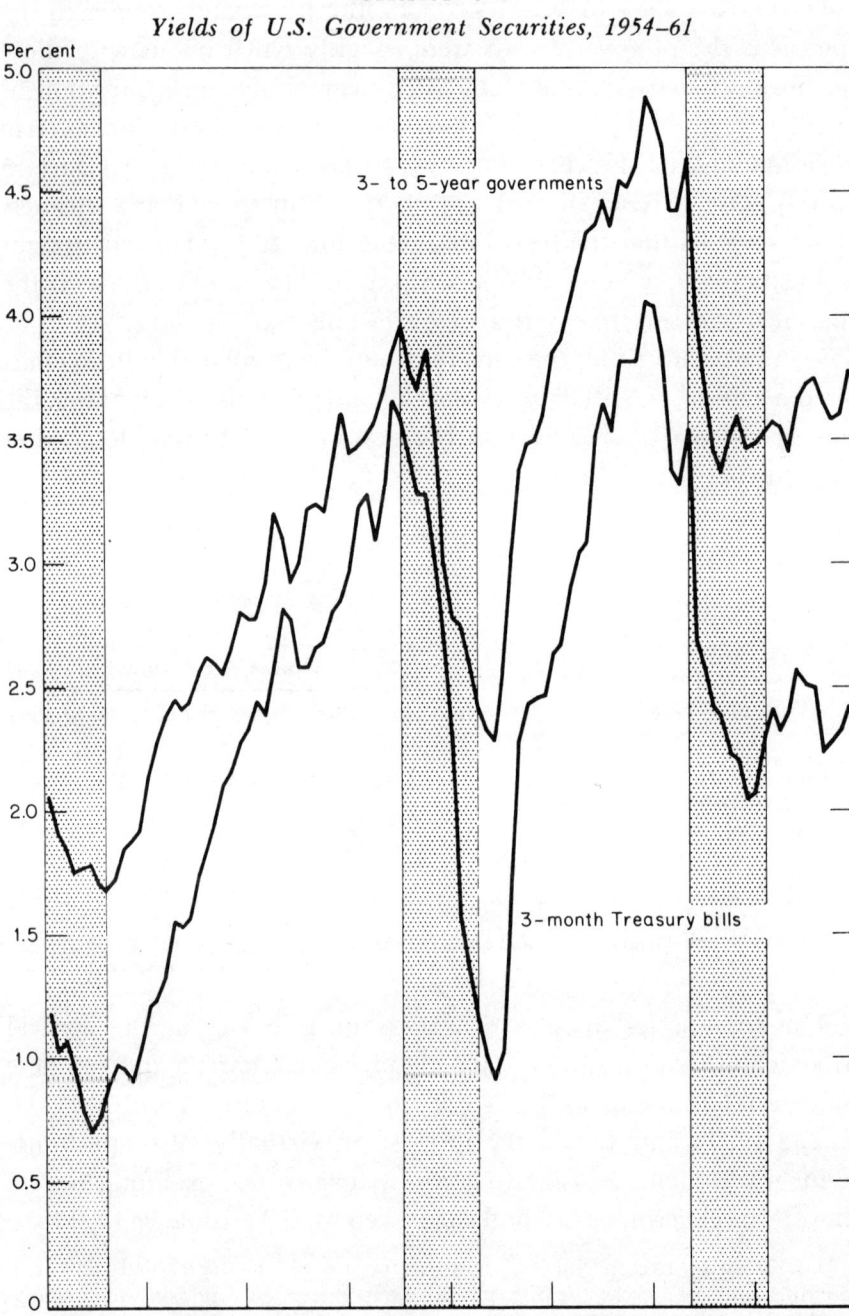

CHART 6
Yields of U.S. Government Securities, 1954–61

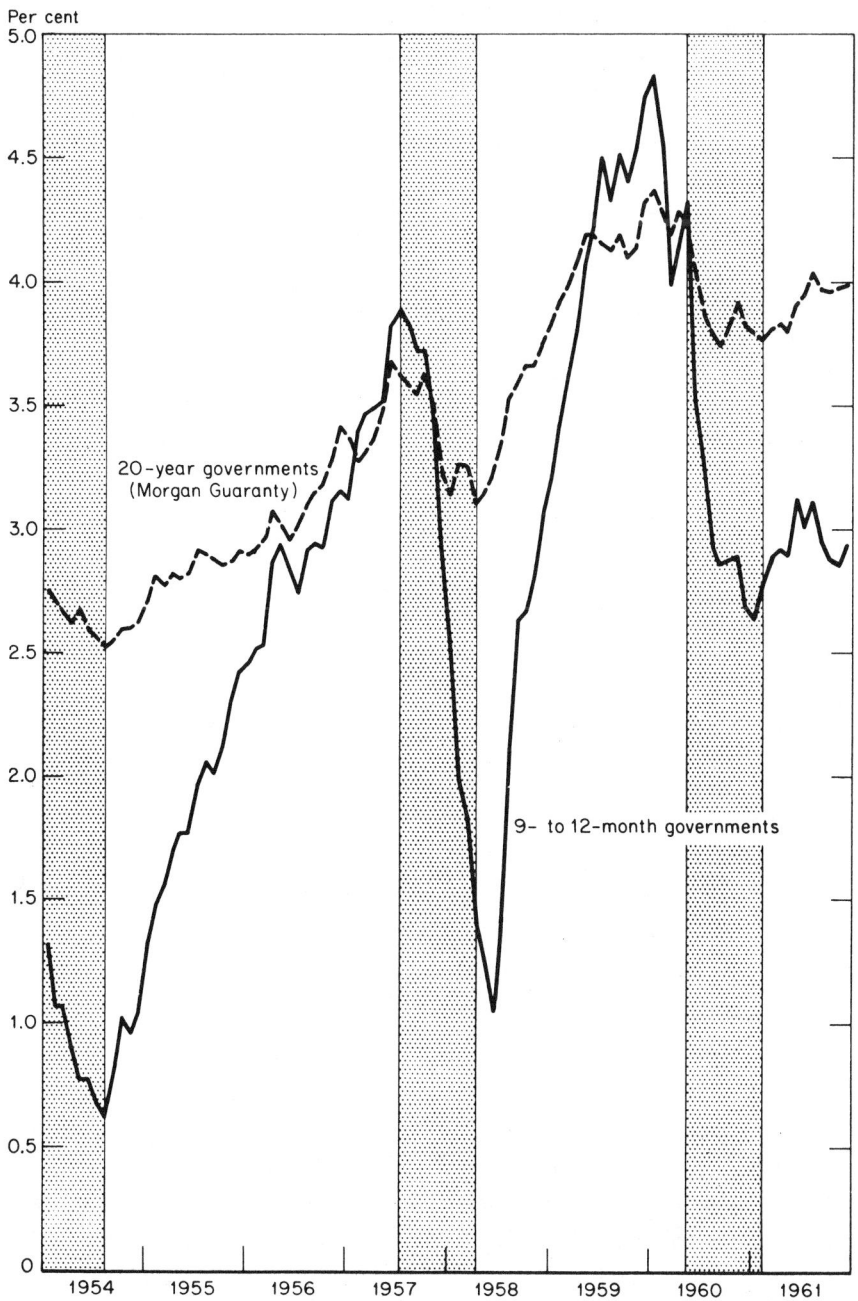

NOTE: Shaded areas represent business cycle contractions; unshaded areas, expansions.

ury bills began in December 1929, but offerings in the following two years were so infrequent and irregular that a continuous series does not begin until 1931. Before 1931, yields on short-term governments could be measured by a series on three- to six-month Treasury notes and certificates that began in 1920 and ended in 1933. The income derived from holding these notes and certificates was fully tax exempt. In summary, prewar data that depict the relative yields of short- and long-term governments over the cycle are not directly comparable to postwar data, and the short-term data for

CHART 7

Yields of U.S. Government Securities, 1920–33

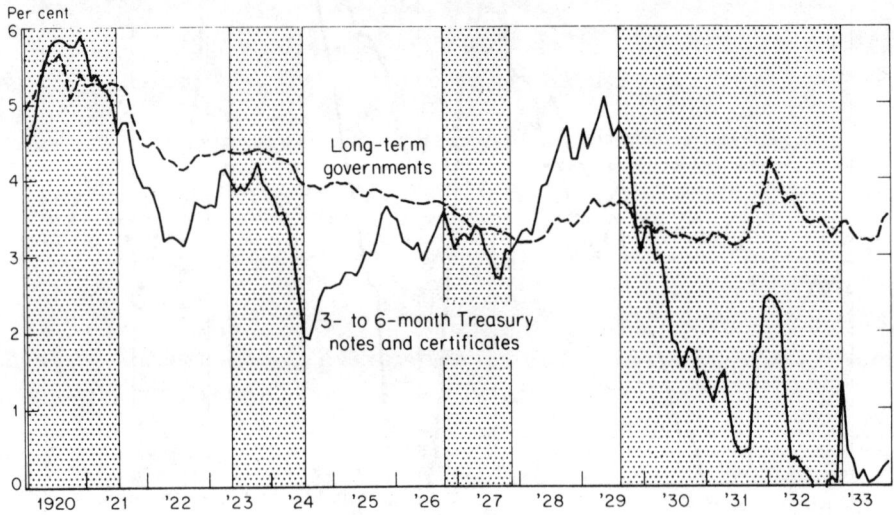

NOTE: Shaded areas represent business cycle contractions; unshaded areas, expansions.

the 1920's are not directly comparable to those of the 1930's. Despite these limitations, this body of data constitutes an important and fruitful source of knowledge. It can reveal how the yields of short- and long-term securities varied cyclically, and the extent to which specific and reference cycles coincided.

Between 1920 and 1956, there were two subperiods when the rate of interest for three- to six-month Treasury notes and certificates was higher than the rate on long-term governments. These were from June of 1920 through March of 1921, and from January 1928 through November 1929. For the balance of this period, short-term government yields were always below long-term yields. The 1920–21 reversal of the usual relationship was both shorter and less pronounced than the later reversal. The maximum yield differential during the 1920–21 reversal was sixty-seven basis points; the average

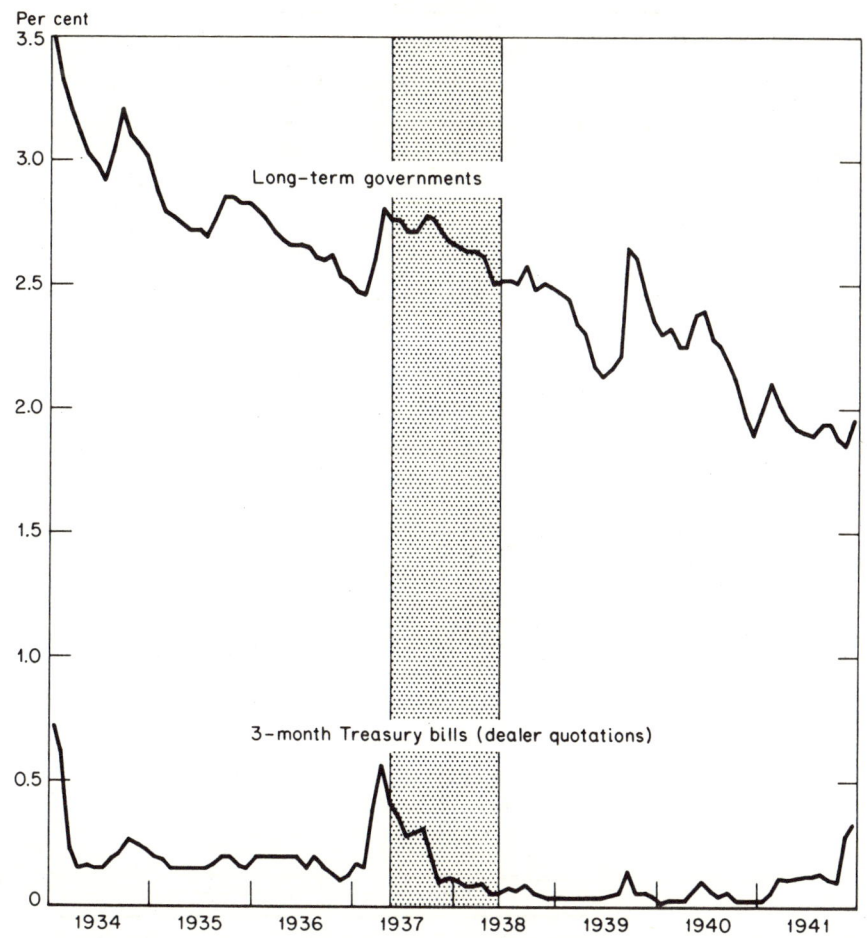

CHART 8

Yields of U.S. Government Securities, 1934–41

NOTE: Shaded areas represent business cycle contractions; unshaded areas, expansions.

differential was thirty-three basis points. For the later period, 1928–29, the maximum differential was 145 basis points; the average was ninety-one. For nine months in 1957 and eight months in 1959 and 1960, nine- to twelve-month government yields were above the

TABLE 10

CYCLICAL CHANGES IN YIELDS OF GOVERNMENT SECURITIES, 1921-45

	Business Cycles			Absolute Values			Changes	
	Trough	Peak	Trough	Trough	Peak	Trough	Trough to Peak	Peak to Trough
A.	Long-term governments[a]			5.26	4.37	3.94	-.89	-.43
	July 1921-May	1923-July	1924	3.94	3.68	3.23	-.26	-.45
	Nov. 1927-Aug.	1929-Mar.	1933	3.23	3.71	3.42	.48	-.29
	Mar. 1933-May	1937-June	1938	3.42	2.80	2.58	-.62	-.22
	June 1938-Feb.	1945-Oct.	1945	2.58	2.38	2.35	-.20	-.03
B.	Short-term governments[b]							
	July 1921-May	1923-July	1924	4.60	3.95	1.92	-.65	-2.03
	July 1926-Oct.	1926-Nov.	1927	1.92	3.58	3.04	1.66	-.54
	Nov. 1927-Aug.	1929-Mar.	1933	3.04	4.70	1.34	1.66	-3.36
	Mar. 1933-May	1937-June	1938	2.29	.65	.02	-1.64	-.63
	June 1938-Feb.	1945-Oct.	1945	.05	.38	.38	.33	0

[a]First Three Cycles: Board of Governors of the Federal Reserve System, *Banking and Monetary Statistics*, Washington, D.C., 1943, Table 128, p. 468.
Last Two Cycles: Federal Reserve Board bill dealer quotations series (average yields on all outstanding fully taxable bonds due or callable after 12 years for March 1933 and after 15 years for May 1937, June 1938, Feb. 1945, and Oct. 1945).

[b]First Three Cycles: Three- to six-month Treasury notes and certificates, *Banking and Monetary Statistics*, Table 122, p. 460.
Fourth Cycle: Treasury bill new issues, *Banking and Monetary Statistics*, Table 122, p. 460.
Fifth Cycle: Three-month Treasury bill dealer quotations series from the *Federal Reserve Bulletin*.

TABLE 11

AVERAGE YIELD AND STANDARD DEVIATION IN YIELDS OF GOVERNMENT SECURITIES DURING FIVE BUSINESS CYCLES, 1921-45

Business Cycle, Trough to Trough	Long-Term Governments		Short-Term Governments	
	Average Yield	Standard Deviation	Average Yield	Standard Deviation
June 1921-July 1924	4.39	.29	3.71	.56
July 1924-Nov. 1927	3.68	.23	3.04	.42
Nov. 1927-March 1933	3.44	.24	2.44	1.63
March 1933-June 1938	2.89	.26	.26	.32
June 1938-Oct. 1945	2.36	.18	.22	.16

Source: See Table 10.

twenty-year bond rate. The maximum differential in 1959–60 was twice that in 1957; seventy-eight basis points compared with thirty-eight (see Charts 6 and 7).

For the prewar cycles, the trough-to-peak and peak-to-trough movements in short-term rates were typically greater than the movements in long-term rates (see Table 10). In this respect, the cyclical behavior of interest rates before and after World War II are similar. Only for the wartime cycle, 1938–45, when the Treasury bill rate was constant for long periods as a result of the government support program, is the variation in the long-term rate greater than in the short-term rate. This seems to be directly attributable to the pegging of the rate on three-month bills by the government.

TABLE 12

TIMING OF SHORT- AND LONG-TERM YIELDS OF GOVERNMENT SECURITIES AT BUSINESS CYCLE PEAKS AND TROUGHS, 1921–45

Government Securities	Lead(−) or Lag(+) in Months, at Business Cycle Peaks and Troughs										
	7/21 T	5/23 P	7/24 T	10/26 P	11/27 T	8/29 P	3/33 T	5/37 P	6/38 T	2/45 P	10/45 T
Short-term	+13	+5	+1	−11	−2	−3	−4	−1	+19	a	a
Long-term	+13	+5	a	a	+4	−5	+47	+5	+40	−7	+6

[a] No specific cycle.

For each of the five prewar cycles shown in Table 11, short-term government yields were, on average, below long-term yields (see Table 11). Hence, for each of the nine complete cycles in the 1921–61 period for which yields of long- and short-term governments are currently available, yield curves for governments probably had a positive slope, on the average. Similarly, the yield variance of short-term governments, with the exception of the wartime cycle, was greater than that of long-term governments.

The association of specific with business cycle turning points is stronger for the postwar cycles than for the five cycles from 1921 to 1945 (see Table 12). Between 1921 and 1945, unlike the later period, there are turning points of interest rate cycles whose association with business cycle peaks and troughs is tenuous at best. In the

THE CAPITAL MARKETS

CHART 9

Average Pattern of Long-Term and Short-Term Interest Rates in the United States During Fourteen Business Cycles, 1858–1914

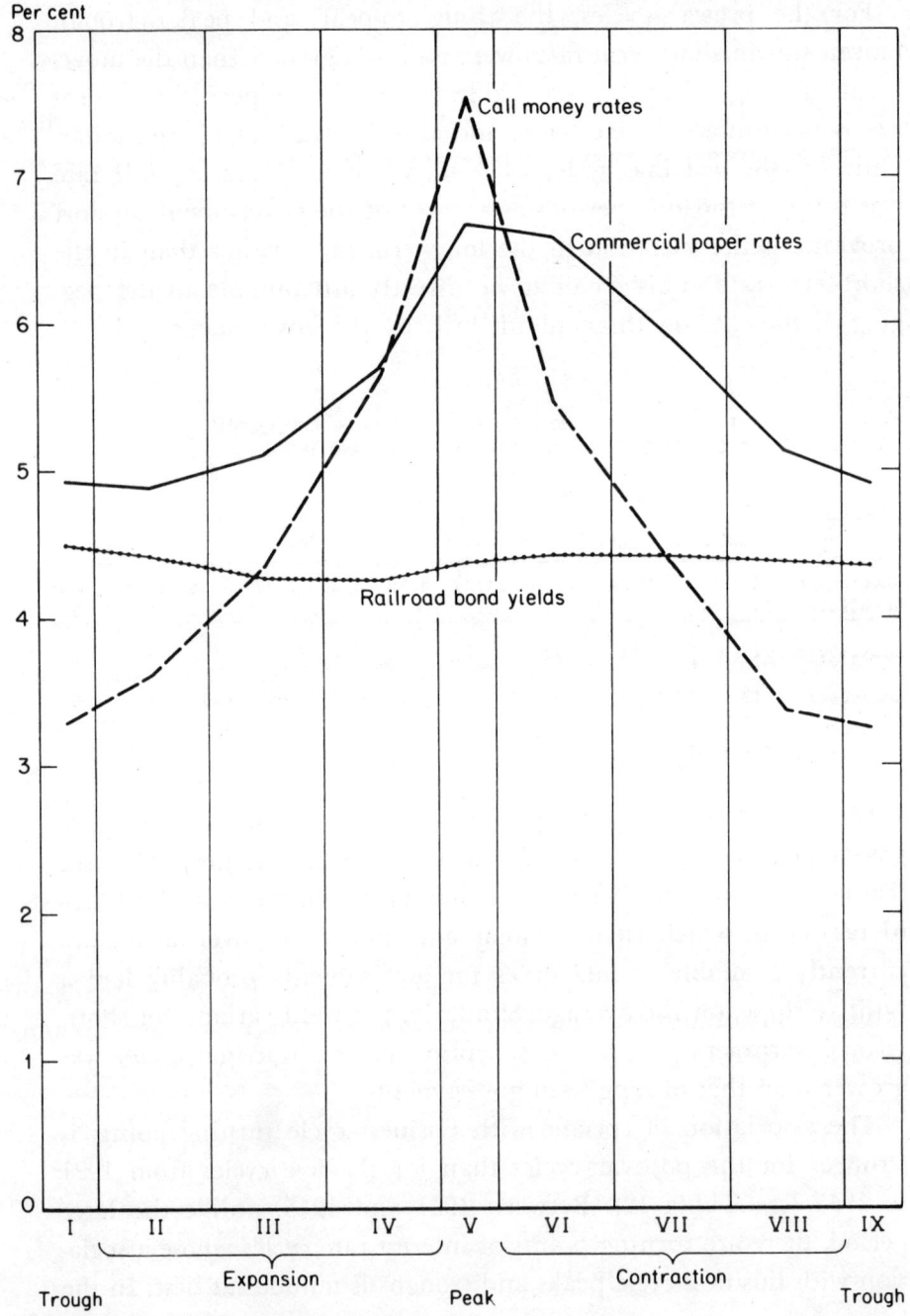

SOURCE: See notes following Chart 12.

CHART 10

Average Pattern of Long-Term and Short-Term Interest Rates in the United States During Five Business Cycles, 1914–33

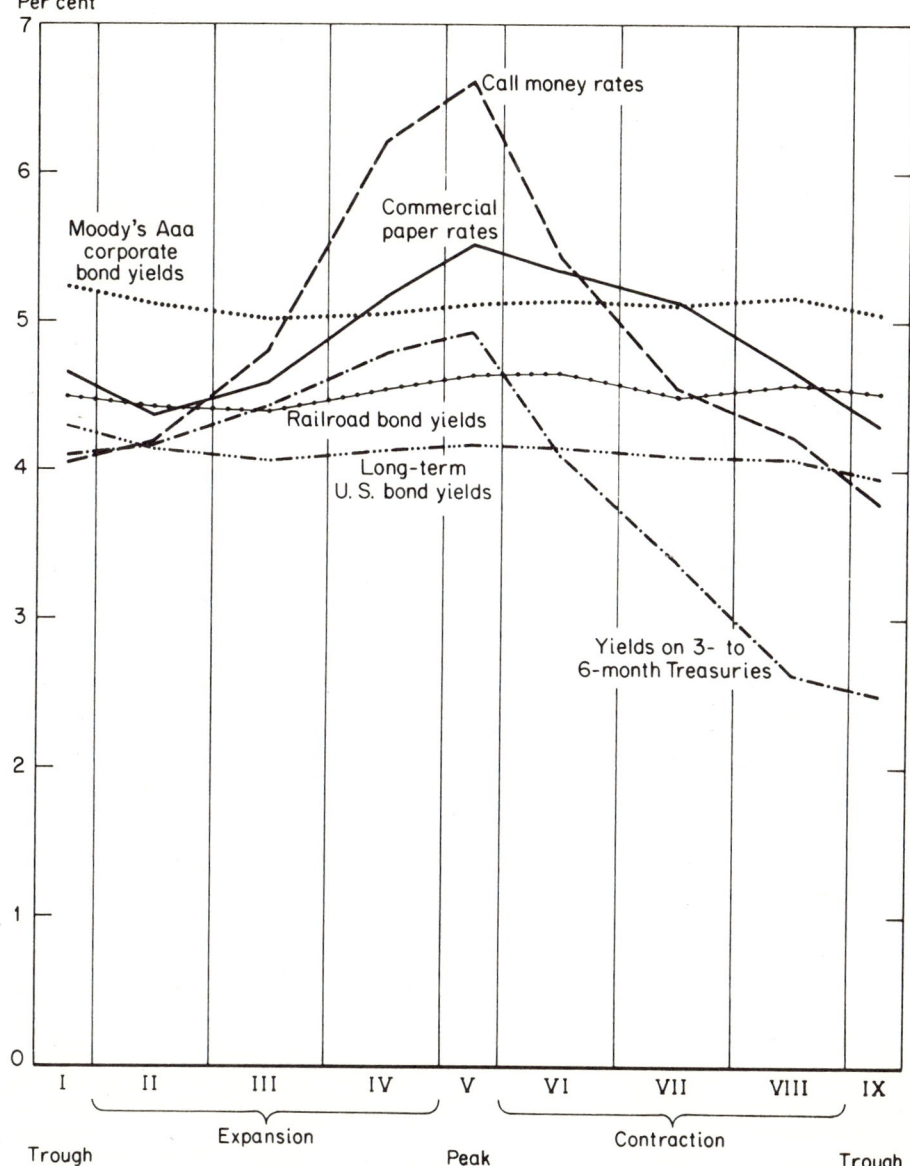

SOURCE: See notes following Chart 12.

NOTE: The following series cover shorter periods: long-term U.S. bonds yields and Moody's Aaa corporate bond yields, four cycles, 1919–33; yields on three- to six-month Treasury notes and certificates, three cycles, 1921–33.

1930's and early 1940's, specific cycles are less well defined than they were during either the 1920's or the post-World War II era. Nevertheless, the generalization that the gap between long- and short-term rates is small when rates are high and large when rates are low still seems to be supported by the data (see Charts 7 and 8).

Yields of nongovernmental obligations can provide insights into the cyclical behavior of interest rates before World War I. Since the issuers of long maturities are not the same as the issuers of short maturities, one hesitates to use these data for comparing the yields on different maturities. The series appear to be more useful for examining the cyclical changes in relative yields. Chart 9 summarizes these data from about the beginning of the Civil War until World War I. For the fourteen cycles in this period, short-term rates rose relative to long-term rates during expansions and fell during contractions. The peaks in the long-term rate occurred about midway in the business contraction, and the troughs occurred about midway in the expansion. The same data are carried forward from 1914 through 1933 in Chart 10. Again, short-term rates rose relative to long-term rates during expansions and fell during contractions. In this period, the peaks in the long-term rate more nearly matched business peaks, although troughs continued to occur after those in business. The same implications for the relative movements of long- and short-term rates during the business cycle may be drawn from these series for the 1945–61 period (see Chart 11). Only for 1933 through 1945, when the yields of governments also behaved anomalously, is the pattern—the relative rise of short-term rates during expansions and their fall during contractions—broken [4] (see Chart 12). This is a period when specific cycles conformed least with peaks and troughs in business conditions.

An independent body of data that reflects the term structure of interest rates from 1900 to date was initiated by Durand and sub-

---

[4] Hicks reports that short-term rates averaged less than long-term rates in England from 1850 through 1930. He uses risk premiums as the explanation for the observed yield differential. See John R. Hicks, "Mr. Hawtrey on Bank Rates and the Long Term Rate of Interest," *The Manchester School of Economic and Social Studies,* October 1939, p. 28.

Hawtrey reports that interest rates have varied cyclically in England, with short-term rates relatively low during depressions and high during booms. See Ralph G. Hawtrey, *A Century of Bank Rates,* London, 1938, pp. 167 ff.

CHART 11

Average Pattern of Long-Term and Short-Term Interest Rates in the United States During Four Business Cycles, 1945–61

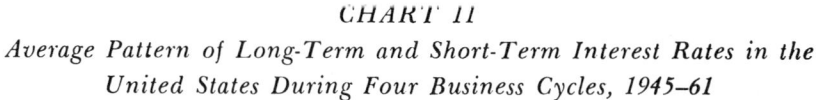

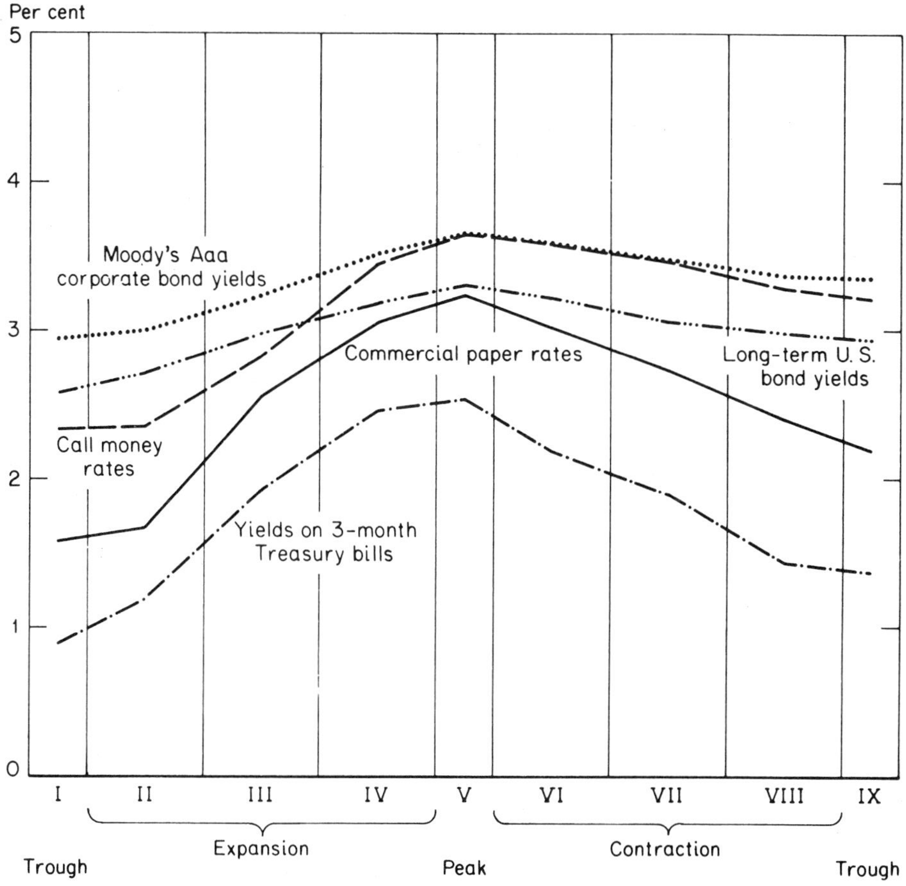

SOURCE: See notes following Chart 12.

CHART 12

Average Pattern of Long-Term and Short-Term Interest Rates in the United States During Two Business Cycles, 1933–45

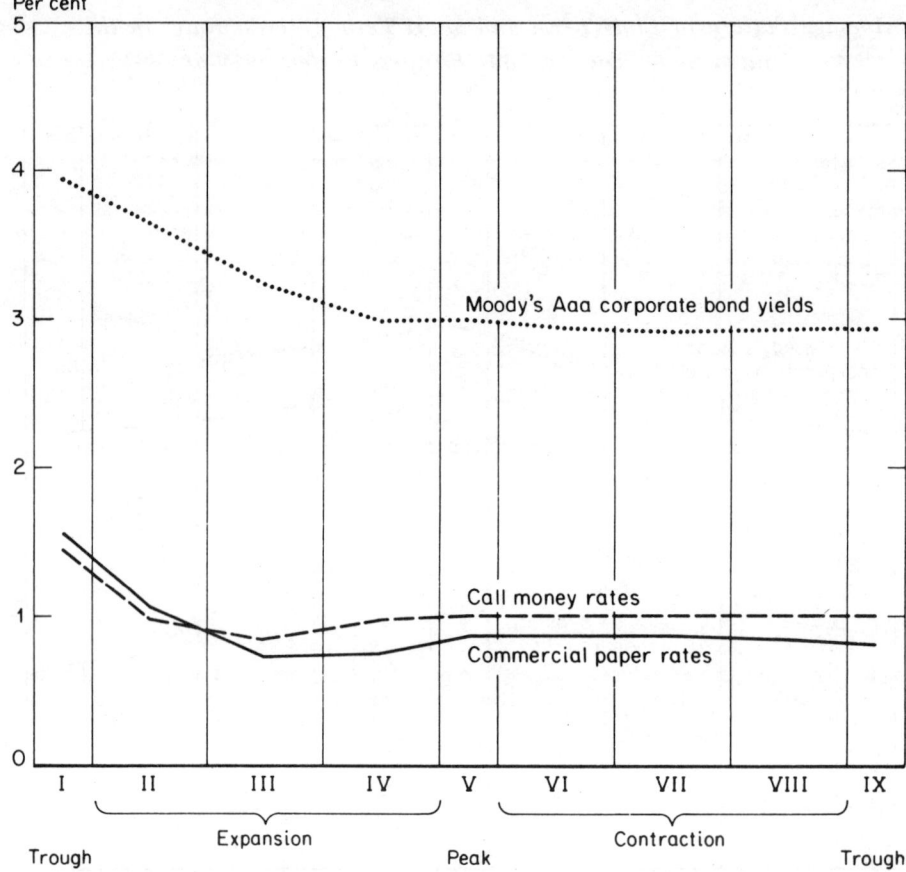

SOURCE TO CHARTS 9 THROUGH 12

Call money rates
  1858–1936: Frederick R. Macaulay, *Some Theoretical Problems Suggested by the Movements of Interest Rates, Bond Yields and Stock Prices in the United States since 1856,* New York, NBER, 1938, Appendix A.
  1937–61: Survey of Current Business, U.S. Department of Commerce.
Commercial paper rates
  1858–Jan. 1937: Macaulay, *Movements of Interest Rates.*
  Feb. 1937–61: Compiled by NBER from weekly rates in *Bank and Quotation Record,* William B. Dana Co.
Railroad bond yields
  Macaulay, *Movements of Interest Rates.* The series used is adjusted for "economic drift."
Moody's Aaa, corporate bond yields
  Moody's Industrial Manual, Moody's Investors' Service
Long-term U.S. bond yields
  Federal Reserve Bulletin, Board of Governors of the Federal Reserve System

The Cyclical Behavior of the Term Structure of Interest Rates

TABLE 13

BASIC YIELDS ON CORPORATE BONDS DURING BUSINESS CYCLES, 1900-61
(per cent)

Business Cycle (fiscal years)			Term to Maturity (years)	Yield at Business Cycle			Change in Yield		Cycle Average[a]
Trough	Peak	Trough		Trough (T)	Peak (P)	Trough (T)	Trough to Peak	Peak to Trough	
1901	1903	1904	1	3.25	3.45	3.60	+.20	+.15	3.39
			5	3.25	3.45	3.60	+.20	+.15	3.39
			20	3.25	3.45	3.60	+.20	+.15	3.39
1904	1907	1908	1	3.60	4.87	5.10	+1.27	+.23	4.37
			5	3.60	3.87	4.30	+.27	+.43	3.75
			20	3.60	3.80	3.95	+.20	+.15	3.66
1908	1910	1911	1	5.10	4.25	4.09	-.85	-.16	4.29
			5	4.30	4.10	4.05	-.20	-.05	4.08
			20	3.95	3.87	3.94	-.08	+.07	3.88
1911	1913	1915	1	4.09	4.74	4.47	+.65	-.27	4.42
			5	4.05	4.31	4.39	+.26	+.08	4.24
			20	3.94	4.02	4.20	+.08	+.18	4.04
1915	1918	1919	1	4.47	5.48	5.58	+1.01	+.10	4.51
			5	4.39	5.25	5.16	+.86	-.09	4.53
			20	4.20	4.82	4.81	+.62	-.01	4.36
1919	1920	1922	1	5.58	6.11	5.31	+.53	-.80	6.16
			5	5.16	5.72	5.19	+.56	-.53	5.70
			20	4.81	5.17	4.85	+.36	-.32	5.10
1922	1923	1924	1	5.31	5.01	5.02	-.30	+.01	5.09
			5	5.19	4.90	4.90	-.29	0	4.97
			20	4.85	4.68	4.69	-.17	+.01	4.72
1924	1927	1928	1	5.02	4.30	4.05	-.72	-.25	4.27
			5	4.90	4.30	4.05	-.60	-.25	4.41
			20	4.69	4.30	4.05	-.39	-.25	4.39
1928	1929	1933	1	4.05	5.27	2.60	+1.22	-2.67	4.01
			5	4.05	4.72	3.68	+.67	-1.04	4.29
			20	4.05	4.45	4.11	+.40	-.34	4.35
1933	1937	1939	1	2.60	.69	.57	-1.91	-.12	1.23
			5	3.68	1.68	1.55	-2.00	-.13	2.33
			20	4.11	2.90	2.65	-1.21	-.25	3.25
1939	1945	1946	1	.57	1.02	.86	+.45	-.16	0.80
			5	1.55	1.53	1.32	-.02	-.21	1.46
			20	2.65	2.55	2.35	-.10	-.20	2.56

(continued)

TABLE 13 (concluded)

Business Cycle (fiscal years)			Term to Maturity (years)	Yield at Business Cycle			Change in Yield		Cycle Average[a]
				Trough (T)	Peak (P)	Trough (T)	Trough to Peak	Peak to Trough	
Trough	Peak	Trough							
1946	1948	1950	1	.86	1.60	1.42	+.74	−.18	1.35
			5	1.32	2.03	1.90	+.71	−.13	1.80
			20	2.35	2.73	2.48	+.38	−.25	2.54
1950	1953	1954	1	1.42	2.62	2.40	+1.20	−.22	2.33
			5	1.90	2.75	2.52	+.85	−.23	2.48
			20	2.48	3.05	2.88	+.57	−.17	2.80
1954	1957	1958	1	2.40	3.50	3.21	+1.10	−.29	2.90
			5	2.52	3.50	3.25	+.98	−.25	2.97
			20	2.88	3.50	3.47	+.62	−.03	3.15
1958	1960	1961	1	3.21	4.95	3.10	+1.74	−1.85	3.92
			5	3.25	4.73	3.75	+1.48	−.98	4.01
			20	3.47	4.55	4.12	+1.08	−.43	4.15

Source: 1900-42, David Durand, *Basic Yields of Corporate Bonds, 1900-1942* New York, NBER, Technical Paper 3, 1942, pp. 5-6.
1943-47, David Durand and Willis J. Winn, *Basic Yields of Bonds, 1926-1947: Their Measurement and Pattern,* New York, NBER, Technical Paper 6, 1947, p. 14.
1948-61, National Industrial Conference Board, *The Economic Almanac 1962,* p. 353.

The business cycle peak and trough dates are from the National Bureau's fiscal year chronology. The basic yields are available only for the first quarter of each calendar year; the yield for the first quarter of 1901 is entered in the fiscal year ended June 30, 1901, etc.

[a]The initial and terminal trough years each receive a weight of 1/2; the intervening years, a weight of 1.

sequently maintained by other observers. These data show yields as of the first quarter of every year for high-grade or default-free corporate bonds as a function of term to maturity. They were assembled by plotting yields of high-grade corporate bonds, fitting curves to the lower bounds of these data, and subsequently observing the points on these yield curves that correspond to particular terms to maturity. These data are summarized in Table 13 and Chart 13.

Durand's observations suggest that the swings in short-term rates are typically greater than the swings in long-term rates. When rates conformed to the business cycle, the term structure was less steeply inclined at peaks and troughs. During the early part of this period, conformity with the cycle was poorer than in the later part.

Durand's observations are consistent with the time series already

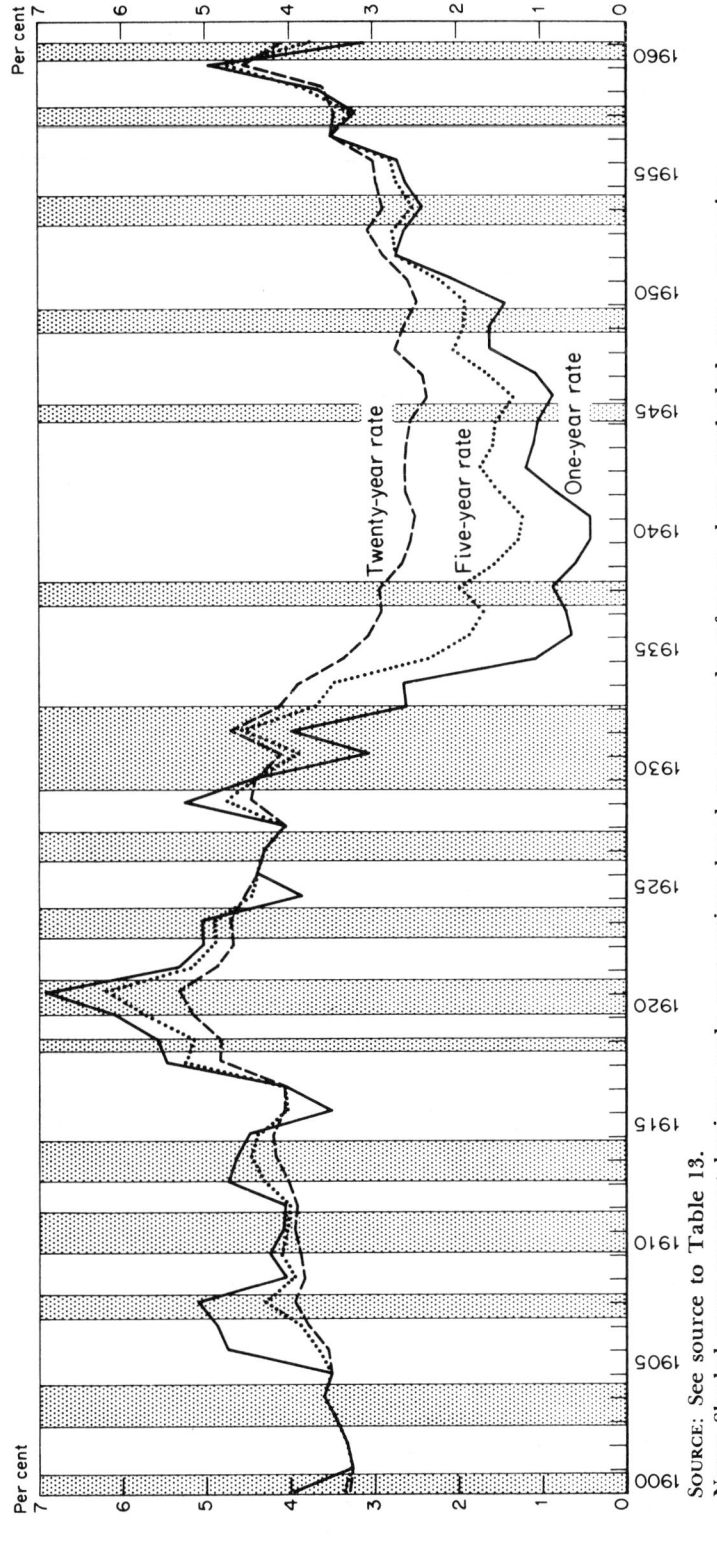

CHART 13

Basic Yields of Corporate Bonds, First Quarter, Durand Data, 1900–1961

SOURCE: See source to Table 13.
NOTE: Shaded areas represent business cycle contractions based on quarterly reference dates; unshaded areas, expansions.

presented, except for the 1920's. During this decade, time series for governments indicate that the average yields of short maturities were below that of long maturities. Durand's findings indicate just the opposite. Durand recognizes the existence of this inconsistency; indeed, for the same year he reports yield curves with opposite slopes but offers no explanation.[5]

---

[5] Two possible lines of explanation, other than errors of observation, come to mind. (1) At this time, long governments were partially tax exempt, short governments totally tax exempt. (2) Transactions costs for short, relative to long, governments are lower than they are for short, relative to long, corporates.

4

THE APPLICATION OF THE LIQUIDITY PREFERENCE AND EXPECTATIONS HYPOTHESES TO THE CYCLICAL BEHAVIOR OF INTEREST RATES

A. *Applications of the Lutz-Meiselman Model*

IF BOTH liquidity effects and incorrect expectations are disregarded, one should expect to find that long-term rates are higher than short-term rates when the latter are low and lower than short-term rates when the latter are high; in the absence of trends in interest rates, the average yields of short- and long-term rates should be equal. Insofar as short-term rates are relatively low about cyclical troughs and high about peaks, yield curves ought to be negatively sloped at peaks and positively sloped at troughs. Peaks and troughs in specific cycles of short-term rates should be anticipated by movements in long-term rates. If the market anticipates increases or decreases in short-term rates, long-term rates should move in advance in the same direction. Hence, if peaks and troughs in short-term rates are coincident with the reference cycle, peaks and troughs in long-term rates ought to lead the business cycle, and the longer the maturity, the greater the lead. The reasoning here is the same as that which led Macaulay to expect time money rates to lead call money rates.

Analytically, the 91-day bill rate can be regarded as a spot or instantaneous rate of interest which reflects money market conditions at specific phases of the cycle. In contrast, the yield on long-term governments represents an average of the current and expected spot rates over the course of three or four reference cycles. Because the term to maturity of long-term governments is longer than the usual reference cycle, the yields of these securities reflect an average of spot rates during both expansions and contractions. Hence, long-term rates vary relatively less than short-term rates. Money market conditions during a specific phase of a cycle are largely "averaged out" (the effects of abnormally low or high spot rates largely cancel) in the determination of the long-term rate. In contrast, money market conditions during specific cycle phases are completely reflected in bill yields. As a result, short-term rates ought to be more variable over the cycle than long-term rates. The expectations hypothesis implies that the shorter the term to maturity of a security, the smaller the number of spot rates that are averaged in order to determine its yield; consequently, the larger its variance over the cycle. Cyclical movements in the short- relative to the long-term rate can be analyzed as if the latter were a permanent or normal rate of interest and the short-term rate contained a large transitory component. This transitory component is largest about peaks and troughs. When positive, at peaks, short-term rates are high relative to long-term rates; when negative, at troughs, short-term rates are relatively low.[1]

The market regards current short-term rates as abnormally high when they are above long-term rates, and expects them to fall in the future. At such times, holders of long-term securities expect

---

[1] This implies that the correlation between a moving average of short-term rates and long-term rates over the cycle would be greater than the correlation between current short- with long-term rates. A moving average would abstract from cyclical effects on short-term rates; it would depict permanent short-term rates and abstract from transitory effects. It also would, of course, reduce the amplitude of the fluctuations in short- relative to long-term rates; in effect, it converts short- to long-term rates.

The view that the long-term rate is an average of short-term rates explains why Hicks found that time series of short- and long-term rates were less strongly correlated than averages of past and present short-term rates (both weighted and unweighted) and long-term rates. Presumably averages reflect expectations of "permanent" short-term rates. Hence they are more like long-term rates than actual short-term rates which embody a transitory component that is negative at troughs and positive at peaks. See Hicks, "Mr. Hawtrey On Bank Rates," p. 28. Hawtrey's position is similar to that of Charles C. Abbott, "A Note on the Government Bond Market," *The Review of Economic Statistics*, Vol. 17, 1935, p. 9. Both reasoned that the forces that affect short maturity yields are largely independent of the forces that affect long maturity yields because fluctuations in short-term rates are much greater than those in long-term rates.

to win capital gains because the passage of time will eliminate the abnormally high short-term rates from the average of present and future short-term rates that is the long-term rate. The opposite occurs when short-term rates are relatively low; i.e., the holders of long-term securities expect to incur capital losses as low short-term rates are eliminated from the average that is the long-term rate.

This does not, in itself, imply that it is more profitable to hold long- than short-term securities when rates are expected to fall. If the expectations of the market are correct, then the high yields of short- relative to long-term securities would just offset expected capital gains on the latter. The yield differential in this case represents what the market thinks is necessary to equalize the holding period yields of these securities, taking into account both coupons and capital gains. Conversely, when short-term rates are abnormally low, they are expected to rise. The abnormally large yield advantage of long-term securities in this case represents what the market thinks is necessary to offset the expected capital losses attributable to holding them. Whether or not the holding period yields of short-term relative to long-term securities are greater or less over the cycle depends upon which way the market erred in predicting future short-term rates. A fall in short-term rates that is larger than anticipated favors the holders of long-term securities, and vice versa.

These implications of the expectations hypothesis for the cyclical behavior of interest rates are in part incorrect because liquidity preference is not an independent variable in the analysis. Yet they go far towards providing an interpretation of the behavior of yield differentials between long- and short-term governments since 1920. In particular, they further our understanding of the sharp movements in short-term rates that occurred during this time.

In the 1920's there were two periods when short-term rates were above long-term rates (see Chart 7). During 1920, and again in 1929, the market anticipated lower future short-term rates. Although the absolute level of short-term rates during 1920 was about seventy-five basis points higher than it was in 1929, the anticipated fall was much greater in 1929. The yield advantage of short-term over long-term securities in 1929 was at least twice as great as it was in 1921. The fall in short-term rates from 1929 to 1931 was about 450 basis points, whereas the fall from 1920 to 1922 was about 275 basis points. Both downward movements were greater than the other declines in short-term rates during this period.

In more recent years (1957 and 1959), short-term rates were again higher than long-term rates (see Chart 6). The absolute level of rates was higher in 1959 but the yield differential between long- and short-term securities was about the same. The subsequent downward movements in short-term rates were of roughly equal magnitude, about 275 basis points, and were the largest declines since the 1920's. In the 1930's, short-term relative to long-term rates were especially low. This was a consequence of abnormally low short-term rates; they were at historical lows.

The implications of a pure expectations model for the cyclical behavior of interest rates are inconsistent with the following observations: (1) short maturities yield less over the cycle than long maturities; yield curves are more often than not positively sloped; (2) short-term rates fail to exceed long-term rates at peaks as much as they fall below long-term rates at troughs; (3) the variance over the cycle in yields of three-month Treasury bills is less than the variance of nine- to twelve-month governments; (4) when short-term rates are above long-term rates, it is not the shortest term to maturity that bears the highest yield, i.e., yield curves at first rise with term to maturity and then fall; (5) long-term rates fail to lead turning points in short-term rates.

B. *Applications of the Hicks Model*

1. CYCLICAL BEHAVIOR OF GOVERNMENTS

To explain these observations, liquidity preference must be added to the analysis. This implies that interest rates no longer measure the total return derived from holding securities. Securities also yield a nonpecuniary or liquidity income to their holders. The evidence presented indicates that the nonpecuniary return from securities is inversely related to term to maturity and directly related to the level of pecuniary yields. The shorter the term to maturity, the larger the fraction of the total return from a security that is nonpecuniary, and vice versa. The higher the level of interest rates, the wider the spread between the total return from a security and its pecuniary yield, and vice versa.

If, abstracting from differences in expectations of future short-term rates, the total return attributable to all maturities is the same, i.e., the sum of pecuniary and nonpecuniary returns is equal for all terms to maturity, then the pecuniary yield must be an increasing function of term to maturity. Therefore, if expectations have a

CHART 14

"Normal" or Average Yield Curve

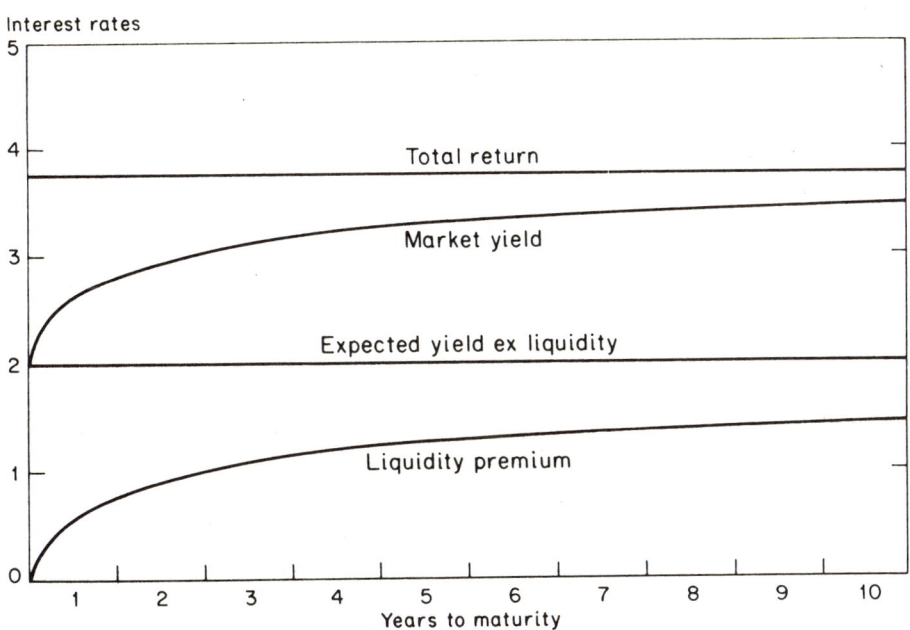

random effect on yield curves, the average yield curve will be positively sloped, and short-term rates will, on the average, be lower than long-term rates. The interaction of expectations and liquidity preference to produce a "normal" yield curve is shown in Chart 14. The "total return" curve is flat; it depicts a market in which future short-term rates are expected to be the same as the current rates. The liquidity yield is the fraction of total yields for any given maturity that is nonpecuniary. Subtracting the nonpecuniary component from total return leaves the pecuniary yield curve, which is the yield curve observed in the market.[2]

Liquidity preference produces asymmetry in the relationship between short- and long-term rates at cycle peaks and troughs. It accounts for the failure of short-term rates to exceed long-term rates at peaks by as much as they fall below long-term rates at troughs.

CHART 15

Yield Curve at Cyclical Troughs

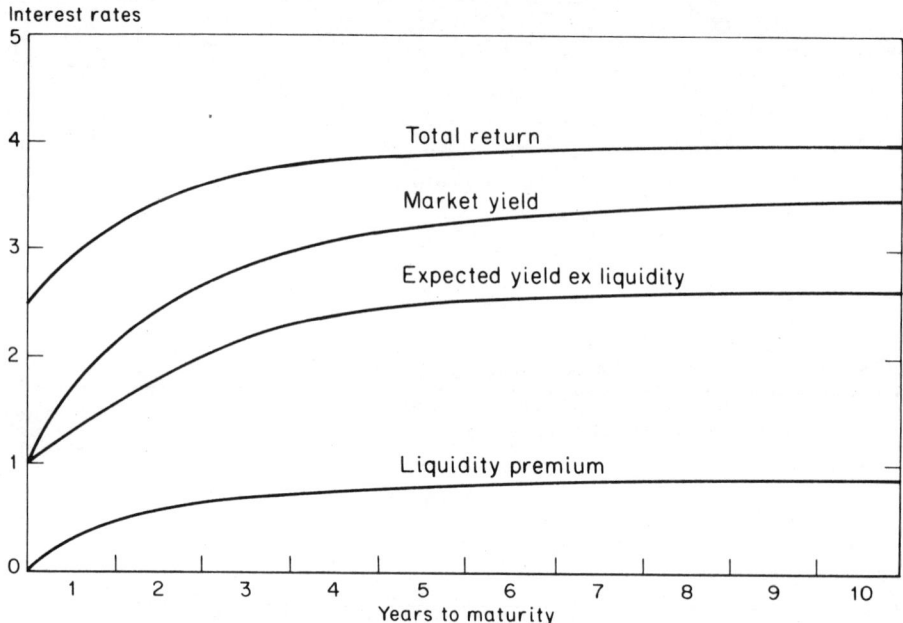

At cyclical troughs, both liquidity and expectational forces operate independently to establish short-term rates below long-term rates. Liquidity preference produces a pecuniary yield differential of long-term over short-term securities. At troughs, the market regards the current short-term rate as abnormally low and expects it to be

[2] Liquidity return as a percentage of total return was obtained by first fitting a yield curve to average yields as a function of term to maturity for the three latest reference cycles. Then the ratios of yields for particular maturities to twenty-year government bond yields were computed. The difference between the ratio for any given term to maturity and one constitutes the fraction of total yield that is nonpecuniary for that term to maturity.

higher in the future. Hence, expectations also push short-term below long-term rates. Both effects operate to widen the spread between these rates (Chart 15). The total-return curve slopes positively because the market expects future yields on short maturities, both pecuniary and nonpecuniary, to be higher than current short maturity yields. Subtracting the liquidity component from the total yield curve produces a market yield curve with a long-short differ-

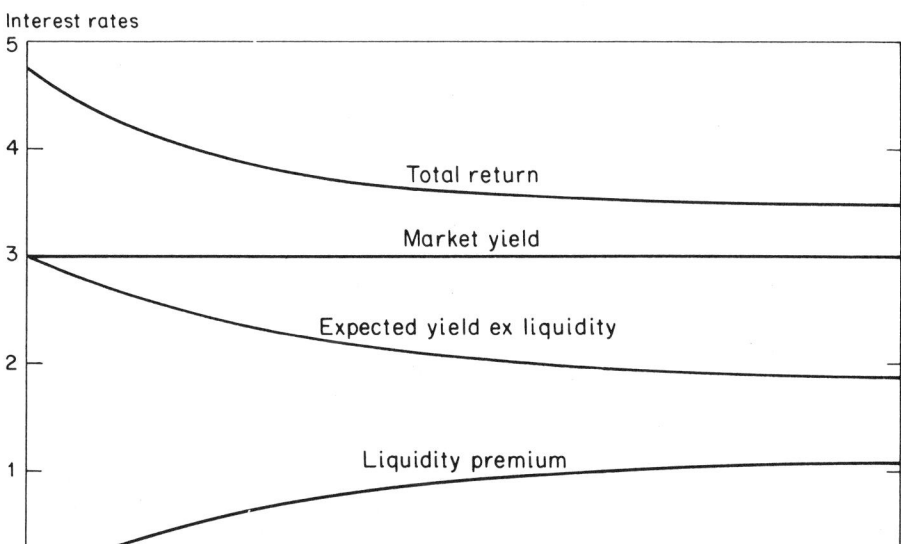

CHART 16
A Flat Yield Curve

ential greater than the differential for the corresponding total yield curve.

At cyclical peaks, in contrast to cyclical troughs, liquidity and expectational forces produce opposite effects on yield curves. Liquidity preference, as always, operates to establish short-term below long-term rates. However, expectations act in the opposite direction. Because the market expects future short-term rates to be lower, the total yield curve declines as a function of term to maturity. Whether or not the resulting market yield curve is rising, falling, or both depends upon the relative strength of these opposing forces. Because these forces work in opposite directions at cyclical peaks but in the same direction at troughs, short-term yields do not exceed long-term yields at peaks as much as they fall below long-term yields at troughs.

The foregoing analysis implies that flat market yield curves should be interpreted as indicating that the market expects future pecuniary yields of short maturities to be lower than current short-term rates. With no change in expectations, the fraction of the total

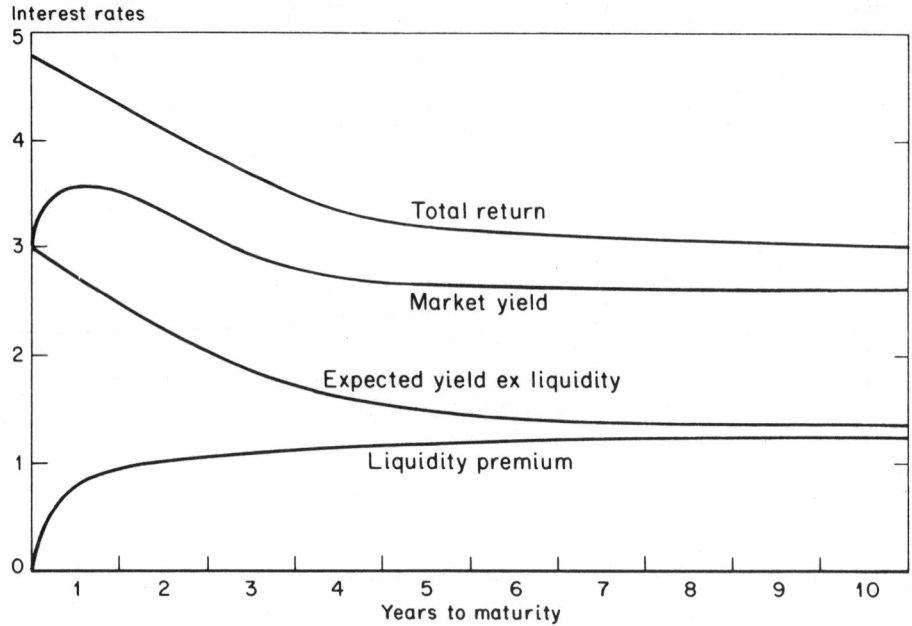

CHART 17
Yield Curve at Cyclical Peaks

return that is nonpecuniary for a forward rate which pertains to a specific period of calendar time will rise with the passage of time. Hence, its pecuniary yield will fall below current spot rates. A flat market yield curve is shown in Chart 16. A falling total-return curve is a necessary condition for its existence.

Charts 17 and 18 depict yield curves with segments that are negatively sloped (yield curves with such shapes are also referred to as humped). Such curves are produced by expectations of sharply falling interest rates, i.e., interest rates that are falling more sharply than those in Chart 15. The more sharply interest rates are expected to fall, the shorter the term to maturity of the peak in yields; the more gradual the expected fall, the further out on the yield curve the peak will be. If the expected fall in short-term rates is very gradual, no negative segment appears. Yield curves with negative segments have been relatively rare, at least since the 1920's; expectations of interest-rate declines are usually not sharp enough to offset the effects of liquidity preference.

CHART 18
Effects of Alternative Expectations of Falling Rates upon the Shapes of Yield Curves

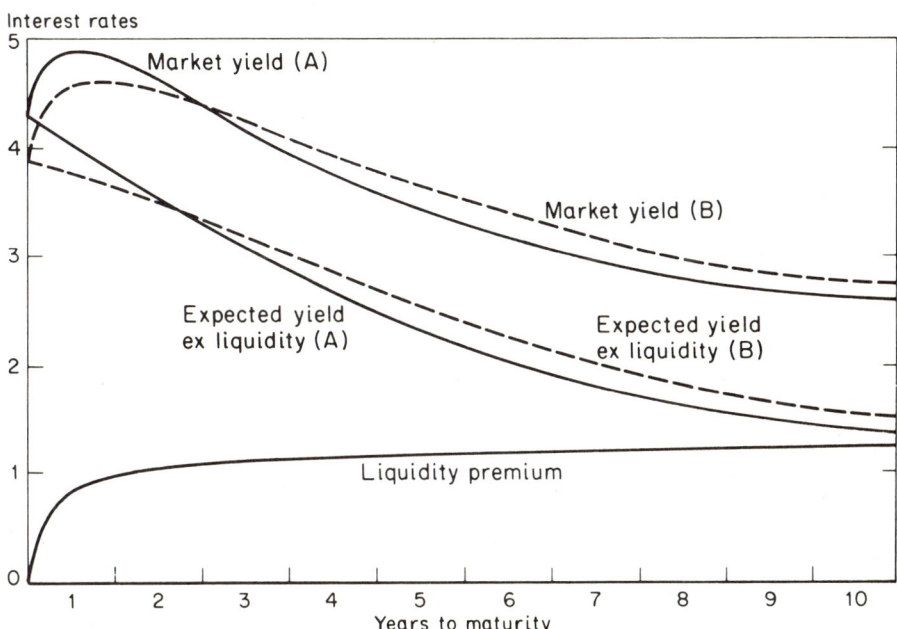

Liquidity preference also explains why the shortest term to maturity is not the highest yielding security in the term structure at cyclical peaks. In order for a yield curve to exist that has the shortest term to maturity bearing the highest yield, expectations of extremely sharp declines in short-term rates are required. Such expectations, while a theoretical possibility, did not exist during the two most recent cyclical peaks and possibly have never existed.

The liquidity preference hypothesis implies that nonpecuniary yields are a decreasing function of term to maturity. Hence, the range of pecuniary yields that will be observed in the market will increase with term to maturity. For example, suppose liquidity yields for Treasury bills and nine- to twelve-month governments are at all times 50 and 25 per cent of total returns. Further, assume that total returns, which are of course not directly observable in the market, range from 4 to 8 per cent. Pecuniary yields will then range from 2 to 4 per cent for bills, and from 3 to 6 per cent for nine- to twelve-month governments. Hence liquidity preference implies that the variance in yields over the cycle increases with term to maturity.

The expectations hypothesis implies just the opposite: that the shorter the term to maturity, the greater the variance. Therefore, the actual variance observed in the market for any specified term to maturity represents a composition of these conflicting forces. The available evidence on variance as a function of term to maturity suggests that liquidity effects dominate expectational effects for governments with maturities equal to or less than nine-to-twelve months. For three- to five-year governments and longer maturities, expectational effects dominate. The absence of time series between these maturity ranges precludes a precise estimate here of the borderline separating the domains of dominance of expectations and liquidity.

During expansions, yield differentials between Treasury bills and nine- to twelve-month governments widen. Insofar as liquidity effects dominate expectational effects, liquidity premiums ought to widen from trough to peak since, according to the liquidity preference hypothesis, they are an increasing function of the absolute level of interest rates. Consequently, if only liquidity effects are at work, the differentials between bills and nine- to twelve-month governments would increase more than the increases observed. Adding expectations to the analysis implies, given the assumption that the market can recognize transitorily high or low levels of spot rates, the addition of an opposing force. Converse implications are implied for contractions. Liquidity operates to narrow, and expectations to widen, the spread between bills and nine- to twelve-month governments. Since liquidity is dominant for this maturity range, the observed spreads decrease during contractions. For evidence on how these differentials have actually behaved, see Charts 5 and 6.

These findings for governments do not necessarily apply to corporates or to the issues of government agencies unless the nonpecuniary component of total yield is the same. In general, governments appear to be more liquid, ignoring the influence of term to maturity, than either agency issues or corporates.[3] Among short-term securities, governments have a comparative liquidity advantage over agencies or corporates. The bill market has very low transactions costs and bid and asked prices are firm for extremely large transactions. This suggests that when yield curves are humped, the peak in yields will have a longer term to maturity for corporates than for governments.

In the absence of liquidity premiums, and assuming the market can forecast turning points in the specific cycles of interest rates, cyclical peaks in long-term rates would precede those of short-term rates and would be observable first. Similarly, troughs in long-term rates would precede troughs in short-term rates. The rationale that Macaulay used to argue that the seasonal peak in time money rates should precede that in call money rates is relevant here. Insofar as the market can predict turning points in short-term rates, the long-term rate (which is an average of future short-term rates) should reach its peak first in anticipation of the peak in short-term rates.

When liquidity preference is introduced into the analysis, however, the sequence in the timing of peaks and troughs of long- and short-term securities becomes less obvious. If liquidity premiums are a function of spot rates, then an amount is added to long-term rates which increases as short-term rates increase and reaches a peak when the latter reach their peak. The peak in long-term rates must

---

[3] The evidence for the proposition that agency issues are less liquid than governments is of two kinds. (1) Agencies have higher transactions costs. The spread between bid and asked prices, as reported in dealer quotation sheets, ranges from two-thirty-seconds for short-term securities to a whole point, the equivalent of ten dollars, for long-term securities. (2) The value of agencies as collateral for bank loans is poorer than is it for governments. Per dollar of borrowing, the market value of collateral in the form of agencies, term to maturity aside, is higher than it is for governments. The Joint Economic Committee *Study of the Dealer Market*, p. 95, reports that the margin requirements for agencies are 5 per cent.

occur later, therefore, than it would have occurred in a world of pure expectations.

How much later this peak will occur can only be partially determined by a priori reasoning. It is clear that the peak in long-term rates should not occur after the peak in short-term rates. Since the maximum amount that will be added to long-term rates because of liquidity preference will occur when short-term rates reach their peak, the peak in long-term rates must either precede or be synchronous with that of short-term rates.

Since the end of World War II, the behavior of time series of governments with various terms to maturity indicates that all securities, irrespective of maturity, reach their peaks and troughs synchronously. Hence, without going further into the question of whether liquidity premiums add enough to long-term rates to delay their peaks until all peaks are synchronous, irrespective of term to maturity, one cannot say, using this evidence alone, whether the market can or cannot predict turning points in interest rates. In view of the inability of the market to predict turning points of other series, on balance, it seems reasonable to interpret these findings as being consistent with the view that the market cannot predict turning points in specific cycles of interest rates.[4]

2. CYCLICAL BEHAVIOR OF AGENCY ISSUES AND CORPORATES

The thesis has been advanced that liquidity premiums are caused primarily by a desire to avoid the risk of capital loss. The evidence indicates that yield differentials, when only liquidity differences exist, increase with the absolute level of rates. The observations of an upward trend in liquidity premiums for the three latest cycles, and regressions of liquidity premiums upon spot rates, show that liquidity premiums increase when interest rates increase. This thesis has implications for the cyclical and secular behavior of other rates of interest. It implies that low-quality bonds ought to yield

---

[4] The highest correlation (.98) of seasonally adjusted time series for three-month Treasury bills with nine- to twelve-month governments was obtained by assuming the two series to be synchronous. The correlations with one-, two-, and three-month leads and lags were: .95 for one month, .90 for two, and .83 for three. No difference, to two decimal places, was observed for leads and lags of equal duration.

more, the cycle aside, than high-quality bonds because they are relatively less liquid, i.e., price variance is greater as a result of the greater default risk. Consequently, it should be possible to observe that high-quality bonds yield less than low-quality bonds generally and that the yield differential between high- and low-quality bonds increases from trough to peak, and decreases from peak to trough. By symmetrical reasoning, the spread between government agency issues and governments, ignoring term to maturity, should increase with the absolute level of interest rates.

To test one of these propositions, yield differentials between governments and government agency issues were regressed against their sums. The results of this test are mixed. For nine- to twelve-month maturities, the spreads between governments on the one hand, and Federal National Mortgage Association, Federal Land Bank, and Federal Home Loan Bank issues on the other, are consistent with the hypothesis advanced; spreads increase as the absolute level of interest rates increase. The same is true for maturities ten years and over. The best results were obtained by regressing the yield differential between a government bond, the three and one-quarter of 1983, and an index of AA utility yields of bonds with coupons of three and one-eighth to three and three-eighths against their sum. The correlation was positive and 40 per cent of the variation in the spread was explained.[5] However, for three- to five-year governments and FLB and FNMA issues, the slopes of the regression coefficients were negative, one significantly so.

The consequences of changes in the level of interest rates for yield differentials between low- and high-quality bonds over the cycle is somewhat more difficult to detect. During contractions, the level of rates falls and the market usually increases its estimates of the risks of default by the issuers of low-quality securities. Conversely, the level of rates rises during expansions and the market usually decreases its estimates of the risks of default. Hence, li-

---

[5] All of the agency issues exhibited a significant downward trend over time in yield differentials compared with governments. Presumably this reflects the diffusion of knowledge about the investment merits of these securities that has occurred in recent years. The data for the agencies consist of incomplete series, mostly for the last decade, compiled by Charles E. Quincey and Co., and Allen Knowles, the fiscal agent of the Federal Home Loan Banks. The AA utility series is compiled by Salomon Bros. & Hutzler.

quidity and cyclical forces work in opposite directions upon yield differentials. During the post-World War II period, the revaluation of risks over the cycle has dominated liquidity forces. Hence, the yields of Baa Moody's bonds, for all categories, have fluctuated less than corresponding Aaa bonds.

The behavior of low- and high-quality bond yield differentials over time seems to support the view that the level of rates and these differentials are related. Since 1945, the spread between Moody's AAA and BAA series has increased with the level of interest rates. The regression of the difference on the sum indicates that the difference rises with the level of rates.

Prewar investigations of the relationship between the yield differential of high- and low-grade bonds and the level of interest rates also conforms to this finding.

Ratios of promised yields (or yield spreads) to the basic rates on high-grade issues deserve more attention than they can be given in this report. According to the classical theory of investment values, the simple yield spread, or algebraic difference between the promised yield and basic rate, would provide the best measure of the risk premium for issues properly priced in the market, since the yield is conceived of as the algebraic sum of the pure rate of interest and the risk premium. It is a matter of record, however, that yield spreads frequently narrow when basic rates fall, and widen when basic rates rise . . . , perhaps because of the efforts of investors to compensate for changes in basic rates.[6]

For any preassigned cyclical downturn in bill rates, yield differentials between low- and high-grade bonds should decrease most during severe and least during mild contractions. Conversely, during strong upturns, the differential ought to increase more for sharp than for mild recoveries. The data on the behavior of differentials between low- and high-grade bonds, since the end of World War II, while they support the view that there has been a secular rise in the differential, do not support the view that the differential is at a maximum at peaks and minimum at troughs. In fact, the maximum differential seems to appear midway between the cyclical peak and the trough. This seems to be accounted for by differences

[6] W. Braddock Hickman, *Corporate Bond Quality and Investor Experience*, Princeton University Press for National Bureau of Economic Research, 1958, p. 288. For further discussion, see following pages.

between low- and high-grade bonds in the timing of their specific cycle peaks and troughs. In the postwar period, specific cycle peaks and troughs of high-grade bonds consistently preceded those of low-grade bonds. Hence, the maximum yield differential between the two could not have been associated with business cycle turning points.[7]

Hickman's investigation of the relationship between low- and high-grade bond yields over time suggests that the long-run rate of return to investors in low-grade bonds is greater than it is for high-grade bonds. He concludes that "the highest returns were obtained by investors who could afford to take the greatest risks."[8] He found that both the variance and the average rate of return was greatest for investments in low-grade bonds. In this respect, his finding is symmetrical with the relationship between long- and short-term government yields, taking into account both capital gains and interest receipts.

---

[7] Part of the increase in the measured yield differential between low- and high-grade bonds is attributable to differences between the economic, as distinguished from the temporal, term to maturity of these bonds. If calendar term to maturity is the same for both grades, then economic term to maturity, which Macaulay termed duration, must be shorter on the lower-grade issues. (See *Movements of Interest Rates,* Chapter II, for a discussion of this point.) The weights assigned to receipts in the near, relative to the distant, future for computing yield to maturity is greater for low- than high-quality bonds. Hence, a rise in rates during an expansion, with no change in investor attitudes towards risk, will increase measured yield differentials for the same reason that yields of three- to five-year governments rise relative to twenty-year governments during an expansion. This same point explains why the market believes that if interest rates are expected to fall, securities with equal yields and terms to maturity will have different relative price rises if their coupons are not the same. The size of the coupons will be inversely related to the rate of change of capital values.

In fact, this phenomenon seems to account for a trivial portion of the cyclical variation in the yield differential between low- and high-quality bonds. To determine the quantitative importance of this effect, a constant risk differential of 1 per cent for all spot and forward rates was assumed for two hypothetical ten-year bonds. At peaks, the higher-grade bond was assumed to consist of a six-month spot rate of 5 per cent, with the first forward rate being 4.5 per cent and all succeeding forward rates, 4 per cent. At troughs, the higher-grade bond was assumed to consist of a six-month spot rate of 2 per cent, with the first forward rate being 3 per cent and all succeeding forward rates 4 per cent. The yield to maturity of these two postulated securities differed by ninety-eight basis points at troughs, and one hundred and two at peaks.

[8] Hickman, *Corporate Bond Quality,* p. 138.

5

CONCLUSIONS AND IMPLICATIONS FOR FURTHER RESEARCH

THIS INVESTIGATION confirms the principal finding of Meiselman—that a relationship exists between expectations of future short-term rates and the term structure of interest rates. The fact that forward rates incorporate predictions of future short-term rates, with an appreciable accuracy in a statistical sense, demonstrates, by an a fortiori argument, that forward rates are a function of expected future spot rates.

Previous investigators, Hickman and Meiselman, have interpreted the difference between forward and subsequently observed spot rates as forecasting errors of the market. (Culbertson found the difference between holding period yields of different terms to maturity to be so large that he rejected the view that the market forecasts, since he found it difficult to believe that the market could forecast as badly as his interpretation of his findings suggests.) Their interpretations can be questioned because it is unreasonable to expect the market to err asymmetrically. The mean error in a long series of observations should be zero. If the work of these investigators is extended or examined closely, it can be shown that what they regarded as forecasting errors were in large part attributable to liquidity premiums, and that the errors of the market were indeed much smaller.

It is the thesis of this study that a forward rate should be viewed, not as an expected rate, but as an expected rate plus a liquidity premium. If forward rates are so interpreted, then the forecasts and forecasting errors of the market can be detected. These forecasts are, within the maturity spectrum studied, accurate to a degree that cannot be rationalized as the workings of chance. The finding that forward rates constitute high estimates of future spot rates is consistent with the Keynesian theory of "normal backwardation." The implications of this theory for the money and capital markets have been developed by Hicks in *Value and Capital*.[1] Hence these results support the Hicksian view that forward rates are equal to expected spot rates plus a liquidity premium.

The existence of liquidity premiums indicates that short and long maturities are not perfect substitutes for one another in the market as the proponents of the pure expectations hypothesis, such as Lutz and Meiselman, have argued. In particular, short and long maturities differ with respect to their value as money substitutes; short maturities are much better money substitutes than long maturities. Consequently, the greater liquidity yield of short maturities leads to a persistent pecuniary yield differential in favor of long maturities. This differential offsets the greater liquidity yield of short maturities. Therefore, the expected value of holding period yields, (with yield defined as total, as distinguished from pecuniary only), is equal for all terms to maturity.

The existence of liquidity premiums has been explained as a consequence of risk avoidance and positive costs for the speculative services required to convert long- into short-term securities. The market is willing to take a lower yield in exchange for a lower variance in the price of governments. The implications of this rationalization are consistent with the observed behavior of relative yields of low- and high-grade bonds, both secularly and cyclically.

Liquidity premiums have moved with the cycle in recent years. Since interest rates also increase during expansions and decrease during contractions, this raises the question: are liquidity premiums a function of the stage of the cycle or the level of interest rates? The upward trend in liquidity premiums over the three latest cycles, when interest rates have also shown an upward trend, indicates that it is the level of interest rates and not the stage of the cycle that determines the magnitude of liquidity premiums.

This finding does not support the theory that liquidity premiums are a development of the Great Depression. It is difficult to understand why evidence of the existence of liquidity premiums was so sparse before the 1930's and so abundant afterwards. If one argues

---

[1] In particular, see p. 147.

that the emergence of liquidity premiums was a consequence of risk aversion caused by the financial losses of the early 1930's, then one ought to observe that liquidity premiums have been declining secularly since that time. The foregoing evidence does not support this view. However, possibly more refined analysis, when the level of rates is held constant, would show that there has been a downward trend in liquidity premiums over time.

The joining of liquidity preference to expectations explains the lack of symmetry in the movement of short- and long-term rates over the cycle. It explains why short-term rates do not exceed long-term rates at peaks by as much as they fall below long-term rates at troughs; why yield curves are positively sloped during most of the cycle; and why yield curves, when short-term rates are unusually high, never seem to be negatively sloped throughout their full length, but show humps near the short end.

The common belief that short-term rates fluctuate more than long-term rates is, in general, correct.[2] However, this generalization conceals an important observation—as term to maturity increases, yield variance first increases, and then decreases. This observation is inconsistent with a pure expectations hypothesis, but is consistent with a hypothesis that combines expectations and liquidity forces.

At any instant of time, the power of the market to predict future spot rates decreases the longer the time span between the moment a forward rate is inferred from the term structure of interest rates and the corresponding spot rate is observed. Clearly it is more difficult to see one year than one week into the future. Hence, as the span of time between the moment a forward rate is inferred and the relevant spot rate is observed increases, the correlations between forward and spot rates ought to decrease. The observations for three- and six-month bills and one- and two-year governments are consistent with this implication of the expectations hypothesis. Other tests for this same period of time, but for different time spans, between forward and spot rates ought to yield results consistent with the foregoing. Indeed, this argument implies that a

[2] This is only arithmetic in a world of perfect certainty. Long-term rates can fluctuate more than short-term rates. The fact that they do not fluctuate as much as short-term rates implies that the market has some powers to recognize when short-term rates are transitorily high or low.

correlation between forward and two-year spot rates that is greater than the correlation between forward and one-year spot rates would contradict the expectations hypothesis.

The data used to show that the expectations hypothesis has predictive content is primarily drawn from one business cycle, 1958–61. Possibly using this particular cycle has produced freakish results and comparable findings could not be obtained for other cycles. Clearly much more work can and should be undertaken to find out just how well the market can predict. In particular, an effort should be made to determine how much of the market's ability to predict is attributable to predicting seasonal changes in rates. The results obtained using one- and two-year maturities indicate that the market can do more than predict seasonal changes in rates.[3]

The explanation of liquidity preference presented here is based on the postulate that the risk of capital loss associated with holding short-term securities is smaller than it is for long-term securities. This implies that in a period free of trends in interest rates, price variance ought to increase with term to maturity. (It should be noted that this implication is not arithmetic. The variance in prices of three-month bills could, in principle, be greater than that of six-month bills.) If variance increases with term to maturity, then mean yields should also increase. Direct evidence of a relationship between means, price variances, and terms to maturity should be sought.

Yield curves published in the *Treasury Bulletin* constitute data that can be used to determine whether or not these propositions about variance in yields, at least to the nine-to-twelve-month range, are correct. These same data can also be used to determine what maturity constitutes the line of demarcation between increasing and decreasing variances as term to maturity increases. Finally, these data could reveal how this boundary line changes from cycle to cycle and whether these changes are correlated with differences in interest rate levels.

Although these results support the view that securities of different

---

[3] Insofar as the market can predict, one should be able to observe that underwriters' spreads increase during expansions, reach a peak at the business cycle peak, and decrease during contractions.

maturities are not perfect substitutes for one another at identical, pecuniary, holding period yields, they do not support the view that it is the time span between maturities that explains less than infinite cross elasticities. Both liquidity preference and expectations imply that the cross elasticity of demand between fifteen- and twenty-year maturities will exceed the corresponding cross elasticity for five- and ten-year maturities. In addition, the expectations hypothesis implies, for coupon bearing securities with fixed maturities, the higher the absolute level of rates, the earlier the maturity at which yield curves will flatten out. This later implication has not been tested.

Durand's findings show that negatively sloped yield curves occurred more frequently before the decade of the 1930's than they have since. This leads to the questions, do his yield curves correctly depict what, in fact, was true, and if so, why this change? Furthermore, it appears that before 1914, long-term yields frequently lagged behind cyclical turns in short-term rates, a result that does not seem consistent with either the recent behavior of these rates or with the implications of the expectations-liquidity preference hypothesis. These questions deserve a fuller investigation than this study has attempted.

DIRECTOR'S COMMENT
Paul A. Samuelson

DR. KESSEL has made a valuable contribution both on the factual and conceptual side. To a first approximation one can consider the dichotomy between (1) the *expectations* hypothesis, which supposes that people will act to make present prices approximate closely to the arithmetic mean of future prices, independently of the dispersion and higher statistical moments of the possible outcomes; and (2) the *liquidity-preference* hypothesis, which supposes that people act as if they disliked dispersion and uncertainty and will sacrifice something of first-moment of money outcome if they can thereby help hedge uncertainties. From the 1920's through 1936, the name of Keynes could be correctly associated with the second view both in the realm of commodities and securities. But to a second approximation, as a close reading of the literature will show, liquidity-preference analysis becomes more general and admits of a wider variety of empirical patterns. Thus, *before* the period of harvest when the desire to play safe is dominated by the need of producers for *long* hedges, the same Keynes-Hicks-Houthakker-Cootner analysis that leads to "normal backwardation" leads instead to its reverse: during those months, a futures price tends to fall in order to coax out risk-taking on the part of speculators. Similarly, as Modigliani, Wehrle, and others have argued, if insurance companies or other blocs of investors have a strong desire or need to "play safe" in terms of, say, eight-year periods ahead, then the yield curve might be expected to depart from its rising pattern and show a characteristic hump. Or, again, if investors in an age of secular inflation want to play safe in terms of real purchasing power, is it really anomalous that stock dividend yields should begin to fall significantly below the yield of allegedly safer fixed-principal bonds? Hence, a priori reasoning cannot itself settle what are the most plausible patterns to look for; and except as a simplifying approximation, mere dichotomy between expectation and liquidity-preference hypotheses would seem overly simple. These remarks, I should add, are of course completely within the spirit of Dr. Kessel's analysis.

APPENDIX A

THREE TESTS of the expectations hypothesis are presented in Hickman's paper. One consists of a comparison of projections of the preceding year's structure of interest rates with theoretical forecasts based on the expectations hypothesis. These results are reproduced in Table A-1.

A second test consists of a comparison between the signs of predicted and actual changes of one-year spot rates. The results of this investigation are contained in Table A-2.

Hickman found ten cases of definite disagreement with the theory. He implies that he found sixteen cases of definite agreement. On balance, this evidence does more to support than deny the validity of the Meiselman version of the expectations hypothesis.

Hickman's third test follows from the assumption that the market can forecast accurately. Hence, changes from year to year in the long-term rate should only reflect the effects of dropping last year's one-year spot rate and adding the estimate of the market for the one-year forward rate which, for the maturity observed, is the rate expected on one-year money fifty-nine years in the future.

Hickman makes the completely *ad hoc* assumption that, at most, such changes in the inputs that determine the long-term rate, according to the expectations hypothesis, will change that rate by a maximum of one basis point. How one basis point was obtained is not explained to the reader. There are no calculations showing the effect of dropping the one-year spot rate of the previous year and adding the expected one-year rate fifty-nine years into the future upon the sixty-year rate of interest. Using plus or minus five basis points as the range that defines no change in the long-term rate (this is what Durand regarded as his measurement error), Hickman found only eighteen of the forty-two years consistent with the assumption that the expectations hypothesis could predict.

Hickman does not observe that the long-term rate, for coupon bonds, is a weighted average of expected short-term rates. These weights decline monotonically as a function of time, with the current short-term rate assigned the highest weight. For a sixty-year bond with a 5 per cent coupon that yields 5 per cent to maturity, the one-year rate relevant for the sixtieth year has about one-twentieth the weight of the current one-year rate. Hence, if the one-year rate that is dropped from the average is relatively high or low compared with the other rates, yields to maturity could easily change by more than five basis points. Such a change would be completely consistent with perfect foresight.

TABLE A-1

COMPARISON OF ACTUAL AND FORECAST TERM STRUCTURES OF INTEREST RATES, MEASURED BY AREAS UNDER CURVES[a]

Year	Type of Curve		Area Under Curve	Difference in Area Between Actual and Forecast Curves
1935	Actual		56.47	
1936	Actual		48.45	
	Projection of 1935		56.47	8.02
	Theoretical forecast from:	1935	62.92	14.47
1937	Actual		45.14	
	Projection of 1936		48.45	3.31
	Theoretical forecast from:	1936	55.00	9.86
		1935	67.30	22.16
1938	Actual		48.42	
	Projection of 1937		45.14	-3.28
	Theoretical forecast from:	1937	50.85	2.43
		1936	60.20	11.78
		1935	70.00	21.58
1939	Actual		41.29	
	Projection of 1938		48.42	7.13
	Theoretical forecast from:	1938	54.08	12.79
		1937	55.39	14.10
		1936	64.07	22.78
		1935	71.97	30.68
1940	Actual		37.42	
	Projection of 1939		41.29	3.87
	Theoretical forecast from:	1939	46.73	9.31
		1938	58.19	20.77
		1937	59.01	21.59
		1936	66.74	29.32
		1935	73.20	35.78
1941	Actual		36.25	
	Projection of 1940		37.42	1.17
	Theoretical forecast from:	1940	42.76	6.51
		1939	51.02	14.77
		1938	61.10	24.85
		1937	61.83	25.58
		1936	68.21	31.96
		1935	74.01	37.76
1942	Actual		41.28	
	Projection of 1941		36.25	-5.03
	Theoretical forecast from:	1941	41.38	.10
		1940	47.13	5.85
		1939	54.31	13.03
		1938	62.98	21.70
		1937	64.13	22.85
		1936	68.88	27.60
		1935	74.28	33.00

TABLE A-2

TYPES OF TERM STRUCTURES, THIRTY-SEVEN SELECTED YEARS (1900-42), AND ACTUAL CHANGES IN ONE-YEAR RATES

Type of Term Structure at Beginning of Year	Number of Years in Which Prevailing	Number of Years in Which Change in Short-Term Rate to Next Year Was		
		Plus	Minus	Zero
Increasing	12	7	4[a]	1[b]
Horizontal	10	6[b]	4[b]	
Decreasing	15	6[a]	9	
Total	37	19	17	1

Source: Hickman, "Term Structure of Interest Rates," Table I, p. III-5.

[a] Definite disagreement of historical pattern with theory.

[b] Partial disagreement of historical pattern with theory.

NOTES TO TABLE A-1

[a] The curves represent three types of structure: the actual structure of interest rates; the structure of rates in the preceding year projected forward one year without change; and theoretical forecasts of structures implied by structures of earlier years. The areas under the curves are computed for the portion covering maturities of from one to twenty-one years. For 1937, for example, the first area in the third column is that under the curve representing the actual term structure in 1937. The second is that under the projected curve (the actual curve in 1936). The third and fourth areas are those under the curves representing theoretical forecasts of the 1937 structure implied by the actual structures in 1936 and 1935, respectively. The term structures of interest rates are represented by curves showing the relationship between interest rates and term to maturity.

Appendix B

YIELDS TO MATURITY OF U.S. GOVERNMENT SECURITIES, BASED ON TREASURY YIELD CURVES

The yields shown in these tables were read from the fixed maturity yield curves published monthly in the *Treasury Bulletin*. The yields in Tables B-1 and B-2 were compiled independently by two different observers. Hence, many of the corresponding figures in the two tables differ by a few basis points. The implied forward rates shown in Tables B-1 and B-3 also differ, for the same reason.

TABLE B-1

SPOT AND FORWARD ONE-YEAR RATES

Date of Treasury Bulletin	Date of Yield Curve	One-Year Rate	Two-Year Rate	Forward One-Year Rate, One Year Hence	One-Year Rate, Observed One Year Later	Difference Between Spot and Forward One-Year Rates	Observed Change in One-Year Rate
3/58	1/58	2.20	2.50	2.83	3.53	+0.63	+1.33
4/58	2/58	1.74	2.09	2.48	3.41	+0.74	+1.67
5/58	3/58	1.75	2.09	2.47	3.53	+0.72	+1.78
6/58	4/58	1.48	1.80	2.16	3.82	+0.68	+2.34
7/58	5/58	1.14	1.66	2.31	3.88	+1.17	+2.74
8/58	6/58	1.41	1.87	2.42	4.08	+1.01	+2.67
9/58	7/58	1.65	2.07	2.56	4.30	+0.91	+2.65
10/58	8/58	2.94	3.42	3.96	4.67	+1.02	+1.73
11/58	9/58	3.35	3.53	3.72	4.89	+0.37	+1.54
12/58	10/58	3.07	3.36	3.67	4.48	+0.60	+1.41
1/59	11/58	3.27	3.48	3.70	4.93	+0.43	+1.66
2/59	12/58	3.17	3.52	3.90	4.97	+0.73	+1.80
3/59	1/59	3.53	3.80	4.09	4.62	+0.56	+1.09
4/59	2/59	3.41	3.69	3.99	4.53	+0.58	+1.12
5/59	3/59	3.53	3.87	4.24	3.73	+0.71	+0.20
6/59	4/59	3.82	4.02	4.23	4.05	+0.41	+0.23
7/59	5/59	3.88	4.21	4.56	4.04	+0.68	+0.16
8/59	6/59	4.08	4.43	4.80	3.27	+0.72	−0.81
9/59	7/59	4.30	4.53	4.77	2.89	+0.47	−1.41
10/59	8/59	4.67	4.87	5.08	2.97	+0.41	−1.70
11/59	9/59	4.89	4.95	5.01	2.93	+0.12	−1.96
12/59	10/59	4.48	4.63	4.78	2.82	+0.30	−1.66
1/60	11/59	4.93	4.97	5.01	3.03	+0.08	−1.90
2/60	12/59	4.97	5.04	5.11	2.65	+0.14	−2.32
3/60	1/60	4.62	4.76	4.90	2.78	+0.28	−1.84
4/60	2/60	4.53	4.68	4.83	3.01	+0.30	−1.52
5/60	3/60	3.73	3.89	4.06	2.91	+0.33	−0.82
6/60	4/60	4.05	4.28	4.52	2.87	+0.47	−1.18
7/60	5/60	4.04	4.26	4.49	2.91	+0.45	−1.13
8/60	6/60	3.27	3.71	4.20	3.04	+0.93	−0.23

(continued)

TABLE B-2

YIELDS OF FIXED-MATURITY TREASURY SECURITIES

Date of Treasury Bulletin	Date of Yield Curve	One-Year Rate	Two-Year Rate	Three-Year Rate	Four-Year Rate	Five-Year Rate	Six-Year Rate	Seven-Year Rate	Eight-Year Rate	Nine-Year Rate	Ten-Year Rate
3/54	1/54	1.23	1.50	1.75	1.97	2.10	2.22	2.34			
4/54	2/54	0.93	1.30	1.50	1.69	1.88	2.04	2.20			
5/54	3/54	1.00	1.30	1.50	1.68	1.84	1.99	2.13			
6/54	4/54	0.80	1.19	1.42	1.62	1.77	1.89	2.02			
7/54	5/54	0.86	1.29	1.56	1.79	1.98	2.11	2.22			
8/54	6/54	0.76	1.21	1.47	1.66	1.81	1.98	2.10			
9/54	7/54	0.70	1.16	1.46	1.67	1.85	2.01	2.11			
10/54	8/54	0.94	1.28	1.50	1.70	1.88	2.04	2.18			
11/54	9/54	1.13	1.47	1.67	1.82	1.97	2.09	2.21			
12/54	10/54	1.23	1.56	1.74	1.89	2.02	2.14	2.28			
1/55	11/54	1.22	1.54	1.75	1.94	2.09	2.22	2.35	2.44		
2/55	12/54	1.22	1.58	1.81	2.01	2.16	2.28	2.38	2.43		
3/55	1/55	1.45	1.81	2.02	2.18	2.29	2.39	2.46	2.52		
4/55	2/55	1.70	2.09	2.29	2.39	2.47	2.53	2.60	2.64		
5/55	3/55	1.67	2.04	2.27	2.39	2.48	2.55	2.60	2.64		
6/55	4/55	1.79	2.10	2.32	2.44	2.54	2.60	2.65	2.69		
7/55	5/55	1.82	2.16	2.34	2.44	2.51	2.59	2.63	2.69		
8/55	6/55	1.92	2.23	2.43	2.54	2.62	2.70	2.77	2.82		
9/55	7/55	2.13	2.43	2.61	2.72	2.82	2.88	2.91	2.92		
10/55	8/55	2.39	2.60	2.74	2.83	2.89	2.91	2.94	2.96		
11/55	9/55	2.30	2.47	2.60	2.69	2.76	2.82	2.85			
12/55	10/55	2.35	2.49	2.59	2.65	2.70	2.73	2.77			
1/56	11/55	2.61	2.74	2.81	2.83	2.84	2.86	2.88			
2/56	12/55	2.70	2.79	2.83	2.85	2.88	2.90	2.92			
3/56	1/56	2.45	2.57	2.64	2.70	2.73	2.77	2.81			
4/56	2/56	2.50	2.62	2.70	2.75	2.78	2.81	2.82			
5/56	3/56	2.59	2.88	2.97	3.00	3.02	3.03	3.05			

(continued)

TABLE B-1 (concluded)

Date of Treasury Bulletin	Date of Yield Curve	One-Year Rate	Two-Year Rate	Forward One-Year Rate, One Year Hence	One-Year Rate, Observed One Year Later	Difference between Spot and Forward One-Year Rates	Observed Change in One-Year Rate
9/60	7/60	2.89	3.11	3.34	2.96	+0.45	+0.07
10/60	8/60	2.97	3.21	3.46	3.04	+0.49	+0.07
11/60	9/60	2.93	3.21	3.51	2.99	+0.58	+0.06
12/60	10/60	2.82	3.18	3.57	2.93	+0.75	+0.11
1/61	11/60	3.03	3.33	3.65	2.99	+0.62	−0.04
2/61	12/60	2.65	2.81	2.98	3.19	+0.33	+0.54
3/61	1/61	2.78	3.15	3.56	3.22	+0.78	+0.44
4/61	2/61	3.01	3.24	3.48	3.14	+0.47	+0.13
5/61	3/61	2.91	3.16	3.43	3.00	+0.52	+0.09
6/61	4/61	2.87	3.10	3.34	3.03	+0.47	+0.16
7/61	5/61	2.91	3.24	3.60	2.99	+0.69	+0.08
8/61	6/61	3.04	3.36	3.71	3.22	+0.67	+0.18
9/61	7/61	2.96	3.33	3.73	3.36	+0.77	+0.40
10/61	8/61	3.04	3.38	3.75	3.13	+0.71	+0.09
11/61	9/61	2.99	3.37	3.79	3.01	+0.80	+0.02
12/61	10/61	2.93	3.32	3.75	2.98	+0.82	+0.05
1/62	11/61	2.99	3.36	3.76	3.09	+0.77	+0.10
1/62	12/61	3.19	3.50	3.83	3.13	+0.64	−0.06
2/62	1/62	3.22	3.58				
3/62	2/62	3.14	3.37				
4/62	3/62	3.00	3.22				
5/62	4/62	3.03	3.30				
6/62	5/62	2.99	3.20				
7/62	6/62	3.22	3.40				
8/62	7/62	3.36	3.49				
9/62	8/62	3.13	3.26				
10/62	9/62	3.01	3.19				
11/62	10/62	2.98	3.18				
12/62	11/62	3.09	3.25				
1/63	12/62	3.13	3.28				

TABLE B-2 (continued)

Date of Treasury Bulletin	Date of Yield Curve	One-Year Rate	Two-Year Rate	Three-Year Rate	Four-Year Rate	Five-Year Rate	Six-Year Rate	Seven-Year Rate	Eight-Year Rate	Nine-Year Rate	Ten-Year Rate
6/56	4/56	3.01	3.18	3.18	3.17	3.16	3.15	3.13			
7/56	5/56	2.78	2.94	2.94	2.94	2.94	2.94	2.94			
8/56	6/56	2.62	2.83	2.90	2.93	2.94	2.96				
9/56	7/56	2.84	3.15	3.21	3.22	3.23	3.23	3.23			
10/56	8/56	3.21	3.45	3.50	3.49	3.48	3.47	3.45			
11/56	9/56	3.32	3.45	3.43	3.40	3.39	3.36	3.34			
12/56	10/56	3.21	3.40	3.46	3.49	3.49	3.49				
1/57	11/56	3.57	3.74	3.69	3.65	3.63	3.60				
2/57	12/56	3.61	3.71	3.70	3.67	3.64	3.62				
3/57	1/57	3.27	3.38	3.38	3.34	3.33	3.30				
4/57	2/57	3.44	3.49	3.47	3.44	3.41	3.38				
5/57	3/57	3.37	3.47	3.48	3.47	3.44	3.41				
6/57	4/57	3.48	3.57	3.58	3.57	3.55	3.53				
7/57	5/57	3.60	3.68	3.72	3.73	3.73	3.72				
8/57	6/57	3.74	3.88	3.90	3.97	3.97	3.96				
9/57	7/57	3.82	3.93	3.98	4.01	4.02	4.01				
10/57	8/57	4.02	4.02	3.97	3.94	3.90	3.86				
11/57	9/57	4.09	4.09	4.07	4.06	4.04	4.03	4.02	4.02	4.01	4.01
12/57	10/57	3.98	4.05	4.06	4.06	4.05	4.03	4.01	3.99	3.98	3.97
1/58	11/57	3.44	3.43	3.40	3.38	3.37	3.35	3.35	3.36	3.40	3.43
2/58	12/57	2.88	2.87	2.85	2.84	2.84	2.87	2.92	2.96	3.01	3.04
3/58	1/58	2.19	2.48	2.68	2.78	2.84	2.92	2.98	3.06	3.12	3.17
4/58	2/58	1.73	2.07	2.31	2.50	2.64	2.75	2.85	2.94	3.00	3.05
5/58	3/58	1.71	2.09	2.33	2.48	2.59	2.70	2.78	2.86	2.92	2.98
6/58	4/58	1.46	1.78	2.07	2.26	2.42	2.57	2.69	2.78	2.86	2.91
7/58	5/58	1.09	1.60	1.98	2.18	2.36	2.50	2.60	2.71	2.79	2.88
8/58	6/58	1.47	1.90	2.25	2.48	2.60	2.71	2.81	2.88	2.95	3.20

(continued)

TABLE B-2 (continued)

Date of Treasury Bulletin	Date of Yield Curve	One-Year Rate	Two-Year Rate	Three-Year Rate	Four-Year Rate	Five-Year Rate	Six-Year Rate	Seven-Year Rate	Eight-Year Rate	Nine-Year Rate	Ten-Year Rate
9/58	7/58	1.68	2.09	2.45	2.70	2.86	2.96	3.05	3.11	3.18	3.21
10/58	8/58	3.01	3.42	3.54	3.59	3.63	3.67	3.70	3.74	3.75	3.77
11/58	9/58	3.38	3.53	3.62	3.70	3.74	3.76	3.78	3.79	3.81	3.82
12/58	10/58	3.09	3.35	3.55	3.70	3.76	3.80	3.81	3.82	3.82	3.82
1/59	11/58	3.29	3.48	3.68	3.64	3.66	3.67	3.68	3.69	3.70	3.71
2/59	12/58	3.20	3.53	3.70	3.80	3.85	3.85	3.85	3.84	3.84	3.84
3/59	1/59	3.52	3.80	3.91	3.97	3.98	3.98	3.98	3.97	3.97	3.96
4/59	2/59	3.42	3.70	3.79	3.83	3.85	3.87	3.88	3.89	3.90	3.90
5/59	3/59	3.52	3.86	3.96	4.02	4.02	4.02	4.02	4.02	4.02	4.02
6/59	4/59	3.81	4.02	4.12	4.18	4.23	4.23	4.23	4.22	4.21	4.20
7/59	5/59	3.92	4.20	4.29	4.28	4.27	4.25	4.25	4.23	4.21	4.20
8/59	6/59	4.08	4.45	4.49	4.47	4.45	4.42	4.38	4.34	4.32	4.29
9/59	7/59	4.28	4.55	4.57	4.54	4.48	4.45	4.42	4.39	4.36	4.33
10/59	8/59	4.67	4.88	4.90	4.84	4.74	4.67	4.60	4.55	4.50	4.47
11/59	9/59	4.90	4.95	4.92	4.84	4.77	4.73	4.68	4.64	4.60	4.57
12/59	10/59	4.47	4.64	4.70	4.67	4.60	4.55	4.49	4.45	4.41	4.37
1/60	11/59	4.94	4.97	4.93	4.84	4.76	4.69	4.62	4.57	4.51	4.47
2/60	12/59	4.97	5.04	5.06	5.05	5.01	4.96	4.90	4.84	4.79	4.73
3/60	1/60	4.60	4.75	4.80	4.79	4.75	4.70	4.66	4.62	4.57	4.55
4/60	2/60	4.52	4.68	4.74	4.74	4.67	4.61	4.55	4.49	4.46	4.44
5/60	3/60	3.67	3.89	3.97	4.03	4.08	4.10	4.10	4.10	4.10	4.10
6/60	4/60	4.04	4.29	4.37	4.40	4.39	4.36	4.33	4.31	4.29	4.28
7/60	5/60	3.98	4.25	4.33	4.37	4.36	4.31	4.28	4.25	4.22	4.20
8/60	6/60	3.21	3.70	3.89	3.97	4.00	4.02	4.02	4.02	4.02	4.02
9/60	7/60	2.86	3.12	3.29	3.41	3.52	3.60	3.66	3.70	3.73	3.77
10/60	8/60	2.93	3.19	3.37	3.50	3.61	3.68	3.72	3.76	3.79	3.80
11/60	9/60	2.92	3.22	3.39	3.54	3.63	3.69	3.71	3.75	3.78	3.80
12/60	10/60	2.86	3.21	3.42	3.58	3.69	3.76	3.80	3.82	3.86	3.88

(continued)

THE CAPITAL MARKETS

TABLE B-2 (concluded)

Date of Treasury Bulletin	Date of Yield Curve	One-Year Rate	Two-Year Rate	Three-Year Rate	Four-Year Rate	Five-Year Rate	Six-Year Rate	Seven-Year Rate	Eight-Year Rate	Nine-Year Rate	Ten-Year Rate
1/61	11/60	3.02	3.37	3.58	3.70	3.79	3.87	3.90	3.95	3.98	3.99
2/61	12/60	2.65	2.93	3.18	3.35	3.48	3.57	3.61	3.65	3.68	3.70
3/61	1/61	2.78	3.13	3.46	3.61	3.68	3.72	3.75	3.73	3.80	3.82
4/61	2/61	2.99	3.23	3.40	3.52	3.58	3.61	3.63	3.66	3.69	3.70
5/61	3/61	2.90	3.12	3.31	3.48	3.59	3.65	3.70	3.75	3.78	3.80
6/61	4/61	2.86	3.08	3.25	3.38	3.48	3.56	3.62	3.68	3.70	3.71
7/61	5/61	2.99	3.26	3.42	3.53	3.64	3.70	3.75	3.79	3.30	3.80
8/61	6/61	2.99	3.34	3.56	3.67	3.75	3.80	3.82	3.87	3.88	3.89
9/61	7/61	2.92	3.32	3.61	3.78	3.88	3.90	3.92	3.92	3.92	3.92
10/61	8/61	3.00	3.40	3.72	3.88	3.94	3.97	3.99	4.00	4.01	4.01
11/61	9/61	2.97	3.38	3.61	3.70	3.74	3.77	3.80	3.82	3.85	3.88
12/61	10/61	2.82	3.29	3.56	3.65	3.72	3.78	3.80	3.82	3.85	3.87
1/62	11/61	2.96	3.37	3.61	3.72	3.82	3.89	3.93	3.96	3.98	3.99
2/62	12/61	3.21	3.50	3.68	3.80	3.86	3.90	3.93	3.96	3.99	4.01
3/62	1/62	3.22	3.59	3.79	3.91	3.97	4.02	4.05	4.08	4.10	4.12
4/62	2/62	3.18	3.38	3.52	3.66	3.77	3.84	3.90	3.96	4.01	4.03
5/62	3/62	3.00	3.22	3.38	3.51	3.61	3.69	3.77	3.82	3.86	3.88
6/62	4/62	3.03	3.27	3.44	3.57	3.65	3.72	3.78	3.82	3.85	3.88
7/62	5/62	3.00	3.22	3.38	3.54	3.64	3.74	3.82	3.88	3.90	3.91
8/62	6/62	3.22	3.40	3.54	3.66	3.77	3.83	3.90	3.96	3.99	4.00
9/62	7/62	3.31	3.48	3.61	3.71	3.82	3.91	3.98	4.01	4.02	4.03
10/62	8/62	3.11	3.25	3.38	3.51	3.65	3.78	3.88	3.92	3.95	3.95
11/62	9/62	2.98	3.18	3.32	3.48	3.65	3.75	3.83	3.90	3.92	3.92
12/62	10/62	2.96	3.16	3.32	3.49	3.63	3.73	3.82	3.88	3.91	3.92
	11/62	3.08	3.24	3.38	3.50	3.59	3.67	3.75	3.82	3.88	3.92

TABLE B-3

SPOT AND FORWARD ONE-YEAR RATES ADJUSTED FOR LIQUIDITY PREMIUMS

Date of Yield Curve	One-Year Rate	Forward One-Year Rate One Year Hence	Estimated Liquidity Premium	Forward Rate Minus Liquidity Premium	One-Year Rate Observed One Year Later
4/58	1.46	2.17	−0.34	2.51	3.81
5/58	1.09	2.34	−0.53	2.87	3.92
6/58	1.47	2.45	−0.34	2.79	4.08
7/58	1.68	2.60	−0.23	2.83	4.28
8/58	3.01	3.88	+0.43	3.45	4.68
9/58	3.38	3.68	+0.62	3.06	4.90
10/58	3.09	3.63	+0.74	2.89	4.47
11/58	3.29	3.68	+0.77	2.91	4.94
12/58	3.20	3.89	+0.87	3.02	4.97
1/59	3.52	4.10	+0.98	3.12	4.60
2/59	3.42	4.00	+0.93	3.07	4.52
3/59	3.52	4.23	+1.04	3.19	3.67
4/59	3.81	4.24	+1.05	3.19	4.04
5/59	3.92	4.50	+1.18	3.32	3.98
6/59	4.08	4.85	+1.35	3.50	3.21
7/59	4.28	4.83	+1.34	3.49	2.86
8/59	4.67	5.09	+1.47	3.62	2.93
9/59	4.90	5.00	+1.43	3.57	2.92
10/59	4.47	4.81	+1.33	3.48	2.86
11/59	4.94	5.00	+1.43	3.57	3.02
12/59	4.97	5.11	+1.48	3.63	2.65
1/60	4.60	4.90	+1.38	3.52	2.78
2/60	4.52	4.84	+1.35	3.49	2.99
3/60	3.67	4.12	+0.99	3.13	2.90
4/60	4.04	4.55	+1.20	3.35	2.86
5/60	3.98	4.53	+1.19	3.34	2.99
6/60	3.21	4.26	+1.06	3.20	2.99
7/60	2.86	3.40	+0.63	2.77	2.92
8/60	2.93	3.47	+0.66	2.81	3.00
9/60	2.92	3.55	+0.70	2.85	2.97
10/60	2.86	3.60	+0.73	2.87	2.82
11/60	3.02	3.76	+0.81	2.95	2.96
12/60	2.65	3.23	+0.54	2.69	3.21
1/61	2.78	3.52	+0.69	2.83	3.22
2/61	2.99	3.48	+0.67	2.81	3.18

6 The Allocation of Mortgage Funds (1969)

The objective of this paper is to study the effects of the following phenomena upon the allocation of mortgage funds: (1) Secular trends in interest rates, (2) the cyclical behavior of the term structure of interest rates, (3) trends in the yields of tax exempt and corporate debt securities, (4) legal ceilings upon mortgage rates, and (5) regional variations in mortgage yields.

1. Secular Trends in Interest Rates

Savings and loan associations may be viewed as performing two functions in the money and capital markets. One is to convert relatively illiquid mortgages into very liquid deposit liabilities. (Liquidity in this context may be measured by the difference between the bid and asked prices for both classes of securities.) The other is to convert relatively long-term assets, mortgages, into short-term deposit liabilities. Needless to say, these functions are not performed free of charge; the economic cost to society of these activities is a function of the difference between mortgage and deposit yields.

Converting long-term assets, such as mortgages, into short-term liabilities is not arbitrage. It is not a risk-free undertaking in a world in which future interest rates are not known with certainty. Any uncertainty, however small, about future rates implies that unanticipated changes in interest rates must occur. Given the way that the money and capital market revises its estimates of future interest rates when new knowledge is acquired, the returns—income flows plus capital-value changes—derived from long-term securities are more variable than the returns on short-terms.[1] Returns are more variable for long-terms because of the greater instability in the prices of long-terms which more than offsets the greater yield-to-maturity variability of short-terms. Reasoning symmetrically, the returns on mortgages are more variable than the costs of deposits; deposits have virtually zero term-to-maturity, and hence exhibit less variability in realized returns than mortgages.[2]

---

[1] It is not a truism that the prices of long term securities will fluctuate more than short-terms. It is caused by the way the market revises its estimates of future short rates; these revisions are positively correlated. On this point, see David Meiselman, *The Term Structure of Interest Rates* (Prentice-Hall, 1962), p. 32.

[2] The economic term-to-maturity of a deposit liability is a function of the frequency with which dividends are declared. Semi-annual declarations are the lowest frequency with quarterly declarations more typical. The effect of the frequency of dividend declarations upon economic term-to-maturity is in large part, but not completely, offset by the ability to borrow using deposits as collateral.

The propositions (1) interest rate changes are not perfectly anticipated, and (2) the market revises its estimates of expected future rates in a manner that leads to greater variability in the economic returns associated with holding long as compared with short maturities, imply that savings and loan associations have greater variance in the economic returns on their assets than in the costs of their deposit liabilities.[3] Unanticipated increases in rates produce a fall in the market value of assets that is not offset by a commensurate fall in the value of liabilities. Therefore, equity, which for savings and loan associations is reserves, falls. Converse implications hold for an unanticipated decrease in rates. In summary, savings and loan associations are long on long-term money (mortgages) and short on short-term money (deposits). Hence, they lose when there is an unanticipated rise in rates and gain when there is a fall.

Since the end of World War II, there has been a secular rise in rates. Yields of tax exempts, treasury bills, long-term governments, deposit liabilities of savings banks and savings and loan associations have all exhibited an upward trend. On average, the yields to maturity of long governments exceeded bill yields during every business cycle, as measured by the National Bureau of Economic Research, during these 22 years. Yet, if one examines quarterly holding period yields, (i.e., coupon yields plus or minus capital value changes computed quarterly), since the end of World War II, on average, bill yields have exceeded bond yields by over 90 basis points.[4] In other words, a steady-state (continuous) investor in bills would on average earn 90 basis points per year more than an investor in long governments.

This evidence clearly indicates that at least some of the secular rise in rates, which was about 17 basis points a year measured by treasury bill yields, has been unanticipated if one is willing to accept either the Hicks or the Lutz theories of the term structure of interest rates.[5] How much of this rise has been unanticipated by the market depends upon which of these theories one is willing to accept. In retrospect, it is evident that the yield-to-maturity of long-terms vis-à-vis short-terms has been too low, i.e., the ex post differential between the cost of savings money and the realized yield on mortgages has been below the ex ante differential. Alternatively, unanticipated capital losses, capital losses not offset by higher yields to maturity of longs vis-à-vis shorts, must have been realized by the holders of longs.

---

[3] In a world of perfect certainty, both longs and shorts would be equally variable in total returns. This is consistent with greater price variability for longs than shorts if yields to maturity reflected expected price changes.

[4] This number was obtained by hypothetically investing in 91-day bills every 91 days and comparing the yield obtained with an investment and disinvestment for the same 91 days in the three longest-term governments. Transaction costs were implicitly assumed to be zero by transacting at an average of bid and asked prices.

[5] The Hicksian view, which is widely accepted, implies that the holding period yields of longs ought to be in excess of shorts with the difference representing a measure of the nonpecuniary yield attributable to the greater liquidity of shorts.

This analysis implies that the receipt streams savings and loans derived from their principal asset, mortgages, must have, on average, been below the current mortgage market. Given the upward trend in rates, receipt streams must have been below what they would have been if past investments in mortgages could have been committed at current yields. For the savings and loan industry as a whole, and this probably applies to other depository institutions as well, interest costs have been noncontractual and reflect the current market. By contrast, revenues have been contractually determined and in entering mortgage contracts, the savings and loan industry failed to fully anticipate the secular trend upwards in interest rates. Consequently, costs but not revenues reflected current market conditions, and operating margins for savings and loans must have contracted as a result of the secular trend in rates.

The effect of the unanticipated trend in rates since the end of World War II upon the returns on savings and loan associations, abstracting from rate of growth, is a function of the term-to-maturity of mortgages.[6] This is not easy to determine. The contracted or programed term-to-maturity of mortgages is typically from 20 to 30 years. However, the mortgagee has the option (this is similar to call provisions for bonds) of paying off his mortgage before the termination of its programed life, and almost invariably exercises this option. Even if a mortgage lives out its programed life, since virtually all residential mortgages are amortizing mortgages, i.e., provide for automatic repayment of the mortgage principal over its programed life, loan size decreases monotonically with time. Consequently, a 30-year mortgage for, say, $10,000 is equivalent to a loan whose average size over its life is about $7,500.

Variables that play a role in determining the expected life of a mortgage are programed life, loan-to-value ratio, and the difference between the contract and the current mortgage rate. Typically, the programed life of a mortgage is terminated when a house is sold and the mortgage on the property is of an unsuitable size for the new buyer. This is most likely to occur when the loan-to-value ratio is low, the programed life short, and there has been a rise in property values.

---

[6] This analysis owes much to a paper by Paul Samuelson, "The Effect of Interest Rate Increases on the Banking System," *The American Economic Review*, March, 1945, p. 28ff. Samuelson analyzes the effects of interest rate increases upon the welfare of the owners of college endowments, life insurance companies, and commercial banks. The premises and conclusions reached here differ from Samuelson's in the following important respects. (1) Samuelson does not explicitly distinguish between anticipated and unanticipated changes in rates although by implication it appears that he is referring to unanticipated rate increases, (2) Samuelson implicitly assumes that a rise in interest rates does not change the cost of deposits to commercial banks; that rising rates affect interest receipts but not the costs of deposits, and (3) concludes that interest-rate increases favor banks. On the analysis followed here, banks would lose as a result of an unanticipated rise in rates but their losses, per dollar of assets, would not be as severe as they are for savings and loan associations because their assets are of shorter duration.

This suggests that mortgages have a shorter life in booming housing markets, where house prices have risen relative to the remainder of the country and conversely. It also suggests that insured mortgages, which typically have relatively longer programed lives and lower down-payment requirements, are longer-lived than conventional mortgages. And among conventional mortgages, the high down payment and short programed life mortgages should have shorter economic lives.

The FHA estimates, based on its past experience, an average life of 14 years for its insured mortgages. Conventional mortgages in the Chicago area, which typically have a programed life of 20 to 25 years with an 80-percent loan-to-value ratio, average about 7 years of actual life. An average life of 7 years implies substantial lags between contractual rates of return on mortgage portfolios and current yields on comparable mortgages.

The effect of the unanticipated secular rise in interest rates has been to reduce the reserves of savings and loan associations below what they would have been if this rise had not occurred. In view of the trend in interest rates, it is reasonable to presume that the book value of mortgages for the industry as a whole is in excess of the market value; unrealized capital losses exceed unrealized capital gains. Therefore, the book value of nonliability or equity reserves must also be in excess of their market value.[7] As a result of the secular change, associations have been less aggressive in bidding for savings money than they otherwise would have been. Net inflows of savings lower reserve ratios; i.e., the ratio of surplus to savings. The greater the rate of growth of savings, the greater the rate of decrease in reserve ratios. (There exists a mandatory reserve requirement of 5 percent.) Consequently, savings and loan associations have sought a lower rate of growth than would otherwise have been true, and the flow of funds into mortgages has been lower than would have been the case if there had been no unanticipated trend upward in rates since World War II.

The empirical magnitude of the effects discussed is revealed by table 1. An unanticipated upward trend in rates implies that interest costs will rise faster than interest receipts for financial institutions that are short on short-term money and long on long-term money. This is in fact what the figures reflecting interest receipts and costs of savings and loan associations show. This table also reveals trends in the spread between what is paid for money by savings and loan associations and interest receipts. From 1950 through 1967, the spread has gone from 210 to 110 basis points, a drop of almost 50 percent. This

---

[7] It is also highly likely that the book value of U.S. Governments held to satisfy the mandatory 6½ percent liquidity requirement is also in excess of market value.

TABLE 1.—COMPARISON OF RATES EARNED ON ASSETS AND PAID ON SAVINGS BY SAVINGS AND LOAN ASSOCIATIONS [1]—1950–67

[In percent]

Year	Interest return on mortgages [2]	Rate earned on assets [3]	Rate paid on savings [4]	Spread (2-3)
	(1)	(2)	(3)	(4)
1950	4.8	4.6	2.5	2.1
1951	4.8	4.6	2.6	2.0
1952	4.8	4.6	2.7	1.9
1953	4.9	4.7	2.8	1.9
1954	4.9	4.8	2.9	1.9
1955	5.0	4.9	2.9	2.0
1956	5.0	4.9	3.0	1.9
1957	5.1	5.1	3.3	1.8
1958	5.2	5.2	3.4	1.8
1959	5.3	5.4	3.5	1.9
1960	5.5	5.5	3.9	1.6
1961	5.6	5.6	3.9	1.7
1962	5.7	5.8	4.1	1.7
1963	5.7	5.7	4.2	1.5
1964	5.8	5.7	4.2	1.5
1965	5.8	5.7	4.2	1.5
1966	5.9	5.8	4.5	1.3
1967	5.9	5.8	4.7	1.1

[1] From Irwin Friend, "Changes in the Asset and Liability Structure of the Savings and Loan Industry", Vol. III of the present study.
[2] Source: Member savings and loan associations of the Federal Home Loan Bank System combined financial statements; interest return on mortgages relative to average mortgages outstanding.
[3] Source: Ibid; gross operating income relative to average assets.
[4] Source: Ibid; dividends distributed relative to average savings balance.

drop is accounted for by a virtual doubling in rates paid to savers while rates earned on assets increased about 20 percent.[8][9]

The effects of the long-term secular trend upward in rates upon savings and loan associations have been analyzed without asking what led to this trend. This question cannot be ignored because the rise in rates could have been caused by an increase in demand for mortgage money which implies an increase in demand for the services of savings and loan associations. Or it could have occurred without any change in the demand for mortgage funds or with a decrease. If either of the latter are relevant, then the rise in rates would cause a curtailment in the quantity of mortgage funds demanded and the effect of the secular rise in rates upon the fortunes of savings and loan associations would be reinforced. By contrast, if the first alternative is relevant, then the effect of the unanticipated upward trend in interest rates could have been, at least in part, offset by an increase in the demand for financial intermediation by savings and loan associations.

Probably the best single piece of evidence on this point is the behavior of housing starts. Judging from the census figures for private

---

[8] Some observers have inferred a much wider spread because they assumed an average life to maturity which is less than the average life cited here. For example, Bloch uses for mortgage yields a 5-year moving average of yearly rates on conventional mortgages. This implies an average life of 2½ years. See Ernest Bloch, "Changes in the Structure of Bank and Nonbank Competition in the United States," *Banca Nazionale del Lavoro Quarterly Review*, No. 84 (March 1968), p. 20.

[9] Another measure shows "profitability" of savings and loan associations declining by two-thirds from 1950 to 1967. See chart 57, p. 107, of *Savings and Loan Fact Book for 1968* U.S. Savings & Loan League, 221 North LaSalle St., Chicago, Ill.

housing starts, the post-World War II housing boom peaked out at or near the end of 1963. By 1966, housing starts were at a level lower than they had been in the past 15 years. Housing starts during the interest rate peak of 1960 were clearly higher than they were in 1966 although they fell sharply from 1958 to 1960. This evidence suggests that the rise in interest rates in recent years, since 1963, cannot be rationalized as a consequence of a housing boom. For the entire post-World War II period, the evidence is not as unambiguous. That part of the secular trend in rates associated with the period from 1950 through 1963 appears to have some rationale in a housing boom. Hence, the effects of the secular trend in interest rates were mitigated by an increase in the demand for the services of savings and loan associations. However, since 1963, this force has been absent. Therefore, the effect of the secular rise in rates has been more severe in recent years abstracting from the rate of change of rates.

2. Cyclical Behavior of the Term Structure of Interest Rates

In addition to the effects of the unanticipated secular trend in rates upon the reserves, and as a consequence, the rate of growth of savings deposits and mortgage portfolios, there exist cyclical movements in rates that also affect these variables. Over the business cycle, interest rates are, in the language of the National Bureau of Economic Research, coincident indicators. They reach their peaks at peaks in business conditions and conversely reach their troughs at troughs in business conditions. Short rates rise relative to long rates during expansions; i.e., the arithmetic difference between long and short rates decreases as the economy moves from business trough to business peak. Symmetrically, short rates fall relative to long rates (rates are internal rates of return or yields to maturity here) when the economy moves from business peak to trough.

The rise in short relative to long rates during business expansions has been strong enough, in recent years, to produce periods of substantial length when short rates were above long rates. For 9 months in 1957, 8 months in 1959–60, and about 15 months starting in January of 1966, short rates as measured by the yields of Treasury bills were above long rates as measured by the yields of long-term governments.

When short rates are high relative to long rates, the market expects future rates of all maturities to be lower than current short rates. Therefore, the purchasers of longs anticipate capital gains. If the expected decline in rates is especially sharp, then the expected capital gains for longs are unusually large. Consequently, short rates are especially high relative to long rates and often are above long rates about cyclical peaks so that the returns on the two classes of securities can be equalized.[1] The cyclical behavior of the term structure of interest implies that the market anticipates capital gains for the buyers of longs about cyclical peaks and capital losses for the buyers of longs about cyclical troughs. This explains the relative variation in the yields to maturity; i.e., internal rates of return, of short and long bonds over the cycle.

About cyclical peaks, if savings and loan associations were to raise their rates on deposits to a level commensurate with other money-market instruments, say Treasury bills or bankers' acceptances, then the returns on mortgage portfolios—i.e., yields to maturity—would for many institutions go below the interest costs of deposits. Hence, unless savings and loan associations anticipate capital gains on mortgages acquired about cyclical peaks, they cannot compete in the market for short-term money at that time. Conversely about cyclical troughs, unless savings and loan associations anticipate capital losses on mortgages acquired, they overestimate the returns on these mortgages and hence compete too vigorously for funds.

However, even if savings and loan associations did anticipate capital gains and losses on mortgages over the cycle, there is the question of what could they do with respect to accounting for such gains and losses. Clearly, unless anticipated capital gains were reflected in income statements, raising yields on deposits during cyclical peaks in order to acquire savings which will be converted into mortgages would deplete reserves. Yet it is difficult to believe that either regulatory authorities, or recognized CPA firms, would approve of statements that included in reserves, anticipated capital gains.

The foregoing suggests that, whether or not capital gains and losses attributable to cyclical fluctuations in interest rates are anticipated by savings and loan associations, it would be difficult to act upon such expectations given the views of the accounting profession and the regulatory authorities. Consequently the cyclical pattern of interest rates will lead to cyclical patterns in the flow of savings into, and mortgage funds from, savings and loan associations. The flow will be contracyclical; it will be at a maximum at cyclical troughs and a minimum at peaks.

In those instances when short rates have gone above corresponding long rates, a process that has been described as financial disintermediation has occurred. Investors have withdrawn deposits from financial institutions when their rates on deposits were no longer competitive. These withdrawn deposits were in turn invested, without benefit of financial intermediation, in governments, often treasury bills or agency notes. As a result, financial intermediaries such as sav-

---

[1] For a discussion of this point, see Reuben A. Kessel, "Cyclical Behavior of the Term Structure of Interest Rates," Occasional Paper 91, National Bureau of Economic Research (New York: Columbia University Press, 1965).

ings and loan associations incurred negative rates of growth of savings. Financial disintermediation is an extreme form of a more general phenomenon that is cyclical in nature. Until short rates went above long rates, it manifested itself in lower but positive rates of growth of savings and mortgage portfolios about cyclical peaks than was true about cyclical troughs, or for the cycle. When short rates went above long rates in 1960 and again in 1966, negative growth rates were observed.

3. Trends in Yields of Tax Exempt and Corporate Debt Securities

The unanticipated rise in rates has had roughly the same effect on all financial institutions that borrow short and lend long. Savings and loan associations, and to a lesser extent savings banks, are unique among financial institutions, in the sense that they are wedded to carrying a particular type of assets, mortgages. By contrast, life insurance companies can easily switch from mortgages to corporate bonds, and the time deposits in commercial banks can go into tax-exempt securities and corporates rather than mortgages. Tax exempts have a special appeal to commercial bankers because most of their institutions have marginal tax rates of roughly 50 percent in contrast to much lower effective rates for both life insurance companies and savings and loan associations. Hence, the willingness of commercial banks and life insurance companies to invest in mortgages is a function of the relative yields of mortgages vis-à-vis corporates and tax exempts. By contrast, savings and loan associations, and possibly savings banks, are not as free to switch. If the relative yields of mortgages fall, they adjust by reducing their rate of growth and not by switching to other assets. The proximate cause that leads to a reduction in the desired rate of growth is a contraction in the spread between the cost of deposits and mortgage yields.

Since the beginning of 1947, Moody's AAA tax exempt 20-year bond yield has risen from about 1¾ percent to slightly over 4 percent. It is currently—January 1968—at or about its all time high. Lower quality municipals, AA and A rated bonds, have exhibited an even greater increase in yield during this period because differentials attributable to quality differences have decreased. The current yield on municipals implies that commercial banks, whose marginal tax rate is roughly 50 percent, can obtain, by buying municipals, a yield equivalent to at least 8 percent on a security whose income is taxable.[1]

---

[1] This needs to be qualified. If municipals are bought at a discount, the difference between the price paid and par, or the resale price if higher than original cost, is subject to a capital gains tax. Needless to say, this is reflected in the prices of municipals. Hence, low-coupon municipals typically sell at higher yields-to-maturity than high-coupon municipals. The opposite holds for low- and high-coupon Federal obligations.

As a result of the great increase since 1960 in the volume outstanding of State and local governmental debt and corporate debt relative to home mortgage debt, relative yields have changed.[2] The after-tax yields of municipals have risen relative to most negotiable instruments in the capital markets and in particular relative to mortgages. The comparative advantage of municipals vis-à-vis mortgages for commercial banks has increased markedly; and at present yields for mortgages and municipals, it appears unambiguous that an absolute advantage for municipals exists.[3]

Life insurance companies, the other large institutional participant in mortgage markets, have found that corporate bond yields have risen relative to mortgage yields. At the end of 1967, the yield of Moody's AAA corporates was about 6.25. In the past 19 to 20 years, this series has risen about 400 basis points, from about 2.30 to its present level. Since corporates are an important competitor for mortgages in the portfolios of life insurance companies, the allocation of mortgage funds is affected by the relative yields of these two classes of assets. During the past 19 years, the yields in the secondary market of insured FHA mortgages rose from about 4.35 to about 6.80. Clearly the comparative advantage of corporates vis-à-vis mortgages has changed in favor of corporates as a function of time. Absolutely, there currently is not much difference in the net yield to the holder of home mortgages and top quality corporates. For home mortgages, the yield quoted is a gross yield out of which servicing costs must be paid. This typically runs about three-eighths of 1 percent for FHA insured mortgages. Consequently, the net yield on FHA's current is about 6.40; this is less than the current yields of medium- and low-quality corporates and about the yields of top quality corporates.

This evidence on the changes in relative yields of tax exempts and corporates vis-à-vis mortgages suggests that commercial banks and insurance companies should have been shifting away from mortgages into these other securities. Hence, the share of savings and loan associations and savings banks in the home mortgage market should have increased. This has been true for the past 10 to 15 years. Since 1947, the mortgage holdings of savings and loan associations for one- to four-family properties have risen at a more rapid rate than they have for either life insurance companies or commercial banks. For savings and loan associations, holdings increased by a factor of 12; for savings banks, holdings increased by a factor of 14. In contrast, life insurance holdings increased by a factor of less than nine, banks by a factor less than 6. Similar results can be obtained using other

---

[2] See *Savings and Loan Fact Book*, op. cit., table 19, p. 32.

[3] Municipals often can be pledged as security for tax and loan accounts of governmental bodies, whereas mortgages cannot. This constitutes a nonpecuniary advantage for municipals and implies that a yield advantage for mortgages is necessary to bring the aggregate yield of the two into equality.

years as bases. For example, since 1955, holdings of savings and loan associations and savings banks increased more than threefold, whereas insurance company holdings less than doubled and commercial bank holdings increased by a factor of about $2\frac{1}{4}$.[4]

4. Legal Ceilings Upon Mortgate Rates

Legal ceilings on mortgage rates exist, in one form or another, in 10 States. In addition, the FHA and VA impose ceilings upon rates for the mortgages they insure. The most well known, and probably the most important ceiling imposed by State law, exists in New York which currently has a 6 percent maximum upon mortgage rates.[1] Whether or not these ceilings have any economic effects depends upon the level of interest rates in the market and the ability of mortgagees and mortgagors to transact business legally at economic rates in excess of ceiling rates.

From the point of view of a financial institution, effective ceilings induce it to invest either in media not subject to the ceiling, or buy mortgages in the secondary market which are typically originated out of State, or buy participations in out-of-State mortgages. Even if a financial institution were willing to forgo higher yields available in the secondary market in order to lend locally at ceiling rates, it would lose its share of the market to institutions that did not forgo higher secondary market rates. Institutions that invested at the higher rates would be able to pay commensurately higher rates of interest and/or spend more on advertising. Hence, willingness to adhere to ceiling rates, under these circumstances, is not a survival property for such institutions.

However, ceilings may not be effective. To illustrate, if ceiling rates are below market rates, can the difference between market and ceiling rates be equalized by appropriate service charges? If not, can a seller of property also provide a mortgage at the ceiling rate which is resold to a financial institution at a yield equal to the market rate? If so, the appropriate service charge is buried in the price of the property. In other words, the borrower appears to borrow at the ceiling rate but in fact borrows at the market rate, and the price of the house is higher by an amount representing the present worth of the difference between interest charges computed at the market and at the ceiling rate. This is typically the way that the FHA and VA ceilings are evaded. For the FHA and VA, another control exists in the form of appraisals by the insuring agency. To the extent that house prices rise

---

[4] These estimates are obtained from the releases of the Federal Home Loan Bank Board. Also see *Savings and Loan Fact Book*, op. cit., table 20 and chart 19, pp. 36 and 37.

[1] Since this paper was first written, many States have revised their mortgage rate ceilings upward.

as a consequence of a discrepancy between insured and market rates, the probability of a loan being approved for governmental insurance decreases because the house price rises relative to the appraisal price. It is because FHA's and VA's mortgages are subject to appraisals that the use of these mortgages decreases when rates rise.[2]

In general, rates in the mortgage market are related to loan-to-value ratios. At any moment in time, poor risks, i.e., high loan-to-value ratios, are associated with higher rates of interest than good risks. Hence, at any moment in time, there exists a structure of mortgage rates that is a function of risk. To the extent that legal ceilings on mortgages are effective, they are bound to bear more onerously upon poor risks. The rates charged to good risks are, for any specified ceiling, more likely to be below the ceiling than the rates charged to poor risks. Moreover, good risks, to the extent that they are precluded from the mortgage market by effective ceilings, are more likely to have other collaterable assets than poor risks. Therefore, to the extent that ceilings are operative, they are more likely to keep poor, in contrast with good, risks from borrowing.

5. Regional Variation in Mortgage Yields

In general, a mortgage appears to be a relatively illiquid instrument as measured by the bid-ask spreads typically observed in securities markets. However, precisely how it compares with other securities in this crucial dimension is difficult to determine. It is difficult to obtain bid-ask spreads for mortgages since dealers that continuously make a market are virtually nonexistent.[1] The FNMA buys and sells mortgages. Unfortunately, it rarely sells when it is buying and conversely. Its objective is market stabilization as defined by mortgage yields, and it typically buys when it judges rates to be low and sells when they are high.[2] In recent years, it has on net balance been a buyer, and its portfolio of mortgages has grown. Consequently, its operations have contributed, insofar as it has had any effect at all, to keeping down mortgage yields relative to the yields of other long-term securities. In effect, the FNMA through expanding its holdings of mortgages and

---

[2] See the supplement to "Business Review," June 1968 of the Federal Reserve Bank of Philadelphia for remarks by Andrew F. Brimmer on "Statutory Interest Rate Ceilings and the Availability of Mortgage Funds," that have much in common with the foregoing discussion.

[1] See Oliver Jones and Leo Grebler, "The Secondary Mortgage Market" (University of California press, 1961), chap. IV.

[2] For every $1,000 of mortgages bought by the FNMA, the seller of these mortgages is required to pay a $5 marketing fee and invest $10 in FNMA stock. At the current price this stock sells for in the secondary market, one-half of this investment is lost. Hence, the effective buying price of FNMA per $1,000 of mortgages is $10 less than the price stated. This is suggestive that bid-ask spreads must be in excess of $10 per thousand.

financing these holdings through the issuance of participation certificates has been, effectively, in competition with the savings and loan industry.

The operation of FNMA has undoubtedly increased the liquidity of the class of mortgages that it buys. To the extent that this has occurred, the yield basis that investors should have been willing to hold such mortgages should decrease. Nevertheless, because of their illiquidity, which in large part stems from the costs of servicing which are unique to this instrument in the capital markets, the market for mortgages is primarily an institutional market with almost no participation by individuals. Part of what a financial institution that invests in mortgages is paid for is to convert illiquid mortgages into more liquid assets that individuals want to hold.

The insurance premiums charged for governmental insurance are independent of the risk of default as conventionally measured by the loan-to-value ratio. Since the terms at which conventional mortgages are made vary with the loan-to-value ratio, with rates positively related to loan-to-value ratios, insured loans have a comparative advantage, for both borrowers and lenders, for high loan-to-value ratio borrowers. Consequently, when insured loan rates are so far away from the market that discounting these loans to bring their effective rate in line with the market will lead to unacceptably high appraisals, it is the poor risks that are most adversely affected. This analysis explains why foreclosure rates and delinquency rates are higher, for most lending institutions, for insured as distinguished from uninsured loans.

The Federal insurance program also has the effect, to the extent that it is used, of producing a relatively standardized commodity. Hence, would-be buyers of unseasoned mortgages in the secondary market can more easily, i.e., at lower cost, estimate the probable receipt stream associated with insured as distinguished from uninsured mortgages. In buying an unseasoned, conventional mortgage, a would-be buyer has a strong interest in obtaining an independent appraisal of the value of the properties securing the mortgages being considered for purchase. This is a costly procedure. Hence, when conventional mortgages are sold in the secondary market, they are more likely to be seasoned. This is to say that they have a demonstrated record of payments by the mortgagee which the would-be buyer places reliance upon.

The foregoing suggests that there exist substantial transactions costs in the secondary market for mortgages. To the extent that transactions take place between institutions in the secondary mortgage market, and there does not exist a permanent relationship between these institutions on a par with the relationship between mortgage banker and insurance company, either seasoned, conventional mortgages, or insured mortgages will be traded. Moreover, bringing money from low- to high-rate areas via the secondary market for mortgages must compete with bringing money directly via higher rates on savings deposits in high-rate areas. This implies that the transactions costs in secondary markets must be compared with the premiums investors demand to keep their funds in institutions hundreds of miles away from their homes. There exists a great deal of evidence that California savings and loan associations, which have been located in high-rate areas, have in fact attracted a great deal of funds from out-of-State investors. To the extent that this has occurred, it has led to a smaller volume of transactions in the secondary mortgage market and the lack of development of this market.[3]

This analysis suggests that to the extent that rates paid to savers are made uniform throughout the country by regulation, then the volume of transactions in the secondary market will increase. Abstracting from the variations in mortgage rates throughout the United States, savings rate regulation will increase the volume of transactions in the secondary mortgage market.

The isolation of particular mortgage markets from interregional lenders appears to be greater for used or existing homes sold by owner-residents as contrasted with typically new homes sold by builders.[4] A common explanation offered for the greater isolation of the used housing market from interregional lenders is:

A possible reason for this result is the greater insulation of the existing house market from the effects of interregional credit supplied through the FHA–VA secondary market and the conventional lending of life insurance companies. The latter two types of financing are most often secured by new houses; existing houses are more heterogeneous and are more likely to be financed in the local, conventional market. Thus, yields on mortgages secured by used houses are more apt to be affected by the relative availability of local credit than are yields on new house mortgages.[5]

An alternative interpretation of this phenomenon turns on the fact that insured FHA and VA mortgages can only be made at rates preassigned by regulatory authorities. These rates often depart from market rates. When they do, and in the postwar period they were on balance below market rates, they must be discounted in order to equalize their attractiveness with conventional mortgages or insured mortgages in the secondary market. However, a lending institution is prohibited from providing, to a borrower, funds less than the face value of an insured FHA mortgage. Hence, if this mortgage is to be discounted, then the seller of the property must obtain the mortgage and add the discount to the price of the house to the buyer. This involves considerable cost and redtape and is most attractive to the

---

[3] This is a point that Jones and Grebler, op. cit., have not recognized.
[4] See Schaaf, A. H., "Regional Differences in Mortgage Financing Costs," *Journal of Finance* (Mar. 1966), p. 85.
[5] Ibid., pp. 92 and 93.

mass production tract builder who can simultaneously make such an arrangement for a number of houses. Used houses are typically sold by individuals who sell first and leave the financing to the buyer or realtor. Once the price is determined, then discounting becomes difficult if not impossible. On this line, the market for used houses is more isolated from the services of national lenders because the costs of evading FHA–VA rate regulations are greater for used than new houses. This explains why regional variations in rates are greater for used as distinguished from new homes and why insured mortgages are more frequently employed for new as distinguished from used houses.[6]

Schaaf found regional variations in yields of 89 basis points for new houses and 106 basis points for existing homes. However, loan-to-value ratios are correlated with high rates; areas that have high loan-to-value ratios also report high mortgage rates. When Schaaf standardized for risk as measured by loan-to-value ratios, regional variations in rates were sharply reduced. He concluded that:

> ... a major share of the total amount of regional mortgage yield variation, particularly in new construction, is not a manifestation of an imperfect mortgage market. Nor does it signify a misallocation of mortgage funds. Rather, it is a manifestation of a necessary allocative device whereby a higher-risk borrower may secure credit by agreeing to pay a higher price.[7]

There is of course considerable evidence that mortgages flow from west to east, and savings money from east to west. Although savings and loan associations on balance buy more mortgages in secondary markets than they sell, the associations in the San Francisco district are on balance sellers of mortgages. Moreover the New York and Boston district associations seem to be especially heavy buyers of mortgages. Consistent with these observations is the fact that San Francisco associations are particularly heavy borrowers of funds from the Federal Home Loan Bank which in turn borrows nationally.[8]

6. Conclusions

The trend in interest rates that has characterized most of the post-World War II period has been, at least in some, if not in large part, unanticipated. Since savings and loan associations are long on long-term funds, and short on short-term funds, they have experienced un-

---

[6] This argument implies: (1) A larger fraction of sales of new homes utilize FHA mortgages than used homes, and (2) the variation in the use of FHA mortgages with variations in interest rates ought to be greater for used as distinguished from new homes. For evidence on this point, see *Savings and Loan Fact Book*, op. cit., chart 68, p. 128.

[7] Ibid., p. 94. Loan-to-value ratios are an imperfect measure of risk because foreclosure costs vary from State-to-State. Hence, mortgages with equivalent loan-to-value ratios are not equally risky. This is a variable that was not entered into the analysis.

[8] Ibid., chart 50, p. 90; table 71, p. 91; table 87, p. 117.

anticipated capital losses, probably unrealized in an accounting sense, during most of this period. Hence, equity reserves and assets in the form of mortgages are carried at book values that exceed market values.

During this time, there has been a pronounced cyclical movement in rates that has been independent of trend. During two of the cyclical peaks in rates, 1960 and 1966, short rates were above long rates, a relationship between long and short rates that is relatively rare. In order to compete in the money and capital markets at these cyclical peaks, savings and loans would have to offer savers rates in excess of current mortgage rates. Such a policy could only be economically rational if one anticipated a decline in both long and short rates with the expectation of capital gains on mortgages acquired during these peaks. Apart from the problems of convincing management to engage in a policy based on such expectations, there exist both regulatory and accounting problems. Either anticipated capital gains would have to be taken into income or reserves as conventionally measured would be depleted by such a policy.

As a consequence of cyclical variations in the attractiveness of deposits in savings and loan associations, the rate of growth of mortgage portfolios and savings also takes on a cyclical pattern. It is comparatively high at cyclical troughs and low at peaks. This implies that the average yield of mortgage-portfolio acquisitions is below the average yield of mortgages over the cycle. Moreover, this pattern of savings flows, as contrasted with a more cyclically uniform rate of flow of savings and funds into mortgages, leads to greater oscillations in mortgage rates over the cycle.

Concurrent with the secular trend in interest rates has been a relative decrease in the effective yield of mortgages vis-a-vis corporates or tax exempts. This implies that the relative attractiveness of mortgages has decreased for both banks and insurance companies. As a result, the share of all home mortgages held by savings and loan associations has risen. The partial withdrawal from the mortgage market by commercial banks and insurance companies suggests that the demand for the financial intermediation of mortgages has not been growing over time. This is consistent with the conclusion one reaches when housing starts are examined directly. However, it is important here to distinguish between the latest 5 years and the preceding 15. During the early part of the postwar period, there was indeed a housing boom and not surprisingly, these were the years of greatest prosperity and growth for the savings and loan industry.

The secular rise in rates has led to market rates above the legal ceilings for mortgages that exist in many States. The effect of these ceilings is to foreclose the acquisition of mortgages by the least credit-worthy members of the community. Moreover, it generally leads to a withdrawal of mortgage funds from local markets and their reappearance in the national market typically through the acquisition by local institutions of discounted insured mortgages originated in another part of the country.

There exists evidence that regional variation in mortgage yields exists. In general, rates rise from east to west with the low-rate area being the northeast. Variations in rates are typically arbitraged through the employment of insured mortgages because of their lower transactions costs. Despite arbitrage, one should expect such variation to exist in a world of positive transactions costs. Hence, the presence of such variations does not imply a malfunctioning secondary mortgage market.

Evidence exists that when one standardizes for risk, as measured by loan-to-value ratios, that local or regional demand and supply conditions for mortgages affect the yields on mortgages for existing homes but have a negligible effect on the yields of mortgages secured by new homes. This finding has been explained as a consequence of the lower costs of arranging for insured mortgages, and tapping national markets, for new as contrasted with used homes. However, apart from this consideration, much of the observed regional variation in mortgage rates can be explained by regional variations in loan-to-value ratios.

7 A Study of the Effects of Competition in the Tax-Exempt Bond Market (1971)

This is a study of the effects of competition upon underwriting costs, reoffering yields, and the financing costs to issuers of tax-exempt bonds. It provides estimates of the marginal effects of changes in the degree of competition, as measured by independent bids submitted by underwriters syndicates, upon the terms of newly issued tax-exempt bonds holding constant default risk, issue size, level of interest rates, etc. The paper is of theoretical interest because it applies Stigler's theory of information to the explanation of phenomena—in particular, the behavior of reoffering yields—that cannot be explained with the neoclassical model of competition which implicitly postulates that information is a free good.

This paper reports the results of a study of two aspects of the tax-exempt bond market. These are (1) the exclusion of commercial banks from underwriting an important class of tax-exempts, revenue bonds;[1] and (2) the effect of variations in the degree of competition in underwriting, as measured by the number of bids submitted for new issues, upon (a) the difference between the buying and selling prices of underwriters, (b) the selling prices or reoffering yields of underwriters to the investing public,

---

I am indebted to (1) Potluri M. Rao, graduate student in the Department of Economics at the University of Chicago for running the regressions used in this study; (2) Paul Tracy of the First National City Bank of New York and Herman Charbonneau of the Chemical Bank–New York Trust Company for supervising the assembly of the data used and for many helpful discussions dealing with the practical aspects of the municipal bond business; and (3) Armen A. Alchian of UCLA, and Merton Miller and George Stigler of the University of Chicago for help with the analysis. The views expressed are not necessarily the views of those named.

[1] See Investment Bankers Association (1968, p. 24). Both general obligation and revenue bonds are obligations of nonfederal governmental units such as states, municipalities, school districts, authorities, etc. The chief difference between these two classes of bonds is the source of the funds to be used to meet payments of interest and principal. Revenue bonds are secured by the income derived from specific taxes or user charges. By contrast, general obligations are secured by the general taxing power of the issuer.

and (c) the costs of borrowing for the issuers of tax-exempts. More specifically, this study attempts to answer the following questions: Is the prohibition of bank underwriting of revenue bonds of any economic significance? And, how sensitive are the costs of underwriters' services for issuers to the intensity of competition among underwriters?

The intensity of competition in underwriting new issues of tax-exempts has the expected effect on underwriters' spreads, that is, the difference between buying and selling prices; spreads decrease as the degree of competition increases. Of far greater interest and importance, both theoretically and empirically, is the somewhat unexpected discovery that a relationship exists between the reoffering prices of bonds to the investing public by underwriters and the intensity of competition in underwriting. More specifically, reoffering yields decline, or prices rise, as the degree of competition increases. This finding is inconsistent with the usual assumption of complete knowledge associated with perfect competition; in a world in which information is free, reoffering yields ought to be independent of the degree of competition. By contrast, in a world in which information is a scarce resource, a postulate of Stigler's economics-of-information theory which is employed to explain the behavior of reoffering yields, bids for a new issue by underwriters can be usefully interpreted as a means of scanning the population of would-be buyers of tax-exempts for that subset for whom a forthcoming issue is most valuable.[2] A bid submitted by an underwriter incorporates his knowledge of what his customers are willing to pay for a prospective issue. Hence, bids reveal the underwriters whose customers will pay the most for a forthcoming issue. Competitive bidding is a way of utilizing "knowledge which is not given to anyone in its totality."[3]

In fact, the variation of reoffering yields with the intensity of competition is substantially greater, as measured in dollars and cents, than the variation of spreads with the degree of competition. Consequently, for the issuers of tax-exempts, the important gains from competition stem from the impact of competition upon the prices at which bonds are sold and, by implication, the prices paid by underwriters to issuers.

In order to answer the questions that have been raised and to show how the conclusions presented were obtained, this paper is divided into three major sections. These deal with (1) the effects of entry restrictions on the number of bids submitted for a tax-exempt bond issue, (2) the effects of variations in the number of bids submitted upon underwriters' spreads, and (3) the effects of variations in bids submitted upon reoffering yields. In this introductory section, the data used in this investigation are described, some summary statistics and the results of previous

[2] Stigler (1961, p. 213).   [3] Hayek (1945, p. 519).

studies are presented, and the nature of the statistical problems encountered is outlined.

The banking legislation of the early 1930s prohibited the underwriting by commercial banks of revenue bonds, that is, tax-exempts secured by specific taxes or user charges.[4] By contrast, general obligation (G.O.) bonds, the other major class, are secured by the general taxing power of the issuer.[5] Studies of the economic effects of the prohibition of bank underwriting of revenues have appeared in hearings of congressional subcommittees and the *Federal Reserve Bulletin*.[6] Articles dealing with issues relevant for resolving this question have appeared in various economic journals.[7]

Two bodies of data are utilized to extract the evidence to be presented. One consists of observations on all new issues, 9,420 in number, reported by the *Bond Buyer* as submitted for competitive bids between spring of 1959 and spring of 1967. This is probably the most extensive body of data on tax-exempt bonds ever assembled. The aggregate value of these issues was roughly 48 billion dollars, with about one-fourth, or 12 billion dollars, accounted for by revenue bonds.[8] For each issue, to the extent that the *Bond Buyer* reports were complete, data were collected that described the economic characteristics of new issues. The variables observed were (1) quality rating, both Standard and Poor's and Moody's; (2) size of issue; (3) average life of issue; (4) amount of prior outstanding tax-exempt bonds of the issuer; (5) absence or presence of call provisions and, if the bonds were callable, the first call date; (6) date of issue; (7) number of bids submitted; (8) G.O. or revenue; (9) dollar cost of issue to underwriters; (10) dollar receipts of underwriters derived from reoffering prices; (11) twenty-year reoffering yield, that is, the yield-to-maturity of the twenty-year bond in an issue, (12) the so-called net interest cost; and (13) whether the manager of the winning syndicate is a commercial bank or an investment banker.[9]

The other body of data constitutes—in effect, if not by design—a test

[4] Commercial banks can neither underwrite new revenue issues nor make a market, that is, operate as dealers, in the secondary market for revenue bonds. However, banks can, and do, buy revenue bonds for their own account or portfolio, either as participants in underwriting syndicates that buy tax-exempts from original issuers, or as customers of underwriting syndicates, or from dealers in the secondary market.

[5] The aggregate value of outstanding tax-exempt bonds is well in excess of 100 million (see Investment Bankers Association 1968, p. 32).

[6] See U.S. Congress (1967), *Federal Reserve Bulletin* (1967), and Smith (1967).

[7] West (1965b; 1967, p. 241).

[8] Revenues constitute about one-third of all new tax-exempts issued but only one-fourth of all tax-exempts submitted for competitive bids.

[9] The data were taken from the so-called sheet summaries to the *Bond Buyer* which are not an integral part of that publication. If the data were incomplete, as they were relatively infrequently, they were, nevertheless, included in the sample and used whenever the missing data were not relevant.

of what would happen if banks were to be permitted to underwrite revenues. These data were a consequence of rulings by a former comptroller of the currency, James J. Saxon. While he held that office, Saxon ruled that a number of issues of tax-exempt bonds, previous issues of which had been regarded as revenue bonds, were, in fact, general obligations. These tax-exempt bonds whose status changed from revenues to G.O.'s were named Saxon G.O.'s by professionals in the bond business.[10] These data enable an investigator to hold the issuer constant and examine what happens to the number of bids submitted before and after its obligations became eligible for bank bidding. Saxon G.O.'s, therefore, represent a test case of what would happen if banks were permitted to underwrite revenue issues. All of the issues Saxon's office redefined were utilized, subject to certain constraints to be described later. The pertinent data on bids, date of issue, etc., for these issues were obtained from published sources.

In general, there appears to be agreement that (1) G.O. bonds receive more bids than revenue bonds when both classes of bonds are submitted for competitive bids; (2) one-third of revenue bonds in contrast with about 6 percent of G.O. issues are negotiated, that is, are not submitted for competitive bids: and (3) G.O. bonds are of higher quality, shorter term-to-maturity, and, on average, issued in smaller amounts. These characteristics must be held constant in order to determine whether there is truly a difference in the number of bids submitted.

An important, if not the most important, study of this question was undertaken by the Federal Reserve Board. The study concluded:

> Since the number of bidders was an important determinant of the net interest cost, and is a topic central to the issue of whether the number of possible underwriters should be increased, the other factors affecting this variable are also relevant. As can be seen from the equations, one may confidently say that issues with higher ratings receive more bids than those with lower ratings, the longer the maturity, the fewer the number of bidders, that general obligations receive more bids than revenues—a full 1.5 on the average—and that the higher the level of interest rates (the "Bond Buyer Index"), the fewer the number of bidders.[11]

The Federal Reserve study suggests that the chief problems confronting investigators are (1) to isolate the effects of difference in average

---

[10] Since Saxon's departure from the office of comptroller of the currency, a number of these issues have reverted to their original revenue status.

[11] See *Federal Reserve Bulletin* (August 1967, appendix, p. 8). The text (see p. 1300) and the article are inconsistent on this point, since the text reports two more bids. Presumably, there is a typographical error in the text, since the bid regression equation has −1.539 as the coefficient for the general obligation–revenue dummy.

maturity, issue size, and rating upon the number of bids submitted for an issue; and (2) if a difference in the number of bids submitted remains after removing the effects of these variables, to determine the relationship, if any, of underwriting costs and the prices paid for bonds by underwriters to the number of bids.

I. Entry Restrictions and the Number of Bids Submitted for New Issues

Is there a difference in the number of bids submitted for G.O. and revenue issues after adjustment for other differences in the economic characteristics of these two classes of issues? The answer to this question, provided by both this and the Federal Reserve's study, is yes. Although somewhat different variables were used, the data were obtained from independent sources, and the fraction of the observed variance explained differed, answers to this question were the same.

As with the Federal Reserve study, a multiple regression model was employed in an attempt to explain the number of bids submitted for new issues. The variables in this analysis were: (1) type of issue (revenue or G.O.); (2) issue size; (3) prior issues outstanding; (4) rating; (5) call provisions; (6) level of interest rates; (7) rate of change of interest rates; (8) Blue List, that is, aggregated value of all tax-exempts listed for sale by dealers during week of issue; (9) number of G.O. issues that came to market, as measured by the number in the sample, during the week of issue; (10) number of revenue issues that came to market, as measured by the number in this sample, during the week of issue; (11) average maturity; and (12) trend.[12] (These variables are described more specifically in the footnote to table 1.)

Bringing variables other than the G.O.-revenue characteristic into analysis represents an attempt to hold differences constant between the two classes of bonds that are not attributable to entry constraints in underwriting. Issue size, time, level of interest rates, Blue List, rate of change of interest rates, and the flows to market of G.O. and revenue issues were entered into the regression equation linearly. Outstandings and average maturity were entered logarithmically, and two series of dummies were used, one for call provisions and the other for rating. Five dummies were entered for five call-date classes with the excluded set being noncallable bonds. Standard and Poor's ratings were preferred to Moody's because Standard and Poor's rates more bonds; hence, less data are lost.[13]

[12] The data for variables 9 and 10 have shortcomings. They do not include (1) negotiated issues, and (2) small issues under 1 million, because they are usually not reported by the *Bond Buyer*.

[13] For some of the regressions to be presented, Moody's was used as an alternative to Standard and Poor's with little or no perceptible difference in results.

One dummy was used for each of the three rating classes, AAA, AA, and A; the excluded set was BBB. Less than 1 percent of tax-exempts in this body of data carry a rating below BBB.[14] Consequently, little was lost by ignoring ratings below BBB.

The resulting regression equation explained about one-third of the observed variance (see table 1). The G.O.-revenue distinction proved significant as it did for the analysis published by the Federal Reserve Board. General obligations received 0.81 more bids than revenues when one abstracts from the other variables in the regression. The regression coefficients, t-values, and partial correlation coefficients are in table 1.

The Federal Reserve study explained 28 percent of the variance in bids. In that study: (1) when continuous functions were used, all were linear; (2) geographical region in which issuer is located was an indepen-

TABLE 1

BID REGRESSION:* COMBINED SAMPLE OF GENERAL OBLIGATIONS AND REVENUES

Variable	Regression Coefficient	t-Value	Partial Correlation
1. Issue size	-0.11×10^{-3}	-33.0	$-.34$
2. Outstandings, in logs	0.80×10^{-1}	6.0	$.65 \times 10^{-1}$
3. Level of White's	-3.5	-17.0	$-.18$
4. Rate of change of White's	-1.4	-6.3	$-.68 \times 10^{-1}$
5. Time, in weeks	0.45×10^{-2}	9.1	$.98 \times 10^{-1}$
6. Flow of G.O. issues	-0.15×10^{-1}	-2.9	$-.31 \times 10^{-1}$
7. Flow of revenue issues	-0.53×10^{-1}	-5.2	$-.56 \times 10^{-1}$
8. Blue List	-0.10×10^{-5}	-2.5	$-.27 \times 10^{-1}$
9. Maturity, in logs	-0.63×10^{-1}	-0.66	$-.71 \times 10^{-2}$
10. Call provisions:			
a) Less than 5 years	-1.7	-10.0	$-.11$
b) 6–9 years	-1.0	-7.6	$-.82 \times 10^{-1}$
c) 10–14 years	-0.33	-9.1	$-.98 \times 10^{-1}$
d) 15–19 years	-0.44	-3.5	$-.38 \times 10^{-1}$
e) 20 or more	-0.10	-0.49	$-.52 \times 10^{-2}$
11. Rating, Standard and Poor's:			
a) AAA	4.5	29.0	$.30$
b) AA	3.8	39.0	$.39$
c) A	1.7	20.0	$.21$
12. G.O.-revenue dummy	-0.81	-7.6	$-.82 \times 10^{-1}$

NOTE.—1, in thousands; 2, in thousands; 3, the level of interest rates is measured by the yield, published weekly, of the highest quality twenty-year bond of current coupon available in the market; this series is known as White's index of 100 and is published by Standard Statistics which is part of Standard and Poor's; 4, this week's minus last week's rate; 5, in weeks; 6, number of new G.O. issues coming to market during week in which issue observed receives bids; 7, number of new revenue issues coming to market during week in which issue observed receives bids; 8, in millions; 9, in years and fractions thereof.

* $R^2 = .332$; constant, 16.3; t-value, 21.4; 8,614 observations; residual variance 8.7; standard error of estimate, 2.9.

[14] The foregoing represents the product of some experimentation combined with intuition. The call provisions yield virtually the same results, if not better, if call-date classes are introduced in continuous form logarithmically, with noncallable bonds regarded as callable on the maturity date. Similarly, ratings yield virtually the same results if entered linearly. The value of all general obligation issues, revenue issues, and all issues coming to market during the week of issues were tried linearly with generally insignificant results.

dent variable; (3) outstandings, rate of change of interest rates, the Blue List, the flow variables, and time were not used; (4) the data were obtained by questionnaire for the years 1964, 1965, and 1966; (5) AAA bonds were excluded on the grounds that there were too few; (6) Moody's ratings were used; and (7) the presence or absence of call provisions was ignored. One difference in results is a negative coefficient for average maturity.

It is, at this point, more useful to consider the separate regressions for G.O.'s and revenues than to dwell on the differences between the results presented here and those of the Federal Reserve Board study. Aggregation of the two classes of bonds into one regression conceals significant differences (see table 2). In particular, the separate regressions reveal that there has been no trend in bids for revenues but a strongly positive trend for G.O.'s (row 5). Over the eight years observed, the number of bids submitted for G.O.'s increased by more than two. During the entire period, G.O. issues received on average 6.82 bids (SD, 3.7) against 4.81 (SD, 2.6) for revenues.[15] Therefore, the bid advantage of G.O.'s over revenues at the end of the period studied, given the G.O.-revenue dummy, is well in excess of two.

For G.O.'s, the trend in bids, that is, the relationship of bids to time, was positive for all rating categories. In addition, the higher the quality rating, the stronger the trend. For AAA's, the trend has been two and a half times; for AA's, twice; and A's, one and a half times the trend for BBB's. In contrast to G.O.'s, evidence of the existence of positive trends in bids for revenues is weak or nonexistent, with the exception of AA revenues (see table 3). Indeed, for BBB revenues, it is likely (t-value, −1.4) that it was negative.

Similarly, separate regressions reveal diversity in the relationship between average maturity and bids. Evidently, investment bankers, probably because of customer preferences, prefer to bid for long relative to short maturities. Converse preferences hold for commercial bankers. Clearly, the longer term-to-maturity of revenues is not an explanation of the observed difference in bids between G.O.'s and revenues. If revenues were of shorter term, the difference in bids observed would be even larger. Average maturity is not significant for the pooled data because the negative relationship of maturity to bids for G.O.'s is offset by a positive relationship for revenues.

---

[15] These are means determined by assuming every issue is just as important as every other issue. When means are weighted by issue size, the average number of bids submitted is smaller and the average maturity greater. (The average life of revenue issues is seventeen years against twelve for general obligations, and the average issue size of revenues is 7 million against 5 million for general obligations.) Whether means are weighted by issue size, general obligation bonds received more bids than revenues and were of shorter average life. Moreover, weighting by size left unchanged the difference between general obligation and revenue means for both bids and average maturity.

TABLE 2
Separate General Obligation and Revenue Regressions:* Bids Dependent Variable

Variables	Regression Coefficient		t-Value		Partial Correlation	
	G.O.	Revenue	G.O.	Revenue	G.O.	Revenue
1. Issue size	-0.12×10^{-3}	-0.81×10^{-4}	-31.0	-15.0	$-.35$	$-.36$
2. Outstandings, in logs	0.91×10^{-1}	0.58×10^{-1}	5.9	2.6	$.71\times10^{-1}$	$.65\times10^{-1}$
3. Level of White's	-3.6	-2.8	-16.0	-7.9	$-.19$	$-.19$
4. Rate of change of White's	-2.3	$+1.9$	-6.7	0.66	$-.80\times10^{-1}$	$+.17\times10^{-1}$
5. Time, in weeks	0.50×10^{-2}	-0.42×10^{-4}	8.8	0.05	.10	$-.12\times10^{-2}$
6. Flow of G.O. issues	-0.22×10^{-1}	0.53×10^{-2}	-3.7	0.58	$-.44\times10^{-1}$	$.15\times10^{-1}$
7. Flow of revenue issues	-0.10×10^{-1}	-0.12	-0.82	-8.1	$-.98\times10^{-2}$	$-.20$
8. Blue List	-0.85×10^{-6}	-0.90×10^{-6}	-1.9	-1.3	$-.22\times10^{-1}$	$-.33\times10^{-1}$
9. Maturity, in logs	-0.39	0.55	-3.6	3.2	$-.43\times10^{-1}$	$.80\times10^{-1}$
10. Call provisions:						
a) Less than 5 years	-2.0	-0.84	-8.5	-2.8	$-.10$	$-.71\times10^{-1}$
b) 6–9 years	-0.86	-0.50	-4.2	-1.8	$-.50\times10^{-1}$	$-.45\times10^{-1}$
c) 10–14 years	-0.82	-0.16	-7.4	-0.57	$-.89\times10^{-1}$	$-.14\times10^{-1}$
d) 15–19 years	-0.36	0.30	-2.5	0.89	$-.30\times10^{-1}$	$+.22\times10^{-1}$
e) 20 or more	0.13	1.4	0.57	2.9	$+.69\times10^{-2}$	$+.73\times10^{-1}$
11. Rating, Standard and Poor's:						
a) AAA	4.9	1.9	30.0	4.5	.34	.11
b) AA	4.3	1.9	39.0	10.0	.42	.26
c) A	1.8	1.1	19.0	7.3	.22	.18

* 8,614 observations: 1,603 revenues, 7,011 G.O.'s. For G.O.'s: $R^2 = .33$; constant, 17.0; t-value, 19.6; residual variance, 9.2; standard error of estimate, 3.0. For revenues: $R^2 = .26$; constant, 13.0, t-value, 9.4; residual variance, 5.1; standard error of estimate, 2.3.

TABLE 3

TRENDS IN BIDS AS A FUNCTION OF RATING*

RATING	REGRESSION COEFFICIENT		t-VALUE	
	G.O.	Revenue	G.O.	Revenue
AAA	0.78×10^{-2}	0.15×10^{-2}	3.3	0.90
AA	0.62×10^{-2}	0.32×10^{-2}	3.0	3.5
A	0.46×10^{-2}	-0.11×10^{-2}	1.6	-0.55
BBB	0.31×10^{-2}	-0.19×10^{-2}	3.3	-1.4

* Measured in bids per week.

Disaggregation also reveals marked differences in the sensitivity of bids to rating; the number of bids submitted for G.O.'s is far more sensitive to rating than it is for revenues (table 2, row 11, a, b, c). For A-rated bonds, the most frequently observed rating, the bid advantage over BBB for general obligations is almost one bid greater than it is for revenues. For AA-rated bonds, the next most frequently observed rating, the general obligation bid advantage over BBB is in excess of two bids greater than the corresponding relationship for revenues.

The foregoing analysis suggests that, even in the absence of a systematic bid advantage for G.O.'s, the issuers of revenue bonds that fall into the first three rating classes would gain additional bids if banks could underwrite their bonds. These additional bids would stem from the apparent comparative advantage of commercial banks, which is implied by the bidding pattern for G.O.'s, in underwriting higher-quality tax-exempts. Conversely, if commercial banks were to drop any of their present business as a result of the removal of legal restraints, the business dropped would be the underwriting of low-quality G.O. issues. This analysis also implies that, to the extent that investment bankers underwrite G.O.'s, they are overrepresented in underwriting low-quality or relatively risky issues. Similar implications follow from the relationship of average maturity to bids for the two classes of underwriters.

The findings displayed in table 2 (rows 10, a–10, e) also indicate a difference between G.O.'s and revenues with respect to sensitivity to call provisions. Callable bonds typically receive fewer bids than noncallable bonds, and the influence of call provisions upon the number of bids submitted is inversely related to the time span to the first call date. The only exception appears to be the fifth call-date class, twenty years and over, for revenues.[16] This is generally consistent with the finding that bids decrease as quality decreases. High quality and noncallability have similar implications for investors; both reduce the variance in money flows. The

[16] About one-third of the general obligations in the sample were callable, whereas 93 percent of the revenues were callable. The behavior of the fifth call-date class is anomalous and generally inconsistent with the explanation presented above.

greater sensitivity of bids for G.O.'s to call provisions is not inconsistent with this explanation. The call provisions for G.O.'s are more stringent than they are for revenues: par calls for callable G.O.'s are frequent, whereas revenues are usually called at premiums.[17]

The inverse relationship shown by the bid regressions between bids and the level of interest rates revealed is consistent with the results obtained by the Federal Reserve.[18] Yields of tax-exempts, like obligations of the federal government, are procyclical; yields are high about cyclical peaks and low at troughs. Commercial banks buy for their own portfolios about 40 percent of the value of all new issues. The acquisition of tax-exempts by commercial banks, like their acquisition of federal obligations, has a contracyclical pattern. They are heavy buyers at cyclical troughs and light buyers—if not, on balance, sellers—at peaks.[19] To the extent that underwriters are specialized in serving commercial bank demands, their willingness to bid for new issues would also exhibit a contracyclical pattern, thereby producing the observed relationship. Moreover, bids for bonds that commercial banks are apt to buy, short maturities and high-quality issues, would decrease more than bids generally. This suggests that bids for G.O.'s ought to be more sensitive to the level of rates than bids for revenues.

The regression coefficients for the level of rates for G.O.'s, -3.6, and for revenues, -2.8, is a weighted average for all four rating classes and conceals important differences. Commercial banks prefer high-quality and short-maturity issues. Hence when commercial banks withdraw from the tax-exempt market about cyclical peaks, their agents in the acquisition of tax-exempts, the commercial bank underwriters, also withdraw from the submission of bids for the type of tax-exempts their customers prefer. This phenomenon is revealed when one observes the coefficients of White's (the yield of the highest-quality twenty-year tax-exempt) for high-quality tax-exempts; for AA-rated bonds, the coefficient for White's is -4.85 for G.O.'s in contrast with -1.64 for revenues.

[17] This suggests that pooling general obligations and revenues to estimate the bid advantage of general obligations will lead to too low an estimate. The stringent par calls for general obligations vis-à-vis revenues and the greater frequency of callable bonds among revenues will lead to too great an estimate of the effect of the callability of revenues upon bids.

[18] See *Federal Reserve Bulletin* (1967, appendix, p. 7). To obtain this interpretation, the variable X_{17}, which is identified as X_{15}, is assumed to be the Bond Buyer Index. The level of interest rates is measured throughout this study by the yield of the highest-quality tax-exempt of current coupon outstanding. In the municipal bond field, this weekly series is known as White's index of 100.

[19] Robinson (1960, p. 159) notes that commercial banks have been volatile investors. Phelps (1961, p. 289) shows that commercial banks acquired, on balance, tax-exempts equal to 81 percent of all tax-exempts issued in the second quarter of 1968. By contrast, commercial banks, on balance, sold tax-exempts equivalent to 25 percent of all tax-exempts issued in the second quarter of 1960.

A Study of the Effects of Competition in the Tax-Exempt Bond Market

There is some reason for believing that the payment for risk bearing, that is, yield differentials as a function of quality differences, is positively related to the level of rates. This implies that low-quality bonds are viewed as being comparatively more desirable when rates are low. Therefore, bids ought to be inversely related to interest rates, and this relationship should be stronger for G.O.'s than for revenues, because bids for G.O.'s are more sensitive to quality considerations. Unfortunately, this relationship is difficult to observe because of another force working in an opposite direction; this is the relationship of commercial bank acquisition of tax-exempts to the level of interest rates. For revenues alone, the evidence on this point is fragmentary but consistent with the hypothesis enunciated; the coefficient for AA revenues (-1.64) is the only one significantly different from the coefficient of BBB's (-3.08), and it is almost one-half of the absolute size of the latter. For G.O.'s, the only significant difference was also between AAs (-4.85), and BBBs (-2.99).[20]

There is a negative relationship between number of bids and the number of new issues. For the regression using all the data, the number of both revenue and G.O. issues coming to market during the week a particular issue comes to market affects the number of bids this issue receives. However, when separate regressions are run for revenues and G.O.'s, the number of bids submitted for G.O.'s is affected only by the flow of G.O.'s during the week of issue; the flow of revenues plays no role. This implies that the underwriters of G.O.'s are not interested in underwriting revenues; this is consistent with the view that investment bankers have abandoned the market for underwriting G.O.'s, and legal constraints preclude the bank underwriting of revenues. This interpretation is also consistent with the finding that bids submitted for revenues are affected by the number of revenue issues coming to market but not the number of G.O. issues. It suggests that the underwriters of revenues do not generally underwrite G.O.'s. In addition, it appears that the number of bids submitted for revenues is more sensitive to the flow of revenues than is true for G.O.'s. Hence, the supply of underwriting services for revenues is less elastic than it is for G.O.'s. These findings suggest that the legal restrictions on bank entry have economic effects; investment bankers can bring resources into the underwriting of G.O.'s, but the converse is not true.

The most interesting difference between the results presented here and those of the Federal Reserve study is the estimate of the G.O.-Revenue dummy, that is, the expected difference in the number of bids submitted abstracting from other differences between the two classes of bonds; 1.5

---

[20] The signs of the coefficients constitute additional evidence on this point. All three high-quality G.O. rating categories had coefficients that were larger, in absolute size, than the coefficient for BBB G.O.'s. By contrast, the coefficient for the three highest-rated revenue classes was smaller than the coefficient for BBBs, with the exception of AAAs.

in the Federal Reserve against 0.81 here, despite the exclusion of AAAs from the Federal Reserve investigation.[21] One reason why the Federal Reserve Board estimate of the bid difference is larger than the one presented here is that they did not abstract from trend. Their data are for the years 1964, 1965, and 1966. On the average for these three years, G.O.'s were receiving about one and a half more bids than in 1959, whereas, for revenues, there were fewer bids in these years than in 1959.

Questions can be raised about the confidence one ought to place upon these estimates of differences in the number of bids submitted for G.O.'s and revenues derived from regressions using pooled data. The regression coefficients for the same variables in the separate regressions are obviously quite different. Yet if the number of bids that would be submitted for revenues is estimated, using the means of the revenue variables and the G.O. regression, virtually the same estimate is obtained.[22]

II. The Relationship between the Number of Bids Submitted and the Difference between the Buying and Selling Prices of Underwriters

The preceding section of this paper dealt with the determinants of the number of bids submitted for an issue. In particular, the role of entry restrictions as a determinant of bids was investigated. Sections II and III study the effects of variations in the number of bids submitted upon the costs of underwriting services for the issuers of tax-exempts. In this section, the relationship of bids to spreads is investigated; in the next, the relationship of bids to reoffering yields is studied.

On average, the spread for G.O.'s is $11.06 (for a $1,000 bond), with a standard deviation of $3.46 about this mean. By contrast, the spread for revenues is $13.77, with a standard deviation of $3.72. This existence of this difference, $2.71, leads to a series of questions: To what extent is it attributable to differences, other than number of bids submitted, in the characteristics of the two classes of bonds? If not, to what extent do variations in the number of bids submitted account for the observed difference? And, how sensitive are underwriting costs to variations in the number of bids? Can bids be viewed as a proxy for competition?

---

[21] This is the bid category for which the comparative advantage for G.O.'s vis-à-vis revenues is greatest. Hence, the measured bid advantage for G.O.'s would have been larger had this category been included. However, this only widens the discrepancy to be explained. Three percent of revenues and 23 percent of G.O.'s are AAA on Standard and Poor's rating.

[22] At the means, the advantage is 0.71. Similarly, using the means of the G.O.'s and the revenue regression, the advantage is 1.2. If the end point for the "variable" time is used, which surely is more relevant for estimating what would happen if commercial banks were to be permitted to underwrite revenues, the bid advantage becomes 1.9.

A Study of the Effects of Competition in the Tax-Exempt Bond Market

The difference between the buying and selling prices, measured in dollars and cents, of tax-exempts is here viewed as a function of:

1. Quality as measured by Standard and Poor's rating; three dummies were entered for the top three rating classes, with the excluded set being BBB;
2. Issue size in thousands of dollars;
3. Volume of bonds already outstanding by the same issuers, measured in thousands of dollars, and entered linearly in logs;
4. Trend variable for underwriting costs of BBB-rated bonds;
5. Trend variables, for each of the top three rating classes, AAA, AA, and A, entered in weeks, with the excluded set being BBB, to measured trends in underwriting costs over time relative to BBB-rated bonds;
6. Interest rates, as measured by twenty-year White's yield for top quality bonds, observed weekly;
7. Change of interest rates; this week's less last week's White's;
8. First call date; noncallable bonds are regarded as callable at maturity, entered linearly in logs;
9. The number of bids submitted, entered linearly in logs;
10. A dummy for type of issue; "0" for G.O., and "1" for revenue issues;
11. Average maturity entered linearly in logs.

The results for the pooled samples of G.O.'s and revenues for which underwriters' spreads were available are displayed in table 4.

These results indicate that forty-eight cents of the observed difference of $2.71 in average underwriting costs is explained by the G.O.-revenue dummy. They also suggest that there exist economies of scale in underwriting; abstracting from bids, underwriting costs decrease with increases in issue size (table 4, row 1). There has been a downward trend in underwriting costs (rows 5 and 10). Abstracting from bids, issue size, etc., underwriting costs have decreased as a function of time.

Before turning to a discussion of the other variables, it is useful to segregate and examine the results of the separate regressions for each of the two classes of bonds. Clearly, bids, average maturity, rating, and White's (the yield of the highest-quality twenty-year tax-exempt) (table 5, rows 10, 6, 8, 3) play the most important roles in explaining variations in underwriters' spreads. The larger the number of bids submitted, the lower the underwriting costs. The fact that the relationship between bids and the underwriting costs is depicted better by a logarithmic than by a linear function suggests that the marginal effect of bids upon underwriting costs declines as the number of bids increases. Similarly, the fact that logs do better than a straight-line function (both were tried) in

TABLE 4

Underwriters' Spread Regression:* Combined Sample of General Obligations and Revenues

Independent Variables	Regression Coefficient	t-Value	Partial Correlation
1. Issue size	-0.31×10^{-4}	-10.0	$-.12$
2. Outstandings, in logs	-0.83×10^{-1}	-7.0	$-.08$
3. Level of White's	3.7	27.0	$.30$
4. Change in White's	5.6	8.4	$.10$
5. Absolute trend of BBB	-0.60×10^{-2}	-10.0	$-.12$
6. Maturity, in logs	3.8	46.0	$.47$
7. Call dates, in logs	-6.5	-6.7	$-.08$
8. Rating, Standard and Poor's:			
a) Underwriting costs of AAA relative to BBB	-3.0	-11.0	$-.12$
b) Underwriting costs of AA relative to BBB	-1.9	-10.0	$-.12$
c) Underwriting costs of A relative to BBB	-1.1	-6.3	$-.07$
9. G.O.-revenue dummy	0.48	5.2	$.06$
10. Trends, in weeks:			
a) AAA relative to BBB	0.27×10^{-2}	2.5	$.03$
b) AA relative to BBB	-0.91×10^{-3}	-1.2	$-.00$
c) A relative to BBB	-0.13×10^{-2}	-2.0	$-.03$
11. Bids, in logs	-1.7	-27.0	$-.30$

* Number of observations, 7,532; G.O.'s, 6,137; revenues, 1,395. $R^2 = .55$; constant, -3.1; t-value, 5.9; residual variance, 6.1; standard error of estimate, 2.5. For some of the issues in the sample, underwriters' spread was unreported. Hence, the number of observations are fewer than the number used for the bid regression.

depicting the relationship between maturity and underwriting costs is consistent with the view that the marginal risk decreases as term-to-maturity increases.[23] These results support the view that the number of bids submitted can be viewed as a proxy for competition, that is, the larger the number of bids, the better off are the issuers.

The results obtained are also consistent with the usual view that underwriters have to be paid for risk bearing; the longer the average maturity, the greater the underwriters' risk and the greater the costs of underwriting an issue. Indeed, these results seem, on the surface, to be paradoxical. Underwriters have to be paid more for risk bearing than the ultimate investor. Underwriters charge more to hold low vis à vis high-quality securities than the investing public; the higher yields of low-quality securities are sufficient inducement for the public to hold them. Yet, in a society in which resources are free to move around, one expects the most willing, that is, the cheapest, risk bearers to become underwriters.[24]

[23] For discussion of this point, see Kessel (1965, p. 49).

[24] Presumably, in the absence of any differences between underwriters and the investing public, underwriting costs would be the same for issues of all ratings. Differences in promised yields would capture differences in the marginal costs of underwriting securities of differing ratings unless marketing costs varied with rating.

TABLE 5

GENERAL OBLIGATION AND REVENUE REGRESSION:[*] UNDERWRITERS' SPREAD THE DEPENDENT VARIABLE

VARIABLES	REGRESSION COEFFICIENT		t-VALUE		PARTIAL CORRELATION	
	G.O.	Revenue	G.O.	Revenue	G.O.	Revenue
1. Issue size	-0.24×10^{-4}	-0.45×10^{-4}	-7.1	-6.6	$-.09$	$-.17$
2. Outstandings, in logs	-0.66×10^{-1}	-0.14	-5.1	-5.0	$-.06$	$-.13$
3. Level of White's	3.3	5.3	23.0	16.1	.28	.40
4. Change in White's	5.9	3.6	8.2	2.2	.10	.06
5. Absolute trend in BBB's	-0.62×10^{-2}	-0.79×10^{-2}	-9.6	-6.1	$-.12$	$-.16$
6. Maturity, in logs	4.0	3.3	43.0	15.6	.48	.39
7. Call dates, in logs	-0.65	-0.68×10^{-1}	-7.6	-0.44	$-.10$	$-.01$
8. Rating, Standard and Poor's:						
a) AAA/BBB	-3.1	-4.0	-11.0	-3.3	$-.14$	$-.09$
b) AA/BBB	-1.8	-2.9	-8.8	-6.6	$-.11$	$-.17$
c) A/BBB	-0.96	-1.9	-5.3	-4.5	$-.07$	$-.12$
9. Trends, in weeks						
a) AAA/BBB	0.31×10^{-2}	0.25×10^{-2}	2.8	0.57	.04	.02
b) AA/BBB	-0.12×10^{-2}	0.23×10^{-2}	-1.5	1.4	$-.02$	.04
c) A/BBB	-0.14×10^{-2}	0.85×10^{-3}	-1.9	0.55	$-.02$	.01
10. Bids, in logs	-1.6	-2.1	-22.0	-14.0	$-.28$	$-.36$

[*] Revenues: $R^2 = .52$; constant, -4.9; t-value, 3.9; residual variance, 6.7; standard error of estimate, 2.6. G.O.'s: $R^2 = .52$; constant, -2.4; t-value, 4.1; residual variance, 5.8; standard error of estimate, 2.4.

This paradox can be resolved if one recognizes that the security of any particular issuer constitutes a smaller fraction of the portfolio of the investing public than it does for underwriters; underwriters, unlike the investing public, forego diversification. Hence, at the margin, the same security is more risky for the underwriter, and this difference is a function of the quality of the marginal security. The lower the quality, the larger the difference. Consequently, AAA G.O.'s are estimated to cost about $3 less to underwrite than BBB G.O.'s; AA G.O.'s, about $2 less; and A's, about $1 less. For revenues, the corresponding figures are $4, $3, and $2. The trend variables suggest that underwriting costs have been going down over time, with the highest-quality bonds decreasing the least (see table 6).

The downward trend in underwriting costs, which is strongest for the lowest-quality securities, is consistent with the view that the payment for holding low- vis-à-vis high-quality bonds has been decreasing. This implies that the economic significance of quality differences must be decreasing and the substitutability between low- and high-quality bonds has been increasing.

Secularly, there has been a positive trend in interest rates and a negative trend in underwriting costs. Yet, cyclically, underwriting costs are positively related to rates. This positive cyclical relationship of underwriting costs to interest rates has the same explanation as the positive cyclical relationship of number of bids to interest rates. About cyclical peaks, commercial banks, which hold about 40 percent of all tax-exempts outstanding, are more likely to be sellers than buyers.[25] Hence, new buyers must be found for tax-exempts coming to market at such times, and it is likely that underwriting costs rise as a consequence.[26] Second,

TABLE 6

DECREASE IN UNDERWRITING COSTS*

Rating	General Obligations	Revenues
AAA	$1.29	$2.25
AA	3.08	2.35
A	3.16	2.92
BBB	2.50	3.28

* In dollars and cents per eight-year span.

[25] Investment Bankers Association of America (1968, p. 25).

[26] Morris Mendelson (1968, p. 223), suggests that the difference in underwriting costs between G.O.'s and revenues may be attributable to differences in transactions size for these two classes of bonds. He contends that the market for G.O.'s is more institutionalized than revenues, that is, commercial bankers buy more G.O.'s than revenues for their own portfolios, and the average transaction size for commercial banks is greater than it is for the market as a whole. Accepting Mendelson's empirical statements, one would expect underwriters' costs for G.O.'s to be more sensitive than

although there has been a secular trend downward in yield differentials between low- and high-quality bonds, these differentials increase during expansions and narrow during contractions. This cyclical pattern implies high-yield differentials at interest-rate peaks, which, during the post-World War II period, have been associated with business peaks, and low differentials at interest-rate troughs, which have been associated with troughs in business conditions. Moreover, the cost of "carrying" bonds is a function of the level of rates.

The relationship of interest-rate changes to changes in underwriting costs indicates that underwriting costs rise when interest rates are rising and conversely. This is an alternative to saying that if bond prices are falling, underwriting costs are rising. Since underwriters buy before they sell, this is not an unexpected result, assuming they have expectations about future rates that are to some degree correct. Costs of underwriting, in fact, rise when rates rise or bond prices fall.

The costs of underwriting G.O. bonds are increased by call provisions. Yet, there appears to be no difference in the underwriting costs of callable and noncallable revenues. This is consistent with a higher probability of par calls for callable G.O. bonds than callable revenue bonds. Hence, the call feature of G.O.'s is regarded as more disadvantageous than the call feature in revenues. This is reflected in relatively higher underwriting costs for callable G.O.'s, whereas the same is not true of revenues.[27]

The regressions presented (table 4, row 11) show that number of bids is inversely correlated with underwriting costs. They also indicate that the marginal value of bids to the issuer decreases as the number of bids increases. (Number of bids is entered linearly in *logs* of number of bids.) However, no evidence is presented to indicate at what number of bids the value of the marginal bid falls to zero. To achieve this end, the independent variable, bids, is replaced in the regressions reported in tables 4 and 5 with eleven dummy variables. These dummies represent one through eleven bids, and the excluded set consists of issues receiving twelve or more bids. In other words, the question is being asked: Is there a significant difference in the underwriting costs between one bid and all bids over eleven, two bids and all bids over eleven, etc.? Since there was

---

revenues to the level of interest rates. Since banks are out of the market as buyers of tax-exempts about interest-rate peaks, Mendelson's empirical propositions imply that underwriting costs for general obligations should be more sensitive to the level of rates than the underwriting costs for revenues. The regressions in table 5—more specifically, the coefficients associated with the level of rates—suggest that underwriting costs for G.O.'s are the less sensitive of the two classes of bonds.

[27] Charlotte D. Phelps (1961, pp. 284-85) argues that a maturity date known with certainty commands a lower rate of interest than a maturity date with uncertainty. Callability imposes upon the investor the additional risk of having to liquidate at a time when he can reinvest only at a lower yield. Here, empirical findings for a combined sample of revenues and G.O.'s confirm this analysis. She does not recognize that there could exist premiums for call provisions that would vitiate her analysis.

virtually no change in the results for the other variables in these regressions, only the findings for the dummies are reported (see table 7). Additional bids clearly have a positive marginal product in terms of reducing underwriting costs through six bids for revenues and nine for general obligations; thereafter, the effects of bids on costs is much more ambiguous. The dummies also show why logs provide a better fit than a linear function; the marginal product falls off sharply as bids increase. Nevertheless, these findings indicate that an increase in the number of bids submitted for revenues (the mean is 4.81) would reduce underwriting costs.

III. The Relationship between the Number of Bids Submitted and the Selling Prices or Reoffering Yields of Underwriters

The evidence presented above showing that underwriters' spreads decrease with number of bids suggests that the prices received by issuers of tax-exempts increase as the number of bids increases if either no changes occur in the terms at which the ultimate investor buys bonds as bids increase or reoffering prices increase with bids. This section will present evidence that shows that selling prices increase as bids increase. Hence, as the number of bids increases, the difference between buying and selling prices of underwriters decreases and the selling prices of underwriters increase. For the issuers of tax-exempts, these effects are additive; both operate to reduce the costs of borrowing.

Those who have speculated about the effect of number of bids upon reoffering yields have typically concluded that no relationship exists.

TABLE 7

UNDERWRITING COSTS AS A FUNCTION OF BIDS*

Bids	Underwriting Costs			t-Values		
	Combined Sample	G.O.	Revenue	Combined Sample	G.O.	Revenue
1	5.74	5.09	6.32	21.8	15.7	10.0
2	2.64	2.50	2.73	16.7	13.9	5.2
3	2.36	2.33	2.38	17.2	15.6	4.7
4	1.63	1.69	1.38	12.5	12.2	2.7
5	0.99	0.95	1.12	7.9	7.2	2.2
6	0.71	0.72	0.58	5.7	5.5	1.1
7	0.52	0.51	0.49	4.0	3.8	0.9
8	0.34	0.29	0.60	2.4	2.0	1.1
9	0.12	0.13	0.10	0.9	0.85	0.2
10	0.23	0.18	0.54	1.4	1.06	0.9
11	0.11	0.13	−0.21	0.6	0.73	−0.3

* More precisely, the mean difference in underwriting costs between the mean costs for each number of bids and for all bids over eleven, measured in dollars and cents.

For example: "The offering price to the public, however, depends basically on the quality rating, the maturity, and other characteristics of the bonds being offered as well as the state of the market at the time of offering. These are the prime determinants of investment demand at a given time. An increase in the number of competitors in the sense of an increase in the number of underwriting groups bidding for the issue, does not alter these basic determinants of the public offering price."[28] By contrast, the work of West suggests that reoffering yields should fall as the number of bids submitted increases.[29]

In order to produce evidence bearing on the relationship between bids and reoffering yields, other variables that affect reoffering yields are introduced in order to isolate the effect of variations in bids. The excess of the reoffering yield of the twenty-year maturity of all new issues over White's is used as the dependent variable. Hence, both variations in the level of interest rates when bonds are reoffered and variations in rates attributable to maturity differences are held constant. The other variables introduced to isolate the effect of variations in bids are issue size, outstanding bonds of the same issuer, rating, call provisions, and trend. (Average maturity is introduced as an independent variable to determine whether in fact it has been held constant.) Outstandings, maturity, and call provisions are included linearly in log form; the ratings and trend variables, in the form of dummy variables. The market interest rates are measured by White's in order to isolate the effects of variations in the market rate on the spreads between top-quality yields and actual yields on new offerings, the dependent variable in the regressions presented in this section of this study.[30] A G.O.-revenue dummy variable is used to measure how much of the difference in reoffering yields between these

---

[28] Fox (1963, pp. 720–21).

[29] See West (1965a, p. 135). Insofar as West is correct, it follows that interest costs to issuers decrease as numbers of bids increase for two reasons. These are the decrease in underwriters' spread and the increase in reoffering prices, or, to use a slightly different language, the fall in reoffering yields. From the point of view of the issuers of tax-exempts, these gains from competition are additive.

[30] The rationale for the expectation of a positive correlation between the difference in yields of bonds of different quality with the level of interest rates may be found in Kessel (1965, p. 85). Briefly, the argument is: The substitutability of a security for money is a function of the variance in its realized rate of return. By this criterion, low-quality bonds are poorer money substitutes than high-quality bonds. Hence, when the level of rates rises and the costs of holding money and money substitutes rise, the yield differential between low- and high-quality bonds ought to increase also. Therefore, yield differentials associated with quality differences ought to be positively related to the level of rates. The change in White's, this week's less last week's rate, is not employed as an independent variable, unlike the underwriters' spread regressions, in the reoffering-yield regressions. The rate of change in rates affects the cost of carrying bonds; however, it should not affect the difference between reoffering yields and White's. By the argument in the preceding paragraph, it should affect the rate of change of the reoffering yield less White's.

two classes of bonds remains unexplained. The results obtained are displayed in table 8.

These results show that reoffering yields go down as number of bids increases. Hence, the change in reoffering yields is additive to the change in underwriting spreads for computing the gains to be derived from additional bids for the issuers of tax-exempt bonds. The G.O.-revenue dummy (.086) indicates that less than half of the average difference in reoffering yields, fifteen basis points, is explained by the variables considered. In this respect, the results obtained appear to be roughly consistent with the findings for underwriting spreads.

The separate regressions exhibit trends which imply a compression in yield differentials as a function of time (table 9). This compression can be seen a little more clearly by converting the data from relative to absolute changes and examining the eight-year period as a whole (see table 10). These findings clearly show that there has been a compression in yield differential attributable to quality differences as a function of time. What has been observed indicates that there has been a secular trend in these differentials over the post–World War II period.[31]

TABLE 8

COMBINED SAMPLE OF GENERAL OBLIGATIONS AND REVENUES:*
REOFFERING LESS WHITE'S, THE DEPENDENT VARIABLE

Variable	Regression Coefficient	t-Value	Partial Correlation
Issue size	-0.14×10^{-5}	-5.9	$-.07$
Outstandings, in logs	-0.41×10^{-2}	-4.8	$-.06$
G.O.-revenue dummy	0.86×10^{-1}	13.0	$.16$
White's	0.18	19.0	$.23$
Absolute trend of BBB's in weeks	-0.95×10^{-3}	-26.0	$-.30$
Maturity, in logs	0.12×10^{-1}	1.5	$.02$
Rating:			
1. AAA/BBB	-0.61	-27.0	$-.32$
2. AA/BBB	-0.46	-35.0	$-.40$
3. A/BBB	-0.24	-21.0	$-.25$
Bids, in logs	-0.14	-31.0	$-.36$
Call provisions, in logs	-0.48×10^{-1}	-8.6	$-.11$
Trends, in weeks:			
1. AAA/BBB	0.78×10^{-3}	9.2	$.11$
2. AA/BBB	0.48×10^{-3}	9.4	$.12$
3. A/BBB	0.17×10^{-3}	3.8	$.05$

* 6,503 observations: 1,279 revenues; 5,224 G.O.'s. The only reason for the difference in the number of observations in the underwriters' spread regression and this one is the failure of many issues to have a maturity as long as 20 years. Constant, 0.53; t-value, 12.7; $R^2 = .64$; residual variance, 0.03; standard error of estimate, 0.16. For those with a taste for high R^2s, this taste can be satisfied by running this regression with reoffering yields alone as the dependent variable.

[31] This suggests that it would be undesirable to relate reoffering yields to an index of bond yields or bond prices when this index reflects yields of bonds of varying quality. The *Bond Buyer* index is indeed such an index; it consists of bonds that range in quality over most of the quality spectrum.

TABLE 9

REOFFERING YIELDS LESS WHITE'S:* GENERAL OBLIGATIONS COMPARED WITH REVENUES

VARIABLES	REGRESSION COEFFICIENT		t-VALUE		PARTIAL CORRELATION	
	G.O.	Revenue	G.O.	Revenue	G.O.	Revenue
Issue size	-0.14×10^{-5}	-0.15×10^{-5}	-5.5	-2.5	$-.08$	$-.07$
Outstandings, in logs	-0.30×10^{-2}	-0.63×10^{-2}	-3.2	-3.2	$-.04$	$-.09$
White's	0.15	0.29	14.0	12.8	.19	.34
Absolute trend of BBB's in weeks	-0.99×10^{-3}	-0.94×10^{-3}	-24.0	-10.8	$-.32$	$-.29$
Maturity, in logs	-0.16×10^{-2}	0.12×10^{-1}	-0.17	0.62	$-.00$	.02
Rating:						
1. AAA/BBB	-0.61	-0.81	-27.0	-6.3	$-.35$	$-.17$
2. AA/BBB	-0.46	-0.45	-32.0	-14.6	$-.41$	$-.38$
3. A/BBB	-0.25	-0.21	-20.0	-7.3	$-.27$	$-.20$
Bids, in logs	-0.14	-0.16	-27.0	-15.7	$-.35$	$-.40$
Call provisions, in logs	-0.76×10^{-1}	0.16×10^{-1}	-12.0	1.4	$-.16$	.04
Trends, in weeks:						
1. AAA/BBB	0.83×10^{-3}	0.11×10^{-2}	9.6	2.5	.13	.07
2. AA/BBB	0.54×10^{-3}	0.33×10^{-3}	9.6	2.7	.13	.08
3. A/BBB	0.22×10^{-3}	0.77×10^{-4}	4.4	0.74	.06	.02

* For revenues: $R^2 = .60$; constant, 0.25; t-value, 2.7; residual variance, 0.03; standard error of estimate 0.17. For G.O.'s: $R^2 = .63$; constant, 0.70; t-value, 14.9; residual variance, 0.03; standard error of estimate, 0.16.

TABLE 10

CHANGE IN REOFFERING YIELDS RELATIVE
TO WHITE'S (DUE TO TREND)*

Rating	General Obligations	Revenues
AAA	− 7	+ 5
AA	−19	−25
A	−32	−36
BBB	−41	−37

* Measured in basis points per eight-year span.

Another way to observe the effect of number of bids on reoffering yields is to employ a series of dummies for bids as an alternative to entering bids as a continuous variable in the foregoing regressions. By using eleven dummies for bids from one through eleven, differences in reoffering yields between (a) yields on issues with any specified number of bids ranging from one through eleven, and (b) yields on issues with twelve or more bids, are compared. If significant differences exist, these would be evidence on the sensitivity of reoffering yields to bids (see table 11). Up to but not including seven bids for revenues and eleven for G.O.'s, the means seem to be significantly different. Hence, the seventh bid for revenues and the eleventh for G.O.'s seem to produce positive marginal products, that is, lower costs for issuers. Beyond these two points, the value of additional bids is more doubtful.

These results lead to the conclusion that it is not true that the "market" determines reoffering yields and the degree of competition among underwriters affects underwriters' spreads only. In this respect, the find-

TABLE 11

REOFFERING YIELDS LESS WHITE'S AS A FUNCTION OF BIDS*

NUMBER OF BIDS	COMBINED SAMPLE		GENERAL OBLIGATIONS		REVENUES	
	Difference in Means	t-Value	Difference in Means	t-Value	Difference in Means	t-Value
1	37	20.3	34	15.1	40	0.5
2	24	20.8	25	18.6	26	7.1
3	20	20.0	21	19.3	21	6.0
4	15	15.3	16	15.4	15	4.2
5	10	10.6	10	10.3	14	4.0
6	6	6.9	7	7.5	7	1.9
7	4	4.2	5	4.9	4	1.0
8	4	3.6	4	3.5	8	2.1
9	3	2.4	3	2.6	5	1.1
10	2	1.7	3	2.3	1	0.2
11	2	1.4	2	1.4	4	0.8

* In basis points, differences in reoffering yields less White's for bids 1–11 compared with differences in reoffering yields less White's for all bids 12 and over.

ings reported here are consistent with the results obtained by West, who used a substantially different method of analysis for arriving at the same conclusion.[32] West explained the decrease in reoffering yields with number of bids by invoking monopoly theory. He argued that there exists collusion among underwriters that limits the number of bids submitted for large issues. The gains from collusion are taken in the form of purchases at the reoffering by members of the conspiracy who are not members of the bidding syndicate and by purchases for their own account—that is, not reoffering to the public—by syndicate members. In other words, West contends that reoffering yields for issues receiving one and to a lesser extent two bids are fictitious yields in the sense that they are not available to the investing public. At the quoted reoffering yields of the syndicate, there exists nonprice rationing, and those in the conspiracy preempt the issue. After the syndicate has dissolved, the conspirators reoffer their bonds at prices higher or yields lower than the original reoffering.[33]

An alternative explanation of the relationship of reoffering yields to number of bids submitted, which is not necessarily competitive with West's, is suggested by Stigler's economics of information.[34] Underwriters possess specialized knowledge of what the customers they serve will pay for a prospective bond issue. This knowledge of customer preferences, that is, knowledge of the "market," is not the same for all under-

[32] West (1965a) examines the differences between the yields of new and seasoned issues of the same issuer. He used the dummy-variable technique also; however, he defined his excluded class to be the population of over three bidders. The findings presented here suggest that West may have inappropriately defined his excluded class. If the excluded class included bids that have positive marginal effects upon reoffering yields, then the probability of detecting differences between the bid categories explicitly considered is lower than it would be if the excluded class constituted a narrower range of bids. West found a range of about twelve basis points going from one to the maximum number of bids he considered. This is about one-third the range observed here. However, this is probably not the most likely explanation of the difference in findings. West's benchmark, yields of already outstanding bonds of the same issuer, is more likely to be affected by the appearance of a new issue than is the yield reported by White.

[33] This does not explain, nor does West explain, why monopoly gains are not incorporated into underwriters' spreads.

[34] Stigler (1961, p. 213). This explanation has other implications that are consistent with the findings presented here. If one accepts the empirical judgment that the "broadness" of the market for tax-exempts is a positive function of quality, with broadness measured by the set of holders of tax-exempts in each of the quality categories, then it follows that the economic resources going into search by underwriters ought also to be a function of the quality of the issue to be distributed. The variation in number of bids submitted with rating, shown by the bid regressions presented earlier, is consistent with this interpretation. Similarly, the trend in bids over time as a function of quality implies, if one accepts the search hypothesis, that the market for high-quality bonds is broadening relative to low-quality bonds. In addition, this hypothesis implies that low-quality bonds will be overrepresented among issues not submitted for competitive bids, that is, negotiated.

writers; their knowledge of the preferences of their "good" customers is better than their knowledge of the preferences of indifferent or poor customers. This knowledge of the market, which is not known to any underwriter in its totality, is incorporated in the prices offered to issuers by underwriters when bids are submitted. Consequently, the larger the number of bids submitted, the greater the probability of discovering the underwriter in possession of the knowledge of who will pay the most for a prospective issue; this is apt to be the underwriter who submits the winning bid. Reoffering yields decline as bids increase, because bids constitute search by issuers for those buyers who most prize the bonds they have to sell. This search is intermediated by underwriters; and the more extensive the search, the higher the price realized.

The foregoing interpretation of the behavior of reoffering yields with respect to bids implies that knowledge of the "market" for tax-exempts is what the issuers of tax-exempts buy when they engage the services of underwriters. This knowledge consists of knowing who will buy and at what price tax-exempts of a given rating, call provision, issuer, maturity, etc., at a particular moment in time. Underwriters pit knowledge of this type against one another when they compete for new issues. This process constitutes a means for searching the market for those buyers for whom a particular issue will be the most valuable.

This dimension of competition among underwriters appears to overshadow all other aspects of competition among underwriters, including those that have been typically emphasized—such as risk bearing, marketing, etc. This view can be supported by comparing the range of underwriters' spreads as a function of bids with the comparable range for reoffering yields. Reoffering yields have a range of $3.40 for G.O.'s and $4.00 for revenues per $1,000 bond per year. (One basis point is equivalent to ten cents in servicing costs per bond per year.) Discounting at a 5 percent rate, which is a very high rate for tax-exempts during the period under investigation, variations in capital costs of from $34.00 to $40.00 are implied for a bond issue with a fifteen-year average life. This is about six times the range for underwriters' spreads. Hence, even if one imputes all of the variation in underwriters' spreads to other aspects of competition among underwriters, for the issuer the search effect is dominant.

The reoffering-yield regressions show that those who have argued that ratings are an incorrect measure of the quality of a bond because one can observe bonds of the same quality rating with different reoffering yields have used an inappropriate argument.[35] Clearly, reoffering yields are

[35] West (1967, p. 249). Lack of continuous variability is a more appropriate argument which West also makes. The findings here suggest that West's use of reoffering yields to measure quality and therefore a determinant of underwriters' spreads along with bids, issue size, etc., constitutes a misspecified model. Reoffering yields and underwriters' spreads are highly correlated because they are determined by virtually the same variables.

A Study of the Effects of Competition in the Tax-Exempt Bond Market

affected by a number of variables wholly or largely independent of quality (that is, default risk), such as callability, number of bids, and issue size.[36] Hence, although the conclusion that ratings are less than perfect may be correct, and probably is, a more sophisticated analysis is required to establish this point.

The investigations of the comptroller of the currency and the Federal Reserve into the effects of increased competition upon underwriting costs have largely ignored the relationship between reoffering yields and number of bids, and focused on the relationship of (1) underwriters' spreads, and (2) the so-called net interest cost to number of bids submitted.[37] The latter relationship is difficult to interpret because the meaning of net interest cost is not economically "sensible." Net interest cost is the criterion by which the lowest bidder is selected in the United States. It is a function of the coupons assigned to a prospective bond issue by underwriters. When a tax-exempt issue is put out for bids, each bidder assigns coupons to every maturity of the issue. (Most tax-exempt bond issues are serial bond issues, that is, have multiple maturities.) The net interest cost is determined by computing the total prospective costs of servicing and dividing by the weighted average maturity. In other words, the undiscounted expenditure stream for servicing is summed and divided by the average amount to be borrowed to determine net interest cost.[38]

The net interest cost method of computing the costs of servicing a bond issue implies that a dollar to be disbursed in the distant future is just as important as a dollar in the near future. To see that this is the case, assume that the same amount of a serial bond issue falls due on every maturity date. Then, if the coupon is reduced from, say, 5 to 4 percent for the ten-year maturity and the coupons for the four- and six-year maturities are increased from 4 to 5 percent, computed net interest cost remains unchanged. However, the present worth of the servicing costs has increased. Hence, this method for evaluating bids leads underwriters to assign high coupons to short, and low coupons to long, maturities. For

[36] Mendelson (1967, p. 426) asserts, without documentation, that yield is a more accurate measure of quality than rating. One suspects that the author regards this statement as so obviously true that documentation is redundant. If quality is defined to be default risk, and not reoffering yield, then the case that rating is a poorer measure than reoffering yield is far from obvious.

[37] Heins (1962, p. 399); West (1966, p. 305); and Phelps (1961) estimate net interest costs only. The difference, perhaps the chief difference, between West's regressions and the others is that Heins and Phelps ignore bids as an independent variable.

[38] Often, last-minute adjustments in bids of underwriters are made by offering to pay an amount in excess of the par value of the securities in cash. This is often done as an alternative to adjusting coupons. Amounts in excess of par value paid by underwriters are deducted from the total expenditure stream to be paid in servicing bonds in computing net interest cost.

underwriters to respond in any other way would be economic suicide. Consequently, the long-term maturities of most serial bond issues with multiple coupons are reoffered by underwriters at less than par; and the short terms, at premiums. Since the bonds of a new issue are in aggregate sold at par, the difference between the reoffering price and the value at maturity is taxable income. These "capital gains," really implicit interest, for the buyers of long terms are taxable as capital gains, whereas the explicit interest is tax free. Hence, some of the tax exemption of municipals is dissipated.[39] Alternatively, the cost of servicing tax-exempts is higher than it would be if a method of evaluating bids were used that led to the reoffering of tax-exempts at par.

These findings also indicate that if one abstracts from the trend in differentials over time, yield differentials between White's and any specified rating class are related positively to the level of interest rates. However, the reoffering-yield regressions do not, and cannot, show what happens to the differentials in reoffering yields caused by rating differences as the level of interest rates varies. To investigate the sensitivity of these differentials to the level of rates, the coefficient of White's was computed for each rating class.[40] If these differentials are sensitive to the level of rates, this sensitivity will be revealed by differences in the magnitude of these coefficients. The coefficients (see table 12) clearly show that differentials increase, after abstracting from trend, with the level of rates.

These findings are consistent with the implications of the money-substitute theory of securities, or the theory of liquidity preference, enunciated by Hicks (1962). Low-quality bonds are subject to greater default risk than high-quality bonds. Hence, the variance in the realized rate of return from holding low-quality bonds is greater. Consequently, they are poorer substitutes for money than high-quality bonds. Since high-quality bonds are better money substitutes, and the opportunity cost of holding money and money substitutes ought to increase simulta-

[39] The market for long-term tax-exempts, selling well below par, tends to be confined to life insurance companies. Capital gains is not included in the definition of life insurance company taxable income (see Percus and Quinto 1956, p. 415, n. 2). Also, Robinson (1960, p. 233, n. 3) reports that the low-coupon terminal maturities are usually not reoffered publicly. However, underwriters report that the yield-to-maturity of these maturities is usually from forty to sixty basis points higher than a comparable maturity reoffered at par. There exists a difference of opinion in the literature on what the foregoing article contains. West (1966, p. 113, n. 12), says: "The article [by Percus and Quinto] also failed to recognize the difference between 'present value' methods of interest computation and the traditional form prevailing in this bidding." Percus and Quinto regard (1956, p. 415) the reoffering yields as "determined by market conditions." Reoffering yields are assumed to be exogenously determined and regarded as given in solving for an optimal pattern of coupons.

[40] More specifically, the coefficient of White's for each rating class relative to the coefficient of BBBs was computed in addition to computing the absolute value of the coefficient for BBBs.

TABLE 12

COEFFICIENTS OF WHITE'S BY RATING CLASS*

Rating	General Obligations	Revenues
AAA	−0.07	0.05
AA	0.02	0.09
A	0.15	0.20
BBB	0.27	0.27

* These coefficients measure the sensitivity of the difference between reoffering yields and White's to the level of White's. The sensitivity of reoffering yields to White's is measured by one plus the coefficients in table 7.

neously, yield differentials associated with quality differences should increase with the level of rates if the Hicks's theory is correct.[41]

IV. Analysis of Saxon General Obligations

In comparison with the data already utilized, the Saxon G.O.'s represent a handful of issues. Hence, if these issues constituted evidence with the same strengths and weaknesses as that already presented, their marginal value here would be nil. The great merit of the Saxon G.O. evidence is: it is a test case of what would be the immediate, if not the long-run, effects of the abolition of the prohibition of bank underwriting of revenue bonds. Because of the abundance of evidence on the relationship of reoffering yields and underwriters' spreads to number of bids, the question asked of the Saxon G.O. data is: Did the number of bids increase as a result of the partial lifting of the ban against bank underwriting of revenues as a result of Saxon's rulings?[42]

For every issuer whose bonds were affected by Saxon's rulings, an attempt was made to compare the number of bids submitted for postruling issues with bids for the immediately preceding preruling issues. Issues following rulings were paired, insofar as possible, with an equal number of issues preceding rulings. If there were, for example, two issues after Saxon's ruling for an issuer, then these two issues were paired with the two issues that just preceded the ruling, subject to the constraint that these issues have the same Standard and Poor's rating.

[41] Hickman (1958, pp. 288 ff.) observed that quality differentials for corporates are also a function of the level of rates. However, he used a wholly different theory to explain his observations. Phelps (1961, pp. 301–2) also finds that yield differentials increase with the level of rates.

[42] These rulings occurred between 1962 and 1966. Another body of data similar to the Saxon G.O.'s will be generated by recent legislation. An amendment to a housing law passed in 1968 makes all bonds issued to finance state university dormitories eligible for bank underwriting. Hitherto, such bonds have been regarded as revenues.

Such a comparison involves obvious difficulties unless one abstracts from other factors that determine the number of bids—such as, issue size, level of interest rates, rate of change of rates, etc.—the variables that were considered in the analysis of bids. The matching process is best for holding quality, the single most important determinant of the number of bids uncovered here, constant. In general, issue size, the level of rates, and outstandings have increased as a function of time. The bid regressions suggest that, on balance, ignoring these variables will bias the comparison against discovering more bids for the post-Saxon issues. Nevertheless, this evidence indicates that the number of bids submitted for post-Saxon ruling issues, on average, exceeded the number submitted for pre-Saxon issues by a factor of 50 percent. Moreover, about half of the bonds affected by Saxon ruling were bid for and won by syndicates led by commercial banks.

There are thirteen issuers for which there were just one pre-Saxon and post-Saxon issue. For this set, two issues received the same number of bids before and after rulings. Three received fewer bids, and eight received more bids after becoming eligible for bank underwriting. Of the three issuers for which two issues were involved, all three issuers received, on average, more bids for post-Saxon issues. The same holds true for issuers with four, five, seven, and eight paired issues. Of the twenty-one issuers of Saxon G.O.'s, three received fewer bids, two the same, and sixteen more bids after Saxon's rulings. Of the forty-six issues studied, there were, on average, in excess of four bids after issues became Saxon G.O.'s in contrast with under three bids when they were defined to be revenues. Table 13 constitutes a listing of the issuers and a summary of the number of bids received by each issuer for the issues compared.

V. Conclusions

The results obtained indicate that the prohibition of bank competition in the underwriting of revenue bonds has led to fewer bids for these bonds and higher underwriting costs. In particular, the issues of revenues that are high quality, short maturity, and offered about troughs in business conditions have been particularly disadvantaged.

Competition in the tax-exempt bond market manifests itself principally through its effects on the terms at which bonds are bought by the investing public. Competition is search; the greater the degree of competition, the more the market is searched by underwriters for buyers. Consequently, the greater the degree of competition, the more extensive the canvass of the market and the higher the prices received by underwriters. Interpreting the results obtained with the aid of Stigler's search hypothe-

TABLE 13
Saxon General Obligations*

Issuers	Pre-Saxon Bids	Post-Saxon Bids
Single issues:		
1. Alabama Public School and College Authority	2	3
2. Detroit Wayne Joint Building Authority	3	3
3. Florida State Board of Education†	2	3
4. Georgia Ports	9	7
5. Georgia State Hospitals Authority	4	9
6. Georgia State Office Building	8	7
7. Georgia Stone Mountain Memorial	5	7
8. Illinois State Office Building	4	4
9. University of Texas—Board of Regents	9	6
10. Georgia Rural Roads	4	13
11. Port of New York Authority	4	5
12. Indiana State Office Building	2	3
13. Wisconsin State Agencies	4	5
Two issues:		
1. Georgia State School Building Authority	4	8
2. Georgia State Highway Authority	8	19
3. Louisiana Capital Construction and Improvement Commission‡	5	8
Three issues:		
State of Washington Public School Plant Facilities Bonds†	7	11
Four issues:		
Ohio Highway Improvement and Major Thoroughfare Bonds†	8	16
Five issues:		
Pennsylvania Highway and Bridge	12	21
Seven issues:		
Pennsylvania State Public Schools Building Authority	13	31
Eight issues:		
Pennsylvania Generals	16	29
Totals	133	218

* All issues were either AA or AAA as rated by Standard and Poor's.
† Reverted to revenue status in 1967 and received two bids on January 24, 1967.
‡ Reverted to revenue status on March 14, 1967 and received three bids.

sis, the bid regressions can be viewed as supply equations, with the number of bids submitted being affected by the size of the market at the time an issue is submitted for competitive bids; the economic profitability of search is a function of market size. On this analysis, there appears to be a trade-off, with respect to search, between a small number of large syndicates and a large number of small syndicates. This suggests that the negative coefficient of issue size in the reoffering-yield regressions is a consequence of bids not measuring a homogeneous unit of search. The larger the issue, the larger the syndicate and conversely. However, the question of what constitutes a better measure of search, and how it ought to be employed, goes well beyond the scope of this paper.

Finding that revenue issues do indeed receive fewer bids than G.O.'s leads to the question: Why should the prohibition of bank underwriting of revenues imply less competition in revenue than in G.O. underwriting? There exist no entry barriers to the underwriting of revenues for other participants or would-be participants in our financial markets; free entry exists for all except commercial bankers.[43] Hence, the level of competition in underwriting revenue bonds ought to be unaffected by the absence or presence of commercial bankers in this market.[44] This line of analysis is based on certain premises about the supply function of underwriting capital and talent which may not be appropriate. Certainly, many would argue that the salaries of professors would be higher if one or another cultural group that has demonstrated survival properties in higher education were excluded by a legal prohibition. Hence, long-run supply inelasticities cannot be ruled out as an answer.

However, there does exist another line of explanations of the results obtained here that does not rest upon supply inelasticities. This is the argument that investment and commercial bankers are complementary resources in producing underwriting services. This complementarity in production stems from the differences in the laws regulating these two classes of enterprises. To the extent that the costs of distribution of financial securities are subject to economies associated with being able to offer a "full line" of securities to the market, investment bankers can distribute more economically than commercial bankers. Typically, investment bankers distribute more than tax-exempts; they also distribute corporate bonds and stocks. By contrast, commercial bankers are precluded from the latter markets by law.

With respect to financing the holdings of inventories of tax-exempt securities in the process of distribution, commercial banks can take the income on these securities as tax free. By contrast, investment bankers can take this income as tax free, subject to an important constraint, that tax-exempts are not used to secure loans. In other words, the value of tax-exempts as collateral is less for investment bankers than it is for commercial bankers. Or, commercial banks have a comparative advantage in carrying tax-exempts.[45]

An implication of this analysis is that syndicates bidding for bonds that both investment and commercial bankers are eligible to underwrite

[43] Mendelson (1967, pp. 425–26) seems to regard the prohibition of bank underwriting of revenues as ipso facto evidence of less competition in revenue relative to G.O. bond underwriting.

[44] A related question is: What would happen to the cost of transacting in federal government securities if banks were barred from this market? Currently, both investment and commercial bankers deal in governments, and no legal entry barriers exist for anyone.

[45] Investment bankers have a strong incentive to pledge anything but tax-exempts to secure bank loans. As a consequence, investment bankers that underwrite tax-exempts exclusively have become a smaller fraction of the market as a function of time.

will consist of both investment and commercial bankers. This implication appears to be correct. Whenever it is possible, in the case of general obligations, syndicates formed to submit bids to buy and distribute tax-exempts usually consist of a combination of both commercial and investment bankers. Moreover, syndicates that underwrite G.O.'s almost invariably allocate to their commercial bank membership the task of carrying undistributed bonds.

Trend was entered into several of the regression equations and was euphemistically referred to as a variable. Clearly, it must be a proxy for an unspecified variable. The trend in bids, which is strong enough to account for an increase in roughly two bids per issue over the period studied, manifested itself in the bid regression for G.O.'s only. Hence, any explanation offered must be specific to G.O.'s or irrelevant for revenues. If the value of this tax advantage is a function of the level of interest rates, this would explain the upward trend in bids, since there has been an upward trend in rates over the time period investigated.

Why should the advantage of banks in carrying tax-exempts be a function of the level of rates? A rise in interest rates increases the difference between tax-free income and deductible expenses. Hence, assuming a constant marginal tax rate for banks over the time interval studied and no change in the ratio of tax-exempt rates to short-term rates such as bill rates (which are relevant for measuring the cost of short-term funds), this conclusion follows. To illustrate, assume that the short-term rate, which measures the implicit interest cost of deposits for banks, is 3 percent and goes to 6 percent, while the tax-exempt rate goes from 2 to 4 percent. The difference in the after-tax income at the beginning of the period, assuming a marginal tax rate of 50 percent, is the difference between 2 and 1.5 percent. At the end of the period, it is the difference between 4 and 3 percent.[46] By contrast, the losses of investment bankers, if they pledge municipals for loans, increase with the level of rates insofar as the difference between tax-exempt and short-term taxable rates widens. Another avenue for explaining the trend in bids for G.O.'s, which is not inconsistent with the tax argument, is the growth in the holdings of tax-exempts by commercial banks as a function of time. The *Federal Reserve Bulletin* (1967) reports that the holdings of tax-exempts by commercial banks grew from about 8 to about 13 percent of loans and investments between the end of 1958 and the end of 1967. If commercial bank underwriters are overrepresented in servicing commercial banks as investors in tax-exempts, as was argued earlier, then the trend in bids can be rationalized as a consequence of the growth in the market served by commercial bank underwriters.

[46] In fact, the ratio of tax-exempt rates to short-term taxable rates has risen over this time period. Hence, the foregoing example understates the improvement over time in the tax advantage of banks in carrying municipals.

The trend in underwriting costs and reoffering yields, the other trend "variable" employed, reveals trends common for both G.O.'s and revenues. There has been a downward trend in underwriting costs and a compression in yield differentials over time. Moreover, the lower the quality, the more robust the trend. The unspecified variable that appears to account for these trends is a persistent difference between the default risk expected by the market and the default risk actually experienced. Consequently, over the period investigated, the market has revised upward its estimates of the quality of tax-exempts. Since a larger fraction of the promised yield of low- relative to high-quality bonds is accounted for by default risk, a similar argument applies to underwriters' spreads; the yields and underwriting costs of low-quality bonds have been most affected.

References

Federal Reserve Bulletin. "Interest Cost Effects of Commercial Bank Underwriting of Municipal Revenue Bonds." *Federal Reserve Bull.* (August 1967), pp. 1287–1302.

Fox, Bertrand. In U.S., Congress, House, Committee on Banking and Currency. *Hearings.* 88th Cong., 1st sess., September 23–30, October 1–11, December 10–13, 1963.

Hayek, Friedrich A. "The Use of Knowledge in Society." *A.E.R.* 35 (September 1945): 519–30.

Heins, A. James. "The Interest Rate Differential between Revenue Bonds and General Obligations: A Regression Model." *Nat. Tax J.* 15 (December 1962): 399–405.

Hickman, W. Braddock. *Corporate Bond Quality and Investor Experience.* Princeton, N.J.: Princeton Univ. Press (for Nat. Bur. Econ. Res.), 1958.

Hicks, J. R. *Value and Capital.* Oxford: Clarendon, 1962.

Investment Bankers Association of America. *Fundamentals of Municipal Bonds.* 6th ed. Washington: Investment Bankers Assoc. America, 1968.

Kessel, Reuben A. *The Cyclical Behavior of the Term Structure of Interest Rates.* National Bureau of Economic Research. Occasional Paper, no. 91. New York: Columbia Univ. Press, 1965.

Mendelson, Morris. "Underwriting Compensation." In *Investment Banking and the New Issue Market,* edited by I. Friend et al. New York: World Book, 1967.

———. "Determinants of Underwriters' Spreads on Tax-exempt Bond Issues: Comment." *J. Financial Quantitative Analysis* 3 (June 1968): 215–24.

Percus, J., and Quinto, L. "The Application of Linear Programming to Competitive Bond Bidding." *Econometrica* 24 (October 1956): 413–29.

Phelps, Charlotte D. "The Impact of Tightening Credit on Municipal Capital Expenditures in the United States." *Yale Econ. Essays* 1 (Fall 1961): 275–321.

Robinson, Roland. *Postwar Market for State and Local Government Securities.* Princeton, N.J.: Princeton Univ. Press (for Nat. Bur. Econ. Res.), 1960.

Smith, W. Paul. *Commercial Bank Entry into Revenue Bond Underwriting: An Appraisal of the Public Benefits of S. 1306.* Washington: Department of Banking and Currency, Office of the Comptroller of the Currency, 1967.

Stigler, George J. "The Economics of Information." *J.P.E.* 69 (June 1961): 213–25.

U.S., Congress, Senate, Committee on Banking and Currency. *Hearing on S. 1306.* 90th Cong., 1st sess., 1967.

West, Richard. "New Issue Concessions on Municipal Bonds: A Case of Monopsony Pricing." *J. Bus.* 38 (April 1965): 135–48. (*a*)

———. "Should Commercial Banks Be Allowed to Underwrite Municipal Revenue Bonds?" *Nat. Banking Rev.* 3 (September 1965): 35–44. (*b*)

———. "More on the Effects of Municipal Bond Monopsony." *J. Bus.* 39 (April 1966): 305–8.

———. "Determinants of Underwriters' Spreads on Tax-exempt Bond Issues." *J. Financial Quantitative Analysis* (September 1967), pp. 241–63.

III Monopoly and Competition

8 Economic Effects of Federal Regulation of Milk Markets*
(1967)

I. ORIGINS OF FEDERAL REGULATION

EXISTING federal control over the marketing of fluid milk is authorized by the Agricultural Adjustment Act of 1937.[1] This act permits the producers of milk eventually sold to the public as fresh milk, to impose marketing controls upon bottlers or dairies, or, in the language of the act, handlers, who market their milk to consumers or other dairies. A proposed marketing order is first presented to the handlers concerned for their signature and approval. However, if those handling most of the milk to be covered by the proposed order fail to sign, an order can nevertheless become effective if either two-thirds of the producers or producers of two-thirds of the output sold within the marketing area approve the proposal. In effect, milk producers can impose controls over the handlers.

Most of the major cities in the United States serviced by handlers who receive milk from producers in more than one state, that is, when interstate commerce is involved, now have federal milk marketing orders. The handlers that supplied milk to such cities as New York, Chicago, and Boston were regulated in the 1930's. By 1940, roughly twenty per cent of all milk shipped from farms passed through the plants of regulated handlers. This fraction rose to twenty-five per cent in 1950, and to about sixty per cent today. Federal controls over milk marketing by handlers spread very rapidly during the decade beginning in 1950. The absence of federal controls does not imply the absence of marketing controls; the handlers in many large markets such as San Francisco and Los Angeles are regulated by state controls.

---

* It is my melancholy duty to acknowledge the assistance which I received on the legal aspects of milk regulation from Mr. Robert M. Schuchman, whose death while holding a law-economics fellowship at the University of Chicago was a serious loss to scholarship. It had been hoped that it would be possible to publish some of Mr. Schuchman's writings on this question, but unfortunately they had not reached a sufficiently developed form to enable this to be done. The research on which this article is based has been supported by Ford Foundation funds made available by the School of Business of the University of Chicago.

[1] 7 U.S.C. § 601-624 (1964); 50 Stat. 246 (1937). This act replaced legislation first passed in 1933 and revised in 1935.

Before federal marketing legislation was enacted, farmers supplying markets such as Chicago, Boston, and New York bargained, through their cooperatives, with handlers over the price to be paid for their milk. Almost invariably, they bargained for a two-price system with a relatively high price to be paid for milk to be resold as fresh milk, and a lower price to be paid for milk used in manufacturing butter, cheese, and other manufactured milk products.[2] Competitive forces often operated to erode away all price differences between milk for manufacturing and fluid use other than those accounted for by cost differences. Fluid milk dealers could find milk producers who would sell their milk at or about what it was worth in manufacturing. Despite the willingness of producer groups to employ milk strikes and violence, two-price systems before the advent of governmental support were unstable and hence produced instability in milk prices to producers and handlers.

As a result of alternation in the determinants of milk prices to producers, with monopoly pricing alternating with price determination by competitive forces, the market for fluid milk was regarded by milk producers as lacking in "order." The suppliers of milk to large urban markets regarded the frequent breakdowns in the two-price system as socially undesirable and described the transition from monopoly to competition as chaotic. They argued that milk strikes and the associated violence and price instability (caused by their efforts to maintain discriminatory pricing for their output) constituted an undesirable consequence of the presence of competition. Unable to eradicate competition privately, they attempted and ultimately succeeded in enlisting the support of governments to suppress competition.[3]

With the advent of the Great Depression and a change in the willingness of the community to accept economic controls, milk producers who supplied large urban markets strongly supported and won legislation that would substitute government for private power as a means of maintaining classified pricing. The purpose of this legislation has been described in a report to the Secretary of Agriculture by the Federal Milk Order Study Committee as follows:

"1. To promote orderly marketing conditions for farmers specializing in

---

[2] See Cassels, A Study of Fluid Milk Prices, (1937), for a history of efforts to organize the milk markets in our major cities before the advent of federal marketing controls.

[3] Although producer groups experienced difficulties in maintaining classified pricing, efforts to win governmental support were relatively weak until the 1930's. During the Great Depression, it became more difficult and costly to privately enforce classified pricing. Consequently milk producers intensified their efforts to obtain support for discriminatory pricing from both state and federal governments. See Harris, Classified Pricing of Milk 27 (U.S. Dep't of Agriculture Tech. Bull. No. 1184, 1958); and U.S. Federal Milk Order Study Committee, Report to the Secretary of Agriculture 8 (Dec. 1962). [Hereinafter cited as Report.]

the production of fluid milk and thereby improve their income situation at least in the long run;

2. To administer and supervise the terms of trade in defined milk markets in such manner as to equalize the market power of buyers and sellers and attain reasonable competition but not local monopoly resulting in undue price enhancement;

3. To assure customers that they will have access to adequate and dependable supplies of high-quality milk from the sources best suited both technologically and economically to supply these demands;

4. To complement the efforts of milk producers' organizations to maintain economic order in their industry, and to bring about the coordination of price structures and market practices within and between marketing areas, between fluid and manufacturing segments of the dairy industry, and between milk production and other lines of farming;

5. To secure equitable treatment of all parties—producers, dealers and consumers, not only within each local or regional market but throughout the system;

6. To establish such terms of trade under the orders as will combine maximum freedom of trade with proper protection of established producers against seasonal or other loss of outlets that would tend to demoralize markets and farming plans."[4]

Why should these farm organizations have bargained for such a complex system that involves patently difficult problems of auditing and policing? Indeed, why should they have any interest at all in the end products which are to be produced out of the raw material they supply? Two classes of answers to this question appear in the literature. One explains this behavior in terms of consumer interests. If consumers are to be assured of a supply of fresh milk throughout the year, then the prices of milk eligible for bottling must be higher than milk eligible only for manufacturing since milk for bottling must satisfy more costly sanitary standards. If a supply of fresh milk is to be assured, then there will be a surplus of milk eligible for bottling that goes into manufacturing. The milk eligible for bottling that goes into manufacturing will be no more valuable than milk ineligible for bottling. Consequently higher prices must be charged for milk that is resold as fresh milk. The other class of answers implies that producers are pursuing their own interest to the detriment of consumers. "Price classification was designed primarily to obtain higher returns for producers."[5] Fluid milk is more expensive to transport than manufactured milk products. It weighs

[4] Report at 12.
[5] Report at 17 n.1.

much more per dollar of product at the source, and it is more difficult, that is, more expensive, to handle because of its perishability and differences in sanitation requirements among communities. Hence fluid milk markets are naturally more isolated from one another than the markets for manufactured milk products. Under competition, butter and cheese prices would vary less, from one part of the country to another, than milk prices. Consequently it is easier for a producer group to control the supply of fresh milk in a market than to control manufactured milk products. These economic considerations, quite apart from any legal restraints on interregional trade, suggest that it is easier to monopolize fresh milk markets than it is to monopolize the markets for manufactured milk products. Hence the adoption of classified pricing by producers supplying a particular market can be rationalized as being a consequence of, on the one hand, a negatively sloping demand curve for fresh milk and, on the other, an infinitely elastic demand curve for milk to be used in manufacturing, since the market for manufactured milk products is national if not international. "Products locally manufactured from excess milk supplies do not enjoy the same protective advantages afforded the less concentrated products, and are sold in markets of national scope."[6]

The purpose of this study is to answer the questions: What are the economic effects of these controls? Do they increase the cost of milk to consumers? Are they in the economic interest of all dairy farmers? How have they affected the efficiency with which resources are employed?

II. THE CONTROL MECHANISM

The Agricultural Adjustment Act of 1937 provides that the producers of fresh milk who normally supply a "marketing area" can enlist the support of the Agriculture Department to work out an "orderly" method of marketing their output. The Department of Agriculture will, if the producers can show that a two-thirds majority desire federal help in marketing their products, appoint a federal milk marketing administrator who will administer the marketing agreement which is referred to as an order. The principal function of the administrator and his staff is to enforce the marketing order. This entails a great deal of auditing of the accounts of handlers. Handlers are taxed by the order to pay the costs of administering a market order. The budget for the Chicago order in 1965 was approximately one-half million dollars.

There are no federal controls over the prices and selling policies of dairies or bottlers that are members of an order. It is the buying practices of dairies with respect to their major input, milk, that is regulated. The federal milk market

---

[6] Report at 19. Also see Report at 20.

administrator sets, monthly, minimum fresh and manufacturing milk prices that dairies must pay at a specified location or base. (In Chicago, this base is City Hall.) Since dairies typically haul the milk they buy from the country to their plants, the milk market administrator also sets what are termed zone differentials, that is, discounts from the base price to be paid for milk acquired by dairies in the country. In Chicago, for example, these discounts are a function of the distance between the points at which dairies pick up their milk, and City Hall.

The milk marketing administrator also computes what is known as the blend price. This is a weighted average of the prices paid for manufacturing and fresh milk. It is what a particular handler, in a market-wide pool, pays his suppliers. In addition, handlers have financial relations with a producers' settlement fund, which is managed by the milk marketing administrator. A handler pays into the fund if his fluid utilization of milk is greater than the over-all utilization for the entire market. Conversely he receives from the fund if his utilization is below the market average. Hence it is a matter of indifference to any individual producer, in a market-wide pool, whether or not his milk is utilized as fluid milk or turned into butter. As long as he sells to a regulated handler, he must receive the blend price. For the Chicago order in 1966, milk sold to dairies to be resold as fresh milk was priced at about $4.24 per hundredweight by the order administrator. In contrast, identical milk used in manufacturing butter, cheese, and dried skim milk was priced at about $3.20. The receipts of each producer in an order are the product of his output and the blend price.

Since the end of World War II, milk market administrators have had very little choice in pricing manufacturing milk. Most of the time, the government has been actively supporting the butter, cheese, and skim milk markets. Hence if manufacturing milk is to be sold, it must be priced at its value in producing manufactured milk products to be sold to the federal government. In effect, the demand for milk to be used for manufactured dairy products has been virtually infinitely elastic at its imputed value in the production of butter and cheese for sale to the government.[7]

III. The Working of the System

Presumably under competition milk of like grade and quality would bring the same price in a market, and therefore the price paid for milk to be resold

---

[7] See U.S. National Commission on Food Marketing, Technical Study No. 3: 286 (1966). [Hereinafter cited as Organization.] CCC expenditures for butter have averaged about a quarter of a billion dollars per year in the last ten years. See Table 3-2, *id.* at 38. "In the summer of 1961, the large accumulation of butter stocks threatened to over-run the available storage facilities." See Spencer, Development of the Federal Milk Order System as Related to National Supplies and Surpluses of Milk, 1947-1963, 1 (Cornell Univ. Dep't of Agricultural Econ., Agricultural Econ. Research Bull. No. 162, 1965).

as fresh milk ought to approximate the value of similar milk used in butter production. The word approximate is used because grade B milk, which is milk produced under less rigid sanitary standards, can be used to produce butter but not fresh milk, and grade B milk is somewhat cheaper to produce.[8] However, this difference is small and for the purposes of analysis can be ignored. Hence the most important difference between an unregulated and a regulated market is the price paid for milk that is subsequently resold as fresh milk. Maintaining prices for milk to be used for fluid purposes that are higher than manufacturing milk prices, and higher than the cost difference associated with differences in sanitary standards for grades A and B milk, is the *raison d'être* for marketing orders.

The foregoing analysis implies that one of the major effects of federal milk order regulation, as contrasted with an absence of regulation, is higher prices to handlers for milk to be resold as fresh milk. Therefore, one ought to be able to observe systematically lower prices in nonregulated markets. Unfortunately, the buying prices of unregulated handlers are difficult to come by because so few cities of any size are unregulated. Moreover, handlers have relatively little incentive to divulge this information. Indeed, if anything, the incentives are probably the other way.

A recent study of the geographic pattern of milk prices by a member of the Department of Agriculture utilized one hundred and thirty-three observations of prices that were classified in four categories: federal order markets, state regulated, federal and state regulated, and unregulated. For the period studied, July, 1960 to June, 1961, there were twenty-four independent observations of unregulated markets, and seventy-six of purely federal order markets. These one hundred observations were pooled and the prices regressed on distance from Eau Claire, Wisconsin, the heart of the milk producing center on the Wisconsin-Minnesota border. In the absence of a systematic difference between unregulated and federally regulated order markets, prices in unregulated markets ought to be randomly distributed

---

[8] Milk that goes into the fresh milk market must meet higher sanitary standards than milk used for manufacturing. To the extent that these differences in sanitary standards are associated with differences in costs of production, the foregoing statements should be qualified. In fact, the marginal costs of meeting fluid sanitary standards are not easy to come by; sanitary standards for manufacturing milk vary from state to state.

There has been a steady increase in the fraction of milk produced that is eligible for Class I use. In 1950, only 39 per cent of the country's milk was grade A. By the end of 1965, the fraction eligible for grade A had risen to 61 per cent. In Wisconsin, the grade A manufacturing price differentials have been averaging approximately 35 cents per hundred pounds. However, at this differential there has been a dramatic conversion from grade B to grade A, and it is clear that the differential at which there would be no conversion is substantially smaller than 35 cents. See Graf, Economic Outlook for One Grade of Milk, presented at the Thirteenth Annual Dairy Manufacturing Conference, University of Kentucky, Dec. 1, 1965.

"Producer conversion from a manufactured milk to a market milk basis is relatively inexpensive and rather quickly accomplished." Report at 57.

about the regression line. In fact, the following pattern of the distribution of residuals was found:

DISTRIBUTION OF RESIDUALS

	+	−	Totals
Unregulated	8	16	24
Regulated	43	33	76
	51	49	100

A = 3.70 (.0602); B = .163 (.00763); R^2 = .823 where A is the constant term and B is the regression coefficient.

The high frequency of regulated markets and low frequency of unregulated markets among the observations with positive residuals is difficult to rationalize as the workings of chance. Application of the X^2 test indicates significance at a level of five per cent for a two tail test.

When regressions are run on distance from Eau Claire for each of the markets, for the regulated and the unregulated, the regression lines appear to be roughly parallel with a lower intercept for the unregulated market. The constant term for the unregulated markets was 3.53 (.1612) and 3.76 (.0575) for the regulated. The regression coefficients were .157 (.00747) for the regulated—dollars per hundred miles—and .175 (.0191) for the unregulated markets. Eighty-six per cent of the observed variance was explained by the first equation and seventy-nine by the second.[9] These findings lead to the question: Should the observed difference in constant terms, twenty-three cents, be attributed to chance? The answer is unclear; there is a probability of about twenty-eight per cent of a difference as large as twenty-three cents occurring by chance.[10]

In the 1964-65 study by Lasley of the relationship between prices and transportation costs, there were only eight unregulated markets. These were:

>Springfield, Illinois
>Eau Claire, Wisconsin
>Bemidji, Minnesota
>Winona, Minnesota
>Jacksonville, Florida
>Galveston, Texas
>Houston, Texas
>Cheyenne, Wyoming

[9] These data were obtained through personal communication with Floyd A. Lasley, the author of Geographic Structure of Milk Prices, 1964-65, (U.S. Dep't of Agriculture Economic Research Service No. 258, 1965).

[10] The test used is described in Lehmann, Testing Statistical Hypotheses 172 (1959). A two tailed test was used. For the slopes, the probability of the difference being significant was about one-quarter.

The Springfield price was 4.09 against 4.26 for Chicago, although Springfield is roughly one hundred miles further from the producing center. The Bemidji and Winona prices were 3.55 and 3.68 respectively against 4.13 and 3.99 for Duluth and Saint Paul respectively. Saint Paul and Winona are approximately the same distance from Eau Claire. The Eau Claire price was the lowest price observed, 3.53. Other Wisconsin prices were 4.20 for Madison and Milwaukee, and 3.75 for Green Bay. The other prices in the unregulated markets seemed to be roughly equal, after adjusting for distance, to the regulated prices.[11]

IV. The Effects of the System

Given that federal milk orders utilize a two-price system for the same product, then it can be shown that orders lead to an increase in milk output. Under competition, there would be a single price for milk eligible for fluid use and a somewhat lower price for manufacturing milk. In the long run, the difference beween these two prices would reflect differences in production costs. In the short run, this price difference would be demand determined. If the suppliers of milk eligible for fluid use organize an order, then they can, given demand inelasticities, increase total receipts by increasing the fluid milk price. Consequently the blend price for a given output must exceed the single price formerly charged. Under orders, output decisions are made individually and blend price will equal marginal costs. Consequently output must rise above the level formerly produced under competition, and the quantities supplied by order producers to the manufacturing milk market must increase. Hence the institution of orders implies an increase in milk output, a fall in the amount supplied to the fluid market, and an increase in the amount offered for use in the production of manufactured milk products.[12]

A two-price system of orders, given no controls over the output decisions of individual producers, with each producer accounting for a small fraction of order output, implies that every order producer will produce some milk that is sold at prices below marginal costs of production. If output decisions are based on blend prices and milk is in fact sold at the manufacturing milk

---

[11] The difference between producer prices in regulated and unregulated markets has implications for retail prices in these markets. These implications are examined in the Appendix.

[12] Presumably, under competition, a certain fraction of milk eligible for fluid use would go into manufacturing. However, the foregoing conclusion still holds as long as demand for fluid use is inelastic and the price of fluid is increased. "[W]here the milk supplies excluded from regulation under the Federal order for the major market were left unregulated, the producers often received flat prices as high or higher than the uniform prices determined under major order. Nevertheless, the net cost to the handler of milk used in his fluid sales was nearly always less than he would have had to pay for Class I milk under an order." Report at 38.

price, then it follows that the replacement of competition in the supply of milk with federal orders produces a system that induces farmers to produce milk individually and collectively at a cost that exceeds the price at which this milk is jointly sold. The foregoing is illustrated by Figure I.

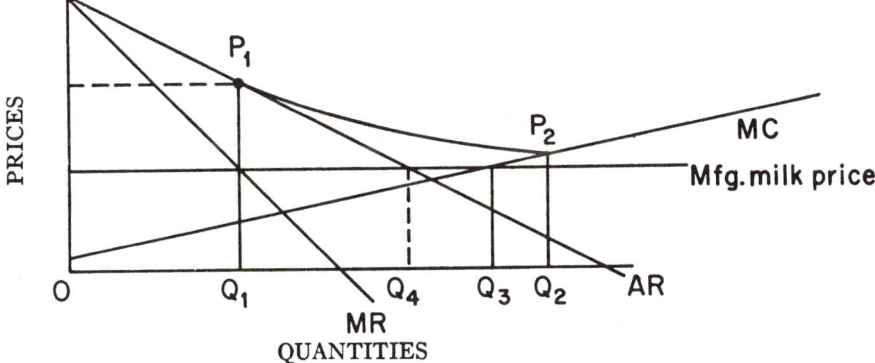

FIGURE I. Optimal Outputs and Prices for Orders

The equilibrium conditions for a marketing order are:
1. Blend price must equal marginal cost.
2. Marginal revenue must be equal in both markets.

The latter condition implies that marginal revenue in the fluid market must equal the manufacturing milk price. The demand for manufacturing milk is assumed to be infinitely elastic because (1) a single order produces a small fraction of all manufacturing milk used, and (2) the government has been, during most of the post World War II years, supporting the manufacturing milk market through its purchases of butter, cheese, and dried skim milk. The intersection of the marginal revenue curve (MR) for the fluid milk market and the demand curve, which is of course also a marginal revenue curve, for manufacturing milk, determines the optimal price and output for the Class I market whose demand curve is depicted by AR. At the optimal price P_1 in the fluid market, there exists the beginning of a locus of points $P_1 P_2$, which becomes asymptotic to the demand curve for manufacturing milk products, that describes the blend prices associated with various total outputs (Q_1 being sold in Class I and the remainder in the Class II market). The equilibrium blend price is determined by the first equilibrium condition, that blend price equal marginal costs (MC). This occurs for output Q_2 and blend price P_2. At blend price P_2, Q_1 is supplied to the Class I market, Q_1Q_2 to the Class II market. Output Q_3Q_2 is produced at out-of-pocket costs in excess of the receipts derived from the sale of this output; this loss is described by the triangle bounded by P_2 and the demand curve for milk for manufacturing. The amount that would have been produced under competition is Q_3 and the amount supplied to the fluid market Q_4 and to the manufacturing milk market Q_4Q_3.

To the extent that order producers increase their output over what would be produced under competition, they depress the price of manufacturing milk. Hence non-order producers receive lower prices for their manufacturing milk than would otherwise be the case. Orders operate to keep the price of manufacturing milk down and hence increase the support purchases of manufactured milk products by the government. Needless to say, they also operate to depress the incomes and outputs of non-order producers below what they would be if order producers operated in a competitive world.

From this analysis, it follows that the replacement of competition by federal milk market orders can be viewed as a negative sum game. It clearly operates to the detriment of the non-order producers as a class, and to taxpayers because it increases the support purchases of manufactured milk products. It produces economic inefficiencies because it induces order producers to produce some output at marginal costs that are in excess of marginal revenues, raises the prices of fluid milk above its true economic costs and, if anything, lowers the prices of milk for manufacturing below its economic costs. Only the order producers can possibly gain from this game. Consequently, insofar as one of the objectives of orders is to help all milk producers, it more than fails in this objective; it makes the producers of almost one-half of all milk worse off.

From the point of view of the consumer, federal orders raise the prices of fresh milk and fresh milk products relative to manufactured milk products. Abstracting from the support program for manufactured milk products, competition instead of federal orders would lead to lower prices for fluid milk vis-à-vis manufactured milk products, lower absolute prices for fluid milk products, and raise manufactured milk prices. In general, the federal order program increases the prices of what many regard as a "necessity," fluid milk, and decreases the prices of "luxuries" such as ice cream, cheese, and butter. Possibly the only exception to the foregoing is the price of dried skim milk which is lowered by the support program.

The behavior of milk prices in central Illinois, before the advent of regulation, constitutes an important piece of evidence that market forces, in the absence of federal, state and private controls, can provide the consumer with a steady supply of fresh milk at prices as low or lower than the prices that would have existed under federal controls. Clearly the consumer of fluid milk is not the beneficiary of federal marketing controls and consumer interests are not the cornerstone of the explanation of the existence of these controls; for the consumer, competition does at least as well, if not better.

Classified pricing with no production controls over the output of order producers leads them to produce more for the manufacturing milk market than they would under competition. However, federal milk market administrators, in setting the Class I price, can influence the amount offered by these producers. If they are willing to lower Class I prices, they can reduce output. Milk market administrators have an unambiguous criterion by which they can evaluate whether or not their Class I prices are too high or too low. This is the output of milk eligible for Class I use that in fact goes into manufacturing. If the key factor in the pricing of Class I milk is "to assure customers that they will have access to adequate and dependable supplies of high quality milk," then prices should be decreased to reduce surpluses and conversely (subject of course to the constraint that Class I prices do not fall below manufacturing milk prices).

What are the facts? Nationally, Class I surpluses have been rising since the end of World War II. It is clear that there exists an upward trend in the size of surpluses, as can be seen from Table 1. However, one may argue that, with the expansion of orders, a more relevant criterion is the fraction of Class I milk that is surplus, not the absolute amount. Since the end of World War II, the fraction utilized in Class I has been about two-thirds of the milk delivered by order producers. Over this same period, Class I order prices have generally risen relative to manufacturing milk prices.[13] They are from 35 to 100 per cent higher than manufacturing milk prices.[14] The decrease in utilization caused by the relative rise in Class I prices has been roughly offset by the expansion of federal price control orders in such areas as Texas, which until the advent of orders did not provide all of the milk sold as Class I from the output of local producers. Hence, the expansion of the federal order program has operated to increase measured utilization for all owners collectively. With respect to the older orders such as those in New York, Chicago, and Boston, there has been a downward trend in utilization. Since Class I prices have been secularly rising relative to manufactured milk prices, it follows that federal milk marketing administrators have set prices that increase surpluses and decrease utilization.[15]

The view that orders increase milk surpluses, which can be defined as milk that is sold to the government in the form of manufactured milk products, has not been accepted by many experts on milk marketing. Spencer concludes his study of the effects of orders upon surpluses with the statement: "The findings of this study indicate, however, that federal orders have been a relatively minor factor in the rapid growth of commercial supplies and

---

[13] Report at 32 and at 72-73, n.8.

[14] Organization at 41.

[15] The effect of bringing in orders to replace competition has been to increase permanently local output. Typically the increase in output has been greatest in the years immediately following the launching of an order. With the spread of orders in the 1950's and 1960's, this country has become regionally more self-sufficient with respect to its milk supplies. Report at 93-94.

national surpluses of milk."[16] Elsewhere he states: "This analysis disclosed no significant relationship between the importance of federal order markets as outlets for milk in the various states and the rate of increase in farm sales of milk during the seven years 1957-1963."[17] Spencer's data, however, suggest somewhat different conclusions. Table A2 in the Appendix, which

TABLE 1
MEASURES OF GROWTH IN FEDERAL MILK ORDER
MARKETS, SELECTED YEARS, 1947-65

			Order Producer Deliveries					
Year	Markets[a]	Handlers[a]	Producers[b]	Volume	Used in Class I	Used in Class I	Of all Milk Sold to Plants and Dealers	Class I Surplus
				Millions of Pounds	Millions of Pounds	Per Cent	Per Cent	Millions of Pounds
1947	29	991	135,830	14,980	9,808	65.5	21.2	5,172
1950	39	1,101	156,584	18,660	11,000	58.9	25.1	7,660
1955	63	1,483	188,611	28,948	18,032	62.3	31.8	10,916
1960	80	2,259	189,816	44,812	28,758	64.2	43.2	16,054
1962	83	2,258	186,468	51,648	31,606	61.2	46.7	20,042
1963	82	2,144	176,477	52,860	32,964	62.4	47.6	19,896
1964	77	2,010	167,503	54,447	33,965	62.4	47.6	20,482
1965[c]	73	1,891	158,118	54,446	34,559	63.5	47.9	19,887

[a] End of year.
[b] Average for year.
[c] Preliminary.
Source: U.S. National Commission on Milk Marketing, Technical Study No. 3: Organization and Competition in the Dairy Industry, at 41.

appears in Spencer's paper, clearly indicates that the growth rate of farm sales of whole milk delivered to order markets was, on an annual basis, greater than it was for the output of whole milk delivered to all markets. Another table, A3, also reproduced in the Appendix, indicates that the states with the greatest increases in farm sales of milk and cream had a relatively high fraction of milk going to federal order plants and conversely. The data contained in this table convinced Spencer that "the degree of dependence upon farm separated cream as a market for milk had much more influence upon the trend of farm sales of milk and cream than did the importance of federal order plants in the two groups of states represented in the foregoing tabulation."[18] By eliminating the states (nine) in which farm sales of cream were

[16] Spencer, *supra* note 7 at 20 & 22.
[17] *Id.* at 20.
[18] *Id.* at 18-20.

important, Spencer was able to produce a table that indicated an increase in farm sales of milk unrelated to the presence of federal orders. (This is Table A4 which is also reproduced in the Appendix.)

The major difficulty with Spencer's analysis is his failure to regard farm sales of cream as responding to weaker price incentives than farm sales of whole milk. Since orders do not cover farm separated cream, virtually all farm separated cream bought by processors is converted to manufactured milk products. Hence the elimination from his data of farm separated cream constitutes the elimination of evidence unfavorable to his thesis.[19]

For Chicago, the fraction going into Class I use was approximately 56 per cent in 1947, 55 in 1951, 52 in 1955, 46 in 1959, 39 in 1964, and 45 in 1965. Chicago had the dubious distinction of being the order market with the largest fraction of its output going into manufacturing. Hence the price paid for Class I milk in Chicago was probably further away from equilibrium than in any other market. Given the evidence on the spreads between dealer costs of milk and prices to consumers, it is highly likely that the costs to consumers attributable to the absence of competition are greater for Chicago than any other midwestern city, and possibly any other large city in the United States.

Federal orders lead to the creation of two classes of producers: order and non-order producers. The order producers have a fluid milk market to exploit and, in the process of exploiting it, produce more milk that is ultimately used in manufacturing than would be true in the absence of orders. The non-order producers do not have fluid milk markets to exploit and hence sell their milk for manufacturing without the benefit of a blend price; it is sold at the prevailing manufactured milk price which, for most of the postwar period, has been the value of milk in producing butter and cheese to be sold to the government at the support prices for these commodities.

Minnesota, Wisconsin, and, to a lesser extent, Iowa have a strong comparative advantage in milk production. Minnesota and Wisconsin produce roughly a quarter of all of the fluid milk produced in the United States. These three states produce over one-half of all the butter, cheese, and dried skim milk produced in this country. Obviously, these states and the upper midwest generally have a comparative advantage in milk production for any purpose. Federal orders clearly depress the price of milk used in manufacturing and consequently induce a lower level of production on the part of non-order producers. Since Wisconsin, Iowa, and Minnesota producers are overrepresented among non-order producers, it follows that federal orders induce the milk producers with a comparative advantage in milk production to

---

[19] The last column in Spencer's table reproduced in the Appendix as Table 2 should reflect changes in farm sales of milk in all forms, both whole and cream. What is essentially being compared is the change in incentives to produce milk generated by orders vis-à-vis the dairy support program.

contract their output and those with a comparative disadvantage to expand. In general, orders work to the disadvantage of the upper midwest and to the advantage of the rest of the country. With the spread of orders, the relative position of the milk producers of the upper midwest has deteriorated.

Between 1946 and 1964, the milk output of Iowa, Minnesota, and Wisconsin producers, as a fraction of all output, increased from 26.6 to 28.5 per cent. In contrast to this increase, the receipts from the sale of milk by producers in these states, as a fraction of all receipts from the sale of milk, declined from 25 to 23 per cent. The output of milk in Iowa declined in absolute terms while the output of milk in Minnesota and Wisconsin sharply increased.[20] Because of the comparative advantage in milk production of Minnesota and Wisconsin, their Congressional representatives have typically been more sympathetic to free interregional access to milk markets than one would predict from the positions taken with respect to other economic issues. Ideology and economic interests seem to be correlated. As a consequence of the conflict between free trade milk states and protectionist states, federal regulation dealing with milk marketing has represented a compromise between these two interest groups; both could agree that the consumer should be exploited; however, they have differences of opinion as to who should do the exploiting. By contrast, state regulations serve the interests of local producers only.[21]

The reduction in the output of efficient producers and the increase by inefficient producers engendered by federal order markets has been exacerbated by the way orders have been administered. The Department of Agriculture has favored local producers over non-local producers in the administration of the law to such an extent that the Department has been overruled by the Supreme Court in one important instance to be discussed. In administering the law, the federal milk market administrators have operated to isolate order handlers from outside competition. To the extent that such competition has been reduced, local monopolies in the distribution of milk have been encouraged. Transportation and location differentials, pool plant requirements, allocation requirements and compensatory payments have all been used to keep

---

[20] Presumably land used for milk production in Iowa has alternative uses not available to owners of land used for milk production in Wisconsin and Minnesota. Why the share of Minnesota and Wisconsin milk in total output increased is more difficult to explain. Clearly, relative price effects dictated a decrease. Did the comparative advantage of these two states in milk production increase over time?

[21] Prices also seem to be higher in state regulated markets than in federal markets. For twenty-two state controlled markets in the 1960-61 study by Lasley, the regression on distance from Eau Claire yielded a constant term of 6.01 (.708), and virtually none of the observed variance was explained; the pattern of prices least resembled those of a free market. The same conclusion appears in Hammond & Christiansen, Marketing Minnesota's Dairy Products: Characteristics, Problems, and Needs 35 (Minn. Agricultural Experiment Station Misc. Rep. No. 63, 1965).

out "foreign" milk and protect local producers. Compensatory payments have also protected local handlers. In addition, milk market administrators have tolerated, if not encouraged, super-pool premiums which have increased already swollen surpluses of Class I milk.[22]

Federal milk market administrators set up a series of concentric zones around the point chosen as the base, and the price paid by dairies depends upon the zone in which milk is picked up by the dairy. The greater the distance from the base, the lower the price paid. These zone differentials are presumed to reflect transportation costs, and, if they correctly reflected transportation costs, would equalize the cost of milk to handlers irrespective of the location of the producer from the base. In fact, zone differentials inadequately reflect transportation costs. The costs of picking up milk from distant producers usually exceed the difference between the base price and the price paid, and this difference increases with distance from the base. Consequently dairies, given these set differentials, have an incentive to buy their milk from close-in producers.

This practice is rationalized on the grounds of economic efficiency. Milk market administrators argue that they do not want handlers to be indifferent between buying from close-in and from distant producers. They want handlers to buy from close-in producers in order to minimize transportation costs. This is probably the only appeal to economic efficiency made by the Agriculture Department in justifying the regulations of milk market administrators. Its use is clearly a piece of economic sophistry.[23] Presumably there exists a set of zone differentials that will lead to the employment of land in the base zone as pasture; transportation costs would be at a minimum if cows were pastured on land surrounding dairies. In fact, economic efficiency would be better, but far from perfectly, served, if zone differentials reflected transportation costs; if in fact processors were indifferent about the location of their producers. Under these circumstances, social costs which in this instance are transportation plus production costs would be lower than they are under the system employed. With the present arrangement, farmers are induced to substitute uneconomically high priced close-in land for land further from the base.

However weak the case for zone differentials that fail to depict transportation costs, it is infinitely stronger than the case for location differentials. These constitute payments to close-in producers from the producers' settlement fund simply because they are close-in producers. These payments, which are a function of the volume of milk delivered by producers eligible for these payments, are made from the producers' settlement fund and are deducted from the gross receipts of the order before computing blend prices.

[22] Report at 24.
[23] *Id.*

Hence location differentials depress blend prices, and favor producers close to the market at the expense of those farther away. Clearly they operate as a deterrent to far-out producers vis-à-vis close-in producers in supplying fluid milk for an order market. Both location and zone or transportation differentials favor one class of milk producers at the expense of another class. These nearby differentials, or location differentials, have existed in many important markets such as Chicago, New York-New Jersey, Connecticut, and other New England orders. In many of the New England orders, nearby differentials are paid on two-thirds to ninety per cent of the milk delivered, and blend prices are depressed by thirty to forty cents per hundredweight.[24]

These differentials are rationalized as an attempt to reproduce the competitive market. Under competition, it has been argued, nearby producers would get more for their milk than distant producers, apart from differences in transportation costs, because of more desirable seasonality, earlier and more dependable arrival at city plants, easier and more economical supervision of producers, etc.[25] This argument, apart from its validity, is a strange defense since the rationale for the existence of orders is that competition produces undesirable results because it pits one producer against another. Yet this defense says the outcome of this undesirable process should be reproduced by regulators.

The rationale presented for the existence of location differentials is quite independent of the reason for their existence. Presumably when orders were being organized, close-in producers were somewhat reluctant to pool their milk with more distant producers, since under competition, apart from transportation costs, they would receive a higher price for their product. Consequently, in order to win the consent of the close-in producers for orders, concessions in the form of location differentials were presumably bartered for their political support in organizing orders.

In addition to lowering the prices of the output of manufacturing milk producers through equating marginal production costs with blend prices, order producers have erected barriers to the admission of non-order producers to milk market orders that are above and beyond the location differentials and inappropriate zone differentials. These barriers are erected because order producers have an interest in high utilization and hence high blend prices. In contrast, non-order producers have an interest in becoming order producers in order to increase their revenues by the difference between manufacturing milk prices and blend prices. Hence, non-order and order producers are constantly engaged in a form of covert warfare through their representa-

[24] Report at 74-75.
[25] *Id.* at 75.

tives in the halls of Congress and elsewhere.[26] Manifestations of this conflict are pool plant requirements, allocation provisions and compensatory payments.

Pool plant requirements constitute a condition for admission to the privilege of having a producer's output pooled and priced under an order. In order to qualify, a producer must have his output move through a plant that has some specified fraction of its milk used for fluid purposes, often during a particular part of the year. (In Chicago, pool plant requirements were twenty per cent, which is relatively low.) Often in order to qualify, producers will, insofar as it is possible to do so and not violate order regulations, absorb processing costs in order to induce regulated handlers to purchase some of their output. Close-in producers have objected to this practice on the grounds of economic inefficiency; milk is hauled uneconomically long distances in coming to market.

What happens when a handler buys milk from producers or from plants whose producers are not eligible to share in an order market? Order administrators have viewed this behavior with horror and have used allocation provisions and compensatory payments to discourage such purchases. Virtually all orders have at one time or another had allocation provisions. These provide that if a handler buys milk from unregulated sources, he must allocate all milk from regulated sources to fluid use before he can pay more than the manufacturing milk price for the unregulated milk. Hence, if any milk from regulated sources is used in manufacturing, then the maximum price that can be paid unregulated milk is the manufacturing milk price. If the most a handler can pay is the manufacturing milk price, then virtually all incentive is eliminated for the sale of such milk by unregulated sources to order handlers.

Compensatory payments deal with the problem of a handler whose sales in a regulated market constitute a relatively small fraction of his total sales. If such a handler is regulated as an order handler, then his producers become eligible for participation in pooling. This would be to the detriment of other order producers because it would lower utilization. However, if such a handler is not regulated with respect to the price he pays for milk, then order handlers may be at a disadvantage. An unregulated handler might be able to buy milk at a lower price than regulated handlers. To solve this problem, unregulated handlers selling in order markets are assessed the difference between fluid and

---

[26] There is also a conflict of interest within an order between the near-in and far-out producers with the near-in producers trying to oust the far-out producers from the order in an effort to raise utilization. Some analysts have attributed to such a conflict the dissolution of the Chicago order which had an unusually low utilization. They believe the object of the dissolution is to eliminate far-out producers through preventing their entry in a subsequent order. If they are eliminated, blend prices would increase and the near-in producers would be better off.

manufacturing milk prices on their sales in the order market regardless of the price actually paid.

Assessing unregulated handlers for the difference between manufacturing and fluid milk prices for all milk sold in an order market regardless of the price in fact paid, led to the famous Lehigh Valley case,[27] and the ruling that the Agriculture Department had exceeded the powers Congress delegated in the Agricultural Adjustment Act. The plaintiffs were handlers with plants in Pennsylvania, who bought most of their milk from farmers located in Pennsylvania, and sold most of their output in Pennsylvania. One, Lehigh Valley, was regulated by the Philadelphia order; the other, Suncrest, was unregulated. One of the plaintiffs had sold its milk in the Phillipsburg area of Northern New Jersey for twenty-two years before this case arose, the other for ten years. Both paid prices for milk that were equal to or higher than the Class I (fluid milk) prices set by the New York-New Jersey order.

In an order effective August 1, 1957, the Secretary of Agriculture extended the area of the New York order to include Northern New Jersey, bringing Phillipsburg and the surrounding area into a federal order for the first time. Under the terms of this order, Lehigh Valley and Suncrest became subject to regulation as a consequence of their sales in the Phillipsburg area. Lehigh Valley was ineligible to join the New York-New Jersey order since it already belonged to the Philadelphia order and more of its sales were in the Philadelphia order market. Suncrest found it unprofitable to join the New York-New Jersey order, assuming it could satisfy pool plant requirements, because most of its milk was bought and sold in Pennsylvania. If Suncrest joined the New York-New Jersey order, it would have to pay to the producers' settlement fund of that order the difference between blend and Class I prices on its fluid sales, and would have to pay Pennsylvania minimum prices to its producers. Hence, it would have higher fluid milk costs than competitors in all markets served.[28]

The rationale for the extension of the New York order into New Jersey is straightforward. Northern New Jersey produced and bottled less milk than it consumed.[29] Hence, the expansion of the New York order would drive out of the market the dairies that supplied this area insofar as they paid prices for fluid milk in excess of the manufactured milk price. As a result of compensatory payments, handlers who did not have plants in the original or expanded area but supplied the area incidental to supplying other markets would be effectively precluded from this market. For the producers already under the New York order, the addition of Northern New Jersey to

[27] Lehigh Valley Cooperative Farmers, Inc. v. United States 370 U.S. 76 (1962).
[28] Record, vol. 1 at 10a, 46a-50a, 86a-88a, 117a-118a, 244a-254a, 285a, 304a-311a, Lehigh Valley Cooperative Farmers, Inc. v. United States, 370 U.S. 76 (1962).
[29] *Id.* at 372a.

the order added more fluid milk consumption than production, hence utilization would rise. Consequently, both the handlers and the producers under the New York order could gain from this expansion at, of course, the expense of other handlers and producers.

Clearly, the experience in Northern New Jersey indicates that until the overthrow of compensatory payments by the Lehigh Valley case in 1962, the Agriculture Department administered milk market orders in a way that isolated handlers supplying a given market from the competition of handlers that primarily supplied other markets. Hence the orders served more than the interest of order producers; it also isolated regulated handlers from some of the hazards of competition. Compensatory payments constitute at least a partial explanation for the rapid expansion of orders and provide an economic rationale for a community of interest between producers and handlers.[30]

In recent years, in approximately one-third of the federal order markets, the price paid for milk by handlers has not been fixed by the federal milk market administrator. Order producers have been permitted to negotiate prices in excess of the price set by the milk market administrator. The difference between prices determined by milk marketing administrators and the prices actually negotiated are called superpool premiums. These premiums varied from 2 to 35 cents per hundredweight in 1965.[31] Presumably Congress in enacting this legislation was dissatisfied with the results of negotiations between handlers and producers and set up an umpire to provide "fair prices" for both handlers and producers. If this function is surrendered, then much of the rationale for the existence of orders disappears. The role of the federal milk market administrator, under these circumstances, is to use the power of the government to enforce prices that he had no direct role in determining.[32] The willingness of handlers to pay superpool premiums is related to the probability that they will have to compete with handlers who can obtain milk at lower costs. Consequently, insofar as handlers are isolated from competition with handlers outside the local markets, the formation of superpool premiums is encouraged.[33]

---

[30] Growth of limited access, high speed interstate highways since the end of World War II helped break down the natural isolation of fluid milk markets and appears to be a very important explanation for the spread of orders.

[31] Hammond & Christiansen, *supra* note 21 at 36.

[32] Presumably in the absence of orders and with competition, superpool premiums would not exist. And zone differentials that inadequately reflect transportation differentials encourage producers to seek superpool premiums. Consequently, insofar as orders replace competition, superpool premiums must be attributed to the existence of orders.

[33] Before the dissolution of the Chicago order, handlers did not have to pay superpool premiums on milk they bought that was to be sold to handlers outside the local market for bottling. The rationale for this discrimination is demand elasticity. Milk going outside the local market often must meet more competition. As a consequence of this discrimi-

V. The Food and Agriculture Act of 1965

The Food and Agriculture Act of 1965[34] enables the Department of Agriculture to set up orders that, in principle, could more effectively exploit the monopoly position of the suppliers of milk under an order. In fact, powers delegated by this new legislation have yet to be utilized in the administration of an order. Consequently, what would occur if these powers were utilized must rest on economic analysis and estimates of how this law will be administered.

The key provision of this legislation deals with the inefficiencies caused by milk producers utilizing blend prices to make their output decisions when their marginal milk was in fact sold at the manufacturing milk price. This legislation assigns market rights to producers to sell Class A milk in a particular market. Presumably, rights will be issued for an output equal to Class I sales at the order price. In the absence of these market rights, milk will be sold by producers at the best price they can get, which will be the manufactured milk price; the blend price is effectively eliminated as a determinant of output. As a consequence, the manufactured milk price should rise as a result of the decline in the output of order producers. Hence, this legislation will make the manufacturing milk producers of the midwest better off. Order producers will stop producing milk at costs in excess of manufacturing milk prices, and they also will be better off.

In contrast to the producers of manufactured milk products of the midwest, the producers of manufactured milk products in the east will be worse off.[35] The costs of milk to eastern producers will rise relative to those of the midwest, if Class I production quotas are established. Federal milk orders have stimulated the growth of a manufactured milk industry in the east as a result of the surplus of milk eligible for Class I use that is diverted to manufacturing. These new manufacturing milk processors were induced to enter this activity by the order policies for selling surplus Class I milk. Often this meant prices to processors for milk to be used in manufacturing that were as much as twenty cents per hundred pounds less than the comparable Minnesota price.[36] The present Secretary of Agriculture, when he was Governor of Minnesota, felt so strongly about these surpluses, and the manufacturing milk industry they induced, that he advocated amending the Agricultural

---

nation, a Saint Louis handler could buy milk in Chicago for less than the price paid by a Chicago handler for milk to be resold locally.

[34] 79 Stat. 1187 (1965).

[35] Between 1946 and 1963, butter production in New England and New York increased by a factor of four while butter production in Minnesota, Wisconsin and Iowa increased by a factor of about two. Needless to say, this increase in the output of butter was not in response to the wishes of consumers; during this period per capita butter consumption fell by a factor of one-third.

[36] Hammond & Christiansen, *supra* note 21 at 34.

Adjustment Act of 1937 in order to bring down Class I prices relative to manufacturing milk prices.[37] He argued:

> We think that it is plain that the New York consumers' payments of high Class I prices constitute, in effect, a subsidy to the New York milk manufacturers in the form of unduly low manufacturing milk costs, and with no advantages to the New York dairy farmers whose blend price is being pulled down by the low manufactured price.[38]

If the rights to sell Class A milk in order markets are negotiable, then trade barriers to interregional sales of milk will be reduced, if not eliminated. Assuming these rights can be freely bought and sold, then their value would be greatest in the hands of those milk producers who can supply milk to a given market at the lowest cost. Consequently, the negotiability of these rights can improve the economic position of all milk producers, and presumably will lead to the expansion of output by producers of the upper midwest for the fluid market and a contraction in the output of present order producers associated with an increase in their net worth.

With respect to the taxpayer, the provisions of the Food and Agriculture Act of 1965 imply that smaller quantities of manufactured milk products will have to be bought by the CCC for any specified level of support prices than would be the case under the legislation of 1937. With respect to the consumer, the implications of the new legislation are less straightforward. Insofar as handlers are no longer protected from the pressures of competition, there would be a gain. However, what will happen to Class I prices is another matter. If surpluses of Class I milk operated as a brake upon Class I prices, then this brake will be removed and Class I prices will be increased. It would seem that, if anything, fluid milk consumers will probably be worse off as a result of this legislation. Insofar as marketing monopolies by dairies are removed, they will gain. But against this gain must be put the adverse effects of higher prices for milk to bottlers and higher prices for manufactured milk products.

V. Summary

In summary, present legislation constitutes class legislation. It favors the suppliers of fluid milk markets and injures the suppliers of milk for manufacturing. The proliferation of orders following World War II led to an increase in the supply of milk for manufacturing as a result of the use of blend prices in making output decisions by order producers. Consequently,

---

[37] Hearings on Investigation of Dairying before the Subcomm. on Dairy Products of the House Comm. on Agriculture, 84th Congress, 1st Sess., Ser. GG, at 443 (1955).

[38] *Id.* Class I prices have continued to rise relative to manufacturing milk prices since Freeman took office.

the higher prices obtained by fluid market suppliers were associated with lower prices for manufacturing milk suppliers. The economic gains of the fluid milk suppliers are considerably smaller than the economic costs incurred by society as a result of orders.

Orders constitute a monopolistic pricing arrangement that produces, not too small, but too large, an output. Typically, monopolists have marginal costs that are less than the price at which their marginal output is sold; the economic costs of monopoly arise because output is too small. In contrast, order producers sell their marginal output at prices below marginal costs. Hence, some of their gains in monopolizing the fluid milk market are dissipated in excessive production of milk at costs that exceed marginal returns. Consequently, if the output of order producers were reduced, the resources relinquished could be used to produce goods and services whose market value would exceed the value of the milk in fact produced.[39] One method of achieving this objective is the replacement of orders with competition. Another is to establish Class I production quotas and sell all other milk at the market, and this is apparently the purpose of the Food and Agriculture Act of 1965.

APPENDIX

The data on prices to producers cited suggested that the retail prices in towns whose handlers are unregulated ought to be lower than they are in Chicago, abstracting from transportation costs. Presumably, unregulated handlers are able to buy their milk for less than regulated handlers. By how much less is a more difficult question. The maximum difference is roughly seventy-five cents per hundredweight. The Springfield-Chicago price differential suggests that this advantage is about twenty-five cents per hundred pounds or a half cent per quart. Illinois is one of the few states with cities of any size whose handlers until recently (December, 1966) have been uncontrolled. These cities exist in the middle of the state. They are bordered on the north by the Chicago and Rockford orders, and on the south by the St. Louis order. This area, uncontrolled until December, 1966, contains the towns of Danville, Champaign, Bloomington, Peoria, Springfield, and Decatur.

The retail prices of milk in stores that are parts of chains operating in Chicago and in these cities were obtained. These stores were the A & P, Kroger, and Eisners. Eisners is part of the Jewel chain in Chicago. The prices are tabulated below.

The prices in the unregulated cities are, if anything, too low relative to those observed in Chicago to be explained by differences in raw milk prices to handlers. The most the difference in raw milk costs could account for is one-half cent per quart. Moreover, there are considerable economies of scale in bottling plants and the trend has been toward larger plants. Hence, if anything, plant processing

---

[39] The fact that the CCC has been an important buyer of this milk only strengthens this conclusion. Presumably the resale price of milk by the government is less than its purchase price.

RETAIL MILK PRICES, CHICAGO & CENTRAL ILLINOIS*

		Quarts	Half Gallons	Gallons	Half Gallons 2%
(1, 2, 3)	Chicago	26	47	89	45
(1)	Decatur	21	40	77	37
(3)	Decatur	22	38.5	69	31.5
(2)	Springfield	23	37.5	69	36.5
(3)	Champaign	23	43	79	33.3
(2)	Champaign	22	39.5	79	38
(2)	Danville	22	43	73	41
(2)	Bloomington	23	42.5	72	37
(1)	Peoria	25	39.5	75	36.5
(3)	Peoria	25	39.5	75	37

1. Kroger
2. Jewel
3. A & P

* Observed November 12, 1965. Prices in cartons.

costs would be smaller in Chicago. These results indicate that more than a difference in dealer costs of milk is being detected. The fact that the Eisner chain downstate carries Dean's milk, the same brand carried by Jewel in Chicago, and that this milk came from the Chicago-area Dean's plant does nothing to weaken the impression that what has been uncovered cannot be entirely explained by the absence or presence of federal orders. Dean's is fully regulated under the Chicago order and hence must pay the minimum order price for milk that is shipped downstate.

There exists other evidence that suggests that marketing margins are relatively high in Chicago. This evidence is summarized below.

AVERAGE FARM PRICES AND TOTAL MARKETING MARGINS ON WISCONSIN FLUID MILK SOLD IN SEVEN MARKETS, 1951-54

	Wis. Farm Price	Total Marketing Margin on Sales Through Retail Stores	Total Margin on Sales in Home Delivery Basis (cents per quart)		
			Single Quart Containers	Two Quart Containers	Discount Basis
Chicago	9.09	13.06	15.67	15.17	13.61
Milwaukee	9.47	10.14	10.75	10.22	9.63
Oshkosh	9.00	10.28	10.28	8.80	8.62
Beloit	9.39	12.00	12.00	10.81	8.66
Kenosha	9.42	11.36	11.30	10.81	10.30
Madison	9.69	10.40	10.86	10.46	9.33
Minneapolis	9.13	8.53	11.54	—	9.25

Source: Wisconsin Legislative Council, *Report of the Special Joint Committee on Dairy Prices Spreads to the 1955 Legislature* 2089 (June, 1955). [Assembled at the direction of the Committee by the staff of the Legislative Council.]

MONOPOLY AND COMPETITION

The foregoing data are consistent with the differentials between retail prices and dealers' prices for major midwest cities covered in the Fluid Milk and Cream Report of the Department of Agriculture in recent years. The data, for the cities of Detroit, Cleveland, Indianapolis, Milwaukee, Minneapolis, Kansas City, St. Louis and Chicago, are summarized in Chart A. They clearly show Chicago with

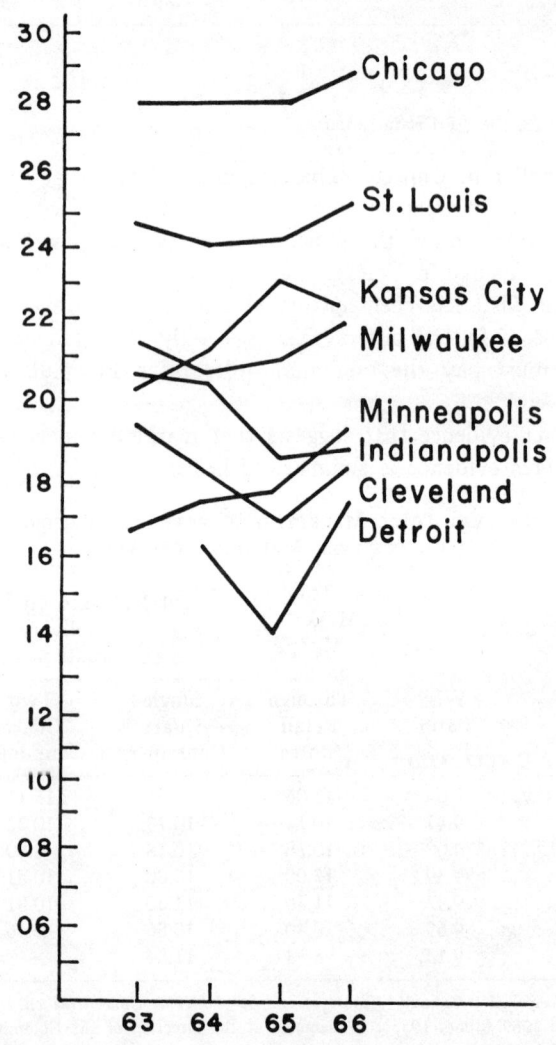

Chart A.
Average Annual Margin Per Half-Gallon Whole Milk, Chicago and Other Cities 1963–1966, in Cents

Source: Fluid Milk and Cream Reports, U.S. Department of Agriculture

the largest distribution margins, approximately three cents per half gallon higher than the closest competitor, St. Louis.

A noteworthy property of the retail prices of milk in Chicago, as compared with other major midwestern cities, that probably is related to the size of the spreads observed in the preceding table, is the relative stability and small range in retail prices reported. Typically, for half gallons of milk sold in cartons by stores, the Agriculture Department reports a range of observed prices for a metropolitan area; for Chicago only a single observation has been reported. (These observations reflect prices in major chains.) Moreover, if one uses the mean of the ranges when several observations are reported, the month-to-month variations in Chicago prices are lower than they are for other major cities in the midwest.

Other observers have found similar evidence of high marketing costs in Chicago. The marketing margins for nine cities (Chicago, Denver, Detroit, Los Angeles, Louisville, Miami, Minneapolis, St. Louis, and Washington, D.C.) are compared for half gallons of milk sold by stores. The price paid to farmers as a fraction of the retail price is lowest, and the absolute size of the difference between dealer costs for milk and retail prices the greatest for Chicago. The ratios ranged from 36.6 to 57.4 per cent, and the absolute difference from .166 to .298 cents.[1]

Another piece of evidence suggestive of unusually large margins is the practice of "stop buying."

In Chicago secret discounts of up to 11% and secret payments to secure an account of up to $50,000 have been proved in cases brought by the federal government.[2]

Such an observation is suggestive of efforts to evade price restrictions.

Still another anomaly of the Chicago market is the failure of prices either to dealers or on the retail level to fall since the abandonment of federal control in Chicago at the end of June in 1966. The evidence presented suggests that dealer buying prices should drop with the abandonment of federal regulations. All this evidence points to the existence of price restrictions other than governmental.[3]

---

[1] See U.S. National Commission on Food Marketing, Technical Study No. 3: Organization and Competition in the Dairy Industry, Table 14-1 at 194 (1966). Wages in Chicago were highest for three of four categories of workers employed by dairies that were also reported in this table.

[2] Wisconsin Legislative Council, Report of the Special Joint Committee on Dairy Price Spreads to the 1955 Legislature, 2089 (June 1955). [Assembled at the direction of the Committee by the staff of the Legislative Council.]

[3] Prices in downstate Illinois towns, which became regulated in December of 1966, continue to be lower than Chicago prices despite the fact that they are farther from Wisconsin. One could also observe price variations among major chains in the same town downstate and "sales," that is, temporary price cuts, which are not observed in Chicago.

TABLE A1
Federal Order Markets: Number of Markets, Producer Milk in Class I, and Total Receipts from Producers. Annual Data for the Years 1947-1963

Year	Number of markets (end of year)	New orders issued	Producer milk in Class I		Total receipts from producers		
			Million pounds	Percentage of nonfarm consumption	Million pounds	Percentage of production	farm sales*
1947	29	1	9,808	24.3	14,980	12.8	21.2
1948	30	1	9,852	24.6	15,020	13.3	21.8
1949	33	3	10,104	24.9	17,049	14.7	23.3
1950	39	6	11,000	26.4	18,660	16.0	25.1
1951	44	7	12.718	29.7	20,117	17.5	27.0
1952	49	5	14,672	33.6	22,998	20.0	29.8
1953	49	1	15,436	34.6	25,896	21.5	30.6
1954	53	4	16,172	35.1	27,140	22.2	30.9
1955	63	10	18,032	37.7	28,948	23.5	31.8
1956	68	5	19,615	39.7	31,380	25.1	32.9
1957	68	3	21,339	42.5	33,455	26.8	34.0
1958	74	6	23,309	46.3	36,356	29.5	36.5
1959	77	6	26,250	52.0	40,149	32.9	39.8
1960	80	3	28,758	56.5	44,812	36.4	43.2
1961	81	4	29,859	59.4	48,803	38.9	45.1
1962	83	3	31,606	61.8	51,648	41.0	46.7
1963	82	0	32,968	63.2	52,868	42.4	47.6

* Receipts from producers at federal order plants as percentage of all whole milk sold by farmers to dealers and plants.

Sources: Market order data: From reports of the Dairy Division, Agricultural Marketing Service, U.S. Department of Agriculture.

Data on milk production, farm sales of milk to dealers and plants, and nonfarm consumption of fluid milk and cream: From reports of the Statistical Reporting Service, U.S. Department of Agriculture, Milk-Production, Disposition, and Income, (Statistical Bulletin No. 282, 1961) and the annual report for 1962-1963 (April 1964).

TABLE A2
PERCENTAGE INCREASES FROM YEAR TO YEAR IN RECEIPTS FROM PRODUCERS AT FEDERAL ORDER PLANTS, IN ALL MARKETS AND IN COMPARABLE MARKETS: ALSO YEAR TO YEAR INCREASES IN U.S. FARM SALES OF MILK TO DEALERS AND PLANTS, 1950-1963

Years	Number of markets		Percentage increase of receipts from producers at federal order plants		Percentage increase of U.S. farm sales of whole milk to dealers and plants
	All markets	Comparable markets	All markets	Comparable markets	
1950-1951	44	22	7.8	0.2	0.4
1951-1952	49	24	14.3	4.8	3.8
1952-1953	49	33	12.6	10.9	9.4
1953-1954	53	35	4.8	3.9	3.9
1954-1955	63	37	6.7	2.8	3.5
1955-1956	68	40	8.4	4.5	5.0
1956-1957	68	40 (41)*	6.6	6.4 (1.6)*	2.9
1957-1958	74	40 (41)*	8.7	2.4 (0.2)*	1.4
1958-1959	77	45	10.4	2.7	1.2
1959-1960	80	49	11.6	3.9	3.0
1960-1961	81	58	8.9	5.3	4.2
1961-1962	83	67	5.7	2.9	2.2
1962-1963	82	68	2.4	1.3	0.4
Averages:					
1950-1956			9.1	4.5	4.3
1957-1963			7.8	3.1 (2.6)*	2.2
1950-1963			8.4	3.9 (3.5)*	3.2

* New York-New Jersey, by far the largest of all federal order markets, was not included among the comparable markets for 1956-1957 and 1957-1958 because its marketing area was expanded substantially in 1957. If New York-New Jersey were included for those years on the basis of estimated receipts and Class I disposition excluding the effect of expansion, the percentage increases would be as indicated by the bracketed figures.

Sources: 1. Producer receipts at federal order markets: Derived from data compiled by the milk Marketing Orders Division, Agricultural Marketing Service, U.S. Department of Agriculture.
2. Farm sales of milk to plants: Derived from reports of the Statistical Reporting Service, U.S. Department of Agriculture. Milk-Production, Disposition and Income, (Statistical Bulletin 282, 1961) and annual report for 1962-1963 (April 1964).

Note: Comparable markets include all which operated under federal orders throughout each 2-year period and whose marketing areas were not changed significantly during that time.

TABLE A3

Item	Averages for 5 states with greatest increases in farm sales of milk and cream	Averages for 5 states with decreases in farm sales of milk and cream
Percentage increase or decrease in farm sales to dealers and plants	29.3	−10.0
Percentage of all farm sales of milk and cream that went to federal order plants	39.7	22.4
Cream sales by farmers as percentage of total farm sales of milk and cream	1.1	35.9

TABLE A4
Increase or Decrease in Farm Sales of Milk to Plants, 1957 to 1963, in States Grouped According to the Percentage of all Farm Sales of Milk that Was Delivered to Federal Order Plants

Percentage of total farm sales of milk to plants that went to federal order plants, 1960		Number of states	Percentage increase in farm sales of milk to plants, 1957 to 1963	
Range	Average		Simple average (per cent)	Weighted average (per cent)
Less than 20	2.1	10	21.2	15.9
20-49	38.5	11	8.1	5.6
50-69	61.1	9	9.6	11.1
70 and over	88.3	9	8.0	12.0
All groups		39	11.8	10.3

Note: States in which farm sales of cream (in milk equivalent) to plants in 1957 were 20 per cent or more of total milk and cream sales to plants, also the new states of Alaska and Hawaii, have been excluded from this tabulation.

Sources: 1. Percentage of farm sales of whole milk delivered to federal order plants, by states: from Federal Milk Order Market Statistics, Supplement for 1961 to Statistical Bulletin 248. Dairy Division, Agricultural Marketing Service, U.S. Department of Agriculture, November 1962.
2. Farm sales of milk and cream to plants: from reports of the Statistical Reporting Service, U.S. Department of Agriculture, Milk-Production, Disposition and Income, (Statistical Bulletin No. 282, 1961) and the annual report for 1962-1963 (April 1964).

9 Competition, Monopoly, and the Pursuit of Money* (1962)

The Problem

GENERALLY speaking, the observations of economists on the subject of monopoly fall into two classes. One set of observations, which flows directly from monopoly theory, is that resources in the competitive sector of the economy would be underutilized if used by monopolists. The other, which does not arise as an implication of either monopoly or competitive theory, consists of a series of observations of empirical phenomena: that monopolistic enterprises, by comparison with competitive enterprises, are characterized by rigid prices, stodgy managements, and relaxed, easygoing working conditions. Alternatively, it is alleged that employees of competitive enterprises work harder, managements are more aggressive and flexible, and pricing is more responsive to profit opportunities.[1]

To regard this second class of observations as not an implication of either monopoly or competitive theory is only partly correct. More correctly, these observations are inconsistent with the implications of the standard profit or wealth maximization postulate. For analyzing the behavior described by Hicks, the pecuniary wealth maximization postulate is clearly inappropriate and should be replaced by a utility maximization postulate.

* Coauthored by Armen A. Alchian.

[1] Hicks concludes: "The best of all monopoly profits is a quiet life." This conclusion appears in a theoretical paper on monopoly; yet it does not flow from the theory presented.

Preceding the foregoing quotation is: "Now, as Professor Bowley and others have pointed out, the variation in monopoly profit for some way on either side of the highest profit output may often be small (in the general case it will depend on the difference between the slopes of the marginal revenue and marginal cost curves); and if this is so, the subjective costs involved in securing a close adaption to the most profitable output may well outweigh the meagre gains offered. It seems not at all unlikely that people in monopolistic positions will often be people with sharply rising subjective costs; if this is so, they are likely to exploit their advantage much more by not bothering to get very near the position of maximum profit, than by straining themselves to get very close to it. The best of all monopoly profits is a quiet life. John R. Hicks, "Annual Survey of Economic Theory: The Theory of Monopoly." *Econometrica*, January 1935, page 8.

Utility Maximization, Not Wealth Maximization

That a person seeks to maximize his utility says little more than that he makes consistent choices. In order to employ this postulate as an engine of analysis, one must also specify what things are regarded as desirable. This is the class that includes all those things of which a person prefers more rather than less: money, wealth, love, esteem, friends, ease, health, beauty, meat, gasoline, etc.[2] Then, assuming that a person is willing to substitute among these variables, that is, he will give up wealth in return for more peace and quiet, or better looking secretaries, or more cordial employees, or better weather, the behavior described by Hicks can be analyzed.

Economics cannot stipulate the exchange value that these things have for any particular person, but it can and does say that, whatever his preference patterns may be, the less he must pay for an increase in one of them, the more it will be utilized. This principle, of course, is merely the fundamental demand theorem of economics—that the demand for any good is a negative function of its price. And price here means not only the pecuniary price but the cost of whatever has to be sacrificed.

For predicting the choice of productive inputs by business firms, where only the pecuniary aspects of the factors are of concern, the narrower special-case postulate of pecuniary wealth is usually satisfactory. But this special-case postulate fails when a wider class of business activities is examined. Therefore we propose to use the general case consistently, even though in some special cases simpler hypotheses, contained within this more general hypothesis, would be satisfactory.[3]

---

[2] The following impression is not uncommon. "To say that the individual maximizes his satisfaction is a perfectly general statement. It says nothing about the individual's psychology of behavior, is, therefore, devoid of empirical content." T. Scitovsky, "A Note on Profit Maximization and Its Implications," *Review of Economic Studies*, 1943, pp. 57-60. But this is also true of profit or wealth maximization—unless one says what variables affect profit or wealth and in what way. And so in utility maximization, one must similarly add a postulate stating what variables affect satisfaction or utility. This leads to meaningful implications refutable, in principle, by observable events. For example, an individual will increase his use of those variables that become cheaper. Utility maximization, like wealth maximization, is not a mere sterile truism.

[3] Failure to give adequate heed to the special-case properties of wealth maximization may have been responsible for some complaints about the inadequacy of economic theory and may even have led to the curious belief that people themselves change according to which postulate is used. For example, Scitovsky says (*ibid.*):

"The puritan psychology of valuing money for its own sake, and not for the enjoyments and comforts it might yield, is that of the ideal entrepreneur as he was

An example of the power of the generalized utility maximizing postulate is provided by Becker.[4] He shows that under the more general postulate a person, deliberately and even in full knowledge of the consequences for business profits or personal pecuniary wealth, will choose to accept a lower salary or smaller rate of return on invested capital in exchange for nonpecuniary income in the form of, say, working with pretty secretaries, nonforeigners, or whites. The difference in money return between what an entrepreneur could earn and what he does earn when he chooses to discriminate is an equalizing difference that will not be eliminated by market pressures. If these persisting, equalizing differences exist, their size, and consequently the extent of discrimination, will differ when institutional arrangements lead to differences in the relative costs of income in pecuniary form relative to income in nonpecuniary form. Thus, if one can determine the direction in which relative costs are affected by activities or variables that en-

---

conceived in the early days of capitalism. The combination of frugality and industry, the entrepreneurial virtues, is calculated to insure the independence of the entrepreneur's willingness to work from the level of his income. The classical economists, therefore, were justified in assuming that the entrepreneur aims at maximizing his profits. They were concerned with a type of business man whose psychology happened to be such that for him maximizing profits was identical with maximizing satisfaction.

"The entrepreneur today may have lost some of the frugality and industry of his forefathers; nevertheless, the assumption that he aims at maximizing his profits is still quite likely to apply to him—at least as a first approximation. For this assumption is patently untrue only about people who regard work as plain drudgery; a necessary evil, with which they have to put up in order to earn their living and the comforts of life. The person who derives satisfaction from his work—other than that yielded by the income he receives for it—will to a large extent be governed by ambition, spirit of emulation and rivalry, pride in his work, and similar considerations, when he plans the activity. We believe that the entrepreneur usually belongs in this last category."

Aside from the dubious validity of (1) alleged differences between the entrepreneurs of the "early days" of capitalism and those of today, and (2) the allegation that the early entrepreneur was one whose utility function had only a single variable—wealth—in it, the more general analysis obviates the urge to set up two different and inconsistent behavior postulates, as if people were schizophrenic types—utility maximizers when consumers and wealth maximizers when businessmen.

The special-case property of the wealth maximizing postulate has been noted by M. W. Reder ("A Reconsideration of the Marginal Productivity Theory," *Journal of Political Economy*, October 1947, pp. 450-458). But in suggesting alternatives he did not postulate the more general one, which includes the valid applications of the special-case postulate as well as many more, without leading to the invalid implications of the special-case postulate.

[4] Gary S. Becker, *The Economics of Discrimination*, University of Chicago Press, 1957.

hance a person's utility, then it should be possible to observe corresponding differences in behavior.

Monopolistic Versus Competitive Behavior

The wealth-maximizing postulate seems to imply that both competitive and monopolistic enterprises pursue profits with equal vigor and effectiveness, that their managements are equally alert and aggressive, and that prices are just as flexible in competitive as in monopolized markets. Both the competitive and monopoly model imply that the assets of an enterprise, be it a monopolist or competitive firm, will be utilized by those for whom these assets have the greatest economic value. One might object to this implication of similarity between competition and monopoly by arguing that, when a monopolistic enterprise is not making the most of its pecuniary economic opportunities, it runs less risk of being driven out of business than a similarly mismanaged competitive enterprise. The answer to this is that despite the absence of competition in product markets, those who can most profitably utilize monopoly powers will acquire control over them: competition in the capital markets will allocate monopoly rights to those who can use them most profitably. Therefore, so long as free capital markets are available, the absence of competition in product markets does not imply a different quality of management in monopolistic as compared with competitive enterprises. Only in the case of nontransferable assets (human monopoly rights and powers like those commanded by Bing Crosby) does classical theory, given free capital market arrangements, admit a difference between competition and monopoly with respect to the effectiveness with which these enterprises pursue profits.[5]

The preceding argument implies that there is no difference in the proportion of inefficiently operated firms among monopolistic as compared with competitive enterprises. (Inefficiency here means that a situation is capable of being changed so that a firm could earn more pecuniary income with no loss in nonpecuniary income or else can obtain more nonpecuniary income with no loss in pecuniary income.) As Becker has shown, discrimination against Negroes in employment is not necessarily a matter of business inefficiency. It can be viewed as

---

[5] For a statement of this position, see Becker, *The Economics of Discrimination*, p. 38. Becker argues that, insofar as monopoly rights are randomly distributed and cannot be transferred, there are no forces operating to distribute these resources to those for whom they are most valuable. Consequently monopolists, when rights are nontransferable, would be less efficient, on the average, than competitive firms.

an expression of a taste, and one's a priori expectation is that discrimination is characterized by a negatively sloped demand curve. From this viewpoint, discrimination against Negroes by business enterprises, whether competitors or monopolists, would not lessen even if managements were convinced that discrimination reduced their pecuniary income. Presumably, the known sacrifice of pecuniary income is more than compensated for by the gain in nonpecuniary income. But if discrimination does not constitute business inefficiency, then the frequency of discrimination against Negroes ought to be just as great in competitive as in monopolistic enterprises, since both are presumed to be equally efficient. This implication is apparently inconsistent with existing evidence. Becker's data indicate that Negroes are discriminated against more frequently by monopolistic enterprises.[6] But why do monopolistic enterprises discriminate against Negroes more than do competitive enterprises? One would expect that those who have a taste for discrimination against Negroes would naturally gravitate to those economic activities that, for purely pecuniary reasons, do not employ Negroes. Free choice of economic activities implies a distribution of resources that would minimize the costs of satisfying tastes for discrimination. Consequently the managements of competitive enterprises ought to discriminate against Negroes neither more nor less than those of monopolistic enterprises.

If there is greater discrimination by monopolists than by competitive enterprises, and if it cannot be explained by arguing either that people with tastes for discrimination also have special talents related to monopolistic enterprises or that monopolists are in some sense less efficient businessmen, what, then, explains Becker's data and similar observations? More generally, what is the explanation for the contentions that monopolists pursue pecuniary wealth less vigorously, do not work as hard, have more lavish business establishments, etc.? It is to this problem that this paper is addressed.

Monopoly and Profit Control

Stigler and others have pointed out that monopolies, both labor and product, are creatures of the state in a sense which is not true of competitive enterprises.[7] Monopolies typically are protected against the

[6] *Ibid.*, p. 40, Table II.
[7] George J. Stigler, "The Extent and Bases of Monopoly," *American Economic Review*, June 1942, Supplement Part 2, p. 1; H. Gregg Lewis, "The Labor Monopoly

hazards of competition, not simply by their ability to compete, but by the state's policy of not permitting competitors to enter monopolized markets. Laws are enacted that encourage and lead to the creation of monopolies in particular markets. Monopolies so created are beholden to the state for their existence—the state giveth, the state taketh away. Accordingly, they constrain their business policies by satisfying the requirements that they shall do what is necessary to maintain their monopoly status.

Public utilities are an example. Under this head one should include not only gas, electric, and water companies, but all franchised and licensed industries. Railroads, busses, airlines, and taxis fall in this category of business for which permission of a public authority is required, and for which rate and profit regulation exists. For many other businesses, entry regulation exists: commercial and savings banks, savings and loan associations, insurance companies, and the medical profession. All these are formally regulated monopolies, since they are licensed and operated with the approval of the state. Their cardinal sin is to be too profitable.[8] This constraint upon monopolists does not exist for firms operating in competitive markets. This difference in constraints implies differences between the business policies of competitive firms and those of monopolies. The remainder of this paper is devoted to indicating specifically the character of the constraints that are postulated and exploring the observable implications of this postulate.

Even a firm that has successfully withstood the test of open competition without government protection may manifest the behavior of a protected monopoly. Thus a firm like General Motors may become very large and outstanding and acquire a large share of a market just as a protected monopoly does. If, in addition, its profits are large, it will fear that public policy or state action may be directed against it, just as against a state-created monopoly. Such a firm constrains its behavior much in the style of a monopoly whose profit position is protected but also watched by the state. This suggests that the distinction between publicly regulated monopolies and nonregulated

---

Problem: A Positive Program," *Journal of Political Economy*, Aug. 1951, p. 277; C. E. Lindbloom, *Unions and Capitalism*, Yale University Press, 1949, p. 214; and Milton Friedman, "Some Comments on the Significance of Labor Unions for Economic Policy," in *The Impact of the Union*, David M. Wright, ed., Harcourt Brace, 1951, p. 214.

[8] The notorious suggestion of the medical profession that doctors not drive around town in expensive Cadillacs when visiting patients is an example of the point being made.

monopolies is a false distinction for this problem. As the possibility of state action increases, a firm will adapt its behavior to that which the state deems appropriate. In effect, state regulation is implicitly present.

The cardinal sin of a monopolist, to repeat, is to be too profitable. Public regulation of monopolies is oriented about fixing final prices in order to enable monopolists to earn something like the going rate of return enjoyed by competitive firms. If monopolists are too profitable, pressures are exerted to reduce profits through lowering prices. Only if monopolists can demonstrate to regulatory authorities that they are not profitable enough are they permitted to raise prices.

Implications

If regulated monopolists are able to earn more than the permissible pecuniary rate of return, then "inefficiency" is a free good, because the alternative to inefficiency is the same pecuniary income and no "inefficiency." Therefore this profit constraint leads to a divergence between private and economic costs. However, it is easy to be naive about this inefficiency. More properly, it is not inefficiency at all but efficient utility maximizing through nonpecuniary gains. Clearly one class of nonpecuniary income is the indulgence of one's tastes in the kind of people with whom one prefers to associate. Specifically, this may take the form of pretty secretaries, of pleasant, well-dressed, congenial people who never say anything annoying, of lavish offices, of large expense accounts, of shorter working hours, of costly administrative procedures that reduce the wear and tear on executives rather than increasing the pecuniary wealth of the enterprise, of having secretaries available on a moment's notice by having them sitting around not doing anything, and of many others. It is important to recognize that to take income in nonpecuniary form is consistent with maximizing utility. What is important is not a matter of differences in tastes between monopolists and competitive firms, but differences in the terms of trade of pecuniary for nonpecuniary income. And given this difference in the relevant price or exchange ratios, the difference in the mix purchased should not be surprising.[9]

[9] Usually in economics consumers are presumed to maximize utility subject to fixed income or wealth. What is the wealth or income constraint here? In one sense it is not merely wealth or income that is the pertinent limitation. Many people have access to the use and allocation of resources even though they don't own them. An administrator can assign offices and jobs; he can affect the way company or business resources are used. In all of these decisions, he will be

If wealth cannot be taken out of an organization in salaries or in other forms of personal pecuniary property, the terms of trade between pecuniary wealth and nonpecuniary business-associated forms of satisfaction turn against the former. More of the organization's funds will now be reinvested (which need not result in increased wealth) in ways that enhance the manager's prestige or status in the community. Or more money can be spent for goods and services that enhance the manager's and employees' utility. There can be more luxurious offices, more special services, and so forth, than would ordinarily result if their costs were coming out of personal wealth.

For the total amount of resources used, these constrained expenditure patterns necessarily yield less utility than the unconstrained. The man who spends a dollar with restrictions will need less than a dollar to get an equivalent satisfaction if he can spend it without the restriction. This constrained optimum provides the answer to the question: If a person does spend the wealth of a business as business-connected expenditures for thick rugs and beautiful secretaries, can they not be treated simply as a substitute for household consumption, since he can be regarded as voluntarily choosing to spend his wealth in the business rather than in the home? The answer is that business spending is a more constrained, even if voluntary, choice. This whole analysis is merely an illustration of the effects of restricting the operation of the law of comparative advantage by reducing the size of the market (or range of alternatives).

Employment policies will also reflect the maximization of utility. Assume that an employer prefers clean-cut, friendly, sociable employees. If two available employees are equally productive, but only one is white, native born, Christian, and attractive, the other will not get the job. And if the other employee's wages are reduced to offset this, it will take a greater cut or equilibrating difference to offset this in a monopoly. Why? Because the increase in take-home profits provided by the cost reduction is smaller (if it is increased at all) in the monopoly or state-sheltered firm. Thus one would expect to find a lower

---

influenced by the effects on his own situation. Therefore to gauge his behavior by the usual wealth or income limitation is to eliminate from consideration a wider range of activities that do not fall within the usual "wealth" or ownership limitation. By straining it is possible to incorporate even this kind of activity with the wealth constraint but we find it more convenient for exposition not to do so. In this paper, in a sense, we are discussing the institutional arrangements which determine to what extent constraints are of one type rather than another.

fraction of "other" employees in "monopolies" and other areas of sheltered competition.

What this means is that the wages paid must be high enough to attract the "right" kind of employees. At these wages the supply of the "other" kind will be plentiful. A rationing problem exists, so that the buyer, when he offers a higher price than would clear the market with respect to pecuniary productive aspects clears the market by imposing other tests, like congeniality, looks, and so on. For the right kind of employee the price is not above the market clearing price. In a competitive situation this price differential would not persist because its elimination would all redound to the benefit of the owners, whereas in monopoly it will persist because the reduction in costs cannot be transformed into equally large take-home pecuniary wealth for the owners.

The question may be raised: Even if all this is true of a regulated monopoly like a public utility, what about unregulated, competitively superior monopolies? Why should they act this way? The answer is, as pointed out earlier, that the distinction between regulated and unregulated monopolies is a false one. All monopolies are subject to regulation or the threat of destruction through antitrust action. And one of the criteria that the courts seem to consider in evaluating whether or not a firm is a "good" monopoly is its profitability.[10] It behooves an unregulated monopoly, if it wants to remain one, not to appear to be too profitable.

The owners of a monopoly, regulated or "not," therefore have their property rights attenuated because they do not have unrestricted access to or personal use of their company's wealth. This suggests that the whole analysis can be formulated, not in terms of monopoly and competition, as we have chosen to for present purposes, but in terms of private property rights. There is basically no analytic difference between the two since an analysis made in terms of monopoly and competition identifies and emphasizes circumstances that affect property rights. The same analysis can be applied to nonprofit organizations, governments, unions, state-owned, and other "non-owned" institutions, with almost identical results.

One word of clarification—the contrast here is between monopoly and competition, not between corporate and noncorporate firms. We

[10] See Aaron Director and Edward H. Levi, "Trade Regulation," *Northwestern Law Review*, 1956, p. 286 and ff.

are analyzing differences in implications for behavior that arise from factors other than the corporate structure of the firm. Although there may be differences between corporate, diffused ownership firms and single proprietorships that may affect the many kinds of behavior discussed in this paper, we have been unable to derive them from the corporate aspect. Nor are those features derived from considerations of size per se—however much this may affect behavior.[11]

The preceding propositions stated that more of some forms of behavior would be observed among monopolies. But more than what and of what? More than would be observed in competitive industries. It is not asserted that every monopolist will prefer more than every competitor; instead, it is said that, whatever the relative tastes of various individuals, all those in a monopolistic situation pay less for their actions than they would in a competitive context. And the way to test this is not to cite a favorable comparison based on one monopolist and one competitor. Rather the variations in individual preferences must be allowed to average out by random sampling from each class.

Tests of the Analysis

What observable populations can be compared in testing these implications? One pair of populations are the public utilities and private competitive corporations. Public utilities are monopolies in that entry by competitors is prohibited. Yet, as indicated earlier, the utility is not allowed to exercise its full monopoly powers either in acquiring or distributing pecuniary wealth as dividends to its owners. The owners therefore have relatively weak incentives to try to increase their profits through more efficient management or operation beyond (usually) 6 per cent. But they do have relatively strong incentives to use the resources of the public utility for their own personal interests, but in ways that will count as company costs. Nor does the public utility regulatory body readily detect such activities, because its incentives to do so are even weaker than those of the stockholders. The regulatory body's survival function is the elimination of publicly detectable in-

---

[11] We were originally tempted to believe that the same theory being applied here could be applied to corporate versus noncorporate institutions, where the corporate form happens to involve many owners. Similarly the size factor could also be analyzed via the effects on the costs and rewards of various choice opportunities. Subsequent analysis suggests that many of the appealing differences between corporate, dispersed ownership and individual proprietorship proved to be superficial.

efficiencies. Furthermore, the utility regulatory board has a poor criterion of efficiency because it lacks competitive standards.

Public utility managements, whether or not they are also stockholders, will engage in activities that raise costs even if they eat up profits. Management will be rational (i.e., utility maximizing and efficient) if it uses company funds to hire pleasant and congenial employees and to buy its supplies from salesmen who have these same virtues. They cost more, of course, but how does the regulatory commission decide that these are unjustifiable expenditures—even though stockholders would prefer larger profits (which they aren't allowed to have) and customers would prefer lower product prices? Office furniture and equipment will be of higher quality than otherwise. Fringe benefits will be greater and working conditions more pleasant. The managers will be able to devote a greater part of their business time to community and civic programs. They will reap the prestige rewards given to the "statesman-businessman" class of employers. Vacations will be longer and more expensive. Time off for sick leave and for civic duties will be greater. Buildings and equipment will be more beautiful. Public utility advertising will be found more often in magazines and papers appealing to the intellectual or the culturally elite, because this is a low "cost" way of enhancing the social status of the managers and owners. Larger contributions out of company resources to education, science, and charity will be forthcoming—not because private competitors are less appreciative of these things, but because they cost monopolists less.[12]

[12] We could compare a random sample of secretaries working for public utilities with a random sample of secretaries working for competitive businesses. The former will be prettier—no matter whom we select as our judges (who must not know what hypothesis we are testing when they render their decision). The test, however, really should be made by sampling among the secretaries who are working for equal salaried executives in an attempt to eliminate the income effect on demand. Another implication is that the ratio of a secretary's salary to her supervisor's salary will be higher for a public utility—on the grounds that beauty commands a price. Other nonpecuniary, desirable attributes of secretaries also will be found to a greater extent in public utilities (as well as in nonprofit enterprises) than in private competitive firms. In a similar way, all of the preceding suggested implications about race, religion, and sex could be tested.

Another comparison can be made. Consider the sets of events in the business and in the home of the public utility employee or owner having a given salary or wealth. The ratio of the thickness of the rug in the office to that of the rug at home will be greater for the public utility than for the private competitive firm employee or owner. The ratio of the value of the available company car to the family car's value will be higher for the public utility than for the private competitive firm. And similarly for the ratios of secretary's beauty to wife's beauty, decorations in the office, travel expenses, etc.

Job security, whether in the form of seniority or tenure, is a form of increased wealth for employees. Since it makes for more pleasant employer-employee relations, it is a source of utility for employers. The incentive or willingness of owners to grant this type of wealth to employees and thereby increase their own utility is relatively strong because profits are not the opportunity costs of this choice. The owners of a competitive firm, on the other hand, would have to pay the full price either in profits or in competitive disadvantage. Therefore the viability of such activities is lower in that type of firm. The relative frequency or extent of job security should be higher in monopolies and employee turnover rates lower. Also, the incidence of tenure in private educational institutions will be less than in nonprofit or state-operated educational institutions—if the foregoing analysis is correct.[13]

The relative incidence of employee cooperatives will also provide a test. Some employee cooperatives are subsidized by employers. This subsidy often takes the form of free use of company facilities and of employees for operating the cooperative. For any given set of attitudes of employers towards employee cooperatives, costs are lower for monopolists with "excess" profits. Consequently their frequency will be greater among these enterprises.

Inability to keep excess profits in pecuniary form implies that monopolists are more willing than competitive enterprises to forego them in exchange for other forms of utility-enhancing activities within the firm. Fringe benefits, cooperatives, and special privileges for certain employees will be more common. Employees whose consumption preferences do not induce them to use the cooperatives or fringe benefits are not necessarily stupid if they complain of this diversion of resources. But their complaints do reflect their differences in tastes and their ignorance of the incentives and reward patterns that impinge upon owners and administrators. Instead of complaining, they might better seek benefits of special interest to themselves. But since this involves a power play within the firm, the senior people are likely to be the ones who win most often. Hence one would expect to find such benefits more closely tailored to the preferences of the higher administrative officials than would be observed in a competitive business.

Wage policies will also differ in monopoly and nonmonopoly enter-

[13] See Armen A. Alchian, "Private Property and the Relative Cost of Tenure," *The Public Stake in Union Power*, P. Bradley, ed., University of Virginia Press, 1958, pp. 350-371.

prises. If business should fall off, the incentive to resort to fringe or wage reductions (unpleasant under any circumstances), will be weaker for a public utility because the potential savings in profits, if profits are not below the maximum permissible level, cannot be as readily captured by the management or stockholders. One would expect to find wages falling less in hard times, and one would also expect a smaller turnover and unemployment of personnel. The fact that these same implications might be derived from the nature of the demand for the utility's product does not in itself upset the validity of these propositions. But it does make the empirical test more difficult.

Seniority, tenure, employee cooperatives, and many other fringe benefits—instead of increased money salaries or payments—can be composed of mixtures of pecuniary and nonpecuniary benefits, though the inducement to adopt them despite their inefficiency is enhanced by the relatively smaller sacrifice imposed on the owners of organizations in monopolistic situations, as defined here. The relative cost of take-home wealth for the owners is higher; hence they are more willing to utilize other consumption channels.[14]

Constraints on the opportunity to keep profits that are above the allowable limit reduce the incentive to spend money for profitable expansion of services. An upper limit on profits, with strong protection from competition but no assurance of protection from losses of overexpansion, will bias the possible rewards downward in comparison with those of competitive business. An implication of this is "shortages" of public utility services. Despite the fact that prices are above the cost of providing some services, the latter will not necessarily be available. It is better to wait until the demand is already existent and expansion is demanded by the authorities. The possible extra profits are an attentuated inducement.

But these implications hold only if the public utility is earning its allowable limit of profits on investment. If it is losing money—and there is no guarantee against it—stockholders' take-home pay will be curtailed by inefficiency. Until profits reach the take-home limit, profit-

[14] The other commonly advanced reasons for such benefits or "inefficiencies" are the income tax on pecuniary wealth and the influence of unions. The former force is obvious; the latter is the effect of desires by union officials to strengthen their position by emphasizing the employee members' benefits to the union administration, as is done in many fringe benefits. But whether or not these latter factors are present, the one advanced here is an independent factor implying differences between monopoly and competition.

able and efficient operations will be desirable. If the state regulatory commission is slow to grant price increases in response to cost increases, the utilities should find their profits reduced below the allowable limit during a period of inflation. As a result there should be a tightening up or elimination, or both, of some of the effects predicted in the preceding discussion.[15] One would expect the opposite to occur during periods of deflation.

The present analysis also suggests that there may be an economic rationale for the "shock theory" of wage adjustments. This theory asserts that the profit-reducing wage increases imposed by labor will shock management into greater efficiencies. Suppose that monopolies are induced to trade pecuniary wealth (because they are not allowed to keep it) for nonpecuniary forms of income financed out of business expenditures. This means that, under the impact of higher wage costs and lower profits, the monopolies can now proceed to restore profit rates. Since some of their profit possibilities had been diverted into so-called nonpecuniary forms of income, higher labor costs will make realized profits, broadly interpreted, at least a little smaller. In part, at least, the increased pecuniary wages will come at the expense of nonpecuniary benefits, which will be reduced in order to restore profit levels. Actually, the shock effect does not produce increases in efficiency. Instead, it revises the pattern of distribution of benefits. Left unchanged is the rate of pecuniary profits—if these were formerly at their allowable, but not economic, limit.

Evidence relevant for testing the hypothesis presented here has been produced by the American Jewish Congress, which surveyed the occupations of Jewish and non-Jewish Harvard Business School graduates. The data consist of a random sample of 224 non-Jewish and a sample of 128 Jewish MBA's.[16] The 352 Harvard graduates were classified by

[15] This analysis suggests that, with the decline in profitability of railroads, the principle of seniority advancement in railroad management has become relatively less viable. Similar arguments are applicable for other fringe benefits. With respect to negotiation with unions, it implies that railroad managements will more vigorously resist giving the unions extravagantly large concessions because these costs are being borne by owners.

The analysis also implies that unions do better in dealing with monopolistic as contrasted with competitive industries.

[16] The existence of these data became known to the authors as a result of an article that appeared in the New York Times on the first day of the conference at which this paper was presented. Subsequently the American Jewish Congress released a paper, "Analysis of Jobs Held by Jewish and by Non-Jewish Graduates of the Harvard Graduate School of Business Administration," which contains the data reported here.

ten industry categories: (1) agriculture, forestry, and fisheries, (2) mining, (3) construction, (4) transportation, communication, and other public utilities, (5) manufacturing, (6) wholesale and retail trade, (7) finance, insurance, and real estate, (8) business services, (9) amusement, recreation, and related services, and (10) professional and related services.

Categories (4) and (7) must be regarded as relatively monopolized. Therefore, if the hypothesis presented here is correct, the relative frequency of Jews in these two fields is lower than it is for all fields combined.[17] The relative frequency of Jews in all fields taken together, in the entire sample, is 36 per cent. These data show that the frequency of Jews—74 MBA's—in the two monopolized fields is less than 18 per cent. If a sample of 352, of whom 36 per cent are Jews, is assigned so that 74 are in monopolized and 278 in nonmonopolized fields, the probability that an assignment random with respect to religion will result in as few as 18 per cent Jews in monopolized fields (and over 41 per cent in nonmonopolized fields) is less than 0.0005. This evidence, therefore, is consistent with the hypothesis presented.

One might object to classifying all finance, insurance, and real estate as monopolized fields. This classification includes the subcategories of banking, credit agencies, investment companies, security and commodity brokers, dealers and exchanges, other finance services, insurance, and real estate. Of these, only insurance and banking are regulated monopolies. If only these two subcategories are used, then there are 6 Jews among a group of 39 or a frequency of less than 15 per cent. If a sample of 352, of whom 36 per cent are Jews, is assigned so that 39 are in monopolized and 313 in nonmonopolized fields, the probability that an assignment that is random with respect to religion will result in as few as 15 per cent Jews in the monopolized fields (and over 39 per cent in the nonmonopolized fields) is less than 0.005. This evidence is also consistent with the hypothesis presented.

Applications to Labor Unions

This application of monopoly analysis need not be restricted to public utilities. Any regulated activity or one that regulates entry into work

[17] Similarly, one would expect Jews and Negroes to be underrepresented among enterprises supplying goods and services to monopolists for the same reason that they are underrepresented as employees.

should show the same characteristics. Labor unions, because of their control over entry or because of exclusive union representation in bargaining, have monopoly potential. Insofar as a union is able to use that potential to raise wages above the competitive level, unless the jobs are auctioned off, the rationing problem is a nonprice one. A "thoroughly unscrupulous" agent could, in principle, pocket the difference between the payment by the employer and the receipts to the employee, where this difference reflects the difference between the monopolistic and the competitive wage. The moral pressures and the state regulation of union monopoly operate against the existence of thoroughly unscrupulous union officers. But so long as the fruits of such monopoly are handed on to the employed members of the union, the state seems tolerant of monopoly unions. Because of the absence of free entry into the "union agent business," competitive bidding by prospective union agents will not pass on the potential monopoly gains fully to the laborers who do get the jobs.

The necessity of rationing jobs arises because the union agents or managers do not keep for themselves the entire difference between the monopoly wage and the lower competitive wage that would provide just the number of workers wanted. If they did keep it, there would be equilibrium without nonprice rationing. If any part of that difference is captured by the laborers, the quantity available will be excessive relative to the quantity demanded at the monopolized wage rate. The unwillingness of society to tolerate capture of all that difference by the union agents means that either it must be passed on to the workers, thus creating a rationing problem, or it must be indirectly captured by the union agents—not as pecuniary take-home pay, but indirectly as a utility derived from the expenditure of that difference in connection with union business.

To the extent that the monopoly gains are passed on, the preceding rationing problem and its implications exist. But to the extent that they are not, the union agents or persons in control of the monopoly organization will divert the monopoly gains to their own benefit, not through outright sale of the jobs to the highest bidder, but through such indirect devices as high initiation fees and membership dues. This ties the monopoly sale price to the conventional dues arrangement. Creation of large pension funds and special service benefits controlled by the unions redounds to the benefit of the union agents and officers in ways that are too well publicized as a result of recent hearings on union activities to need mention here.[18]

The membership of monopoly unions will tolerate such abuses to the point where the abuses offset the value of monopoly gains accruing to the employed members. We emphasize that these effects are induced by *both* the monopoly rationing problem and by the desire to convert the monopoly gains into nonpecuniary take-home pay for the union officers or dominant group. We conjecture that both elements are present; part of the monopoly gain is passed on to the workers, and part is captured as a nonpecuniary source of utility. When the former occurs the rationing problem exists, and the agents or those in the union will exclude the less desirable type of job applicants—less desirable not in pecuniary productivity to the employer but as fellow employees and fellow members of the union. Admission will be easier for people whose cultural and personal characteristics conform to the interests of the existing members.[19] And admission will be especially difficult for those regarded as potential price cutters in hard times or not to be counted on as faithful members with a strong sense of loyalty to the union. Minority groups and those who find they must accept lower wages because of some personal or cultural attribute, even though they are just as productive in a pecuniary sense to the employer, will be more willing to accept lower wages if threatened with the loss of their jobs. But these are the very types who will weaken the union's monopoly power. All of this suggests that young people, Negroes,

---

[18] Relevant for the analysis of monopoly power is the character of the protection afforded by the state. For utilities the state actively and directly uses its police powers to eliminate competition. For other monopolies—and this is especially relevant for union monopoly—the state permits these monopolies to use private police power to eliminate competition. The powers of the state passively and indirectly support these monopolies by refusing to act against the exercise of private police power. This suggests that there ought to exist a link between those who have a comparative advantage in the exercise of private police powers (gangsters), and monopolies that eliminate competition through "strong arm" techniques.

[19] If the employer is the nonprice rationer, i.e., if the employer does the hiring and not the union, as is true for airplane pilots, he too will display a greater amount of discrimination in nonpecuniary attributes than with a competitive wage rate. If the wage rate has been raised so that he has to retain a smaller number of employees, he will retain those with the greater nonpecuniary productivity. If the wage rate would have fallen in response to increased supplies of labor but instead is kept up by wage controls, then the supply from which he could choose is larger, and again he will select those with the greater nonpecuniary attributes—assuming we are dealing with units of labor or equal pecuniary productivity.

Jews, and other minority or unorthodox groups will be underrepresented in monopolistic unions.[20]

There exists a symmetry in effects between nonprice rationing of admission to monopolistic trade unions and the allocation of rights to operate TV channels, airlines, radio stations, banks, savings and loan associations, public utilities, and the like. In the absence of the sale of these rights by the commission or government agency charged with their allocation, nonprice rationing comes into play. This implies that Negroes, Jews, and disliked minority groups of all kinds will be underrepresented among the recipients of these rights. The symmetry between admission to monopolistic trade unions and the allocation of monopoly rights over the sale of some good or service by a government agency is not complete. The rights allocated by the government, but not by trade unions, often become private property and can be resold. Therefore this analysis implies that entrance into these economic activities is more frequently achieved by minority groups, as compared with the population as a whole, through the purchase of outstanding rights.

The chief problem in verifying these implications is that of identifying relative degrees of monopoly power. If the classification is correct, there is a possibility of testing the analysis. A comparison of the logic of craft unions with industry-wide unions suggests that the former have greater monopoly powers. Therefore if this classification is valid, the preceding analysis would be validated if the predicted results were observed.

For classic economic reasons, we conjecture that the craft unions are more likely to have monopolistic powers than industry-wide unions. Therefore we would expect to observe more such discrimination in the first type of union than in the second. And included in the category of craft unions are such organizations as the American Medical Association, and any profession in which admission involves the approval of a governing board.[21]

Conclusions and Conjectures

This analysis suggests that strong nonrestrained profit incentives serve the interests of the relatively unpopular, unorthodox, and individualistic

[20] See Reuben A. Kessel, "Price Discrimination in Medicine," *Journal of Law and Economics*, 1958, p. 46 and ff.
[21] For evidence of the existence of discrimination, see H. R. Northrup, *Organized Labor and the Negro*, Chap. I, New York, Harpers, 1944; and Kessel, *Price Discrimination in Medicine*, p. 47 and ff.

members of society, who have relatively more to gain from the absence of restrictions. Communists are perhaps the strongest case in point. They are strongly disliked in our society and, as a matter of ideology, believe that profit incentives and private property are undesirable. Yet if this analysis is correct, one should find communists overrepresented in highly competitive enterprises. Similar conclusions hold for ex-convicts, disbarred lawyers, defrocked priests, doctors who have lost their licenses to practice medicine, and so forth.

The analysis also suggests an inconsistency in the views of those who argue that profit incentives bring out the worst in people and at the same time believe that discrimination in terms of race, creed, or color is socially undesirable. Similarly, those concerned about the pressures toward conformity in our society, i.e., fears for a society composed of organization men, ought to have some interest in the competitiveness of our markets. It is fairly obvious that the pressures to conform are weaker for a speculator on a grain or stock exchange than they are for a junior executive of A.T. and T. or a university professor with or without tenure.

COMMENTS

GARY S. BECKER, Columbia University

I

Sociologists, psychologists, and other social scientists have tried to explain why people differ in their prejudices or, better still, attitudes, towards others and have also tried to determine the extent of observable discrimination. There has, however, been little interaction between these investigations, so that scant attention has been paid to how attitudes get translated into actual discrimination. The economist is singularly well prepared to analyze how attitudes combine with different structural and institutional arrangements to produce actual discrimination, but, unfortunately, he has not considered this a worthwhile or manageable problem, and has made only a few contributions to its solution.[1]

In their fine paper Alchian and Kessel consider this problem worthy of attention and fill part of the void by analyzing how one important

[1] In this connection it is interesting to note that sociologists in the South are preoccupied with the racial question while economists there almost completely neglect it.

institutional arrangement—governmental restrictions on profits—combines with attitudes towards minority groups and with other attitudes to produce discrimination, nepotism, and other types of nonpecuniary choices. The theoretical argument showing why these restrictions on profits induce firms (or unions) to choose more nonpecuniary income is carefully laid out, and numerous empirical tests of the analysis, ranging from pretty women to seniority rules, are indicated. While they do not try to demonstrate empirically that their analysis is important, I am inclined to believe that it is sufficiently important to merit much further attention from economists.

An empirical measure of these nonpecuniary effects that yields a more quantitative estimate of their importance than do the measures suggested by Alchian and Kessel can be developed. Suppose a firm was using $100 worth of real capital and that the competitive rate of return was 5 per cent. If the firm was in a competitive industry its equilibrium income would be $5 per annum and its market value would be $100. If the firm had monopoly power its income would be greater than $5; let us assume that it would have an income of $10 in the absence of government restrictions. If the monopoly power were perfectly transferable, competition in the capital market would establish a market value for this firm equal to $200 and a market rate of return equal to 5 per cent (10/200), the competitive rate. Government regulation might limit the monopolist to receiving no more than, say, $5 of money income, and this would induce him to take some nonpecuniary income. Let it be assumed that he could get $3 worth of nonpecuniary income. The total income of the monopolist would be $8, and if this monopoly power were also perfectly transferable, the equilibrium market value of the firm would have to be $160. The market rate of return on total income would still be 5 per cent (8/160), but the observed money rate of return would only be about 3 per cent (5/160), *less than* the competitive rate. This positive difference of 2 percentage points between the competitive and monopolistic money rates of return would measure the importance of nonpecuniary income to the monopolist.[2] It would be larger the greater the monopoly power, the greater the restrictions on money income, and the greater the ease of substitution between pecuniary and nonpecuniary income.

[2] More generally, it measures the difference between the nonpecuniary income in monopolistic and competitive firms, for firms may receive nonpecuniary income even in the absence of government restrictions on money income.

The assumption of perfectly transferable monopoly power requires, among other things, that capital markets operate smoothly, and that any separation between owners and managers is limited. Dropping this assumption would affect many details of the analysis, but the principle would tend to remain the same. For example, if there were separation between owners and managers, the difference between competitive and monopolistic money rates of return would appear in the price that could be obtained for control of a firm by those in control, be they some owners or some managers. The apparent paradox of monopolists receiving less than the competitive money return would still be with us, and the difference between these returns would still tend to measure the greater nonpecuniary income in monopolies.

II

Although the authors emphasized the effects of government restrictions on monopoly profits, many other private as well as public institutions also encourage a substitution between pecuniary and nonpecuniary income. In the remainder of this comment, I try to fit their discussion into a framework of general institutional influences on nonpecuniary behavior, with especial emphasis on discrimination.

Any restriction on the money incomes of working persons, be they employees or employers, would tend to induce a substitution of psychic for monetary income. It is well known that the ordinary income tax provides an incentive for all earners to take more psychic income since it is not taxable. It is seldom mentioned, however, that this includes an incentive to discriminate in employment against minority groups. Many private institutions also tend to limit money income and induce a substitution towards psychic income. For example, I have argued elsewhere[3] that the use of nonprice techniques to ration entry into certain unions encourages this kind of substitution and yet could not entirely be explained by government influence.

Perhaps an even more important example can be found in the separation of owners from managers in modern corporations. If managers really had *complete* control they would have little incentive to maximize profits less diligently than owners, but they would keep the profits for themselves in the form of salaries, bonuses, etc., rather than distribute them to owners. The more interesting situation arises when managers

[3] See my "Union Restrictions on Entry," *The Public Stake in Union Power*, Philip H. Bradley, ed.: University of Virginia Press, 1959, pp. 209-224.

do not have such complete control and when open attempts to capture profits would lead to their being turned out of office. Nevertheless, they might succeed in capturing profits if their income could be concealed, say, by complicated stock options or large expense accounts. Another way to conceal it would be to take psychic income since this is less readily observed or quantified than money income. (The argument in the Alchian and Kessel paper is really based on the same consideration, since governments want to limit the total income of monopolies but can limit the monetary part more readily.) So it would seem that much of the economic content in the separation of owners from managers lies in the impetus given to psychic income, be it from discrimination, nepotism, or corporate support of education.

It is possible to generalize the analysis still further to include a wider variety of situations by looking at the problem differently. A group would try to offset any prejudice against them by offering compensating advantages. For example, in the market place they would receive lower wages than equally productive persons not subjected to prejudice, so that the difference between these wages could be offered to offset the prejudice against them. It has been seen that restrictions placed on money incomes received, such as profit restrictions or the income tax, prevent discriminators from collecting the income difference offered them and thus make it difficult or impossible for disadvantaged groups to offset prejudices. Precisely the same situation occurs when restrictions are placed on the money income gain that can be *offered* by a disadvantaged group.

Institutions limiting the amount offered, like those limiting the amount received, appear in very different clothing. Take the "equal pay for equal work" movement which is exceedingly popular and resulted in legislation in some states and countries. The aim of the movement and legislation is to prevent various minorities, especially working women, from receiving lower wages than other apparently equally productive workers; that is, the aim is to reduce discrimination against them. But the direct[4] effect is quite different, for by preventing disadvantaged groups from offsetting the prejudice against them, the legislation tends to increase rather than decrease the observable discrimination. Legislation is not the only source of a direct restriction on the incomes of minorities. Trade unions have reduced the dispersion

---

[4] I abstract here from indirect, although possibly very important, effects of this legislation, such as the effect on attitudes.

in wages among union members and may well have reduced the dispersion between disadvantaged members and others. The important point is that, whatever the *intent* of the legislation, unions, or other institutions, the *effect* may well be to increase the observable discrimination, and in precisely the same manner as the previously discussed restrictions on the "collection" of money income.

The analysis can be further generalized by introducing the concept "cost of discrimination." The money cost of discriminating against a particular group is, at the margin, equal to the difference between the money cost of associating with this group and another equally productive one. In a private-enterprise competitive system with no controls on income it would also equal the difference between the unit wages of these groups. Controls placed on the money incomes that can be received by discriminators, such as the income tax, reduce the cost of discrimination below the difference in wages and thus encourage discrimination; controls placed on the wage difference, such as equal pay for equal work legislation, directly reduce the cost of discrimination and encourage discrimination.

All the institutions discussed so far either reduce the money incomes received by or offered to discriminators, and thereby reduce the cost of discrimination and increase discrimination. But the effects of some institutions are quite different: laws of the type administered by the Fair Employment Practices Commission, for example, tend to have just the opposite effect. Through litigation, fines, unfavorable publicity, imprisonment, etc., they increase the cost of not hiring some disadvantaged groups, which discourages discrimination against them. Thus that type of legislation has a very different direct effect on observed discrimination than equal pay for equal work legislation, although both are often strongly supported by the same persons.

I have reviewed the effects of various institutions on nonpecuniary choices, especially on discrimination against minorities. This review was motivated by the discussion by Alchian and Kessel of the effects of a government restraint on money profits. We are indebted to them not only for working out many implications of this restraint, but also for emphasizing that the phrase "nonpecuniary motive" is more than just a camouflage for ignorance; it can be given empirical content. Progress in this field has been hindered not so much by an intractable concept as by the economist's reluctance to take the concept seriously.

MARTIN BRONFENBRENNER, Carnegie Institute of Technology

Alchian and Kessel raise the simple question: When a monopolist chooses not to maximize profits, or when regulation prevents his maximizing profits, in what ways will his behavior as a buyer of inputs differ from the behavior of a competitive firm with the same profit level?

Their answer to this question is also simple. Or rather, it involves a multiplicity of illustrations, which can be boiled down to one or two simple propositions. Let us call the sort of firm Alchian and Kessel have in mind a potential rather than an actual monopolist. Then the basic Alchian-Kessel proposition is that a potential monopolist (unless specially regulated) will run his business in such a way as to satisfy his noneconomic preferences for pretty secretaries and sumptuous offices, or his noneconomic prejudices against Jewish or Negro employees, under circumstances where a competitor would be guided by purely economic considerations. This is particularly true if the extra costs of these noneconomic preferences and prejudices can be passed on to the public on a cost-plus basis.

A second proposition, a corollary of the first, is that the potential monopolist (unless specially regulated) will pad his costs with unnecessary and inefficient employees, reputable expenditures for charity, education, publicity, and "research," fancy landscaping and interior decoration, whereas the competitor will not.

These propositions are both more or less interesting. Their interest to the labor economist is naturally concentrated on their implications for the potential monopolist's demand for labor inputs, but their interest to the general economist transcends this limitation. These propositions are also more or less obvious. Simply raising them among one's friends with or without professional training in economics will suffice to show how obvious they are. It is not a happy comment on the development of economics that they retain their interest nonetheless.

Special cases and corollaries of the Alchian-Kessel propositions are in many cases testable in principle. This adds to their interest to the empirically-minded economist. Alchian and Kessel have in fact tested only one of them here. Their paper would have been more significant if tests had not only been considered feasible in principle but had actually been carried out for a few more of the various specific statements they make.

I have no doubt that the Alchian-Kessel propositions would emerge unscathed from statistical testing of most of the special-case conclusions to which they lead. If they did not, my initial impulse would be to suspect the test procedures rather than the propositions themselves. I should, however, like to concentrate here on one important corollary which Alchian and Kessel might have to modify as a result of testing on a sufficiently large scale. This is their argument that employment of minority groups subject to racial or religious prejudice will be concentrated in competitive rather than monopolistic industry.

This argument was formulated with special reference to the Negro in America; I am not inclined to doubt its validity there. But the American Negro minority is a special kind of minority, which I should like to call a "manual labor" minority. The stereotype of the Negro makes him out too stupid, lazy, irresponsible, and shiftless for anything but unskilled manual labor. It is easy to see how this stereotype arose. Negroes were brought to a relatively advanced America as slaves from a relatively primitive Africa. They were put as slaves to manual labor jobs in which they had no interest and which they performed inefficiently. They have not yet overcome the handicaps with which they were burdened over 300 years ago. One can find plenty of similar "manual labor" minorities all over the world—the Indian "untouchables" are examples—to whom, as well as to the American Negro, the Alchian-Kessel argument applies. Excluded by prejudice from monopoly industry they congregate in the competitive sectors of the economy.

At the same time there are despised minorities aplenty with different characteristics and greater economic resources. These are the "business" minorities who are or have traditionally been more advanced economically than the majority among whom they live. The Jews are a western example; the overseas Chinese are an eastern one. Their stereotypes involve such traits as craftiness, dishonesty, clannishness, heartlessness, and scorn for physical labor. Does the Alchian-Kessel argument apply to these business minorities as well as to the manual labor ones? My suggestion is that it must be modified to take account of the "countervailing power" of these minorities to set up little monopoly enclaves of their own. Their position may accordingly be found less rather than more competitive than the position of the majority which discriminates against them.

Consider a business minority, subject to racial or religious prejudice and excluded from the more reputable monopolies and potential monopolies of their economy. These monopolies include the civil service, the public utilities, the educational system, absentee ownership of the land, "the Army, the Navy, the Church, and the stage." Where do such people make their living?

As owners or employees in competitive business, say Alchian and Kessel, and they are partially correct. But I should like to call your attention to another sort of business in which they congregate, which I propose to call the racial or religious cartel. Here their countervailing power is exercised. Here they themselves monopolize opportunities in their turn, excluding and exploiting members of the majority. It often happens that these racial or religious cartels, these originally despised and neglected occupations, increase in importance as economic development progresses. When this occurs, the business minorities often find themselves charged with stifling and strangling the entire economy for their own selfish benefit—meaning the maintenance of their monopoly power.

Gambling, banking, money lending, wholesale and retail trade are the most usual examples of racial or religious cartels in both eastern and western culture. In some cases, the service trades and "foreign" types of manufacturing also are included in the general category of middleman's services and get into minority hands. Thus barbering, tailoring, and rice milling are all characteristically "Chinese" trades throughout much of Southeast Asia. The several racial or religious cartels, moreover, are accused of interrelations which exclude the majority. In the Southeast Asian case, the Chinese banks, money lenders, wholesale traders, and retailers are allegedly in league with each other against outsiders. No Filipino or Thai or Occidental retailer can get credit from the Chinese banker or money lender on the same terms as his Chinese competitor. Nor can he get merchandise from the Chinese wholesaler on the same terms as this same Chinese competitor. The Filipino or Thai or Occidental banker or wholesaler, on the other hand, is tacitly boycotted by the whole Chinese business community. And as is well known to immigrants from Central and Eastern Europe, these charges against the Chinese of Southeast Asia have their counterparts in charges against the European Jews. Nor, for that matter, is the overseas American community exempt from identical charges, particularly in Latin America.

It is no part of my intention to become involved here in the Chinese problem of Southeast Asia, the Jewish problem of Central Europe, or the Yankee problem of Latin America. I simply wish to present the overseas Chinese, the European Jew, and the Latin American Yankee as three examples of economic minorities who react against discrimination (or anticipate it) by forming racial or religious cartels of their own as well as concentrating in competitive industry. My suggestion as to the Alchian-Kessel argument is therefore one of limitation to a particular sort of minority—the noneconomic or manual labor sort typified by the American Negro. When it comes to the economic sort of minority, the argument should be expanded to take account of the minority's countervailing power as exercised through racial or religious cartels.

IV Inflation

10 Redistribution of Wealth through Inflation*
(1959)

Economists have long speculated about the effects of inflation upon the economic welfare of the owners of business enterprises. This speculation has almost invariably led to the conclusion that business firms gain through inflation. This conclusion has been reached through two independent arguments. One, enunciated by both J. M. Keynes and I. Fisher, is that inflation enables business firms to discharge their debts with depreciated money, the creditors' losses being the debtors' gains (1). Strictly speaking, the validity of this conclusion depends upon two propositions: (i) that business firms are debtors, and (ii) that interest rates reflect biased estimates of the future course of prices when prices are rising. The other argument, advanced by E. J. Hamilton and W. C. Mitchell, is that inflation causes prices to rise faster than wage rates (2). Consequently workers are systematically underpaid during inflation, this loss by the working class being a gain for the entrepreneurs (3). This explanation rests upon special assumptions about the character of labor markets that are generally regarded as invalid in other markets.

Practical men of affairs, in particular investment advisers, have been much less confident than professional economists that the owners of business enterprises gain through inflation. They have generally concluded that investors can maintain their capital intact during inflation by investing in common stocks, such an investment being roughly equivalent to an investment in inventories. (Common stocks are ownership or equity shares in a corporation, while bonds represent debt obligations of the corporation.) In other words, an investor in common stock could expect neither to increase nor to decrease his wealth, whereas an investor in bonds and other cash-type investments would suffer a real loss.

This cautiousness of investment counselors is traceable to the experience of investors in equities during the great inflations that have occurred in countries with organized stock markets. It was found dur-

* Coauthored by Armen A. Alchian.

ing the German runaway inflation following World War I, during the Austrian and French inflations of the 1920's, and more recently during the inflation in Chile that the owners of business firms did not obtain the gains that might have been expected on the basis of the hypotheses set forth by Keynes and Fisher, on the one hand, and Hamilton and Mitchell on the other. These observations are also consistent with the behavior of stock price indexes in the United States during the inflations associated with world wars I and II.

What was especially puzzling was the fate of the owners of banks. Banks are typically enormous debtors, larger debtors, in fact, than most business firms by an order of magnitude. Furthermore, banks employ relatively more labor per dollar of invested capital than is characteristic of business firms generally. Consequently, it is an implication of both hypotheses that banks ought to be enormous gainers through inflation. Yet the available evidence suggests that one of the regular results of inflation is that the owners of bank shares suffer. The experience of the owners of bank shares in the United States, Germany, Austria, Chile, and France suggests that the real value of bank shares declines during inflation. (Real value is simply price divided by an index number reflecting changes in the price level. Consequently, if the price of an asset rises more than the price level, then its real value has increased, and conversely.)

Reconciling Hypotheses with Experience

How can this evidence be reconciled with either of these hypotheses? A step toward reconciling the Keynes-Fisher reasoning with the lessons of experience as revealed by the stock market was taken by Kessel when he showed that, despite the enormous debts owed by banks to depositors, there exist offsetting credits that are even larger than these debts (4). These credits are bank assets which are almost entirely (with the exception of bank buildings and business machines) either money or money-type assets such as notes and other obligations payable to banks by either private customers or the government. The existence of these credits led Kessel to argue that one should do more than merely look at the credit that business firms have extended to their customers. What business firms gain from bondholders may be lost to those to whom these firms have extended credit and may never redound to the interests of the owners.

From his analysis emerged a classification for determining whether or not a business firm is, on *net* balance, a debtor or creditor. Kessel classified assets and liabilities into categories, monetary and real. A monetary asset was defined as an asset whose market value is independent of changes in the price level. These would include money, accounts and notes receivable, government and corporate bonds, life insurance, prepaid taxes, and so on. A monetary liability was defined as a liability whose amount is independent of changes in the price level; these would include accounts payable, notes payable, mortgages, bonds, preferred stock, and so on. Preferred stock, although called a stock, is typically corporate debt rather than equity. A net monetary debtor was then defined as a firm whose monetary liabilities exceeded its monetary assets; and conversely for a net monetary creditor. The net monetary status would indicate the magnitude of the gain or loss a firm would incur from a given amount of inflation. However, firms with the same amount of indebtedness but of unequal size, where size is measured by the aggregate value of the equity of the owners, would have unequal movements in absolute stock prices. Therefore, in order to compare corporations of unequal size, the ratio of net monetary debt to equity, as measured by the market price of shares times the number of shares outstanding, is used as the measure of net monetary debtor or creditor status (5). The effects of stock dividends, stock splits, and rights offerings were held constant and did not affect measurements of changes in stock prices. "Stock dividends" and "splits" increase the number of shares of common stock without changing the total investment, whereas "rights" entitle existing stockholders to increase the investment in the corporation by purchasing new shares at a price below existing market prices, thereby also involving some dilution in per-share value. And it was assumed that dividends were continuously reinvested in the shares of the companies that issued them, because this would eliminate variations caused by differences in the extent to which profits were reinvested.

For the United States, Kessel found in his preliminary study that banks were typically net monetary creditors, and that the real value of their shares actually did decline during the World War II inflation, in accordance with the Keynes-Fisher hypothesis. Furthermore, the real value of bank shares seems to have gone down during inflation for every country for which data are available.

Kessel also examined the balance sheets of a small random sample of industrial firms whose stock is traded on the New York Stock Exchange. (Railroads, utilities, and investment companies were omitted. Railroads and utilities were not included because it was supposed that their very close regulation might conceal the effects of inflation upon their stock prices. Investment companies were omitted because of the magnitude of the problems encountered in evaluating the debtor-creditor status of their assets.) In 1939, about 40 percent of the observed firms were creditors and could be expected to lose through inflation, according to the Keynes-Fisher reasoning. After the firms had been divided into the two categories, debtor and creditor, and after the changes in share prices between 1939 and 1946 had been examined, a significant difference was detected between the rise of share prices in the two categories. The share prices of net monetary debtor firms rose significantly more than the prices of net monetary creditor firms. For a period of deflation, 1929–1933, the reverse was found to be true. The share prices of net monetary creditors fell significantly less than the share prices of net monetary debtors.

The behavior of the stock prices of bank shares during the inflation associated with World War II was indistinguishable from the behavior of the shares of equivalent industrial creditors. Other evidence indicates that banks were characterized by large amounts of labor per dollar of invested capital as compared with enterprises generally. This evidence casts doubt upon the validity of the Hamilton-Mitchell reasoning, that inflation causes real wages to fall. If the wage lag had been operative, the value of bank shares would have risen more than the value of the shares of equivalent industrial creditors.

This evidence validated the proposition that during inflation interest rates are systematically lower than they ought to be if inflation is not to transfer wealth from creditors to debtors, but it also challenged the assumption that business firms are, in large part, debtors. The mechanism for redistribution that Keynes and Fisher envisaged was correct, but their assumption that business firms were generally debtors was wrong, and it was this that led them to the erroneous conclusion that business firms gain through inflation. This evidence also explains the behavior of stock-price indexes during inflation. If a substantial fraction of all business firms were net monetary creditors, then an index number of stock prices that was composed of both net monetary debtors and net monetary creditors would not necessarily rise in real value during inflation. Indeed, if the debtors just balance out the creditors, one would expect stock prices generally to keep pace pretty closely with the general price level. These results led to a much larger-scale investigation, designed both to provide stronger evidence of the validity of the mechanism for redistribution envisaged by Keynes and Fisher and to enlarge our empirical knowledge of stock prices (6).

New Evidence for Mechanism of Redistribution

The population of firms investigated includes all of the industrials whose common stock was traded on the New York Stock Exchange at any time between 1914 and 1952. For 1933–1952, the American Stock Exchange was also included. Furthermore, four separate industries were studied for the period 1940–1952—chemicals, steels, retailing, and textiles—in order to hold constant any industry differences. The period of the study, 1915–1952, includes two inflations (world wars I and II), two deflations (1921–22 and 1928–1933), and two periods of relative price stability (1923–1930 and 1933–1940). The number of firms observed in a year ranged from a minimum of 71 to a maximum of 885. In all, nearly 14,000 firm-years of data were observed and analyzed.

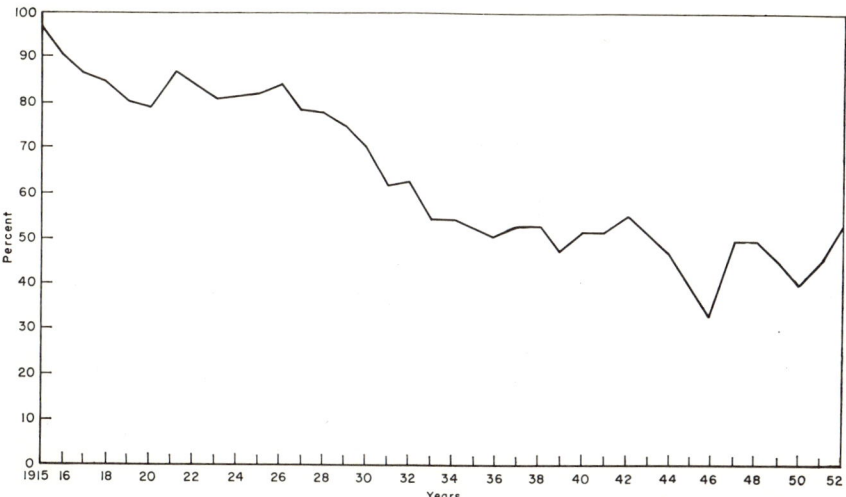

Fig. 1. Net monetary debtor firms as percentage of all firms. [Based on New York Stock Exchange data for 1915 to 1952 and on American Stock Exchange and "over-the-counter" data for 1940 to 1952]

What do these data show? The distribution of firms by net monetary debtor and net monetary creditor status has changed spectacularly since 1914. The percentage of firms in each category is shown in Fig. 1. These data are based on the New York and the American Stock Exchange samples. The shift from predominantly net monetary debtor status, around the time of World War I, to a ratio of approximately 50:50 in 1952 may explain why Keynes and Fisher made the assumption they did about business firms being debtors.

Apparently individual firms usually did not shift their net monetary status frequently. A firm that was a net monetary debtor in one year was very likely to be one in the next year, despite a gradual shift of the population as a whole. A classification of firms during the 1915–1920 inflation according to net monetary status shows that 78 of the firms were net monetary creditors during at least 4 years of the 6-year span, while 22 were net monetary debtors during at least 4 of the 6 years. A few did not retain their status for as long as 4 years. According to Keynes and Fisher the net monetary debtors should have had an increase in the values of their stocks relative to the net monetary creditors. The observed data show that $1 of equity of the net monetary debtors increased to $2.66, while the net monetary creditors' dollar increased to only $1.60; the superiority is 57 percent and one which would have less than 1 chance in 1000 of occurring by an unusually favorable random selection of firms if there really were no transfers of wealth from creditors to debtors.

Table 1 contains more details, as well as the results for the inflation of 1940–1952, for each of the populations of firms studied. In every instance the net monetary debtors did better. In Fig. 2 these results are given in the form of a graph. The probability sampling levels are sufficiently small to make it extraordinarily difficult to attribute such results to random sampling. And when the probability levels are combined by the R. Fisher chi-square method, the sampling probability falls to below 1 chance in 10,000.

To test whether the results are attributable to inflation rather than to a hidden factor which makes the better firms become net monetary debtors, the deflationary episodes were also considered. In the two deflations of 1921–22 and 1928–1933, the firms were again classified according to whether they were persistently net monetary debtors or creditors. In the short deflation of 1921–22, each firm in the sample maintained its monetary status during the entire period. In the 1928–1933 episode, one deviation was permitted. In both deflations the net monetary creditors did better than the net monetary debtors—just the opposite of the finding for inflations and in conformance with the predictions of the Keynes-Fisher model. The sampling probability levels are small, being less than 5 percent for the short deflation of 1920–22 and less than 0.1 percent for 1929–1932. The combined sampling probability is less than 0.01. Finally, for the periods of price stability of 1923–1930 and 1933–1940, a similar classification of firms revealed no difference in performance between the net monetary creditors and the net monetary debtors, again in conformance with the Keynes-Fisher hypothesis as modified here. These results are also given in Table 1.

But what about the Mitchell-Hamilton wage-lag hypothesis and its implications for business profits? Possibly labor intensiveness is correlated with net monetary status. Under these circumstances, the wage lag, while unrevealed, might yet be operative. To explore this possibility as well as the possibility that growth might be correlated

Table 1. Observed stock price values (with reinvested dividends) for episodes of inflations, deflations, and stable prices, by exchanges and industries. [From *Moody's Industrials* (1914–1953); *Commercial and Financial Chronicles* (1921–1953); *Bank and Quotation Journals* (1928–1953); and *New York Times* (1915–1953)]

Population sampled	Kind and No. of firms*		Mean resulting equity value† ($)	Mean of debtor minus creditor‡ ($)	t §	p ‖
Inflations						
1915–1920:						
New York Stock Exchange	Debtors	78	2.66	+ 1.06	3.27	.001
New York Stock Exchange	Creditors	22	1.60			
1940–1952:						
New York Stock Exchange	Debtors	29	5.93	+ 1.47	1.80	.05
New York Stock Exchange	Creditors	35	4.46			
American Stock Exchange	Debtors	57	11.30	+ 3.25	1.65	.05
American Stock Exchange	Creditors	70	8.05			
Over-the-counter	Debtors	22	9.38	+ 2.93	1.19	.12
Over-the-counter	Creditors	45	6.45			
Steel industry	Debtors	29	6.92	+ 0.25	.15	.44
Steel industry	Creditors	27	6.67			
Chemical industry	Debtors	19	7.17	+ 2.53	1.24	.12
Chemical industry	Creditors	19	4.54			
Textile industry	Debtors	29	16.33	+ 6.67	1.45	.07
Textile industry	Creditors	22	9.66			
Department stores	Debtors	29	8.96	+ 4.81	2.64	.007
Department stores	Creditors	22	4.15			
New York Stock Exchange wage firms	Debtors	50	7.85	+ 2.07	1.76	.04
New York Stock Exchange wage firms	Creditors	32	5.78			
Deflations						
1921–1922:						
New York Stock Exchange	Debtors	118	1.48	− 0.30	− 1.73	.045
New York Stock Exchange	Creditors	24	1.78			
1928–1933:						
New York Stock Exchange	Debtors	63	.49	− 0.60	− 3.17	.001
New York Stock Exchange	Creditors	35	1.09			
Stable prices						
1923–1930:						
New York Stock Exchange	Debtors	50	2.78	+ 0.45	1.08	.14
New York Stock Exchange	Creditors	15	2.33			
1933–1940:						
New York Stock Exchange	Debtors	56	4.31	− 0.80	− .89	.81
New York Stock Exchange	Creditors	54	5.11			
American Stock Exchange (curb)	Debtors	17	6.44	+ 1.72	+ .71	.52
American Stock Exchange (curb)	Creditors	20	4.72			

* Number of firms that maintained debtor (or creditor) monetary status during at least ⅔ of the episode.
† Mean price plus reinvested dividends at the end of the episode, per dollar of 1940 stock prices.
‡ Mean equity value for net monetary debtors minus mean value for net monetray creditors.
§ Student's t test coefficient:

$$t = d \bigg/ \left(\frac{s_1^2}{N_1} + \frac{s_2^2}{N_2} \right)^{1/2}$$

‖ Sampling probability of t (one-tailed) based on Welch approximation. [B. L. Welch, "The generalization of student's problem when several different population variances are involved," *Biometrika* **34**, 28 (1947). Two-tailed test is used for periods of price stability]

INFLATION

with debtor-creditor status, a sample of 113 firms listed on the New York Stock Exchange was obtained. These firms were the entire population of industrials that reported wage bills some time during the interval 1940 to 1952. Three variables—(i) net monetary debtor or creditor status per dollar of equity, (ii) wages paid per year per dollar of equity, and (iii) yearly sales per dollar of equity—were evaluated for potential predictive content by means of partial correlation analy-

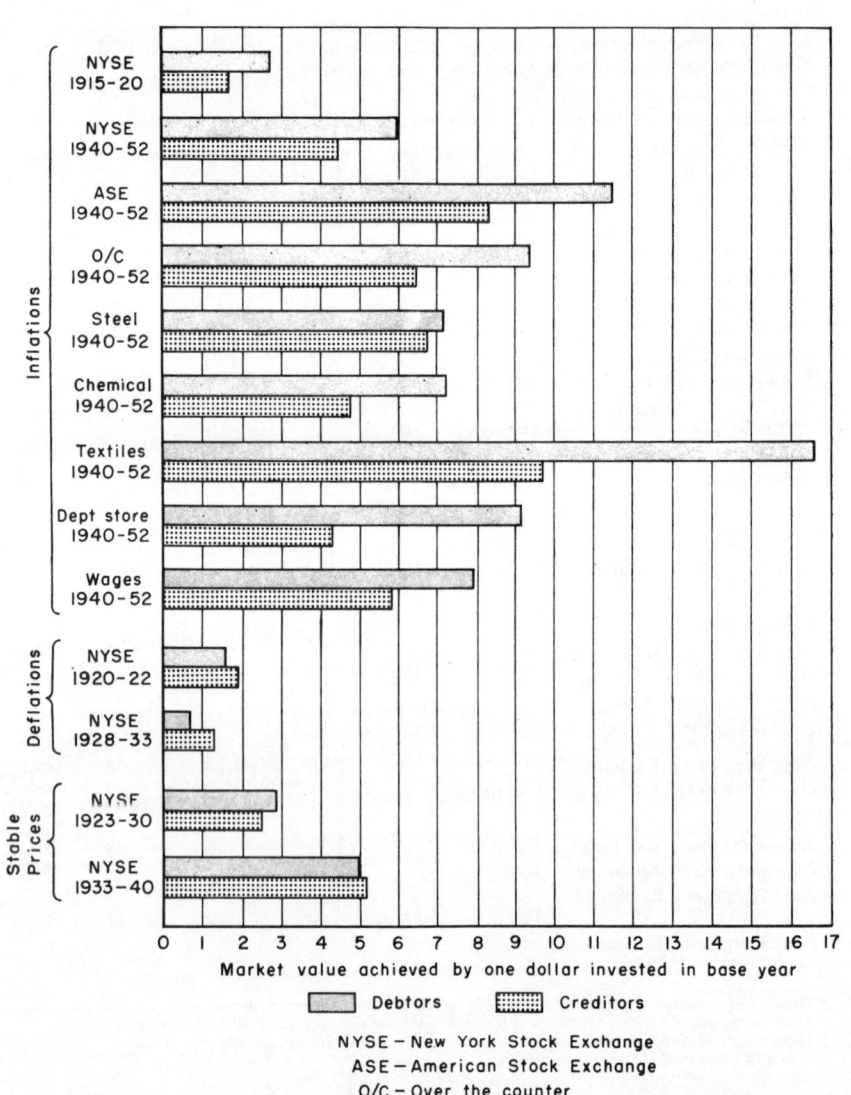

Fig. 2. Market value of equity for debtors as compared to that for creditors (per dollar of base-year common stock value).

sis. (Equity values were determined by the market price of shares.) And in order to avoid violating assumptions underlying probability tests of significance for correlation analysis, ranks for the three independent variables were used.

The results of this analysis revealed that *only* net monetary status was correlated with relative stock price changes, and that this correlation was in the predicted direction. Moreover, the chance that this observation would be produced by random sampling from a population characterized by an absence of this correlation is less than 1 in 1000. This evidence is completely consistent with the hypothesis that the wage lag is inoperative—that is, that the imperfection of the labor market postulated by the wage-lag theorists is nonexistent. Consequently, these results must be regarded as evidence against the hypothesis that a wage lag increases business profits during inflation. However, one must not lose sight of the fact that this is only partial evidence, from a nonrandom sample consisting of 113 firms.

Conclusion

These results, reported here for the first time, while constituting overwhelming evidence in support of the Keynes-Fisher reasoning about the bias in interest rates during inflation, fail to support their conclusion that business firms gain through inflation. The frequency of debtors in the business population is not great enough to justify Keynes and Fisher's sweeping statements about the gains of business enterprise through inflation. This evidence also suggests that the Keynes-Fisher theorizing about the effects of inflation is not specific to business enterprises; it is a general theory of wealth transfers caused by inflation and is equally applicable to individuals. What count are monetary asset and monetary liability positions and not the type of economic activity in which one engages.

Especially pertinent to much of the current discussion of the consequences of inflation is that the present evidence, by validating the wealth-transfer effect from monetary creditors to monetary debtors (and rejecting the wage-lag hypothesis), verifies the implication that inflation is basically a "tax" on creditors in favor of debtors. Inflation constitutes a tax on the wealth of individuals to the extent that they are holders of money-type assets rather than savers, wage-earners, businessmen, widows, orphans, or retired schoolteachers.

These results have implications for the adjustment of personal investment and wealth portfolios (including not only stocks, but bonds, life insurance, mortgages, charge accounts, cash holdings, and so on) in order to hedge against inflation or to profit if inflation comes. Similar reasoning applies to the management of investment, pension, and trust funds.

References and Notes

1. J. M. Keynes, *Tract on Monetary Reform* (London, 1923), p. 18; I. Fisher, *The Purchasing Power of Money* (New York, 1920), pp. 58–73, 190–191.
2. E. J. Hamilton, *J. Econ. Hist.* 12, 325 (1952); W. C. Mitchell, *A History of the Greenbacks* (Chicago, 1903), pp. 347–348; ———, *Gold, Prices, and Wages under the Greenback Standard* (Berkeley, 1908), pp. 275–276.
3. Some economists and noneconomists also contend that anyone who holds inventories gains through inflation. Since the price of inventories rises above their cost, this difference is regarded as a real gain in economic welfare. But holders of inventories cannot acquire with their inventories any more of the world's goods and services than they could in the absence of inflation.
4. R. A. Kessel, *Am. Econ. Rev.* 46, 130 (1956).
5. This is one of the respects in which the present study is an advance over Kessel's early work. While his concept of net debtor or net creditor was correct, his criterion of *intensity* of debtor or creditor status was wrong, and consequently the measurements based upon his criterion were also wrong.
6. This study was undertaken with the aid of a research grant from the Merrill Foundation for the Advancement of Financial Knowledge. The article, from this point on, constitutes the first statement of some of the results of this study.

11 The Meaning and Validity of the Inflation-Induced Lag of Wages behind Prices*
(1960)

Many economists write as if the proposition that inflation causes prices to rise faster than wages were well established. From this proposition at least two important classes of inferences have been derived.

1. A lag of wages behind prices as a result of inflation produces extraordinarily large business profits. These swollen profits generate a high rate of capital formation. In this role, the wage-lag axiom constitutes the foundation of a theory of industrial development.

2. The lag of wages behind prices caused by inflation accentuates oscillations in the general level of economic activity. The failure of wages to keep pace with prices reinforces disequilibrating movements in the general level of economic activity. In this capacity, the wage-lag axiom functions as an integral part of both overinvestment and underconsumption business cycle theories [14, p. 137 and ff.].

The contention that inflation causes real wages to fall appears frequently in the literature of economics. Those who make this contention argue in effect that inflation produces a negative correlation between real wages on the one hand and money wages and prices on the other. As a practical matter, it is extremely difficult to employ this idea as a tool of analysis for understanding observed movements of time series of wages and prices. This difficulty stems from the fact that, as almost everyone would agree, the level of real wages can be affected by such real forces as the relative supplies of labor and capital, the quality of the labor force, the pattern of final demands in the economy, and the state of the arts. Furthermore, increases in the general price level can be produced by changes in the real stock of goods, e.g., by droughts, plagues, wars, etc., even with a fixed money stock. For any time series of real wages, there exists a fantastically difficult problem of imputing changes in the level of real wages to one or the other of two classes of

---

* Coauthored by Armen A. Alchian. This paper is one of a series reporting the results of a study of inflation made possible by a grant from The Merrill Foundation for the Advancement of Financial Knowledge. The authors are indebted to Karl Brunner, Gregg Lewis, William Meckling, Albert Rees, and William Taylor for improvement in analysis and exposition.

variables, i.e., real or monetary forces. Only if one is able to abstract from the effects of real forces can one determine the effect of inflation upon an observed time series of real wages.

To illustrate this problem, consider the data showing real wages, money wages, and prices in the United States since 1889 [39, pp. 15-16]. These data indicate a high positive correlation between real wages on the one hand and money wages and prices on the other. Are these positive correlations to be interpreted as evidence against the proposition that inflation causes real wages to fall? Surely not. Real wages rose during this time, according to most observers, because of the per capita increase in capital, improvements in technology, and improvements in the skills of the labor force. Those who believe that inflation causes real wages to fall would not deny this. Their position would be that real wages rose despite inflation and that if the effects of real forces upon real wages were properly abstracted, one could observe a fall in real wages attributable to inflation.[1]

I. *Some Alternative Wage-Lag Hypotheses*

What, then, is the wage-lag hypothesis? To answer this question, we have turned to the works of those economists who have used this idea. The most important "explanation," importance being measured by either the extent to which it has been used or its deviation from the way economists explain behavior in nonlabor markets, is the belief that wages have more "inertia" or "sluggishness" than other prices because of custom, weak bargaining power of labor, or lack of foresight of workers. For example, Hamilton states: "The chief factor in the failure of wages to keep pace with soaring prices in the second half of the eighteenth century was the 'natural' inertia of wage movements in both directions. History records few instances of wage movements in unison with rapidly changing commodity prices" [18, p. 259]. And:

> There have been no such offsets to the strong tendency during most of the last four hundred years for wages to lag behind prices whenever they were rising. This lag has benefited capitalists as a class at the expense of laborers as a class and awarded gains that dwarf into insignificance the profits from inventory appreciation and from declines in the real value of debts. A tendency for wages to lag behind falling prices has inflicted losses on businessmen, discouraged saving and investment, and aggravated commercial crises [20, p. 327].

Mitchell also contended that an imperfection exists in the labor market. He wrote:

---

[1] Or for a less recent inflation, consider the Black Death period. During this time prices rose and real wages rose. Clearly what explains this phenomenon is the decrease in the stock of labor which also produced a fall in rents. See Lipson [30, pp. 93 and *ff*.].

In the '60's and, though in somewhat less degree, in the '70's, the labor market of the United States was one in which individual bargaining prevailed. Now the individual laborer is a poor bargainer. He is ignorant of the possibilities of his situation, exposed to the competition of others with the same disabilities, more anxious to sell than the employer to buy. Moreover, custom in the form of rooted ideas about what is a "fair wage" has a peculiarly tenacious hold upon the minds of both parties in the labor market, weakening the wage-earner's aggression and strengthening the employer's resistance [35, pp. 275-76].

In his study of the Civil War, Mitchell concluded: "All of the statistical evidence that has been presented in the preceding pages supports unequivocally the common theory that persons whose incomes are derived from wages suffer seriously from a depreciation of the currency" [34, p. 347]. Basically, the rationale for this position is that there exists a flaw in the labor market which, during times of inflation, lowers the wage rate below the marginal product of workers. In effect Mitchell and Hamilton are saying that the same principles economists use in explaining what happens in other markets are invalid for explaining what happens in labor markets during inflation.[2]

Bresciani-Turroni enunciated, in his famous study of German inflation, a hypothesis that could explain declines in real wages during inflation and be consistent with a perfectly functioning labor market.[3] This hypothesis rests on the postulate that employees, as a condition of employment, are almost invariably creditors of their employers. And as creditors, employees lose to their employers for the same reason that creditors generally lose to debtors as a result of inflation. Therefore, even if wage rates correctly represented the marginal product of workers, the fact that wages accrue, i.e., that wages are paid after they are earned, implies that workers extend credit to their employers and incur a loss on this account.

There exists strong prima facie evidence for accepting the wage-accrual hypothesis of Bresciani-Turroni. This explanation rests upon a debtor-creditor relationship that is essentially similar to debtor-creditor relationships between, say, department stores and their charge customers, finance companies and the credit purchasers of automobiles and other appliances, corporations and their bond holders, etc. Since there already exists evidence that supports the belief that interest rates are biased downward during inflation, because of the public's lack of

[2] Explanations of this type may be found in [31, p. 7 and ff.] [41, p. 213] [6, p. 380] [29, p.222] and [32, p. 88].

[3] "In fact, wages were fixed on the basis of an index number of prices which, at the time of payment, no longer represented actual conditions" [7, p. 310]. It failed to represent actual conditions because of the bias in interest rates. Also he argued that wage earners lost because they held cash during inflation [7, p. 302]. Both of these are of course special cases of the proposition that creditors lose during inflation.

knowledge of the course of future prices, there appears to be a reasonable basis for accepting the proposition that wealth is transferred from employees to employers when inflation occurs.[4]

As a practical matter, it does not appear that this relationship between employees and employers, at least in modern times, has the potential for transferring a great deal of wealth from employee to employer. Consider a case that is most favorable for sustaining the proposition that accrued wages constitute an important source of business profits during inflation. Assume that cash is acquired for wage payments at the very instant these payments are made by a business firm. Therefore this firm may be regarded as a consistent net debtor with respect to its employees.

What can be said about the magnitude of such profits under these assumptions? Of all industrial firms listed on the New York Stock Exchange in 1952, approximately 200 reported the size of their aggregate wage bills, or more properly the size of their aggregate wage and salary bills, for at least one year between 1939 and 1952. Among these 200 firms, the ratio of total annual wages to equity (equity being measured by the market value of outstanding shares) ranged from a low of .1 to a high of about 4, depending upon firm and industry. If it is assumed that wages are paid biweekly, then the average amount of wages and salaries accrued is 1/52 of the annual wage bill. Consequently it follows that accrued wages range from a low of about .2 per cent to 8 per cent of equity. This analysis implies that if the price level doubled in any given year, the real value of stock prices would rise from a minimum of .1 per cent to a maximum of 4 per cent.[5]

Using this same debtor-creditor relationship, Fisher had earlier set forth still another explanation of why real wages would fall during inflation. Like the Bresciani-Turroni explanation, Fisher's was consistent with a perfectly functioning labor market. Fisher contended that relations between employer and employee can be viewed as being contractual, just as are economic relations between, say, bondholders and those who incur bonded debt [10, p. 185 and *ff*.]. The same lack of foresight that would lead to too low an interest rate to permit debtor creditor relations to be unaffected by inflation would lead to an effective

---

[4] This of course does not imply that business firms gain through inflation. Such a statement would be correct only if an examination of all of their debtor-creditor relations, of which relations with employees are only a part, revealed that business firms are on balance debtors. On this point, as well as for evidence that interest rates are biased during inflation, see Kessel [23, p. 128]. Nor does the "bias" of interest rates imply any defect in the capital market; instead it reflects people's inability to predict future prices.

[5] The Bresciani-Turroni hypothesis also appears in Meyer [33, p. 17]. "Creditors lost in inflation. Wage-earners and salary-earners normally work before they are paid. They lend their labour until pay day; their work is work given on credit." Meyer also asserts that wages lag because of contractual arrangements between employers and employees.

wage below the marginal product of labor when prices are rising. Only at the time wage contracts are signed would wages be equal to the marginal product of labor. Between contract negotiations, real wages would fall as a result of rising prices.

Prima facie evidence does not support this hypothesis. Wage contracts are typically nonenforceable when broken by employees. Consequently, the legal reasons for arguing that contracts between employers and employees are on a par with contracts between creditors and debtors are of dubious validity. As far as employees are concerned, wage contracts have generally been continuously renegotiable, at least until relatively modern times. Employees can almost always leave their current jobs in favor of alternative employment possibilities in complete freedom from legal sanction by employers. Consequently, in the absence of other evidence there is very little basis for accepting Fisher's hypothesis.

However, there is more to a substantive hypothesis than its logical structure. In its broader aspects, the Fisher hypothesis implies that during inflation there exists a differential in the movements of wage rates of workers under contract as compared with workers employed without contract. It also implies that the longer the life of a contract, the greater the differential in the movements of real wages during inflation. No evidence is contained in this paper for evaluating these two implications.

If one abandons a legalistic frame of reference and argues, as Fisher has, that custom plays a great role independent of contractual arrangements, then this hypothesis becomes indistinguishable from the argument of Hamilton and Mitchell, namely, that a flaw exists in the labor market which manifests itself during times of inflation by a fall in real wages.

The use of inflation as a means of taxation appears to have created a belief that inflation causes real wages to fall. Inflation is a means of taxation, and has been used by those who control the stock of money as an alternative to explicit forms of taxation, such as income taxes, excises, tariffs, etc. Using their power to create money, governments have exchanged money for real resources. Such an exchange reduces the volume of real resources available to the private sector of the economy. The mere existence of an exchange of this character has led many observers to conclude that a fall in real wages is necessarily implied [e.g. 25, pp. 171-74]. Yet it can and has been shown that taxation through inflation is consistent with no reduction in real wage rates.[6]

---

[6] A discussion of the mechanism by which the government acquires resources from the rest of the community through inflation has been presented in [1]. For the first published analysis of this mechanism that the authors have encountered, see the revised portion of Friedman [11, p. 263]. See also Cagan [8].

Inflation constitutes a tax upon monetary wealth and not upon wages or other factor incomes. This tax affects the real functional returns of the cooperating agents of production if inflation is anticipated, i.e., when the increased cost of holding money caused by rising prices is recognized and enters into the calculations of the community. Under these circumstances, both velocity and the nominal or money rate of interest rise. These higher costs of using money are ultimately reflected in a rise in product prices relative to the sum of the returns to the cooperating agents of production. Whether or not real wages fall depends upon the cross elasticity between the price or cost of holding money and the quantity of labor demanded. If one is prepared to argue that capital is a better substitute for money than labor, and to assume that the alternative to inflation as a means of taxation is no tax or a wealth or income tax, then the argument that anticipatory inflation can cause real wages to fall can be sustained.

However if inflation is not anticipated, then the losses of the money holders are on a par with an *ex post facto* penalty or Knightian profits and do not affect resource allocation. In general, it appears that the inflations associated with our Civil War in the North and our two world wars were unanticipated. If excise taxes or turnover taxes are regarded as the alternative to taxation through an unanticipated inflation, then inflation implies a higher level of real wages than would otherwise be true.

II. *The Empirical Evidence*

The remainder of this paper falls into two parts: (1) a review of the statistical evidence that has been used to support the Mitchell-Hamilton hypothesis and (2) a new test of this hypothesis based on differences in the labor intensiveness of business firms and the performances of their stock prices during inflation.[7]

---

[7] The field of income and employment theory contains still another hypothesis that implies the existence of a lag of wages behind prices when prices are rising. It stems from the observation that less than full employment, where full employment is defined as a labor market in which everyone who wants a job at the prevailing wage rate can find one, implies nonprice rationing of employment opportunities. This is consistent with an infinitely elastic supply function of labor that relates the quantity of labor offered with money wages if rising prices will restore full employment. Under these assumptions, increases in prices at times of less than full employment imply a fall in real wages.

This hypothesis is clearly relevant to the present discussion, if it is relevant at all, only for inflations or portions of inflations associated with less than full employment. Since the authors cited believe that inflation causes wages to lag behind prices independently of whether full or less-than-full employment exists, this is not a hypothesis they considered extensively although it appears in the work of Mitchell and Bresciani-Turroni.

This model leads to difficult questions. One is: Shouldn't the wages of unemployed workers be considered in the wage index? If they are included in the wage index, then it is not clear that real wages decline under these circumstances. Another difficulty is that we do not know enough about how an economy returns to full employment to impute to inflation a fall in real wages of those continuously employed. Possibly real supply conditions have not

What is the empirical evidence used to support the hypothesis that inflation, independently of real forces, causes real wages to fall when prices are rising? Major data used to support this hypothesis have been collected for six inflationary episodes: (1) the period from 1350 to 1800 in Spain, (2) the early days of the industrial revolution in England, (3) the U.S. Civil War in the North, (4) the U.S. Civil War in the South, (5) the German inflation following the first world war, and (6) the inflation in the United States associated with the first world war.

A. *Spanish Data*

E. J. Hamilton probably has contributed more to the acceptance of the hypothesis that inflation causes real wages to fall than has any other single economist.[8] His evidence consists almost entirely of time series of wages and prices. In order to use such data as evidence of a wage lag, the impact of real forces must be distinguished from that of inflation. Hamilton is not unaware of this difficult problem of imputation. Throughout his monumental three-volume work on Spanish wages and prices, which covers the interval from 1350 to 1800, are references to real forces and their impact upon the price level and real income [17, pp. 100-4]. Yet, as far as we can discover, he consistently forgets about real forces when using his time series to test the hypothesis; any fall in real wages when prices are rising he interprets as evidence supporting the wage-lag hypothesis.

Yet even with this implicit assumption that real forces are constant during inflation and consequently any change in real wages is attributable to inflation, Hamilton's data in his study of Spanish wages and prices fail in large part to support his thesis.[9] Of the three areas studied in the first episode from 1350-1500, Valencia, Aragon, and Navarre, only Navarre incurred inflation during this time. He concludes: "The greatest anomaly disclosed by the present study is the complete failure of wages to lag behind prices in any of the kingdoms during a single period of upheaval. In fact, Navarrese wages advanced much faster than prices in the last decade of the fourteenth century" [17, p. 203].

For the second period, 1501 to 1650, he concludes: "With few interruptions, the trend [in real wages] was downward from 1520 to 1600" [16, p. 280]. And, "The calamitous depreciation of the inflated Castilian vellon and debased Valencian silver coinage in 1623-1650 impaired the economic welfare of workers no less catastrophically than had the

---

changed but demand conditions have changed. Real aggregate demand could increase, through an increase in the nominal monetary stock, and with an infinitely elastic aggregate supply function, full employment would be restored with no fall in real wages.

[8] This view runs through most of his works. See particularly [18, p. 256] [20, pp. 335-36].

[9] In the ensuing examination of his statistical results, the reported data will be taken at face value. However, the statistical procedures employed merit more extended critical examination than is possible here.

TABLE 1—COMPOSITE INDEX OF REAL WAGES*
Base 1571–1580, Period 1501–1650

Year		Year		Year		Year		Year		Year	
1501	112.78	1526	105.66	1551	100.27	1576	103.47	1601	100.88	1626	101.15
1502	115.55	1527	102.26	1552	98.64	1577	106.52	1602	108.68	1627	97.82
1503	118.96	1528	106.62	1553	102.76	1578	102.95	1603	112.80	1628	102.44
1504	111.56	1529	100.15	1554	108.40	1579	97.81	1604	111.94	1629	104.22
1505	108.62	1530	91.35	1555	110.41	1580	102.86	1605	112.10	1630	109.31
1506	92.47	1531	94.39	1556	109.60	1581	104.43	1606	116.80	1631	110.89
1507	99.68	1532	99.40	1557	100.66	1582	101.12	1607	119.60	1632	107.79
1508	102.75	1533	106.25	1558	101.75	1583	100.09	1608	121.35	1633	111.11
1509	117.06	1534	102.43	1559	111.05	1584	102.48	1609	127.83	1634	113.47
1510	127.84	1535	114.03	1560	110.75	1585	102.22	1610	125.49	1635	114.60
1511	120.80	1536	104.49	1561	102.02	1586	106.01	1611	130.56	1636	111.63
1512	126.85	1537	108.19	1562	96.50	1587	103.14	1612	127.96	1637	105.83
1513	125.48	1538	99.82	1563	100.96	1588	111.63	1613	128.09	1638	105.86
1514	122.04	1539	104.06	1564	102.12	1589	107.31	1614	122.85	1639	110.81
1515	118.56	1540	102.30	1565	101.27	1590	105.85	1615	126.57	1640	111.59
1516	120.62	1541	103.73	1566	99.22	1591	107.70	1616	121.45	1641	106.13
1517	123.87	1542	98.23	1567	103.37	1592	104.12	1617	119.81	1642	98.07
1518	118.36	1543	97.24	1568	105.80	1593	107.07	1618	122.90	1643	101.30
1519	119.77	1544	101.45	1569	108.14	1594	106.47	1619	127.08	1644	102.45
1520	125.56	1545	105.14	1570	105.56	1595	106.29	1620	121.61	1645	105.91
1521	112.61	1546	98.36	1571	99.58	1596	103.84	1621	122.11	1646	102.07
1522	104.81	1547	99.28	1572	100.02	1597	99.00	1622	121.85	1647	103.10
1523	109.89	1548	95.54	1573	97.40	1598	93.02	1623	120.16	1648	98.20
1524	109.36	1549	93.61	1574	100.11	1599	91.40	1624	114.64	1649	97.53
1525	106.87	1550	97.61	1575	94.18	1600	91.31	1625	113.82	1650	93.30

* Reproduced from Hamilton [16, p. 278], with permission of Harvard University Press.

influx of American gold and silver in the last eight decades of the sixteenth century" [16, p. 282]. However again, and once more holding real forces constant, Hamilton's conclusion is not supported by his data. While it is strictly true that real wages as reported by Hamilton were lower in 1600 than they were in 1520, the trend he reports is absent from his data. The reason he gets the results that he does is that 1520 is a year when real wages were exceptionally high when compared with the years immediately preceding and succeeding 1520. On the other hand, 1600 appears to be a year when real wages were exceptionally low when compared with the years immediately preceding and succeeding 1600. If real wages in 1522 are compared with real wages in 1602, then one can conclude that real wages rose. The results Hamilton obtained can be obtained from random series. There is no downward trend in real wages nor any coincidence of wages lagging with inflation.[10] Hamilton's data for the episode are reproduced in Table 1.

[10] Alternatively one might say that the base year for Hamilton's observations had a strong plus random factor and the final year a strong minus random factor, and what he attributes to inflation can be attributed very easily to sampling error. In statistical jargon, he commits the regression fallacy.

The Meaning and Validity of the Inflation-Induced Lag of Wages behind Prices

In his third volume, Hamilton covers the time interval from 1651-1800 and he finds that real wages declined in the urban areas, Madrid and Valencia, in the second half of the eighteenth century. What happened to real wages for the country as a whole is unclear since real wages rose in some rural areas and presumably the country as a whole was predominantly rural [19, p. 210]. The second half of the eighteenth century was characterized by rising prices. However it was also a time when the Spanish population was increasing sharply; it doubled during this century, and was associated with migration from rural to urban areas [19, p. 216]. Consequently one would expect, in the absence of any imperfections in the labor market, that such a population increase would lower real wages. Yet Hamilton did not disentangle the effects of this population increase from the effects of inflation upon real wages, and he concluded in the final sentence of his last volume:

> By involuntarily sacrificing real income through the price-wage squeeze, the laboring class bore the burden that implemented material progress, just as laborers and peasants in Soviet Russia, sacrificing through governmental directives, have largely financed the mechanization of industry that was instrumental in the recent expulsion of German invaders [19, p. 225].

B. *English and French Data*

Hamilton buttresses his conclusions about the effect of inflation upon industrial development by citing similar effects for England and France during inflations that occurred in these countries. Specifically, in his third volume he says:

> The concurrence of profit inflation and of rapid economic development in England and France tends to confirm the thesis that the lag of wages behind prices was an important factor in the great material progress in Spain during the second half of the eighteenth century [19, p. 224].

Again, even if the potential impact of real forces upon wage-price relationships is ignored, can it be said that wages fell during the inflation in England?

Hamilton's study of the movement of prices and wages in London between 1729 and 1800 indicates that real wages fell.[11] Mrs. Gilboy, however, who also studied prices and wages in England at this time, supports Hamilton's findings of fact but not his conclusions [12, pp.

---

[11] [18, p. 259]. One of the relevant problems for analyzing Hamilton's data, which he fails to discuss, is the fact that he has more observations, typically, in his price than in his wage index. Consequently, if the price and wage observations change with the same degree of frequency, say once a year, it will appear, falsely, as if wages were lagging behind prices. This error accounts for much of the intuitive appeal of the wage-lag hypothesis. If during inflation one sees prices moving up day by day whereas one's own wage rate changes once a year, the conclusion that wages lag behind prices during inflation is difficult to resist.

TABLE 2—INDEX NUMBERS OF PRICES AND WAGES IN ENGLAND, 1500–1702*
(Index for 1451–1500 = 100)

Period	Prices	Wages
1501–1510	95	95
1511–1520	101	93
1521–1530	113	93
1531–1540	105	90
1541–1550	79	57
1551–1560	132	88
1561–1570	155	109
1571–1582	171	113
1583–1592	198	125
1593–1602	243	124
1603–1612	251	124.5
1613–1622	257	134
1623–1632	282	138.5
1633–1642	291	152.5
1643–1652	331	175
1653–1662	308	187
1663–1672	324	190
1673–1682	348	205.5
1683–1692	319	216
1693–1702	339	233

* Reproduced from Hamilton [15, p. 352], with permission of London School of Economics and the author.

191-215]. She found that real wages fell in London and rose in the north of England [12, pp. 191-215]. Therefore she concluded: "Generalizations as to what happened to English wages as a whole must at present meet no little skepticism."[12] Her findings were particularly damaging to Hamilton's interpretation of the implications of a fall in real wages during inflation. Capital formation in the north of England was especially high, whereas Hamilton's hypothesis implies that capital formation ought to have been particularly low in this area.[13]

Hamilton has also examined data for an earlier period of English history, 1500 to 1702 [15, p. 351, Chart 1]. Will these data support the hypothesis that inflation causes wages to lag behind prices if one abstracts from the effects of real forces? (See Table 2.) Taking the period as a whole, Hamilton is right. Real wages declined. However, virtually all of the decline occurred during the first 50 years of this period, and it is unclear whether this shorter time interval ought to be regarded as being on net balance inflationary or deflationary. Prices

[12] [12, p. 227]. In a paper dealing with this same issue, Mrs. Gilboy puts the case even more forcefully. "Sufficient data are not at present available to make any statements concerning the movement of real wages in England as a whole for this period" [13, p. 141].

[13] For a partially overlapping time period, 1790-1830, Ashton does not believe that real wages declined [4, p. 158].

TABLE 3—INDEX NUMBERS OF PRICES AND WAGES IN FRANCE, 1500–1700*
(Index for 1451–1500=100)

Period	Prices	Wages
1501–1525	113	92
1526–1550	136	104
1551–1575	174	103
1576–1600	248	113
1601–1625	189	113
1626–1650	243	127
1651–1675	227	127
1676–1700	229	125

* Reproduced from Hamilton [15, p. 353], with permission of London School of Economics and the author.

were about 17 per cent lower at the end of these 50 years than they were for the base observation. The first 40 years were inflationary, and real wages fell. However, the next 10 were deflationary, and real wages fell even more. Again these data will not support even this very simple conception of the wage-lag hypothesis.[14]

Tucker studied real wages in London during the latter half of the eighteenth century but has no data for the country as a whole [40]. In view of Gilboy's findings, his data are not of great relevance for England as a whole. Tucker, for reasons quite different from Hamilton's, was interested in testing the hypothesis that real wages fall as a result of rising prices. However, every time he observes a fall in real wages, he is able to explain this fall by real factors such as poor crops, resources consumed by wars, etc. [40, p. 82, for example]. Yet he ignores these explanations when drawing his conclusions.

For France, Hamilton does have data that unambiguously show that real wages fell [15, p. 353]. (See Table 3.) However his explanation of why they fell is not supported by related evidence. His hypothesis implies that the larger the fall in real wages, the greater the rate of industrial development. Differences in the rates of capital formation between England and France ought, therefore, to be related to differences in

[14] Using time series of wages and prices as Hamilton does involves the vexing question of how to choose one's starting point or base observation. Presumably one wants to start observations when prices start to rise. But the trough of a price series is usually determined by random components. This produces a transitory peak in the real wage series; the subsequent decrease, if interpreted as a lag, provides an example of the regression fallacy. Only by averaging out transitory or random variations about some turning point can one avoid part of this problem.

Only after acceptance of this paper for publication did we discover the following corroboratory conclusion, "It follows that Keynes was misled when he argued in the *Treatise* that the general rise in prices had stimulated industrial growth by widening profit margins," in E. H. Phelps Brown and S. V. Hopkins, "Wage-rates and Prices: Evidence for Population Pressure in the Sixteenth Century," *Economica*, Nov. 1957, N.S. *24*, 299.

either the observed fall in real wages or the rates of change of prices. Nef was unable to explain differences between the rates of capital formation in France and England with Hamilton's hypothesis.[15] Similarly, the failure to find "correlation between inflation, or its absence, and variations in the rate of economic growth" has led another student of industrial development, Felix, to reject Hamilton's theory of development.[16]

C. *The Civil War in the North*

Mitchell's basic time series of wages and prices for the North during the Civil War [34] are substantially better than the data for the early days of the industrial revolution. And there is little doubt that real wages truly fell during the Civil War; most of Mitchell's results cannot be rationalized as an artifact resulting from the choice of the time period said to be inflationary. Moreover, these data [34, p. 343] indicate that a substantial fall in real wages occurred.

One might quarrel with Mitchell's use of a wholesale price index as a deflator of real wages. This index was in large part composed of commodities like opium, mercury, zinc, soda ash, tin plate, blue vitriol, etc. A mere count of such items indicates that an unweighted index overrepresents their effect on the cost-of-living index. Rent, as is typically the case for wholesale price indexes, was absent. But it is easy to make too much of this point. Mitchell also computed a cost-of-living index for this period, and when either this index or one computed by Ethel Hoover, who used the same source material, is used as a deflator, the results still indicate a substantial fall in real wages, although smaller than when wholesale prices are used.[17] (These data are reproduced in [24, p. 102]).

These results led Mitchell to conclude that: "All of the statistical evidence that has been presented in the preceding pages supports unequivocally the common theory that persons whose incomes are derived from wages suffer seriously from a depreciation of the currency" [34, p. 347]. They also led Mitchell to embrace the hypothesis that the labor market in the 1860's and 1870's was imperfect and that this imperfection was of a kind that virtually no serious student of industrial organization asserts exists in any other factor or product market [35, p. 276]. However, there is an alternative explanation of the fall in real wages in the North during the Civil War that is con-

---

[15] J. Nef has collected evidence that fails to show a relationship between the magnitude of the lag and the rate of industrial development. He also has evidence that Hamilton's data exaggerate the magnitude of the fall in real wages [37].

[16] See also Felix's discussion, "Hamilton's *Tour d'Horizon*" [9, pp. 457-59].

[17] Ethel Hoover's index [22, p. 40, Table 1] is better than Mitchell's CPI because it uses more of the available data and better techniques for accounting for gaps in the data.

sistent with the way economists explain changes in price relationships in markets other than labor and it explains more of the relative price movements that occurred. Indeed, this explanation is consistent with the postulate that the labor market was operating perfectly during the inflation associated with the Civil War. Because it has none of the *ad hoc* character of the explanation employed by Mitchell and Hamilton, it is to be preferred.[18]

The outbreak of the Civil War substantially destroyed a triangular trading relationship among the North, the South, and England. The South earned foreign exchange through its exports of cotton, which accounted for roughly two-thirds of all U. S. exports. It, in effect, traded these foreign exchange earnings for Northern goods and services, and the North in turn used this foreign exchange to purchase imports. The outbreak of hostilities, in addition to destroying a mutually profitable trading relationship between the North and the South, presented the North with what would be regarded today as an extremely difficult balance-of-payments problem. This problem was aggravated by a capital flight of foreign investments during the early years of the war.

That this important problem confronting the North has been largely unrecognized is in large part to be explained by the fact that it was solved unobtrusively and successfully by a measure designed for a largely unrelated function. During the war, the North engaged in the printing of greenbacks; and the resulting inflation and the maintenance of convertibility at the prewar exchange rate were incompatible. In consequence, the North abandoned the gold standard in favor of an inconvertible paper standard and a freely fluctuating exchange rate which inadvertently solved the balance-of-payments problem.

The rise in the prices of imports relative to the rise in domestic prices and wages inevitably produced a fall in real factor incomes of all types. In so far as money wages are deflated by a price index that includes international goods, particularly imports, real wages decline. Since Mitchell's wholesale price index was more heavily weighted by imports than his consumer price index, the use of the former as a deflator produces a greater fall in real wages than does the latter. And of course if imports are excluded from his consumer price index and what remains is used as a deflator of money wages, a still smaller fall in real wages in measured.

However, this is only part of the explanation of the fall in real wages that Mitchell observed. The North, in addition to taxing through inflation, also employed turnover taxes and tariffs as means of war finance. The severity of these taxes increased during the course of the

---

[18] The analysis which follows is more fully developed in a paper which appears elsewhere. See [24].

war. These taxes produced a divergence between the sum of the payments to agents of production and final product prices, because unlike retail sales taxes today, they became a part of final product prices. One would also expect for this reason to find that real wages, as measured by Mitchell, declined during the course of the Civil War.

Both the balance-of-payments problem and the turnover taxes would have produced a fall in real wages whether or not inflation had occurred. If the government's increased expenditures had not been financed by inflationary methods, some other means of taxation would have been required. Had tariffs or turnover taxes in any part replaced the inflation tax, an even greater fall in real wages would have occurred. The inflation tax implies that real wages were higher than they otherwise would have been.

D. *The Civil War in the South*

In a number of respects, Eugene Lerner's study of the Confederacy [27] [28] is parallel to Mitchell's work. In particular, both found that real wages declined. In neither case can most of the decline be attributed to the special characteristics of the base or terminal years for the time period defined as inflationary. Like Mitchell, Lerner attributes the fall in real wages to the lag of wages behind prices and accepts the extraordinary profitability implication of the wage-lag argument. "Prices rose much faster than wages in the Confederacy, and southern businessmen made large profits" [28, p. 31]. His paper contains virtually no evidence on profits.

The acceptance by Lerner of the wage-lag explanation of the fall in real wages is inconsistent with another interpretation of the events of the time that may be found in his own papers. He indicates that much of Southern capital was highly specialized to the production of cotton for an international market and that the Northern blockade sharply reduced the productivity of this capital. Lerner also reports that excises, either in the form of taxes or payments in kind, constituted an important means of war finance. In fact, Lerner implicitly presents a hypothesis that explains the fall in real wages by nonmonetary phenomena, but he explicitly accepts the thesis that the fall in real wages is attributable to inflation.

E. *The First World War*

Hansen's study is concerned with real wages and price changes in the United States from 1820 to 1923 and thus includes the inflation associated with the first world war. His position is much like that of Mitchell and Hamilton. "Rising prices cause a gap between the marginal productivity of the various factors employed by the entrepreneur

TABLE 4—HANSEN'S SERIES OF MONEY WAGES, COST OF LIVING AND REAL WAGES*
(1913=100)

Year	Index of Money Wages	Index of Cost-of-Living	Index of Real Wages
1910	94	94	100
1911	95	92	103
1912	98	96	102
1913	100	100	100
1914	102	102	100
1915	104	104	100
1916	118	111	106
1917	134	131	102
1918	168	159	106
1919	193	183	105
1920	232	208	112
1921	207	182	114
1922	201	168	120
1923	220	171	129

* Reproduced from Hansen [21, p. 32].

and the return that each receives. Indeed in such periods it is literally true that 'labor does not receive the full value of its product'" [21, p. 40].

However, even if real forces are assumed to be constant, as Hansen presumably assumed, the data do not support the wage-lag hypothesis. Indeed, they can be just as easily construed as undermining the hypothesis. Only if one chooses the year 1916 as a base and compares it with 1919 or 1917, can one show that real wages fell.[19] (See Table 4.) If one uses 1913 as a base, and every succeeding year through 1920 as a terminal point, there is nothing to indicate a fall in real wages. In fact, Hansen's data show that real wages were almost 10 per cent greater in 1920 than in 1917.

These data of Hansen's contain an unfortunate bias in favor of the wage-lag hypothesis for the entire time interval with which he was concerned. Starting with 1890, Hansen uses weekly earnings rather than hourly earnings. If leisure is a superior good, and if real hourly earnings per capita rise, then weekly earnings understate real wages because of the substitution of leisure for income from work. Consequently, evidence collected to reveal a fall in real wages can be explained, at least in part, by the hypothesis that they were in fact rising. This bias is particularly unfortunate in a study of secular inflations

[19] Hamilton in a parenthetical remark [15, p. 355] selects 1916 as a base year and observes that "... American profiteers reaped [income] from a similar divergence between prices and wages from 1916 to 1919." Hansen's data, reproduced as Table 5, show a less than one per cent fall in real wages for this period.

because the longer the time period considered, the greater the error it introduces into the calculations.

F. *The German Inflation*

Bresciani-Turroni contends that real wages declined as a *result* of the inflation in Germany following the first world war [7].[20] For the entire inflationary episode, he concluded: "But it may be said that on the whole the inflation generally favoured the entrepreneurs and the owners of material means of production, especially strengthening the positions of industrial capitalists; that it caused a lowering of the real wages of workmen . . ." [7, p. 286]. However, leaving aside questions of the impact of real forces upon real wages, Bresciani-Turroni's wage data, which consist almost exclusively of miners' wages, show that real wages sometimes declined and sometimes rose during the course of the inflation. Over the period as a whole, real wages did not fall [7, pp. 307, 309].

During the later stages of the inflation when the real value of the nominal stock of money declined sharply, or during the time that velocity increased at a rate more rapid than the rate of increase of the monetary stock, Bresciani-Turroni found that real wages fell. This rise in velocity was attributable to the recognition by the community of the increased cost of holding cash balances caused by rising prices. In this respect the German hyperinflation was unlike the inflations examined by Mitchell, Hansen, Hamilton, Gilboy, and Tucker, and it led to a marked reduction in the effective stock of capital in money form. Under these circumstances, the higher marginal cost of using money is an additional cost of doing business, and this implies that the share of the final output of the economy going to the other cooperating agents of production has decreased. Consequently, a fall in real wages during an inflation that is generally anticipated is consistent with a perfectly functioning labor market and does not imply an increase in business profits. In fact this analysis is consistent with Bresciani-Turroni's data on share prices, which do not support the thesis that business firms are extraordinarily profitable as a consequence of inflation [7, p. 253].

In general, it appears that a highly selective sampling from the population of all inflations has produced two important unambiguous cases of a fall in real wages for indivdual economies, those of the North and the South during the Civil War. For these cases, the wage-lag hypothesis has to compete with price theory. For the one case that has been studied in great detail, that of the North during the Civil War, price theory offers a more satisfactory explanation.

[20] "The increase in nominal wage rates was slower than the increase in prices caused by monetary inflation. In other words, real wages fell" [7, p. 305; also pp. 186-88]. This fall in real wages, according to Bresciani-Turroni, continued until the summer of 1922.

Whether or not available data indicate that real wages fell during inflation for some particular economy does not in itself establish or disprove the existence of an inflation-induced wage lag unless one assumes real forces to be inoperative. A time series of wages and prices can be made relevant evidence for testing the wage-lag hypothesis only after the effects of real forces are controlled. Unfortunately, the wage-lag theorists have generally ignored real forces. In the case of the North during the Civil War, the real forces ignored are substantial in magnitude and capable of producing the effects upon real wages imputed to the wage-lag hypothesis. When one considers the implications of this hypothesis, as the wage-lag theorists have not, the differences between industrial development in the North and South of England during the early days of the industrial revolutions, along with the Nef findings, must be regarded as still more evidence against this hypothesis.

III. *New Evidence*

In an effort to bring some new evidence to bear on the validity of wage-lag hypothesis, the annual wage bills for 56 industrial corporations listed on the New York Stock Exchange during the time interval 1940 to 1952 have been collected. These were all the industrial firms listed that reported their wage bills during this entire period.

The proposition tested was that the firms with large annual wage bills would experience an increase in profits (and wealth) relative to firms with smaller annual wage bills. That is, for any given rise in prices, sales and costs other than wages rise by the same proportion, whereas total wages [W] rise by less, e.g., by only some fraction, α, of the general price rise. Thus, $W(1-\alpha)$ constitutes the size of the gain in profits for any firm. The relative magnitude of the gain is a function of the size of a firm's wage bill relative to its equity, as measured by its market value. In other words, the ratio of wages to equity is an indicator of the relative rise in stock prices attributable to a lag of wages behind prices.[21]

The ratio of wages to equity was obtained for each of the years from 1940 to 1952 through the use of the annual wage bill and the market value of stock outstanding at the end of the year. Unfortunately, testing for a relationship between the relative change in market value and the wage-to-equity ratio produces a bias in favor of finding a positive correlation because ratios with the same denominator are being corre-

[21] Hamilton evidently regards the ratio of wages to total costs as the correct indicator of the size of the gain attributable to the lag of wages behind prices [18, p. 262]. However, two firms with identical equity values and identical ratios of wages to total costs might have different mark-ups and consequently different aggregate wage bills. (For example, consider a jewelry store and a supermarket grocery.) What is relevant is the size of the wage bill. And for interfirm comparisons, the relationship of the wage bill to total equity is the appropriate one.

lated. To reduce this bias, the annual wage-to-equity ratios, one for each year in the 1940 to 1952 period, were averaged for each corporation and then used as a predictor of relative changes in equity values.[22]

The use of this average seemed reasonable because the differences between firms with respect to this average were significantly greater than the variations of any given year from the average for any firm. (The wage-to-equity ratios exhibited no trend over time.) The standard deviation of the ratio of wages to equity for any given year was about 20 per cent of the average for any firm. On the other hand, the average ratio varied, from firm to firm, from a low of 1 to a high of 7.[23] And because the interfirm variation was so much greater than the intrafirm variation, it seemed sensible to enlarge the size of the sample by using data for firms that reported annual wage bills for as little as two years of the time-span studied. This brought the sample to 113 firms. (A listing of the firms and other relevant data may be obtained through personal communication with the authors. Unfortunately, space constraints do not permit us to publish them here.)

By trying to detect a correlation between wage-to-equity ratios and changes in stock prices, the effects of a lag of wages behind prices caused by inflation can be disentangled from the effects of real forces upon real wages. After all, if one believes that real and monetary forces can operate independently and concurrently, the wage lag should be operative regardless of whether time series of wages and prices during inflation show that real wages fell, rose, or were constant. Given independence between real forces and the wage-to-equity ratio of a firm, this test ought to reveal the presence of the effects of inflation upon real wages.

According to the wage-lag hypothesis, the greater the wage-to-equity ratio, the larger should be the rise in equity values as a result of inflation.[24] To test whether or not this implication is in fact correct, firms were ranked according to their average ratio of wages to equity. The percentage increase in equity for firms with an average ratio of annual wages to equity below .5 were compared with those above 1. The results of this comparison are presented in summary form in Table 5. The

[22] This also buys some insurance against committing the regression fallacy. If the wage-to-equity ratio at the beginning of the time period were used, firms with large wage-to-equity ratios might be those with transitorily small equity valuations and conversely.

[23] This ratio is affected by the financial structure. A firm with large debts and small equity financing will have a high wage-to-equity ratio and conversely.

[24] For example, if a firm's stock sold for $4 at the end of 1939 and $40 at the end of 1952, the equity increase is shown as a ratio, 10. Dividends paid are assumed to be reinvested into more shares of the same firm, and thus their growth was compounded. In this way, differences in dividend payout policy were held constant.

average equity rise was greater the lower the wages-to-equity ratio. Such a difference in the wrong direction clearly does not support the wage-lag hypothesis. Dividing the sample into two equal parts, one consisting of firms with the larger wage-to-equity ratios and the other of firms with the smaller wage-to-equity ratios, yields similar results.

In any attempt to impute the absence of causality to the absence of correlation between two variables, there always exists the danger that still another variable is so correlated with what is regarded as the independent variable that the effects of the independent variable upon the dependent variable are concealed. Relevant to this problem is the fact that a relationship is known to exist between the net monetary status

TABLE 5—MEAN EQUITY INCREASES OF FIRMS CLASSIFIED BY WAGE-TO-EQUITY RATIO*

Ratio of Wages-to-Equity	Average Increase in Equity (1939-52)	Number of Firms	Variance
Under .5	8.41	34	48.4
.5 to .99	7.40	30	39.1
1. and over	6.19	49	26.5
"t" for 8.41−6.19=+1.58			
P(t≥1.26)=.12			

* *Sources:* Moody's *Industrials* [36], *Annual Reports* [3], and *New York Times* [38].

of a firm and the relative change in its stock prices during inflation [23, p. 128]. The increase in the equity of the 43 firms in the sample that were net monetary debtors at least two-thirds of the time from 1940 to 1952 was greater than that experienced by the 29 firms in the sample that were net monetary creditors at least two-thirds of the time.[25] These results are consistent with known effects of debtor-creditor status upon stock-price changes during inflation.[26] Consequently, if firms that were large net debtors were also firms that had

[25] There were 43 debtor and 29 creditor firms. The mean rise for the debtor firms was 8.25 with a variance of 39.67; for the creditor firms, the mean was 5.94 and the variance 19.20. $\bar{x}_d - \bar{x}_c = 2.31, t = 1.82, P\ (t \geq +1.82) \approx .04$ Sources: [3] [36] [38].

[26] Possibly this is too strong a statement. Bach and Ando [5] report that they were unable to detect the debtor-creditor effect. There seem to be two reasons for the apparent difference between the outcome of Kessel's early work and the results reported here on the one hand, and the results reported by Bach and Ando on the other. Bach and Ando used several different criteria for determining whether or not the debtor-creditor effect existed. Only one of these criteria was implied by the hypothesis being tested. On that one pertinent criterion their results do verify the debtor-creditor wealth transfer. But they relied on the rule of the majority rather than the rule of a decisive test. This error was compounded by their erroneous use of a "two-tailed" probability calculation instead of a one-tailed calculation. For additional evidence, published subsequent to the Bach and Ando paper, see [2, p. 537].

large wage-to-equity ratios, debtor status would counteract the effect of the wage lag upon stock prices, and the consequences of inflation-induced lags of wages behind prices would go undetected.

In order to determine whether or not debtor-creditor effects were masking the effects of inflation upon business profits, the relationships among (1) changes in equity values, (2) annual wage-to-equity ratios, (3) debtor-creditor status, and (4) annual sales-to-equity ratio (for those who think that sales are correlated with wage-to-equity ratios) were explored by means of a multiple correlation analysis. As a measure of a firm's net monetary creditor or debtor status over the interval 1940 to 1952, the average of debtor-creditor status in each year was

TABLE 6—MATRIX OF SIMPLE AND RANK CORRELATION COEFFICIENTS AMONG EQUITY RISE, WAGE-TO-EQUITY RATIO, NET MONETARY STATUS, AND SALES-TO-EQUITY RATIO*

	(1)	(2)	(3)	(4)
Equity Rise, 1952/1939 (1)	1.	.04 (−.09)	.01 (.24)	.10 (.02)
Ratio of Wages-to-Equity (2)		1.	.33 (.15)	.51 (.83)
Net Monetary Status (3)			1.	.10 (.36)
Ratio of Sales-to-Equity (4)				1.
Partial Correlation Coefficients	$r_{12.34}=$	−.09 (−.11)		
	$r_{13.24}=$	.04 (.36)		
	$r_{14.23}=$	.16 (.08)		

* The rank correlation coefficients are in parentheses. For the ranks, the one-tailed 5 per cent probability value is .16, the two-tailed probability value is .22, $P(r>.36)<.001$.

weighted by the price rise for the year as measured by the change in the consumer price index of the Bureau of Labor Statistics.[27] For each of 113 firms there are observations with respect to four variables. The simple correlation coefficients among these four variables are presented in Table 6 along with the partial correlation coefficients of each predictive variable with the other two predictive variables held statistically constant. Results of this partial correlation analysis do not support the wage lag.[28] However, these correlation coefficients are difficult to interpret because the necessary conditions for computing their sampling distribution are not satisfied. In particular, the predicted or dependent variable is not normally distributed.[29] Therefore, no reliable probability tests of significance can be applied.

[27] Subsequent examination indicates that an unweighted average, which is cheaper to compute, would have given essentially similar, but not quite as effective, results.

[28] Since these are the same data used in the previous test, these results cannot be construed as new independent evidence against the wage-lag hypothesis.

[29] One objection to this procedure that does not seem warranted is the objection that correlations among ratios, such as these are, must be invalid because they are subject to biases. But it is the ratios themselves that are interesting in an economic sense. Secondly,

To obtain a probability test, the values associated with each of the variables were converted to ranks, and rank correlation coefficients were computed. These are reported in Table 6. These calculations indicate a positive partial correlation between net monetary status and increases in equity values. And there is only one chance in 1,000 that such a result could be obtained by randomly sampling from a population characterized by an absence of this relationship. The negative partial correlation of wage-to-equity ratios and changes in stock prices still persists; however, this correlation can be easily rationalized as the result of random sampling from a population characterized by an absence of this relationship. Again the wage-lag hypothesis is not supported after the potential masking effects of two variables are specifically eliminated. The absence of a relationship between sales and changes in equity values is probably the result of using the level of sales rather than the rate of change of sales as an independent variable.

If neither a regression phenomenon nor a masking effect from monetary status is operating, can the results obtained be attributed to a correlation among specific industries? Relative price changes have possibly favored industries consisting of low wage-to-equity firms. Eight of the 34 firms in the low wage-to-equity class are oil firms. The removal of these firms from the sample failed to alter significantly the results obtained. The average equity rise, with the oil firms removed, of the low wage-to-equity firms was still greater than for the other class by a 6.76 to 6.19 margin. Needless to say, there exists an indefinitely large number of variables that might be so correlated with wage-to-equity ratios that the effects of the wage lag upon changes in equity values would be concealed. All any investigator can do is to eliminate only the most promising candidates in the light of his knowledge of the economics of the problem.

IV. Conclusions

One of the important advances in economic analysis in the postwar period has been the formal incorporation into theory of the effects of wealth upon consumption expenditures. Previously it seemed reasonable to argue that wages must lag behind prices during inflation if the government acquired resources through inflation. The logic of this argument has been shown to be false.

Another independent line of argument for the proposition that inflation causes real wages to fall is based on sluggishness or flaws in the labor market whereby wage-earners receive less than their marginal

---

even if one thinks in absolute terms, the weighting of observations by the inverse of their standard deviation eliminates the bias. Moreover, the bias of ratios, if present, would work in favor of the wage-lag hypothesis, not against it.

product when prices are rising. But much of the data which investigators have collected to show a fall in real wages during the course of selected inflations simply fail to support the hypothesis. By one selection of beginning and terminal points for an inflation it can be shown real wages fell; by another selection it can be shown that real wages rose. The fall in real wages reported by these observers is a product of the arbitrary way the time period during which inflation occurred was defined.

However, data do exist, particularly in Mitchell's work, that unambiguously indicate a fall in real wages. But before such data can be seriously considered as supporting the wage-lag hypothesis, one must first show that even after price theory has done all it can to explain the altered price-wage relationship, there is still something left to explain. The advocates or investigators of the wage-lag hypothesis have never shown this. As for the time period studied by Mitchell, it appears that known and measurable real forces can and do explain the fall in real wages that he has observed.

Efforts to detect the existence of the wage lag during inflation through the examination of stock prices of firms that differed with respect to the volume of labor hired per dollar of invested capital by owners have also failed. This evidence contradicts the wage-lag hypothesis. Still, it is easy to make too much of this evidence since it was based on a nonrandom sample and was obtained for only one inflation.

In general, it appears that unwarranted validity has been assigned to the wage-lag hypothesis, given the character of the evidence that has been used to support it. A rereading of this evidence suggests that the wage-lag hypothesis ought to be regarded as essentially untested.

References

1. A. Alchian and R. Kessel, "How the Government Gains from Inflation," *Proceedings of the Thirtieth Annual Conference of the Western Economics Association (1955)*, Salt Lake City 1956, pp. 13-16.
2. ———, "Redistribution of Wealth through Inflation," *Science*, Sept. 4, 1959, *130*, 535-39.
3. *Corporation Annual Reports*, Godfrey Memorial Library (New Haven, Yale University), 1939 to 1952.
4. T. S. Ashton, "The Standard of Life of the Workers in England, 1790-1830," in *Capitalism and the Historians*, ed. F. A. Hayek, Chicago 1954, pp. 127-59.
5. G. L. Bach and A. Ando, "The Redistributional Effects of Inflation," *Rev. Econ. and Stat.*, Feb. 1957, *39*, 1-13.
6. E. M. Bernstein and I. G. Patel, "Inflation in Relation to Economic Development," *Internat. Mon. Fund Staff Papers*, Nov. 1952, *2*, 363-98.
7. C. Bresciani-Turroni, *The Economics of Inflation*. London 1937.

8. P. CAGAN, "The Monetary Dynamics of Hyperinflation," in *Studies in the Quantity Theory of Money*, M. Friedman, ed., Chicago 1956, pp. 25-117.
9. D. FELIX, "Profit Inflation and Industrial Growth: The Historic Record and Contemporary Analogies," *Quart. Jour. Econ.*, Aug. 1956, *70*, 441-63.
10. I. FISHER, *The Purchasing Power of Money*. Rev. ed. New York 1926.
11. M. FRIEDMAN, "Discussion of the Inflationary Gap," *Essays in Positive Economics*, Chicago 1953, pp. 251-62.
12. E. GILBOY, *Wages in Eighteenth Century England*. Cambridge, Mass. 1934.
13. ———, "The Cost of Living and Real Wages in Eighteenth Century England," *Rev. Econ. Stat.*, 1936, *18*, 134-43.
14. G. HABERLER, *Prosperity and Depression*. 3d ed. New York, United Nations, 1946, pp. 137-41, 481.
15. E. J. HAMILTON, "American Treasure and the Rise of Capitalism (1500-1700)," *Economica*, Nov. 1929, *9*, 338-57.
16. ———, *American Treasure and the Price Revolution in Spain, 1501-1650*. Cambridge, Mass. 1934.
17. ———, *Money, Prices, and Wages in Valencia, Aragon, and Navarre, 1351-1500*. Cambridge, Mass. 1936.
18. ———, "Profit Inflation and the Industrial Revolution, 1751-1800," *Quart. Jour. Econ.*, Feb. 1942, *56*, 256-73; reprinted [26, pp. 322-36].
19. ———, *War and Prices in Spain, 1651-1800*. Cambridge, Mass. 1947.
20. ———, "Prices as a Factor in Business Growth," *Jour. Econ. Hist.*, Fall 1952, *12*, 325-49.
21. A. H. HANSEN, "Factors Affecting Trend of Real Wages," *Am. Econ. Rev.*, 1925, *15*, 40-53.
22. E. D. HOOVER, *Prices in the United States in the 19th Century*. (Mimeographed and unpublished manuscript presented at a National Bureau Conference on Research in Income and Wealth, Sept. 4-5, 1957.)
23. R. A. KESSEL, "Inflation-Caused Wealth Redistribution: A Test of a Hypothesis," *Am. Econ. Rev.*, Mar. 1956, *46*, 128-41.
24. R. A. KESSEL AND A. A. ALCHIAN, "Real Wages in the North during the Civil War: Mitchell's Data Reinterpreted," *Jour. Law and Econ.*, Oct. 1959, *2*, 95-113.
25. J. M. KEYNES, *A Treatise on Money*. Vol. 2. New York 1930.
26. F. C. LANE AND J. C. RIEMERSMA, ed., *Enterprise and Secular Change*. Homewood, Ill. 1953.
27. E. M. LERNER, "The Monetary and Fiscal Programs of the Confederate Government, 1861-65," *Jour. Pol. Econ.*, Dec. 1954, *62*, 506-22.
28. ———, "Money, Prices, and Wages in the Confederacy, 1861-65," *Jour. Pol. Econ.*, Feb. 1955, *63*, 20-40.
29. W. A. LEWIS, *The Theory of Economic Growth*. Homewood, Ill. 1955.
30. E. LIPSON, *The Economic History of England*. Vol. 1, 4th ed. London 1926.
31. A. MARSHALL, "Answers to Questions on the Subject of Currency and Prices Circulated by Royal Commission on the Depression of Trade and

Industry (1886)," *Official Papers by Alfred Marshall*, London 1926, pp. 3-16.
32. G. M. MEIER AND R. BALDWIN, *Economic Development: Theory, History, Policy*. New York 1957.
33. F. V. MEYER, *Inflation and Capital*. Cambridge, Eng. 1954.
34. W. C. MITCHELL, *A History of the Greenbacks*. Chicago 1903.
35. ———, *Gold Prices, and Wages under the Greenback Standard*, Berkeley 1908.
36. *Moody's Manual of Investments, American and Foreign, Industrial Securities*. Moody's Investor's Service, New York. Annually from 1939 through 1953.
37. J. NEF, "Prices and Industrial Capitalism in France and England, 1540-1640," *Econ. Hist. Rev.*, May 1937, *7*, 155-85, reprinted in [26, pp. 292-321].
38. *The New York Times*, daily ed., 1939-1952.
39. A. REES, "Patterns of Wages, Prices and Productivity," in *Wages, Prices, Profits and Productivity*, The Fifteenth American Assembly, New York 1959, pp. 11-59.
40. R. S. TUCKER, "Real Wages of Artisans in London, 1729-1935," *Jour. Am. Stat. Assoc.*, 1936, *31*, 73-84.
41. H. P. WILLIS AND J. M. CHAPMAN, *The Economics of Inflation*, New York 1935.

Bibliography of Major Publications by Reuben A. Kessel

1956 "How the Government Gains through Inflation." With Armen A. Alchian. In *Proceedings of the Thirtieth Annual Conference of the Western Economics Association* [1955]. Salt Lake City.

"Inflation-Caused Wealth Redistribution: A Test of a Hypothesis." *American Economic Review* 46:129–41. Reprinted in *Theory of Business Finance*, edited by J. Fred Weston and Donald J. Woods. Belmont, Calif.: Wadsworth Publishing Company, 1956.

1958 "Price Discrimination in Medicine." *Journal of Law and Economics* 1:20–53. © 1958 by The University of Chicago. Reprinted in *Readings in Microeconomics*, edited by William Breit and Harold M. Hochman. New York: Holt, Rinehart & Winston, 1968. 2d ed., 1971. Reprinted also in *Microeconomics: Selected Readings*, edited by Edwin Mansfield. New York: Norton, 1971. Reprinted also in *The Daily Economist*, edited by Harry G. Johnson and Burton Weisbrod. Englewood Cliffs, N.J.: Prentice-Hall, 1973.

1959 "Redistribution of Wealth through Inflation." With Armen A. Alchian. *Science* 130:535–39. Reprinted in *The Investment Process*, edited by John M. Lishan and David T. Crary. New York: International Textbook Company, 1970. Reprinted also in *Economic Forces at Work*, edited by Armen A. Alchian, Indianapolis: Liberty Press, 1977.

"Real Wages in the North during the Civil War: Mitchell's Data Reinterpreted." With Armen A. Alchian. *Journal of Law and Economics* 2:95–113. Reprinted in *The Economic Impact of the American Civil War*, edited by Ralph Andreano. 2d ed. Cambridge, Mass.: Schenkman Publishing Company, 1967. Reprinted also in *The Reinterpretation of American Economic History*, edited by Robert W. Fogel and Stanley L. Engerman. New York: Harper & Row, 1971. Reprinted also in *Economic Forces at Work*, edited by Armen A. Alchian.

1960 "The Meaning and Validity of the Inflation-Induced Lag of Wages behind Prices." With Armen A. Alchian. *American Economic Review* 50:43–66. Reprinted in *Economic Forces at Work*, edited by Armen A. Alchian.

1961 "The Measurement and Economic Implications of the Inclusion of Indirect Taxes in the Consumer Price Index." In *The Price Statistics of the Federal*

Government, edited by George J. Stigler. New York: National Bureau of Economic Research.

1962 "Competition, Monopoly, and the Pursuit of Money." With Armen A. Alchian. In *Aspects of Labor Economics.* Special Conference Series, National Bureau of Economic Research. Princeton: Princeton University Press for the National Bureau of Economic Research. Reprinted in *Economic Forces at Work,* edited by Armen A. Alchian.

"Effects of Inflation." With Armen A. Alchian. *Journal of Political Economy* 70:521–37. Reprinted in *Economic Forces at Work,* edited by Armen A. Alchian.

1965 *The Cyclical Behavior of the Term Structure of Interest Rates.* National Bureau of Economic Research Occasional Paper no. 91. New York: National Bureau of Economic Research. Reprinted in *Analytical Methods in Banking,* edited by Kalman J. Cohen and Frederick S. Hammer. Homewood, Ill.: Richard D. Irwin, Inc., 1966. Reprinted also in *Essays on Interest Rates,* vol. 2, edited by Jack M. Guttentag. New York: National Bureau of Economic Research, 1971.

1967 "An Economist Views Hospital Economic Trends." *Hospitals: Journal of the American Hospital Association* 41:63–64, 134. Reprinted in *Trustee: Journal for Hospital Governing Boards* 20 (1967): 5–10.

Comment on "Debt Management and the Term Structure of Interest Rates: An Empirical Analysis of Recent Experience," by Franco Modigliani and Richard Sutch. Supplement, *Journal of Political Economy* 75:592.

"Economic Effects of Federal Regulation of Milk Markets." *Journal of Law and Economics* 10:51–78. © 1967 by The University of Chicago.

1969 "The Allocation of Mortgage Funds." In *A Study of the Savings and Loan Industry,* prepared under the direction of Irwin Friend for the Federal Home Loan Bank Board. Washington, D.C.: U.S. Government Printing Office.

1970 "The A.M.A. and the Supply of Physicians." *Law and Contemporary Problems* 35:267–83. Published by Duke University School of Law, Durham, North Carolina. © 1970, 1971, by Duke University.

1971 "A Study of the Effects of Competition in the Tax-Exempt Bond Market." *Journal of Political Economy* 79:706–38. © 1971 by The University of Chicago.

"Expectations and the Demand for Bonds." *American Economic Review* 56: 231.

1972 "Higher Education and the Nation's Health: A Review of the Carnegie Commission Report on Medical Education." *Journal of Law and Economics* 15: 115–27. © 1972 by The University of Chicago.

"The 1972 Report of the President's Council of Economic Advisors: Inflation and Controls." *American Economic Review* 62:527–32.

1974 "Transfused Blood, Serum Hepatitis, and the Coase Theorem." *Journal of Law and Economics* 17:265–89. © 1974 by The University of Chicago. Reprinted in *Blood Policy: Issues and Alternatives,* edited by David B. Johnson. Washington, D.C.: American Enterprise Institute for Public Policy Research, 1977.

1975 Discussion. "Corporate Altruism and Individualistic Methodology." In *Capitalism and Freedom: Problems and Prospects: Proceedings of a Conference in Honor of Milton Friedman,* edited by Richard Selden. Charlottesville, Va.: University Press of Virginia.

1976 "A Study of Expectational Errors in the Money and Capital Markets." With Truman A. Clark. *Journal of Law and Economics* 19:1–15.

1977 "Ethical and Economic Aspects of Governmental Intervention in the Medical Care Market." In *Markets and Morals,* edited by Gerald Dworkin, Gordon Bermant, and Peter G. Brown. Washington, D.C.: Hemisphere Publishing Corporation. Also issued as Reprint No. 67 of the Center for Health Policy Research. Washington, D.C.: American Enterprise Institute for Public Policy Research, 1977.

Index

Abbott, Charles C., 184 n
Advertising, in marketing medical care, 26–27, 51
Agricultural Adjustment Act of 1937, 272–87
Allen, R. M., 11 n
AMA (American Medical Association): control of medical education by, 12–15, 41–49; control of pricing by, 12–15; history of, 8–12; opposition of, to group medical plans, 8–12, 32–42, 49; opposition of, to product liability law, 87. *See also* Discriminating monopoly model; Discrimination, price; Discrimination, social; Medical societies
American Association of Blood Banks, 75
American Red Cross, 75 n, 76, 92; opposition of, to product liability law, 82, 86–88
Ando, Albert, 355 n
Arrow, Kenneth J., 70, 71

Bach, George L., 355 n
Banks: as creditors and debtors, 328–29; in inflation, 329, 330; as mortgage holders, 224–26; as underwriters of tax-exempt bonds, 235–36, 242. *See also* Bonds, tax-exempt; Revenue bonds; Underwriting
Bass, Kenneth, 83 nn 1, 2
Becker, Gary S., 299, 300–301, 315–19
Bennett, Ann J. E., 73 n, 76 n, 78 n, 91 n, 92 n
Bevan, 11 n
Bids: number of, for general obligation and revenue issues, 237–44; ratio of, to average maturity, 239
Blacks. *See* Negroes
Bloch, Ernest, 221 n
Blood assurance programs, 79
Blood banks: accreditation of, 87; litigation involving, 81

Blood, commercial: legislation concerning, 80–82; opposition to use of, 80; quality of, 69, 75–76, 78; regional differences in use of, 80. *See also* Blood banks; Blood donors
Blood delivery systems: in England, 70; in U.S., 70–71, 75
Blood derivatives: commercialism in market for, 79 n; exemption of, from liability, 88
Blood donors: paid, 69, 79; unpaid, 69. *See also* Blood, commercial
Blood labeling law, effect of, 75, 81–82
Blood transfusions, as a service, 88–89
Blue Cross–Blue Shield. *See* Medical insurance
Bonds, agency, 194–95
Bonds, corporate, 155; as competitors for mortgages, 225–26; cyclical behavior of interest rates of, 194–97. *See also* Durand data
Bonds, government, long- and short-term, 155–56
Bonds, tax-exempt: general obligation, 233–64; as investments, 224–25; revenue, 233–64; spread in prices of, 234, 244–50, 252
Bresciani-Turroni, Constantino, 339, 352
Bronfenbrenner, Martin, 320–23

Calabresi, Guido, 83
Call provisions: differences in, 241–42; effect of underwriting cost on, 249–50
Capital markets, 103–232, 233–65
Carnegie Commission on Higher Education: recommendations of, for medical education, 55–67; relationship of, to medical profession, 38–39
Ceilings on mortgage rates, 226–27
Charity: as an argument for discriminatory pricing, 5–8; interpretation of, by medical profession, 42–43
Civil War, inflation during, 348–50

365

INDEX

Coase, Ronald H., 83, 84 n, 92–93
Coase Theorem, application of, 83–91
Colwell, N. P., 10, 39
Commodity market, 156–57. *See also* Normal backwardation
Competition: effect of, on price discrimination, 36; effect of, in sale of tax-exempt bonds, 260–62; lack of, in medical profession, 29, 36; in medical profession, 8; in milk marketing, 281–82
Competitive enterprise, 300–301, 308, 316–17
Conard, Joseph, 107 n, 110 n
Cooper, Michael H., 70, 71 n
Creditors. *See* Net monetary status
Culbertson, John N., 110, 111, 198
Culyer, Anthony J., 70, 71 n
Cunningham v. MacNeal Memorial Hospital, 81–82. *See also* Liability, product
Cyclical behavior of interest rates. *See* Interest rates

Debtor-creditor hypothesis, definition of, 328–29. *See also* Net monetary status
Deflation, 330, 332; effect of, on wealth maximization, 310
Discriminating monopoly model: application of, 12–34; evidence supporting, 12–36; implications of, 25–34
Discrimination in employment, 300–301, 310–14, 321–23; in competitive enterprises, 300–301; in monopolies, 301, 311–14
Discrimination, price: in medicine, 5–7, 50–51; in milk marketing, 270
Discrimination, social, 40–41, 63; effect of, 42; by medical groups, 29–34. *See also* Jews, discrimination against; Negroes, discrimination against; Women, discrimination against
Disintermediation, 223–24
Dollard, John, 9 n, 11 n, 12 n
Durand data: analysis of, 119–20, 136, 138–39, 141, 180, 182; methodology used for analysis of, 138–39, 143; use of, by Hickman, 122–23; use of, by Meiselman, 121–24

Education. *See* Medical education
England: inflation in, 345–48. *See also* Inflation
Entry restrictions: for internship, 12–14; for licensure, 41, 44; for medical schools, 9–12; for medical societies, 14–15; for tax-exempt issues, 237–44; for unregulated milk producers, 284–86. *See also* AMA; Discrimination in employment; Discrimination, social; Medical societies; Milk market
Error term: interpretation of, 116–24, 128, 134, 141. *See also* Expectations hypothesis; Forward rates; Liquidity premium; Meiselman, David
Expectations hypothesis: contradictions of, 124–45; Culbertson's test of, 110–11; definition of, 103, 107–8; Hickman's test of, 109–10, 119, 121; and liquidity premium, 127–45; Macaulay's test of, 109, 141–43; Meiselman's test of, 114–24; Walker's test of, 111–12, 123. *See also* Forecasting; Forward rates
Expectations–liquidity preference hypothesis, 103; test for, 186–97. *See also* Hicks, John R.

Federal Reserve Board, 248
Feldstein, Martin S., 77 n
FHA (Federal Housing Authority). *See* Ceilings on mortgage rates; Mortgages
Fisher, Irving: wage-lag hypothesis of, 340–41; wealth-transfer-in-inflation hypothesis of, 327–28, 329–30, 331–32. *See also* Wage-lag hypothesis; Wealth
Flexner, Abraham, 10–11, 38–39, 42 n
Flexner Report, 55, 56, 60, 62–64; recommendations of, 10
—effects of: on entry into medical school, 11, 40–42; on medical school curriculum, 11, 48; on Negro medical schools, 40; on supply of physicians, 11, 37–38; on tuition, 64–65
FNMA (Federal National Mortgage Association). *See* Bonds, agency; Ceilings on mortgage rates; Mortgages
Food and Agriculture Act of 1965, 288–89
Forecasting: in expectations hypothesis, 109–45; in expectations–liquidity preference hypothesis, 186–93. *See also* Forward rates; Spot rates
Forward rates: definition of, 108 n; forecasting of, 109–45, 154, 186–93; relationship of, to spot rates, 124–37, 141, 157. *See also* Expectations hypothesis;

366

Expectations–liquidity preference hypothesis; Forecasting; Spot rates
France: inflation in, 328, 345–48. *See also* Inflation
Franklin, Marc A., 70 n, 80 n, 82–83 n, 90 n
Friedman, Milton, 11 n, 16 n
Futures market. *See* Forecasting; Forward rates; Risk; Speculation; Spot rates

General obligation bonds. *See* Bonds, tax-exempt; Tax-exempt securities
Germany: inflation in, 328, 339–40, 352–53. *See also* Inflation
Gilboy, E., 345–46
Grady, George F., 73 n, 76 n, 78 n, 88–89, 91 n, 92 n
Group medical plans. *See* Medical plans, group

Hamilton, Earl J.: evidence of, in support of wage-lag hypothesis, 338, 341–48, 353 n
Hansen, Alvin, wage-lag hypothesis of, 350–52
Hawtrey, Ralph G., 113 n, 176 n
Hepatitis, serum: effects of, 72–73; incidence of, 70, 75, 77–78; source of, 69, 75; test for, 71–72. *See also* Liability, product; Titmuss, Richard
Hickman, W. Braddock: test of, for expectations hypothesis, 109–10, 119, 122–23, 205–7. *See also* Expectations hypothesis; Meiselman, David
Hicks, John R.: expectations–liquidity preference theory of, 103, 105–6, 118 n, 176 n, 184 n, 186–97, 297 n, 298

Income, nonpecuniary, 298–300; effect of regulation on, 298–315. *See also* Competitive enterprise; Discrimination in employment; Monopolies; Utility maximization
Income, pecuniary, 298–300, 301–3, 309–10; choice of, 302–3, 310
Income tax: effect of, on minority groups, 317; effect of, on wage earners, 317
Inertia hypothesis, 130, 134, 136. *See also* Expectations hypothesis; Forward rates; Spot rates
Inflation: in Austria, 328; in Chile, 328; effects of, on nonpecuniary and pecuniary income, 309–10; in England, 345–48; in France, 328, 345–48; in Germany, 328, 339–40, 352–53; redistribution of wealth through, 327–36; in Spain, 343–45; during U.S. Civil War, 348–50; during World War I (in U.S.), 331, 350–52; during World War II (in U.S.), 329–30. *See also* Banks; Debtor-creditor hypothesis; Net monetary status; Wage lag; Wealth
Information, economics of, 234, 255–56. *See also* Stigler, George J.
Insurance. *See* Malpractice; Medical insurance
Interest rates: cyclical behavior of, 136–38, 161–82, 224–26; effect of bond quality on, 242; fluctuations in, during business cycles, 161–82; forecasting of, in expectations hypothesis, 109–45; and liquidity premiums, 127–45, 187–91; relationship of long- to short-term, 108, 111, 113; seasonal adjustment in, 137–38, 218–22; short-term movement of, 217–24. *See also* Forward rates; Spot rates; Yields
Interns, control of, by AMA, 12–13
Ireland, Marilyn J., 82 n

James, William, 9
Jennings, E. R., 70 n
Jews, discrimination against, 29–34, 310–11, 314, 321–23; in medical profession, 31–34
Johnson, David B., 82 n

Kessel, Reuben A., 336 n
Keynes, John M.: expectations hypothesis of, 107; liquidity preference hypothesis of, 103, 146–53; normal backwardation theory of, 156–58; wealth transfer in inflation hypothesis of, 327, 328, 330, 331, 332.
Knight, Frank H., 157
Knowles, John, M.D., 37–38
Koepke, John A., 77
Kuznets, Simon, 11 n, 16 n

Labeling. *See* Blood labeling law
Labor unions, discriminatory practices in, 310–14
Lehigh Valley Cooperative Farmers, Inc. v. United States, 286–87
Lerner, Abba, 147 n
Lerner, Eugene: wage-lag hypothesis of,

367

350. *See also* Civil War, inflation in; Inflation
Liability, product: avoidance of, 80; opposition to legislation for, 86–87; responsibility for, 81–93. *See also* Coase theorem; *Cunningham v. MacNeal Memorial Hospital*
Licensure laws, medical: effect of, 61–62; as entry restriction, 43–44, 48; quality of, 41, 65–66, 67; state participation in, 9
Life insurance companies as mortgage holders, 224–26
Liquidity preference hypothesis: analysis of, 186–97; rationale for, 146–60. *See also* Forecasting; Hicks, John R.; Interest rates; Keynes, John M.; Liquidity preference; Liquidity premium; Yields
Liquidity premium: definition of, 186–87; effect of absence of, 185, 193; effect of presence of, 186–91; and expectations hypothesis, 127–45; use of, in analysis, 186–91. *See also* Income, nonpecuniary; Income, pecuniary
Lusher, David, 147 n
Lutz, Friedrich A.: expectations hypothesis of, 107–8, 112 n, 118 n; and Meiselman's expectations hypothesis, 158–59, 183–86. *See also* Culbertson, John N.

Malkiel, Burton G., 114 n, 151 n, 152 n. *See also* Expectations hypothesis
Malpractice, 44–45, 90
Market segmentation hypothesis, 112, 123–24, 144–45. *See also* Meiselman, David; Walker, Charls E.
Mayo Clinic, 76, 80, 91
Means, J. H., 5 n
Medical education: control of, by AMA, 9–15, 31–33, 46–47; curriculum for, 61; financing of, 62–65, 66–67; foreign, 42, 58–60, 272 (*see also* Physicians, foreign-trained); history of, 8, 38–39; investment in, 58–60; subsidies for, 58–60. *See also* Carnegie Commission on Higher Education; Flexner Report
Medical insurance: advertising for, by medical profession, 26; fee-for-service, 15–16, 65; position of, for blood costs, 79, 89; prepaid, 15–25, 65. *See also* Medical plans, group; VA

Medical plans, group: opposition to, by AMA, 15–25, 49; prohibition of, by state law, 24, 25, 49; relations of, with medical societies, 23–24; surgical procedures under, 49–50. *See also* Medical insurance; Medical societies
Medical societies: control of, by AMA, 14–15; effect of, on group medical practice, 16–24; non-price rationing by, 34; protection of members by, 27–28. *See also* AMA; Entry restrictions; Medical plans, group
Meiselman, David: evidence of, for market segmentation hypothesis, 123–24, 158–59; expectations hypothesis of, 183–86; use of error term by, 116–24, 128, 134, 141. *See also* Durand data; Hickman, W. Braddock; Lutz, Friedrich
Mendelson, Morris, 248 n
Meyer, F. V., wage-lag hypothesis of, 340 n
Milk market: regulated, 269–90; unregulated, 274–90
Mitchell, Wesley C.: evidence of, in support of wage-lag hypothesis, 338–39, 341, 342, 348–50. *See also* Hamilton, Earl J.; Inflation; Wage lag
Money market, 103–232, 233–65
—use of: by banks, 224–26; by life insurance companies, 155, 225–26; by savings and loan associations, 155, 217–24
Monopoly. *See* Discriminating monopoly model
Monopolies, 297–315; effect of regulation on, 300–305; employment policies of, 304–9, 321; labor unions as, 310–14. *See also* Labor unions; Public utilities
Mortgage market, 217–32; effect of ceilings on, 226–29; secondary, 226–30. *See also* FHA; FNMA; Mortgages
Mortgages, 217–32, effect of business cycle on yields of, 217–32; effect of secular trends on, 217–22; regional variation in rates of, 226–30

Nef, John U., 348, 353
Negroes, discrimination against, 34, 40–41, 44, 313–14, 321. *See also* Flexner Report; Medical education
Net monetary status, 328–35; shift in, 331–32. *See also* Inflation; Stock, common

Normal backwardation, 156–58, 203. *See also* Commodity market; Keynes, John M.; Risk; Speculation

Order market, milk. *See* Milk market
Organized medicine. *See* AMA

Phelps, Charlotte D., 249 n
Physicians: foreign-trained, 42, 46, 58–60, 62 (*see also* Medical education, foreign); supply of, 55, 56–58, 60–63; women, 40, 44
Prepaid medical plans. *See* Medical plans, group
Price control. *See* Discriminating monopoly model; Discrimination, price
Prices, milk: effect of supports on, 273–77; federal control over, 272–76; as a function of zone and location differentials, 283–84; in unregulated market, 274–76, 278–90
Price supports, milk, 273–77
Prices of tax-exempt bonds, 245, 250. *See also* Bonds, tax-exempt; Tax-exempt securities; Underwriting
Product liability. *See* Liability, product
Public utilities: as monopolies, 302; use of nonpecuniary income in, 306–7. *See also* Income, nonpecuniary; Income, pecuniary; Monopolies

Regulation, effect of: on competitive enterprise, 300–305, 313 n; on milk market, 269–90; on monopolies, 300–309, 313 n; on underwriting of tax-exempt bonds, 262–63
Reilly v. King County Blood Bank, 81 n
Revenue bonds, 233–64; definition of, 233 n. *See also* Banks; Bonds, tax-exempt; Tax-exempt securities
Risk avoidance, 150–53, 156–58. *See also* Normal backwardation; Speculation

Samuelson, Paul A., 147 n, 203–4, 219 n
Savings and loan associations, 217–32; effect of rise in cyclical rates on, 222–24; effect of rise of secular rates on, 218–22; function of, in money and capital markets, 217–18; growth of, 220, 224
Saxon general obligation bonds, 236, 259–60. *See also* Bonds, tax-exempt; Saxon, James; Tax-exempt securities

Saxon, James, 236
Scitovsky, Tibor, 298 nn 2, 3
Seasonal adjustment. *See* Interest rates
Secular trends, 217–22. *See also* Interest rates; Mortgages
Shryock, Richard, 38, 40 n, 41
Simons, Henry C., 160
Social cost. *See* Coase Theorem
Social discrimination. *See* Discrimination, social
Solow, Robert, 70, 75
Speculation, 156–59. *See also* Commodity market; Normal backwardation; Risk avoidance
Spencer, Leland, 273 n, 279–81
Spot rates: definition of, 108 n; relationship of, to forward rates, 120, 124–37, 141, 157. *See also* Forward rates
Spreads. *See* Yield differentials
Stigler, George J., 301; Economics of Information Theory of, 234, 255–56
Stock, common, in inflation, 327–28, 329–30, 355–56
Stock, preferred, in inflation, 329–30
Strict liability in tort. *See* Liability, product

Tax-exempt securities: call provisions for, 241–42; 249–50; effect of liquidity preference theory on, 258–59; entry restrictions for, 237–44; prices of, 245–59; quality of, 241, 243; use of, by commercial banks, 224–25. *See also* Bonds, tax-exempt; Capital market; Money market
Telser, Lester G., 157
Term structure of interest rates, 103–204
Titmuss, Richard M., 69–71, 74–75, 79, 80 n, 91–92
Tucker, R. S., wage-lag hypothesis of, 347

Underwriting: costs of, for tax-exempt securities, 245–50; of revenue bonds, 233–35. *See also* Information, economics of
Utility maximization as a form of nonpecuniary income, 163, 299, 303

VA (Veterans Administration): opposition by AMA to medical-care plan of, 22

Wage lag: Hamilton-Mitchell hypothesis of, 327–28, 330, 332, 334–35, 338, 341; in inflation, 337–58

Wage-to-equity ratio, 353–57

Walker, Charls E.: expectations hypothesis of, 11–12, 123; market segmentation hypothesis of, 145

Wealth: Keynes-Fisher hypothesis of transfer of, in inflation, 327–36; maximization of, 297–300. *See also* Income, nonpecuniary; Income, pecuniary; Utility maximization

West, Richard, 251 n, 255 n, 256 n

Women. *See* Physicians, women

World War I, inflation during, 331, 350–52

World War II, inflation during, 329–30

Yield differentials: for bonds, 149–50, 152, 154, 156; in tax-exempt bonds, 234, 242, 244–50, 249, 252

Yields, mortgage: FHA, 225; FNMA, 227–28; regional differentials in, 227; VA, 226–27

Yields, reoffering, 251–58; on long- and short-term securities, 161–82. *See also* Interest rates; Yield differentials